USING EVIDENCE

How research can inform
public services

Sandra M. Nutley, Isabel Walter and Huw T.O. Davies

First published in Great Britain in 2007 by

The Policy Press
University of Bristol
Fourth Floor
Beacon House
Queen's Road
Bristol BS8 1QU
UK

Tel +44 (0)117 331 4054
Fax +44 (0)117 331 4093
e-mail tpp-info@bristol.ac.uk
www.policypress.org.uk

British Library Cataloguing in Publication Data
A catalogue record for this book is available from the British Library.

Library of Congress Cataloging-in-Publication Data
A catalog record for this book has been requested.

ISBN 978 1 86134 664 3 paperback
ISBN 978 1 86134 665 0 hardcover

Sandra Nutley is Professor of Public Management at the University of Edinburgh and Director of the Research Unit for Research Utilisation (RURU) at the Universities of Edinburgh and St Andrews. **Isabel Walter** is Research Fellow in the Social Dimensions of Health Institute at the Universities of Dundee and St Andrews. **Huw Davies** is Professor of Health Policy and Management in the School of Management at the University of St Andrews, and Director of the Social Dimensions of Health Institute at the Universities of Dundee and St Andrews.

Cover design by Qube Design Associates, Bristol.
Front cover: photograph supplied by kind permission of Magnum Photos.
Printed and bound in Great Britain by MPG Books, Bodmin.

Contents

List of boxes, figures and tables

Boxes

Figures

Tables

Acknowledgements

This book pulls together the work that we have been engaged with over the last five years through the Research Unit for Research Utilisation originally at the University of St Andrews (RURU; www.ruru.ac.uk/). Along the way there were many agencies and individuals who have been critical in providing resources, offering encouragement or shaping our thinking. We cannot hope to recreate a full map of the journey that we have travelled, but we would like to thank at least some of the more obvious companions and supporters who have been instrumental in keeping us on the road. In doing this imperfectly we hope that those neglected will forgive our selectivity.

First, the Economic and Social Research Council (ESRC) invested heavily through their Research Resources Board in building capacity for evidence-based policy and practice in the UK. We were fortunate enough to secure two tranches of money that underpinned the founding of RURU in 2001, and we are very grateful for the ESRC's financial support over the ensuing four years. RURU was, however, just one of several centres funded by the ESRC as part of this initiative, and the interactions within and between these various centres and, in particular, with the *Evidence Network* 'hub' originally at Queen Mary, University of London (www.evidencenetwork.org) were very helpful to us in shaping some of our ideas.

Early in the life of RURU, two research commissions for review work helped focus our work on synthesis for practical application. We are grateful to the Learning and Skills Development Agency (LSDA, as it then was) and the Social Care Institute for Excellence (SCIE) for their important seed funding and for their constructive dialogue around these two very successful projects (Nutley et al, 2003a; Walter et al, 2003a, 2004b). As part of the second of these projects with SCIE, Janie Percy-Smith, Di McNeish and Sarah Frost helped us in articulating the models of research use in practice elaborated in Chapter Seven.

As RURU developed, we planned a programme of research support activities, including a series of research seminars in 2002-04 (see RURU website for further details of these). These drew on a rich variety of practical and theoretical know-how from a wide range of seminar participants. At each of these events we learned much and expanded our grasp of matters relating to social research and its use. We are very grateful to all of the seminar participants for sharing so willingly their experience and expertise. Where these ideas have filtered through into our own understanding and are reproduced in this book without clear acknowledgement we can only apologise – and plead in our defence the essentially uncertain percolation of knowledge, a theme that forms an important strand of this book.

Beyond supporting RURU, the ESRC has been influential in several further ways. In May 2005, it ran a seminar to explore the means of assessing non-academic social research impact, to which we were invited to contribute a discussion paper (Davies et al, 2005). This paper, enhanced by drawing on the expert contributions of the seminar participants, enabled an early articulation of the ideas subsequently elaborated in Chapter Nine. We are very grateful to the ESRC and the seminar participants for this prompt to our thinking and for the insights we were able to gain through the seminar interactions. In addition, the ESRC Teaching & Learning Research Programme (TLRP), in which one of us (SN) was an active participant, provided more opportunities for exploration of key ideas. Some of these were again road-tested with a variety of agencies in a range of guises, for example with the National Education Research Forum; the NHS Service Delivery and Organisation R&D Programme; the Scottish Executive; NHS Health Scotland; the Scottish Funding Council; the Cancer Care Research Centre; the NHS Health Technology Assessment Programme; the Home Office Crime Reduction Programme; and many other UK agencies. Overseas discussions took us to the US, Canada, Australia, New Zealand and Scandinavia to engage with policy makers, research funders and a wide variety of research users. For all of these opportunities to engage in grounded discussions about knowledge transfer, evidence uptake and research impact we are deeply grateful, and to all of those evidence advocates who shared their time and their knowledge we say thank you indeed.

In our own institution (the University of St Andrews at the time of writing) we would like to express our gratitude to those colleagues in the School of Management and more widely who have been so supportive. Special thanks also go to Liz Brodie (RURU administrator, 2001-06) for helping with manuscript preparation and for so much more; to Jennifer Morton who was our part-time information specialist; and to all our doctoral students in the field of research use who have encouraged, challenged and supported us throughout recent years, notably Gail Greig, Tobias Jung, Joanne McLean, Alison Powell, Karen Tosh and Joyce Wilkinson. We would also like to make special mention of Peter Smith (University of York) who, during a relatively brief period at the University of St Andrews in the mid-1990s, initially helped prompt our interest in this fascinating field, worked with us on our early explorations (Davies et al, 2000a), and has been unfailingly supportive and encouraging ever since.

Finally, we would like to acknowledge the debt of gratitude we have to the many people – researchers, policy makers, practitioners, change agents and research brokers – whose work and writings we have drawn upon in developing this text. We have tried so far as possible to source ideas so that due credit is given; where this has not satisfactorily been achieved we ask for forgiveness, and plead in mitigation that uncited use is better than no use at all.

Sandra Nutley, Isabel Walter and Huw Davies
January 2007

ONE

Using evidence – introducing the issues

Research (sometimes) matters

Research on children's early years tells us that people's life chances are heavily influenced by their experiences from a very early age (Schweinhart and Weikart, 1993; Ramey et al, 2000). Growing recognition of this has fed into important debates that range far beyond an academy of scholars to encompass a wide range of stakeholders, such as agencies, service providers and – perhaps most importantly of all – policy makers, including those at the UK Treasury. Changes in thinking off the back of these debates can be seen to have informed radical changes to the provision and financing of public services since the late 1990s, for example with the setting up and subsequent development of 'Sure Start' – a major UK government programme bringing together early education, child care, health care and family support (Eisenstadt, 2000). The activities and impacts of such initiatives have in turn been investigated and evaluated, with the findings from this newer research further feeding the debates, policy choices and practice arrangements (for example, NESS, 2005). Thus, research can sometimes clearly be seen to influence policy debates, the policy choices that flow from these, and the practical implementation of those choices. And policy and practice changes in turn can stimulate and shape the research that is planned, funded and executed in various settings (university, government, and public service arenas, including the third sector).

However, it is not always so. Researchers, as well as other stakeholders, often despair that clear findings are sometimes *not* heeded when decisions are made about the direction and delivery of public services. Indeed, policy and practice decisions sometimes seem to fly in the face of what is considered to be the best available evidence about 'what works' (Davies et al, 2000a). In health care, for example, researchers have long known that medical practice often lags behind summations of best evidence (Antman et al, 1992), that evidence is only rarely seen to support much of management decision making (Walshe and Rundall, 2001; Pfeffer and Sutton, 2006), and that structural reorganisations (such as hospital mergers) are pursued as solutions to organisation failings even though the evidence base is far from supportive (Fulop et al, 2002, 2005). In other areas too, policy and practice can sometimes be significantly out of step with robust research-based knowledge. For example, in the US many local school districts continued to offer the Drug Abuse Resistance Education (DARE) programme even when an increasing number of research and evaluation studies found it to be ineffective in reducing drug abuse (Weiss et al, 2005).

Introducing this text

Although the influence of research, as in the opening example, may sometimes be inferred, it can be far from easy to see *how* such influence occurs. It is also often unclear how any influence is mediated, blocked or amplified, or more instrumentally, how any research influence might be enhanced. These, in essence, are the themes of this book. Importantly, we are interested not only in the direct use of research to make decisions, but also in the many ways that research is used indirectly, for example through conceptual applications that begin to reshape thinking around policy problems, or through political applications where research is used to support arguments, direct action or justify inaction. That means that we are interested not just in the use of research findings *per se*, but also in the broader assimilation of research ideas, theories and concepts into discourse and debates.

In the book we discuss what we know about the influence of research on national and local policy actors and front-line practitioners. We do this because we believe that the ways in which research is combined with other forms of evidence and knowledge could have important impacts on the nature, distribution, effectiveness, efficiency and quality of public services. Indeed, we would go further, to assert that it is reasonable to suppose that more deliberative and judicious engagement with high-quality research may be sufficiently advantageous to be an important goal of public service reform.

Of course the irony here is that the evidence base confirming any benefits (or indeed, dysfunctions) of an evidence-based[1] approach to public policy and service delivery is actually rather thin. This is certainly the case if the search for such evidence is aimed narrowly at linking research use with better service outcomes; much more is known about the processes of research use (see Chapters Two to Four). The current absence of strong evidence linking research use to improved service outcomes need not deflect us from our central tasks, however, which are (a) the unpacking of research use processes and (b) an exploration of the ways in which these processes might be improved. Later in the book, in Chapter Nine, we go on to explore the very significant challenges of demonstrating broader service impacts of research use, and suggest that learning about processes remains a more attainable goal than assembling robust evidence of direct service change. What such an analysis suggests is that the current lack of evidence about the impact of research on policy and practice outcomes reflects more an absence of evidence rather than evidence of absence.

We will proceed therefore with the working assumptions that it is worth unpacking how research interacts with policy and practice, and it is worth considering how such interactions can be made more frequent, deeper and more constructive. We do this because we believe it is reasonable to suggest that certain ways of developing new knowledge may be better than others, and that research-based ways of knowing are worthy of particular attention. This rather complex and contestable set of assumptions is something we will return to more critically in the closing chapter of the book.

This is not entirely untilled ground to us. We began our exploration of the use of research in an earlier book devoted to understanding the development of the evidence-based policy and practice agenda across a wide range of public services – *What works? Evidence-based policy and practice in public services* (Davies et al, 2000a). In that book we discussed the role played by research evidence in a range of public policy areas (health care, social care, education and criminal justice; welfare, housing, transport and urban renewal). We also examined several recurrent cross-sectoral themes relating to the generation and interpretation of evidence, and the emergence of strategies to increase its use. It is a more detailed exploration of this final issue – one that builds on research from the intervening years, and draws on a wider social science literature – that concerns us here.

The current book arises therefore from our identification of 'research use' as a very significant practical and intellectual challenge, and from our subsequent and ongoing work in the ESRC-funded Research Unit for Research Utilisation (RURU; www.ruru.ac.uk). RURU was established in 2001 as a unique cross-sector resource devoted to documenting and synthesising the many diverse strands of conceptual, empirical and practical knowledge about the use of research. It has engaged with a very wide range of stakeholders from academic, policy and practitioner communities, and other agencies interested in research use, such as research funders, research brokers and charitable organisations. RURU has produced many articles and discussion papers in support of extending knowledge about research use, and many of these outputs are available from the website. This book represents the distillation and integration of our learning thus far, and we are indebted to the many people who have collaborated with us along the way for their support and their many insights.

Throughout this book then, we will explore what it means to 'use' research in policy and practice settings, and we will describe key models of the research impact process. We also discuss ways of promoting and improving the use of research: what approaches have been tried and what seems to work. Our purpose is not only to increase understanding of these issues but also to summarise the emerging implications for those actively concerned with promoting research use and assessing its impact. At all times we seek to draw on the specific literatures that have explored research and evidence use, as well as on the broader social science literatures which have relevance to our core concerns: that is, to understand the role of (research-based) knowledge in shaping thinking and influencing action.

Settings of interest

Our discussion draws on studies of 'research use' mainly in four key public service areas: health care, social care, education and criminal justice. These areas not only consume high levels of government resource and political attention but they also display some structural similarities, such as hierarchical relations between central policy and local service delivery, and the employment of staff both with and without professional qualifications to provide services to individuals or groups. These four areas have also witnessed the emergence of significant discourses around the importance of evidence in shaping policy and practice (Davies et al, 1999, 2000a) and each has seen very significant investment in growing and synthesising a relevant research base (see, for example, initiatives noted in Box 1.2 on p 17). There are, of course, also some important differences between these sector areas, particularly in the ways in which research is understood, created, synthesised and used (see Table 1.1 for some brief examples of similarity and difference). These variations provide some diverse contexts within which research use dynamics are played out, and this diversity is often helpful to us, both in providing richer contextualised understandings and in offering opportunities for cross-sector learning.

Table 1.1: Contrasting approaches to evidence creation and practitioner use – some examples from four UK sectors

	Health care (especially clinical services)	Social care	Education (especially schools-based education)	Criminal justice
Methodological preferences and debates	'Gold Standard' of experimental methods (randomised control trials) in relation to 'what works' evidence. Growing interest in qualitative methods to give complementary view.	Quantification and experimentation less often used (although more diverse evaluative efforts of late), and sometimes also viewed with suspicion or even hostility. Emphasis on the importance of practitioner expertise.	Through the 1990s much research considered less than robust, paradigm wars seen between methodological camps, and eclectic methods seen as competing rather than complementing. Since 2000 more attention paid to research quality and research synthesis.	Some acceptance of experimental methods in determining what works, but debate about how this is best achieved. Interest in theory- as well as method-driven approaches to evaluation, alongside use of routine performance data.
Nature of evidence base	Extensive and accessible via national and international initiatives such as the Cochrane Collaboration and the National Institute for Health and Clinical Excellence (NICE), and through local clinical effectiveness strategies.	Growing availability of research summaries and guidance through the Social Care Institute for Excellence (SCIE) and through other intermediaries and collaborations such as Making Research Count, and Research in Practice.	Initially a fragmented research community and few systematic reviews. However, significant investment by the Higher Education Funding Council for England (HEFCE) and some government departments led to the ESRC Teaching & Learning Research Programme, and the funding of systematic review work through the EPPI-Centre. Increasing accessibility of online resources through, eg the National Foundation for Educational Research.	A growing research base. More recent efforts to collate and make available this knowledge, eg internationally through the Campbell Collaboration and the Office of Community Oriented Policing Services (COPS). Home Office research reports are an additional UK research resource.

(continued)

5

Table 1.1: Contrasting approaches to evidence creation and practitioner use – some examples from four UK sectors (continued)

	Health care (especially clinical services)	Social care	Education (especially schools-based education)	Criminal justice
Dominant research use strategies (see Chapter Seven for further elaboration of models)	Largely push of information out from centre (clinical guidelines, National Service Frameworks), sometimes with considerable efforts at local adaptation; some local initiatives to increase practitioner pull. Research-based practitioner model still a pervasive rhetoric.	Diverse strategies in place but not always fully coherent. Rhetoric most seen around 'research-based practitioner' ideas, but also some collaborative and interactive approaches and some systematising of evidence into practice tools.	Considerable focus on 'research-based practitioner' model but also significant investments in interactive and collaborative approaches to research use.	Some push of information from the centre (Home Office), with evidence becoming embedded in programme accreditation and research-based tools and protocols. Web-based guidance, professional associations, formal training courses and networks also important.

Within each of these sectors we are concerned to understand the nature of research use, first of all, in *policy settings*. This means national, regional and local policy making, where we are interested in how research interacts with policy thinking and influences both policy directions and specific policy choices. As policy becomes more local this highlights a second arena of interest to us: that of the *organisation decision maker*, often those located in service delivery organisations. Here we are interested to explore how research influences overall strategy, local priorities, operational procedures, service design and managerial decision making. Finally, we are concerned to unpack the use of research by *practitioners* (individually and collectively) as they deliver services to service users. In many cases these practitioners will be autonomous, highly skilled and professionalised (for example, teachers, probation officers, doctors or nurses), at other times they will be less autonomous practitioners without professional qualifications (for example, classroom assistants or care assistants). As we shall see, such distinctions matter in understanding the nature of research use in practice settings.

Throughout much of the book we shall often draw fairly sharp distinctions between policy and practice arenas. This reflects both the somewhat divergent nature of these two contexts and the largely separate sets of literatures addressing each. However, this distinction between policy and practice is not always so neat: policies are developed locally as well as nationally, and may be formed as much by an accretion of local decisions than through any formal policy process. Moreover, policy making at all levels is often influenced from the bottom up, as well as practice being influenced from the top down. Thus, while the distinctions can sometimes be useful in structuring our material we should be alert to how these distinctions may break down or be more fluid at certain times and in certain contexts (Parsons, 1995; Nutley and Webb, 2000).

While policy and practice are often separated out, we refer much less often in specific terms to the middle group outlined above: organisation decision makers. This is in part because many of the concerns and preoccupations of this group are often best considered using a broad interpretation of the policy literature (that is, policy with a small 'p', rather than the big 'P' of Policy set at government and national department level). It is also because much of the specific literature on research use either collapses this group into the broader mass of 'policy makers' or includes local managers in with a consideration of practice-based issues. One of the conclusions that we touch upon in the final chapter is that this 'meso-level' set of service actors – those managing and shaping local service delivery organisations – are worthy of more specific and sustained study of their habits of research use.

At every level, from policy, through organisation tiers, to practice settings, there are many potential 'users' of research. These include not just those working within public services, but also: the national and local media; opposition, back-bench and local politicians; pressure groups and other stakeholders; other researchers and research brokers; and service users. However, much of the literature we review in subsequent chapters assumes two main user communities for research: policy makers (government ministers, specialist advisors and civil servants with formal responsibilities for policy development, as well as their regional and local counterparts) and practitioners (those who deliver front-line services, and their local managers). We too have focused primarily on those potential research users who are actors operating *within* public services, while noting that much of the ground that we cover will be of interest to the broader array of potential research users listed at the start of this paragraph.

Cast in this way there can be a tendency to view research use as primarily a matter for individual actors within the system. Yet throughout the book we will endeavour to keep in sight the organisational context within which these individuals are embedded. Most obviously, this will involve highlighting the enabling or inhibiting aspects of context for individual behaviour. More than this, however, we will also try to draw attention to organisation- and system-level uses of research. This means paying attention to the ways in which research gets embedded in collective processes, practices and cultures. Throughout the book then, we shall be interested in both individual and more collective processes of research use.

Many of the examples and research studies cited in the book are from the UK, and given that this is where we are located, our understanding and analysis is inevitably influenced by this context. Contextual arrangements – including cultural factors (such as attitudes towards large-scale policy experimentation and/or rational policy analysis) and constitutional issues (such as unitary or federal government structures and the degree of subsidiarity) – are vital in understanding research use. Hence we need to be careful about drawing general conclusions from context-specific analyses. Nonetheless, we do try to draw out general lessons about research use mechanisms where these seem to resonate across contexts, and we hope and believe that the material presented will have value not just in the UK but also internationally.

Having explained in some depth the settings and focus of our interest in exploring the use of research, it may also be worth noting some of the related issues which, while important, are not pursued in great detail. We do not, for example, address how research findings are produced, collated, synthesised, stored, accessed or communicated – except where variations in these arrangements have direct bearing on research use processes. Nor are we very concerned with exploring the methodologies that underpin the production of research findings, or explaining the skills necessary to appraise completed research (although the absence of such critical appraisal skills is sometimes identified as one of the barriers to increased research use – see Chapter Three). By extension, this text also does not engage in much discussion about operationalising participatory research methods such as 'action research' (Gomm and Davies, 2000; Waterman et al, 2001) or 'practitioner evaluation' (Harvey et al, 2002), nor does it explore the role and development of the 'scientific practitioner' (Hayes, 1981; Wakefield and Kirk, 1996), an approach that focuses on practitioners themselves developing small-scale local experimentation as a means of deciding local practice. While all of these may have relevance – for example, they emphasise the co-production of knowledge and may contribute to a local culture of 'research mindedness' – we have taken the view that the details of their accomplishment are not central to our concerns. Therefore our focus remains fixed on the mechanisms by which research findings (which may or may not be externally generated) get integrated into policy and practice in public services.

Having set out the scope of our interest in research use (ie where we shall focus, as well as some of the issues that we do not explore in depth) we will now go on to place our discussion of research use within its historical context, in particular, its relationship to debates about evidence-based policy and practice. Following this we will explore issues arising from a consideration of the nature of evidence, and in doing so we will home in on our preoccupation with research-based evidence, and especially that emanating from social research studies. We conclude by outlining the structure of the book, the content of the remaining chapters, and the processes by which we have come to this summation of the field of research use.

Research use and the evidence-based policy and practice agenda

Some historical context: boom and bust cycles in the social sciences

The massive expansion of the social sciences after the Second World War was a response to an increased appetite for social knowledge. University social science departments flourished and a range of other organisations (such as think tanks and research foundations) emerged to feed the growing demand for social knowledge. The conviction was that research could and should be of direct use to government in determining and achieving its social policy objectives, establishing what has been called a 'social engineering' role for research (Janowitz, 1972). However, early enthusiasm was followed by increasing disillusionment during the 1970s and 1980s about the ability of research to provide answers to complex social problems, bringing into question the whole enterprise of creating social knowledge for direct use by governments (Finch, 1986). One symptom of this was the near-demise of the UK Social Science Research Council (SSRC) in 1982, and its renaming as the Economic and Social Research Council (ESRC), thus losing the imprimatur of 'science'.

Enthusiasm for the insights offered by social research began to gain ground again in the 1990s and this was epitomised in the UK by the rhetoric of Tony Blair's Labour government when it won the 1997 general election. Its slogan – 'what matters is what works' – was intended to signal an end to ideologically-based decision making in favour of evidence-based thinking. As one of the ministers in Blair's first government commented:

> Social science should be at the heart of policy making. We need a revolution in relations between government and the social research community – we need social scientists to help to determine what works and why, and what types of policy initiatives are likely to be most effective. (Blunkett, 2000)

The Labour government duly launched a range of programmes under the evidence-based policy banner, such as the Crime Reduction Programme[2] and Sure Start,[3] and there were growing indications of a developing evidence-based agenda in many parts of public sector service delivery (Davies et al, 2000a). These programmes, and this wider and growing interest in evidence-based policy and practice, provide an important context for our consideration of the use of research. For this reason we will outline some of the key developments underpinning this agenda.

But first an important caveat: while the rhetorical context matters, it should be noted from the outset that research can be, and indeed often is, used in ways that transcend the evidence-based policy and practice agenda. For example, while social research can play an important and positive role in informing or even supporting policy and practice decisions, this is not always the case. Research can also seek to critique and challenge established policy and practice frameworks. Box 1.1 defines some potential roles for researchers in influencing public policy, and demonstrates the wide scope for research use beyond the instrumentalist 'evidence-based' agenda. Our discussion of research use in the remainder of this book seeks to encompass these wider and sometimes critical understandings of the potential uses of research. This reflects, at least in part, concerns that a narrow evidence agenda may be focusing research funding and activity too much on the first of the areas outlined in Box 1.1 at the expense of the more challenging approaches described subsequently. We would suggest therefore that research can have an important role to play in actually *shaping values*, and it should not therefore be relegated to a purely technical role of helping to decide between competing options that seek to operationalise fixed and pre-existing values. These more challenging and contentious research activities have important roles to play in promoting the democratic and intellectual health of society, but are somewhat sidelined in more usual understandings about the evidence-based policy and practice agenda.

Box 1.1: Public policy and the researchers' stance

It is possible to identify three key stances for researchers to adopt in relation to influencing public policy:

(1) The consensual approach

The consensual approach refers to situations where there is broad agreement among policy makers and researchers about the main issues of concern and the ways in which these should be addressed. Researchers then work within the existing paradigm, aiming to provide policy makers, practitioners and other stakeholders with knowledge about how best to improve service delivery and service outcomes. Their focus is on improving the efficacy of decision making and the outcomes of service activities. Such an approach is the mainstay of the evidence-based policy and practice agenda.

(2) The contentious approach

In the contentious approach, researchers place themselves more on the sidelines of public policy. They may not always contribute to policy development directly, but maintain a critical stance in relation to government, society and its institutions. The role of researchers in this approach is to act as 'moral critic'. Examples abound of researchers pursuing such an agenda not just through academic journals but also through articles and letters in the general media. For example, there is a long tradition of critique, commentary and analysis of the government's performance measurement and management approaches and the development of a target culture (Smith, 1995; Mannion et al, 2005; Bevan and Hood, 2006).

(3) The paradigm-challenging approach

More radically, researchers might take a stance outside the prevailing paradigm, using their work to problematise established frameworks and ways of thinking. They may, for example, propose new principles for action for which they hope political support will follow. Examples include: the body of work on '*positive psychology*' (Seligman et al, 2004) that seeks to redirect the agenda for mental health away from one focused on ill-health and dysfunction to one focused on wellness, wellbeing, and happiness (see for example, www.ppc.sas.upenn.edu); or the work of the New Economics Foundation that seeks to 'improve quality of life by promoting innovative solutions that challenge mainstream thinking on economic, environment and social issues' (www.neweconomics.org).

Source: Adapted and augmented from Rein (1976) and Weiss (1995)

Defining the evidence-based policy and practice agenda

Definitions of 'evidence-based policy and practice' range from rather narrow interpretations of its meaning to broader, all-encompassing views about what it represents. A fairly common narrow definition sees it as a movement that promotes a particular methodology for producing a specific form of evidence: systematic reviews and meta-analyses of robust (often experimental) research studies aimed at assessing the effectiveness of health and social policy interventions. Such a 'movement' is also sometimes seen as primarily about promoting the translation of systematic review evidence into guidelines for practice, which may ultimately be transformed into centrally imposed, evidence-based programmes of intervention. This view of research aligns most closely with the 'consensual approach' outlined in Box 1.1. Such views have taken deep root in health care (Davies and Nutley, 1999) and are also seen, to a lesser extent, in criminal justice (Nutley and Davies, 1999).

At the broader end of the spectrum, evidence-based policy and practice has been defined as an approach that 'helps people make well-informed decisions about policies, programmes and projects by putting the best available evidence from research at the heart of policy development and implementation' (Davies, 2004, p 3). Under this broader view, which we would both endorse and ultimately broaden still further, what counts as evidence is more wide-ranging than just research from evaluations of 'what works'. It encompasses a more diverse array of research methods exploring a wider variety of research questions – not just what works, but also what is the nature of the problem, why does it occur and how might it be addressed. This broader view of evidence can therefore accommodate a more challenging role for research (Box 1.1). Under this broad view, 'fitness for purpose' acts as the main criterion for determining what counts as good evidence. Thus, evidence from a range of research and evaluation studies sits alongside routine monitoring data, expert knowledge and information from stakeholder consultations.

Since the publication of our earlier review of the extent to which the evidence-based policy and practice agenda had taken root in various parts of the public sector (Davies et al, 2000a), there has been much debate around this agenda, including the launch of an international journal dedicated to exploring the issues that it raises (*Evidence & Policy*, published by The Policy Press). However, an emphasis on the positive role to be played by research, and a desire to see an increase in research use, has not always been wholly welcomed. In fact a substantial critical literature has flowered, calling into question some of the basic assumptions underpinning narrower views of research use in both the policy and practice settings (Trinder and Reynolds, 2000; Clarence, 2002; Holmes et al, 2006). Such a literature is clearly 'paradigm challenging' to evidence-based policy and practice in the terms set out in Box 1.1, and we next elaborate on this challenge, looking first at the policy critique, then at practice.

Critique of the evidence-based policy agenda

In the policy arena, concerns have been expressed at the 'inherently conservative' nature of evidence-based policy (perhaps leading to the perpetual delay of reform; Davey Smith et al, 2001), while other critics have focused on what are seen as the 'dual follies' that underpin the very idea of policy being evidence-based (Clarence, 2002). The first of these 'follies' is the assumption that evidence, including research evidence, can provide objective answers to inherently political policy questions. Evidence, it is said, can never be objective as all knowledge is relative and developed in social contexts. The second alleged 'folly' concerns the assumption that policy making can become a more rational decision-making process, one that is influenced primarily by the weight of evidence. Politics and the art of muddling through, it is argued, overwhelm and undermine attempts to introduce these more deliberative processes (Leicester, 1999; Clarence, 2002; Parsons, 2002).

The response from the proponents of evidence-based policy to the first folly has been to acknowledge that research and evaluation rarely provide definitive answers, especially when questions relate to what works in what circumstances in tackling complex social problems (Sanderson, 2002). There is also ready recognition from many proponents that what counts as evidence is inextricably bound by our ways of thinking about the social world (Mulgan, 2003). The conclusion drawn is that expectations of what research and other forms of evidence can tell us need to be managed carefully, but this does not mean that research has nothing of importance to say.

The response to the charge that it is politics and not evidence that drives policy processes has been to emphasise that evidence is only one of the many factors that influence the policy process (Nutley and Webb, 2000; Mulgan, 2003; Davies, 2004). Terms such as evidence-informed, evidence-influenced and evidence-inspired can be seen as reflecting this rebalancing. The aim of an evidence-informed process is to try to increase the relative prominence given to evidence during the policy process, with due acknowledgement that other factors, such as ideology, professional norms, expert views, personal experience, media interest and politics, will all remain influential. Encouragement in this aim is derived from the observation that many governments are currently more pragmatic than ideological, and hence more open to arguments based on evidence of what has been found to work elsewhere (Stoker, 1999; Mulgan, 2003). Moreover, in many places reformed policy processes and the development of a stronger 'research intelligence' function have been used to try to ensure greater and more structured engagement with research-based evidence (Cabinet Office, 1999).

Studies of the extent to which policy processes are in fact influenced by evidence have provided some limited support for the idea of evidence-informed policy in the UK (Coote et al, 2004; Fear and Roberts, 2004) and in the US (Auspos and Kubisch, 2004), but they also show the many ways in which research and other evidence are used selectively to support an ideological argument or promote pre-existing plans. Moreover, there is often a gap between the rhetoric of evidence-based policy and what happens on the ground. In Sure Start, for example, it was noted that research and evaluation evidence were used to get the idea adopted, but that these were then 'largely ignored in the design of the programme' (Coote et al, 2004, p 17). There were claims that the programme was 'politically driven and value driven' (Coote et al, 2004, p 18). Thus, despite official assertions to the contrary, social programmes tend to be designed 'on the basis of informed guesswork and expert hunches, enriched by some evidence and driven by political and other imperatives' (Coote et al, 2004, p xi). That this is the case partly reflects the nature of the policy process but it is also due in many instances to the lack of appropriate evidence on which to base the detailed planning and commissioning of social programmes. It is also compounded by widely differing views about what constitutes 'evidence' (Coote et al, 2004) – an issue to which we will return shortly.

Thus we note that the extent and precise nature of research use in policy are often the subject of competing opinions and claims, but that the dispute is often not so much about *whether* research has been used, but more about *how* it has been used. The example of Sure Start also illustrates that research use may take several forms, including an indirect influence on ways of thinking about social issues, a direct influence on the design of social programmes, and as a means of providing political support to an argument or proposal. Thus despite the sustained critique of evidence-based policy it seems reasonable to conclude that evidence will continue to feature in the knowledge-swirl that underpins policy thinking, policy choices and programme implementation.

Critique of the evidence-based practice agenda

Many questions have also been raised about the appropriateness and realism of evidence-based practice (Trinder and Reynolds, 2000; Miles et al, 2002; Holmes et al, 2006). Critics have objected to, for example, the overshadowing by research of practitioner expertise and judgement, and the relatively fixed criteria for assessing the quality of research evidence. They have also pointed out the impracticability of practitioners seeking out, appraising and applying research findings in busy practice settings. In any case, the notion that practitioners are uninfluenced by good evidence is sometimes seen as insulting, and evidence-based medicine in particular has been called 'nothing more than a neologism, seductive in nature ... a re-branding exercise', with its protagonists labelled as 'intractably deaf and increasingly arrogant' (Miles et al, 2002, pp 87 and 90). Similarly, querulous debates have also been seen in social care (Macdonald, 2000) and education (Hammersley, 2001).

It is true that much of the early literature on evidence-based practice made rather naïve assumptions that there were stocks of knowledge (mainly in the form of research and evaluation evidence) on the one hand, and potential users of this knowledge (in the shape of practitioners) on the other. Evidence use, it was argued, depended on finding effective ways of communicating and disseminating existing knowledge to practitioners, who would then integrate this explicit knowledge with their own tacit understandings. Such a view of evidence-based practice has been criticised as being overly simplistic (Nutley et al, 2003b) and unrealistic (Hammersley, 2001). There have been many calls for thinking to move beyond ideas of simple dissemination in order to capture the complexities of what happens when evidence influences practice (Desforges, 2000; Halladay and Bero, 2000). Others have gone further, to assert that the very idea of 'bodies of evidence' is itself flawed (preferring the term 'bodies of discourse'), that research is rarely self-evident to practitioners, and that good practice depends more on accumulated experience together with local ideas, attitudes and discussion (Wood et al, 1998).

Such stinging criticism is often based around one particular characterisation of evidence-based practice – a rather narrow view first alluded to above, where 'the contexts of practice, experiences and narratives of practitioners, ... [and] values and societal perspectives' are 'banished to subsidiary places beneath the throne of evidence' (Upshur, 2002, p 118). Not surprisingly, such a view is unappealing to many in the field who are otherwise supportive of an evidence-informed approach. As we shall see in subsequent chapters (especially Chapters Two, Four and Seven), there are other models of research use that engage with broader and richer pictures of evidence and take greater care to address the integration of these different sources of evidence with existing practitioner knowledge and situated practitioner action. These too are issues we shall return to shortly in the next section.

Notwithstanding dissenting voices, work has nonetheless gone on apace to promote, enable and support the evidence-based practice agenda. Box 1.2 lists a number of high-profile UK and international initiatives all aimed at developing the research supply side and making this evidence available to practitioners and other stakeholders. Not all of this work is aimed at narrow conceptions of evidence-based practice (in social care especially there is considerable sensitivity to balancing research with practitioner expertise) but some undoubtedly is orientated that way (for example, The Cochrane Collaboration and NICE). Thus, despite the emergence of a significant critical literature on evidence-based practice (Trinder and Reynolds, 2000; Miles et al, 2002), there remains considerable energy, ingenuity and resources expended on collating, synthesising and sharing the burgeoning research base on effective practice. In that sense, the 'evidence-based practice' juggernaut rumbles on, largely undeterred.

Box 1.2: Collating and sharing the evidence base

Several enduring initiatives have been launched to promote, enable and support the evidence-based practice agenda at the international level:

The Cochrane Collaboration (founded in 1993) produces and disseminates 'systematic reviews of health care interventions and promotes the search for evidence in the form of clinical trials and other studies' (www.cochrane.org).

The Campbell Collaboration (launched in 2000) is a non-profit organisation 'that aims to help people make well-informed decisions about the effects of interventions in the social, behavioral and educational arenas' (www.campbellcollaboration.org).

Within the UK, several other organisations have been established with the aim of collating the evidence base underpinning practice and sharing research summaries with local service deliverers:

The Social Care Institute for Excellence (SCIE; established 2001) aims to 'collect and synthesise up-to-date knowledge about what works in social care, and to make that knowledge available and accessible' (www.scie.org.uk).

The National Institute for Health and Clinical Excellence (formerly known as the National Institute for Clinical Excellence, but both incarnations are now referred to as NICE) is an independent organisation responsible for 'providing national guidance on the promotion of good health and the prevention and treatment of ill health' (www.nice.org.uk).

Similar initiatives exist in education (for example, the Evidence for Policy and Practice Information and Co-ordinating Centre at the London Institute of Education, known as the EPPI-Centre – http://eppi.ioe.ac.uk) and for criminal justice social work (for example, the Criminal Justice Social Work Development Centre for Scotland; www.cjsw.ac.uk).

Evidence-based policy and practice: commitment re-questioned?

As we write this book there are fresh questions in the UK about whether the government's earlier enthusiasm for evidence-based policy is now beginning to fade as a result of disappointments in the early outcomes of several high-profile policy programmes. For example, in April 1999, the UK government launched the Crime Reduction Programme (CRP), a three-year £400 million cross-government commitment to achieving a sustained reduction in crime. At the time it was described as 'the biggest single investment in an evidence-based approach to crime reduction which has ever taken place in any country' (Home Office, 1999, p 3). A review of the implementation of the CRP (Homel et al, 2004) has documented many problems and a failure of the programme to achieve a number of its overt goals. Several commentators have dubbed it as an overall failure (Hope, 2004; Maguire, 2004; Tilley, 2004) and the fact that it was not extended to run for 10 years, as was originally intended, may be a signal of its failure in political terms.

Possibly of greater political significance in the UK is the fate of Sure Start. Between 1999 and 2005 the government invested £3.1 billion in the establishment of 500 Sure Start local programmes (*The Economist*, 2005). However, the stage one evaluation findings were disappointing (NESS, 2005; Williams, 2005). The publication of the evaluation report was delayed, but its findings were leaked to a journalist, Polly Toynbee at *The Guardian*. According to the newspaper's reports (Toynbee, 2005; Ward, 2005), the only significant positive difference between Sure Start programme areas and comparison communities was the manner in which principal carers were observed to treat their children. Sure Start had, seemingly, failed to boost children's development, language and behaviour, with the children of teenage mothers apparently actually doing worse in Sure Start areas than elsewhere (Ward, 2005). These findings – for all that they might be contested – have led to a debate over whether Sure Start 'works' (Williams, 2005; *The Economist*, 2005). There are also questions about the ongoing political commitment to Sure Start, especially when Sure Start's aims and objectives seem to have been undermined by the government's own welfare-to-work agenda, which focuses on providing child care for working mothers rather than on the children themselves. Taken together, disappointment with delivered outcomes and dissonance with other more ideological directions of travel may serve to undermine such high-profile commitments to 'evidence-based' programmes.

Disillusionment also arises from the sometimes unrealistic expectations about what research can tell us. Despite a lot of valuable effort to improve research and evaluation methods, research rarely provides definitive answers, particularly in the field of health and social problems and the social programmes designed to combat these. However, with large increases in funding for social research come increased expectations about the contributions that such research should make to improving the success of policy interventions and day-to-day practice (Commission on the Social Sciences, 2003). Some of these expectations are likely to prove unrealistic and to result in disappointment.

A more positive diagnosis is that evidence-based policy has entered the 'mature phase of its policy life cycle' (Ferlie, 2005, p 193). It may have a lower political and rhetorical profile than in the late 1990s but there has been an institutionalisation of evidence-based approaches through the establishment of organisations such as NICE and SCIE (see Box 1.2) – with guidance emanating from these organisations increasingly being seen as having some directive force. In addition, the revised registration requirements of many public service professions have also served to institutionalise the expectation that these professions will operate in an evidence-informed way. Regulatory and oversight agencies too now place greater store on assessments against defined evidence-informed standards. Thus, in both policy and practice arenas evidence has achieved a prominence and an embedding that is unlikely to diminish greatly in the immediate future.

The 'evidence-based' agenda therefore provides an important context within which we consider research use, and many of the activities associated with that agenda are potentially important drivers of research use. However, as we stressed earlier, broader debates about research use transcend the narrow evidence-based policy and practice agenda. That agenda can sometimes seem overly focused on direct instrumentalist uses of research to underpin decision making, whereas indirect influences that reshape problem framing and adjust basic conceptualisations are also of keen interest to us, as are critical perspectives and paradigm challenges that might feed into broader debates about values.

But what of the future for the UK 'evidence-based' agenda? In our view, whether or not government continues to stress the importance of basing policy and practice on the best available evidence, research will continue to both influence, and be influenced by, policy and practice concerns. And many researchers and research funders will continue to be keen to ensure that they understand how they can improve the impact of their research. In this sense we are confident that this book can both make an enduring contribution whatever the fate of the 'evidence-based everything movement', and make a contribution considerably broader than any constraints suggested by an analysis of that somewhat narrow agenda.

How does research fit with evidence?

The foregoing discussion on the evolving evidence agenda has highlighted a central concern about the nature of the evidence that can be used to influence policy and practice. This is an important question as this book is most explicitly concerned with *research* use, and research is usually conceived as being only one part of evidence. Moreover, research and evidence both sit as only part of wider knowledge. Thus we need to be clear both about what research actually is, and about how it fits with the wider concerns to use evidence and knowledge.

Research, and social research

To explore this further we will take first the issue of research. Given the four core service areas of interest (health care, social care, education and criminal justice), much of the research of interest to us will be *social* research. We define social research as that research aimed at understanding the social world, as well as the interactions between this world and public policy/public service. There are several social science disciplines that offer different approaches to understanding these concerns (for example, anthropology, economics, political science, social psychology and sociology) and all are relevant here. Social research may be rooted in one main discipline, or different disciplinary approaches may be combined in multidisciplinary teams or in interdisciplinary fields of study such as 'management' or 'health services research' (Steuer, 2003). It is the use of the research emanating from all of these, where it is relevant to public policy and public service delivery, that is our central focus.

Our emphasis on social – as compared with natural science – research matters because such research is often contentious, may be reliant on controversial theories, draws on multiple and sometimes disputed methods, and may lead to contestable and at times ambiguous findings. In addition, multiple studies may compete and diverge rather than offering any neat accumulations of knowledge. Whereas medical research (such as trials of clinical effectiveness and systematic reviews of the same) may at times provide relatively unproblematic and uncontested findings, this is less common for the social research that exists alongside medical research in health care and is the dominant form of research in the other three sector areas. The complex and contested nature of social research thus poses particular challenges when would-be research users try to interpret research findings as 'evidence' or 'knowledge'.

Given that much of our focus is on social research, we are less interested in the use of wider forms of research, information and evidence, such as the use of research evidence from the natural sciences, the information and evidence produced by performance monitoring and inspection systems, or the evidence supplied by expert or other stakeholder consultations. However, these *are* considered in so far as we need to understand the use of social research in the context of these other forms of evidence and influence, and, as we shall see, the distinctions between these different categories may not be as simple as they first appear.

Our understanding of what constitutes the nature of research is also broad and, like others, we have found it unhelpful to provide any overly specific definition (Court et al, 2005). Thus we regard research as any investigation towards increasing the sum of knowledge based on planned and systematic enquiry. This includes any systematic process of critical investigation and evaluation, theory building, data collection, analysis and codification relevant to the social world (Court et al, 2005). Despite the breadth of this characterisation, it still leaves unspecified issues such as the ontologies that underpin the research, the epistemologies by which research knowledge emerges, and the methodologies that define appropriate systematic processes of data gathering. In these we are entirely eclectic, recognising that the appropriateness of each will be a function both of the questions asked and the context of research use (that is, what is persuasive in one setting may be rather less so in another). In any case, each of these aspects will most likely be contested as part of any research use process.

The expansiveness of our characterisation of 'what counts as research?' has an additional consequence. It could be interpreted as being inclusive of other systematic approaches to enquiry that might not usually be classified as research: for example, the reports and evidence created through systematic enquiries by regulatory authorities, or well-managed and systematic stakeholder consultations. This ambiguity does not unduly concern us: first, because we feel no compulsion to defend research as being only those activities of academic researchers in academic settings; and second, because the interpretation of what counts as research will always, to some extent, be socially situated. Ultimately, therefore, it is our hope that this book will have wider relevance across broader conceptualisations of evidence than just research, and this is a theme we return to in the closing chapter.

Areas where social research can contribute

It may be appropriate at this point to say something about the areas or topics of research enquiry that we believe fall within the purview of social research. Too often evidence-based policy and practice has been thought of as mobilising research evidence simply in the area of effectiveness or cost-effectiveness – that is, addressing the 'what works?' agenda. However, our understanding of the sort of social research whose use we should be considering is much broader than that. It covers, for instance, basic understanding about the structuring of society and the nature of social problems, as well as their sources and interrelationships; and it relates to better understanding about social programme implementation, client experience of those programmes, and the sources and causes of implementation failure. We are also concerned throughout the book to highlight the potential use of research that reshapes the ways in which policy problems are conceptualised or framed as a precursor to enabling more novel policy solutions to make their way onto the agenda. Some of these different sorts of research areas are highlighted in Box 1.3. Of course, research-based knowledge is not the only contributor addressing these sorts of knowledge deficits and it is to a consideration of these other types of knowledge that we now turn.

Box 1.3: Knowledge requirements for effective social policy

Know-about problems: for example, the current policy efforts directed at social inclusion reflect a considerable knowledge base on health, wealth and social inequalities.

Know-what works: that is, what policies, strategies or specific interventions will bring about desired outcomes, at acceptable costs and with few enough unwanted consequences.

Know-how (to put into practice): knowing what should be done is not the same as being able to do it effectively; knowledge about effective programme implementation is also needed.

Know-who (to involve): such knowledge covers estimates of client needs as well as information on key stakeholders necessary for potential solutions.

Know-why: knowledge about why action is required, for example the relationship between values and policy directions.

Source: Adapted from Ekblom (2002)

Can we separate out research from evidence from knowledge?

The links between research, evidence and knowledge are difficult and complex, yet it is common to view them in a hierarchical relationship. Research is often seen as one form of evidence, and evidence as one source of knowledge. Others have taken a narrower view of evidence, seeing it as just one component of research, namely, the empirical findings (Culyer and Lomas, 2006). Knowledge, on the other hand, has sometimes been defined as the *interpretation* of research (Marston and Watts, 2003). However, any hierarchical understanding of the links between the three concepts runs the risk of oversimplification. For example, 'research' is a description of a production process that leads to one form of knowledge, whereas 'evidence' is a value-based label attached to particular types of knowledge.

In considering different types of knowledge, it is possible to highlight three rather different ways of knowing (Brechin and Siddell, 2000):

- *Empirical knowing* – the most explicit form of knowing, which is often based on quantitative or qualitative research study.
- *Theoretical knowing* – which uses different theoretical frameworks for thinking about a problem, sometimes informed by research, but often derived in intuitive and informal ways.
- *Experiential knowing* – craft or tacit knowledge built up over a number of years of practice experience.

It is not, however, all that easy to maintain strict distinctions between these categories: 'the boundaries between the practical, the empirical and the theoretical are always in a state of flux' (Pawson et al, 2003, p 73). While research is usually thought of as providing empirical support for (or refutation of) the more abstract and theoretical forms of knowledge, in fact research studies may themselves be purely theoretical in focus. Experiential knowing in turn may be both a source of ideas for testing in formal empirical studies, as well as the rocks on which research 'knowledge' comes to grief.

Whether and how these different ways of knowing can be combined and integrated is a source of considerable debate. In particular, the dynamics of integration of explicit and tacit knowledge by practitioners are highly complex – there is no simple sense in which this integration can take place (Hammersley, 2001). The privileging of explicit knowledge over tacit will often be contested and resisted, and any accommodation will involve difficult processes of 'unlearning' as well as learning (Rushmer and Davies, 2004), leading to reshaped, but nonetheless still internalised, experiential knowledge. Even relatively clear-cut and persuasive research evidence gets further transformed 'in use', for example innovations usually get adapted before adoption in specific settings, involving trade-offs and integration between local and external knowledge (Ekblom, 2002). All of these observations suggest that it will not always be easy to 'source' ideas and knowledge in any clear-cut way to categories such as 'empirical', 'theoretical', or 'experiential'. Nor will any such categorisation – even if initially possible – remain secure for long: leakage, contamination and fluidity between categories are always likely to occur.

This ambiguity in the classification of different types of knowledge has important implications for research use. Research findings cannot then 'speak for themselves': they will be interpreted. As we shall go on to argue in later chapters, this is most likely to happen effectively through dialogue and engagement. But, however systematic such processes, the inevitable elements of interpretation cannot be said to be neutral. This in turn challenges notions of research use as simply the 'dissemination' or 'knowledge transfer' of pre-packaged research findings to passive and accepting user audiences. There is a transformation process that happens alongside any translation and transfer. This further complicates any neat distinction between 'research', 'evidence' and 'knowledge'.

It will be clear by now that although we have tried to comment on some of the distinctions between research (especially social research), other types of evidence and wider knowledge, such an analysis reveals complexity, fluidity, ambiguity and a degree of circularity in the account. That is to say, definitions of any of research, evidence and knowledge invariably invoke implied accounts of at least one other. In some senses, all of this – while not immaterial to our central preoccupation with research use – may not be worth trying to untangle any further. Indeed it may not be possible to do so with any degree of stability: any definitions we may come to are unlikely to be wholly shared, and will in any case contain the seeds of their own undoing. Throughout this book therefore, we have tended to talk in terms of 'research use', and we leave it to the reader to infer when our arguments might be germane to broader categories such as evidence or even knowledge.

One final comment is necessary if our view is sustained that assessing 'what counts as evidence' or 'what counts as research' involves not just technical objective judgements but also subjective and contextualised assessments. The attaching of labels such as 'evidence' or 'research' to particular types of 'knowledge' are in fact political acts. This is so because using such labels means that problems become defined and visible by those able to assert such labelling, and solutions are then proposed that advance the interests of some at the expense of others. We need to recognise then that knowledge, evidence and research are all privileged terms that reflect the perceptions, priorities and power of those who use them (Polanyi, 1967; Foucault, 1977; Giddens, 1987). In this way the refusal to accept labels such as 'research' and 'evidence' can be seen as an act of resistance. Thus the playing out at ground level of debates about what counts as research is by no means always a rational/technical matter, but instead involves a complex deployment of both technical expertise and power dressed up in the guise of rationality. Taken together then, the foregoing arguments suggest that there are no easy or value-free ways in which research can be defined separately from the context of its use. Such a view should be taken to permeate this book.

Structure of the book

The preceding discussion has laid out our aim and scope, located our work in the historical context of the evidence-based policy and practice agenda, and surfaced a number of critical issues that will recur throughout this text. Suitably primed we hope that the ensuing nine chapters will flesh out these concerns for the reader in ways that allow the development of a sophisticated and nuanced understanding of the issues arising when considering the assimilation and application of social research in public policy and service delivery.

To help readers orientate themselves in this complex field we outline briefly the structure and contents of the remainder of this book. As presentation of material is always rendered rather linear by the constraints of written language, Figure 1.1 aims to depict visually the interconnectedness of the various chapters. There are many connections to be made within and between chapters, and although certain themes do recur, we hope that we have been able to collate cogent accounts of the different aspects of research use in each chapter. In that sense, readers with particular interests may well find it useful to focus first on the chapters of key interest, following threads into other chapters as their interests take them. To aid this process we have tried to make

Figure 1.1: A framework for understanding, improving and assessing research use

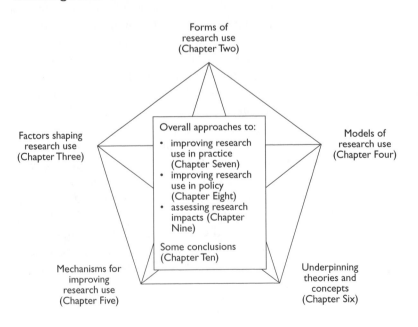

each chapter more-or-less freestanding, with abundant cross-referencing between chapters providing linkages to related material. Of course, we have also tried to arrange our material logically from beginning to end so that subsequent chapters do in some ways build on the preceding materials. Reconciling these two quite different aims has not always been easy, and we hope that the reader will forgive the occasional repetition and not find the cross-referencing too irksome.

As we progress through subsequent chapters we move from an examination of the basic building blocks (what is research use? what shapes its uptake? and how has research use been modelled?) to a synthesis of what this understanding can mean for increasing or influencing research use 'in the field' (for example, what mechanisms seem to be at work? and what strategies for improving research use are available and likely to be effective?). In closing the book we address the challenges facing those who seek to assess the wider impacts of social research, before drawing some conclusions from the arguments that build and interlink throughout.

In brief, the chapters consist of the following:

Chapter Two: What does it mean to 'use' research evidence? Here we begin to define what is meant by research use. We distinguish between various different definitions and conceptualisations, and begin to consider some models that help identify different forms of use, noting along the way how research use has been defined and assessed in empirical studies. In closing this chapter we introduce questions of replication and innovation in relation to research use, arguing that refinement and adaptation of findings in local contexts is a necessary and natural part of research use.

Chapter Three: What shapes the use of research? Here we unpack the processes through which research enters policy and practice, before outlining the sorts of conditions and circumstances that seem to support better use of research. We discuss what we know about the extent to which research is used, and what studies have revealed about the key barriers to – and enablers of – that research use.

Chapter Four: Descriptive models of the research impact process. This chapter explores the many and different ways in which the relationships between research and policy and research and practice have been conceptualised and modelled. In this account we note that earlier rational and linear models are now being rejected in favour of more interactive approaches that draw on interpretivist accounts of the social construction of knowledge. Postmodern frameworks provide an additional critical edge to these analyses.

Chapter Five: Improving the use of research: what's been tried and what might work? Moving on from our basic building blocks on understanding research use processes, we now examine the more applied agenda that is concerned with improving the use and impact of research. We review some of the key strategies and activities that have been used to try to enhance the use of research, and consider the evidence that exists about the effectiveness of these different approaches. In concluding, we highlight the importance of interactive approaches to research use and uptake.

Chapter Six: What can we learn from the literature on learning, knowledge management and the diffusion of innovations? At this point we move out and beyond the specific research use literature. This chapter provides an overview of three bodies of theory and evidence that have the potential to inform research use strategies and activities: learning, knowledge management and the diffusion of innovations. It draws out the research use implications of current thinking and evidence in each of these fields.

Chapter Seven: Improving research use in practice contexts. Continuing our trend of building out from the basic understanding of earlier chapters, we now discuss multifaceted approaches that are aimed at getting research to have an impact on practice, and we review the extent to which there is evidence about their effectiveness. This chapter also considers how different combinations of interventions are likely to be underpinned by particular ways of thinking about research-informed practice. Three emergent models of research-informed practice are discussed: the research-based practitioner model, the embedded research model and the organisational excellence model.

Chapter Eight: Improving research use in policy contexts. In examining how research use can be improved in policy settings we first note the relative dearth of properly evaluated studies. Nonetheless, we identify strategies that address both research supply and research demand issues, and the interplay between them. We also discuss strategies that draw on broader models of the policy process and highlight the role of wider policy networks. Interaction and intermediation are seen as key in shaping how research and policy connect.

Chapter Nine: How can we assess research use and wider research impact? This chapter returns to one of the assumptions that we made at the start, that an evidence-informed approach to both policy and practice is worthwhile, and asks how we could test such a proposition. Three different perspectives are identified: tracking from completed research through to actual and potential consequences;

focusing on understanding the use of research in research user communities; and assessing initiatives that have been designed to increase research impacts. Each of these is elaborated, drawing on the discussions and models laid out in earlier chapters.

Chapter Ten: Drawing some conclusions on *Using evidence.* Our concluding chapter draws together and provides some additional commentary on the themes that have emerged throughout the book. We revisit the idea that research use matters, outlining the sorts of contributions that can be made by more effective engagement with research. In summarising the insights about research use, we draw out the implications for enhancing that use in policy and practice settings. Because of our rather inclusive definition of social research we also highlight the implications of these insights for wider conceptualisations of evidence. Finally, we touch on the areas for further research that might enhance our growing knowledge about research use.

Our own ways of knowing

Given that this book explores research and its impacts, and is itself built around an understanding of a research field, it is perhaps helpful to apply some of our arguments reflexively. *How have we come to know what we aim to explain in this text?* We referred earlier to three different ways of knowing: empirical knowing, theoretical knowing and experiential knowing (Brechin and Siddell, 2000). We have drawn on all three of these in articulating the ideas contained here. First, our empirical knowledge is based on the growing database of empirical studies held in RURU (www.ruru.ac.uk) and especially on the reviews using systematic methods that we have carried out from this resource for such agencies as SCIE (Walter et al, 2004b) and the Learning and Skills Development Agency (Nutley et al, 2003a; Walter et al, 2003a). Second, we have reviewed theoretical ways of understanding research use, both those discussed in reported empirical work on research use, as well as the theories and evidence drawn from a wide social science literature where these have appeared germane (Nutley et al, 2003b). Third, in collating, synthesising and integrating knowledge from the first two categories we have inevitably been influenced and assisted by both our own experiential knowledge around research use and through our interactions with many other actors and stakeholders in the research use arena. These multiple interactions and extensive dialogue, especially around a series of RURU-hosted seminars and workshops (see RURU website noted earlier) have been an essential component of making sense of this complex and challenging area.

Thus the contents of this book could fairly be said to be evidence aware and evidence influenced, but we would make no strong claims that they are necessarily evidence based in the narrow sense that this term is often understood.

Concluding remarks

We started by noting that research may sometimes appear to have quite significant impacts on policy and practice, whereas at other times it may not. This seems to us an issue worthy of further exploration, theoretically and empirically. Such an argument rests on the assumptions that some ways of knowing are better than others – whatever the difficulties associated with that statement – and that research-based ways of knowing are worthy of particular attention. From such beginnings we have laid out the ground this book intends to cover, taking particular care to locate our interest in 'research use' as being more wide-ranging than the often limited scope inferred by the expression 'evidence-based policy and practice'. Along the way, we have taken time to identify research, and especially *social research*, as the core knowledge that we want to track through social systems, but we have then acknowledged that definitions of 'research' may turn out to be either artificially restrictive or ambiguous. Thus, throughout the book, 'research use' can be interpreted broadly (but of course, always contingently), we hope further widening the appeal of our discussions. We trust that, suitably primed, the reader will find our summation of research on research use not just stimulating, and at times challenging, but also, ultimately, of some practical *use*.

Notes

[1] Notwithstanding the title of our earlier text (Davies et al, 2000a), we would prefer the term 'evidence informed', 'evidence influenced' or even 'evidence aware' to the more usual – and over-egged – tag of 'evidence based'. More recently, and in similar vein, the UK government Chief Social Researcher introduced the term 'evidence-*inspired* policy' (author's emphasis; Duncan, 2005).

[2] The Crime Reduction Programme, launched in 1999, was a three-year, £400 million cross-government commitment to achieving a sustained reduction in crime in the UK that drew on a quarter of a century of accumulated crime research and experience (Goldblatt and Lewis, 1998; Nutley and Homel, 2006).

[3] Sure Start is a multi-billion pound investment by the UK government in a programme of support for early years, bringing together early education, child care, health care and family support, and based, at least in part and certainly rhetorically, on extensive evidence about the potential impacts of pre-school experience (Eisenstadt, 2000).

TWO

What does it mean to 'use' research evidence?

This chapter examines what we mean when we talk about 'using' research. Research use is a complex and multifaceted process, and the use of research often means different things to different people. For example, does using research involve simply reading the findings from research as part of general background briefings? Does it mean examining research in making a decision – even if the evidence scanned is ultimately rejected as unhelpful? Or is it necessary for research to have had a direct impact on policy choices or practice behaviours for us to be able to say that research has been 'used'?

This chapter sets out to address these kinds of questions about what it means to 'use' research evidence. We begin by exploring the different ways in which the use of research has been conceptualised and assessed. The common image of research use is that the findings from research have a direct impact on the actions of front-line practitioners or local or national policy makers. Empirical studies have shown, however, that research use is rarely a straightforward process of simple application to policy and practice decision making. More often the use of research is a subtle and complex process, difficult to trace and resulting in equally subtle and complex outcomes. Webber (1991, p 15) characterises the process of research use as 'ambiguous, amorphous, incremental and meandering', and the form that research use takes is likely to be varied and unpredictable. Developing some clarity and consistency around what it means to use research is important to enhance understanding of the field. Where research use is defined in particular ways, however, such definitions will shape how the process is understood, promoted and assessed. Fixed definitions may therefore be less helpful in making sense of the 'ambiguous, amorphous' process of using research. We also look in this chapter at what it might mean to 'misuse' research. Finally, we consider the extent to which using research means replicating precisely the findings of a study, and the implications of adapting or refining such findings in the process of their use.

The different ways research can be used

The most common image of research use is of an instrumental process that involves the direct application of research to policy and practice decisions. At macro policy level, research would then be used to develop and choose between particular policy options. For local policy makers, research would be applied in deciding on local priorities and service configurations, or to define a strategic direction. Among practitioners, research would define the most appropriate course of action to take. The current evidence-based policy and practice (EBPP) agenda is often seen as being focused on these kinds of instrumental uses of research. In reality, however, research is often used in much more indirect, diverse and subtle ways. Research can alter knowledge and understanding, and the use of research may be as much about shaping attitudes and ways of thinking as having a direct influence on decision making. For example, extensive research helped identify the important and varied role played by informal carers in the delivery of health and social care, and such research helped establish the term 'carer' in policy and practice discourse (Parker, 1990). Research has thereby helped to change fundamentally the ways in which the delivery of health and social care in the UK is conceptualised and understood. Using research may also be a political act, to engender support for a particular position or else undermine an opponent's stance. As we noted in Chapter One, research need not always work with the grain of policy or professional orientations, but can play a critical or challenging role in relation to social institutions or dominant currents of thought. Finally, the process of conducting research – or the mere fact that research is being done – can be 'used' within the policy and practice communities, for example to stall making a decision at all.

Widely varying figures emerge when we attempt to pin down the extent to which policy makers and practitioners actually use research, and this probably reflects the diverse definitions both researchers and users have ascribed to research 'use'. Several studies report that only around 10% of their respondents – both policy makers and practitioners – *never* used research (for example, Sunesson and Nilsson, 1988; Rickinson, 2005). Some suggest that 'pockets' exist of individuals within policy and practice communities who regularly seek out research and use it in their day-to-day work (for example, Weiss, 1987; Hillage et al, 1998; Walter et al, 2004b). Others paint a more pessimistic picture of the use of research in policy and practice (for example, Lovell and Kalinich, 1992; Albaek, 1995). However, a scan of studies of research use reveals that such 'use' has been assessed in diverse ways – not only in terms of what this entails, but how frequently or regularly 'use' takes place as well. For example, Rickinson (2005), reviewing studies of teachers' use of research, notes that surveys find that teachers regularly consult and use research. However, more detailed studies demonstrate that their engagement with research is in fact often limited, and may lack depth (Rickinson, 2005).

Studies of the use of research also highlight the diverse ways that research can have an impact on policy and practice. For example, Court and Young (2003) reviewed 50 case studies of policy uses of research, mainly within the developing world, and identified a huge range of ways in which research had influenced policy development and implementation. Research had located priorities for action and pushed particular issues onto the policy agenda as well as influenced key decisions and actions at government level. It had led to new processes and activities on the ground – for example through action research – which sometimes in turn encouraged wider policy changes through much more 'bottom-up' influences. Research had also had an impact on ways of working and not just on the content and substance of policy itself. Further, the use of research had involved not only explicit and codified knowledge (for example in the form of research reports), but the tacit knowledge held by researchers as well, through face-to-face interactions and ongoing exchange between policy makers and researchers. Sometimes researchers had reached a wider audience and encouraged policy change through public pressure. And research had shaped policy in much more subtle and implicit ways as well: enhancing knowledge and understanding, supporting the development of networks, and contributing to the wider societal debates within which policy was made (Court and Young, 2003)

In the practice arena, Rickinson's (2005) review of teachers' uses of research highlights a similar diversity and complexity of ways in which evidence can have an influence. He notes that teachers use research in active and selective ways, which depends on and informs their own values and experiences. Rickinson's (2005) review found that teachers had used research in multidimensional ways. They had drawn on research to improve their day-to-day practice – to develop more effective activities in the classroom – as well as more broadly in designing their methods and curricula. They had also used research to find ways to deal with specific problems. Further, research had encouraged teachers to reflect on their own practices. It had played a role in challenging and changing ways of thinking, sometimes in emotional ways. At a local level, research had also prompted further study, such as to see whether findings could be replicated in teachers' own classrooms. In this way, using research had encouraged additional research and inquiry, and additional evidence use. Finally, teachers had used research to validate certain practices. For example, research had helped support or justify applications for grants for practice development. It had also been used to affirm – either personally or more publicly – the value of existing practices. Rickinson concludes that for teachers, research use is not just about what happens in the classroom but reflects the varied professional roles that teachers hold, 'as planners, thinkers, leaders, coaches, researchers and learners' (Rickinson, 2005, p 23).

Identifying these different types of research use alerts us to the fact that using research means much more than the simple and direct application of specific findings to a specific policy or practice decision. Those advocating more or better use of research tend to see instrumental forms of use as their main goal, but this neglects the range of roles that research can play within the policy and practice communities.

Research use typologies

Research use typologies have emerged in the literature to try to pin down more clearly what the use of research might entail. While they typically originate from empirical work in specific fields, they have been widely applied across different policy and practice contexts.

A key distinction is often made between instrumental and conceptual uses of research (for example, Caplan, 1979; Webber, 1986; Huberman, 1990; Cousins and Leithwood, 1993). Broadly, *instrumental use* refers to the direct impact of research on policy and practice decisions. It identifies the influence of a specific piece of research in making a specific decision or in defining the solution to a specific problem, and represents a widely held view of what research use means. *Conceptual use* is a much more wide-ranging definition of research use, comprising the complex and often indirect ways in which research can have an impact on the knowledge, understanding and attitudes of policy makers and practitioners. It happens where research changes ways of thinking, alerting policy makers and practitioners to an issue or playing a more general 'consciousness-raising' role. Such uses of research may be less demonstrable but are no less important than more instrumental forms of use.

In fact, on the whole it seems that research is much more likely to be used in conceptual than in instrumental ways – changing perceptions and understanding rather than directly influencing policy or practice change (for example, Caplan, 1979; Albaek, 1995; Hemsley-Brown and Sharp, 2003; Reid, 2003). Policy makers say that while research is often interesting and helpful – and is rarely completely ignored – it most often 'informs' policy, rather than providing a clear steer for action (Reid, 2003). This is supported by Innvaer et al's (2002) review of health policy makers' use of research, which found that up to 60% of studies' respondents reported conceptual use, compared to 40% at most reporting instrumental uses of research. Even where research is locally commissioned and might be expected to influence policy more directly, this is not always the case (for example, Sunesson and Nilsson, 1988; Barker, 1994; Innvaer et al, 2002; Greenberg et al, 2003). While there are exceptions (for example, Hutchinson, 1995), it does seem that research is mainly used by policy makers in indirect, conceptual ways.

Practitioners similarly emphasise the conceptual value of evidence. They describe how research can enhance their understanding of key issues in their fields, provide a source of motivation or new ideas, offer a perspective on service users' experiences, challenge existing ways of thinking and doing, and promote informed discussion and debate. On the whole, however, they are less likely to identify examples where research has had a more direct and visible impact on practice (for example, Fisher, 1997; Williams et al, 1997; Walter et al, 2004a; Rickinson, 2005).

Among policy makers in particular, research use may also be *strategic* or *tactical*. Research can be used as an instrument of persuasion, to support an existing political stance or to challenge the positions of others. It can also be deployed to legitimate a decision or a course of action. Alternatively, commissioning or conducting research can be used to push through a decision – with a promise to evaluate the outcomes – or else to defer taking any action at all (for example, Lovell and Kalinich, 1992; Anderson et al, 1999; Dahler-Larsen, 2000). Policy makers describe how research can provide themselves, their agencies and their policies with a level of credibility and weight (for example, Reid, 2003). The same body of research may be seen and used very differently by different actors within the policy environment; and different groups may manage and fund research in order to use it for their own ends (Selby Smith and Selby Smith, 2002). The evidence suggests that these strategic forms of use may also be more prevalent than instrumental uses of research within policy contexts (for example, Lovell and Kalinich, 1992; Innvaer et al, 2002). Strategic forms of use have been identified among practitioners as well, for example to validate what they do, whether personally or publicly (Rickinson, 2005). Such strategic uses of research are, however, more likely to be concealed by research participants, making them difficult to identify empirically (Dahler–Larsen, 2000).

Finally, we can identify the *process use* of research. Originating in the evaluation field, this type of research use emphasises how the design and conduct of research, rather than just its findings, may be used by both policy makers and practitioners (for example, Patton, 1997, 1998; Shulha and Cousins, 1997). Simply engaging in a research or evaluation project can lead to change in ways of thinking and in ways of behaving, among individuals but also more collectively throughout projects and organisations. These changes take place as a result of the learning that occurs through engaging with the process of research (Patton, 1997). This 'process learning' can lead to enhanced communication and understanding between policy makers or practitioners and their stakeholders, or to changes in the design or outcomes of the programme being assessed (Shulha and Cousins, 1997; Patton, 1998). Barker (1994) has identified this kind of process use of research among policy makers engaging with Research & Development (R&D) evaluations in the UK and the European Community, in ways that have supported closer orientation of R&D programmes to current policy needs. Conducting research may also be a way for policy makers to get stakeholders involved and on board, and this may be as important as the findings themselves (Patton, 1997; Reid, 2003). Process learning can persist beyond the shelf life of a single set of findings, with the possibility of sustained policy and practice impact from research (Patton, 1998). Although the focus of this type of research use has been in the evaluation field, it may be as important a consideration for any research that closely or collaboratively engages policy makers and practitioners.

Weiss (1979) has elaborated a more sophisticated typology of research uses which begins to examine these roles for research in more depth (see Box 2.1). This typology derives from empirical work on policy makers' use of research, but has heavily influenced accounts of research use in practice contexts too.

Box 2.1: Seven different 'meanings' of research use

(1) The knowledge-driven model

Basic research identifies knowledge of potential value to the policy or practice community. Applied research tests this knowledge out in real-world contexts, research-based technologies are developed and implemented and research use occurs.

(2) The problem-solving model

Research helps policy makers find a solution to a particular problem. Researchers and policy makers agree about the nature of the problem and the goals to be achieved, and social science provides evidence and ideas to help clarify a way forward – drawing on existing research or commissioning new work.

(3) The interactive model

Policy makers actively and interactively search for knowledge to help support their work, drawing on multiple sources of information – including their own experience – alongside research. The relationship between policy and research is typically iterative, messy and dynamic, and progress is gradual, involving 'mutual consultations' between policy makers, researchers and other players in the political process.

(4) The political model

Where political opinions are long standing and fixed, or where interests have firmly coalesced, research is unlikely to have a direct influence. Instead it may be used politically, to support a particular stance, or else to destabilise opposing positions.

(5) The tactical model

Sometimes, the findings from research are irrelevant: what matters is that research is being done. Funding or conducting new research can be a way for policy makers to avoid taking action. Researchers may be blamed for unpopular policy outcomes; or else research 'experts' can be drafted in to give legitimacy to an agency or its policies.

(6) The enlightenment model

Over time, research will have a gradual and cumulative influence on the public policy sphere. Ideas, theories and ways of thinking that derive from the broad body of research-based knowledge gradually seep into the policy-making process through diverse and indirect routes, such as interest groups, journalists and the mass media. Research can thereby shape the ways both problems and their solutions are framed and can ultimately lead to fundamental shifts in the prevailing policy paradigm.

(7) Research as part of the intellectual enterprise of society

New policy interest in an issue may be stimulated by a wider social concern, and policy makers offer funds for its further research. Researchers are thereby drawn to study it, and may develop and reconceptualise the issue. This in turn shapes ways of thinking by both policy makers and at a broader societal level as well. The process is one of mutual, ongoing influence between policy, research and the social context within which both are embedded.

Source: Adapted from Weiss (1979)

Weiss's (1979) models of research use link and overlap with the more simple typologies of research use already defined, but broaden and extend these by paying more attention to the routes and processes through which research may come to influence public policy. These may in turn depend on the ways in which policy is made. For example, the focus of both the knowledge-driven and problem-solving models is primarily on instrumental uses of research. However, while in the knowledge-driven model it is the research itself that determines policy – 'the sheer fact that knowledge exists presses towards its development and use' (Weiss, 1979, p 427) – the problem-solving model involves an active search for knowledge where policy goals are already in place. While they both place research at the forefront of policy making, Weiss (1979) notes that these models are, however, rare on the ground. By contrast, the political and tactical models reflect more strategic types of research use. They differ, however, in the extent to which the content of the research is seen to play a role in its use, and the tactical model also begins to encompass some process uses of research.

The interactive, enlightenment and intellectual enterprise models offer somewhat different visions of research use, which allow the possibility that evidence will be used in more conceptual ways. They alert us to the fact that research use may be a complex, indirect and lengthy process, that will in turn interact with diverse other forms and sources of knowledge circulating in the policy arena. For example, in the model of research use as part of the intellectual enterprise of society, research and policy interact not just with each other, but with the broader social context in which they operate, including the prevailing discourses and systems of thought of the time. These three models additionally highlight the ways in which uses of research need not be as conscious or deliberate as the other models imply. Policy actors may thus not always be aware that they are drawing on research in their deliberations. Weiss (1979) suggests that, in fact, the enlightenment use of research is the most common model on the ground. While subtle, this kind of use can be substantial, with the potential to redefine a whole policy agenda. Despite its appeal, however, Weiss (1979) sounds some cautionary notes about the enlightenment model. For example, it provides no way of filtering out poor-quality or outdated research: all and any findings will be thrown into the mix. Research use also depends on 'natural' processes of knowledge percolation, which may be inefficient. For these reasons, Weiss (1979) suggests that the process may be as much one of 'endarkenment' as enlightenment.

Ways of thinking specifically about practice uses of research are on the whole less well developed in the literature. Based on a review of studies of the use of evaluation research in education, Cousins and Leithwood (1986) identified four key ways of operationalising research 'use':

- use as decision making: for example to support decisions about programme funding or about the content or management of a programme;
- use as education: primarily conceptual uses of research, for example to shape perceptions about a programme, to enhance understanding among staff or to improve morale;
- use as the simple processing of evaluation results: where 'use' simply means that findings have been given some thought or consideration, including basic understanding of evaluation data; and
- potential for use: such as the extent to which individuals agree with evaluation recommendations. Cousins and Leithwood (1986) suggest this category may be better construed as antecedents to use.

Cousins and Leithwood's (1986) definitions are primarily concerned with the use of research in organisational settings. On the basis of a review of studies of teachers' use of research referred to earlier, Rickinson (2005) has identified five different processes that help us understand how individual practitioners engage with research (see Box 2.2).

Box 2.2: Teachers' use of research

(1) An active process

Teachers actively engage with the concepts and findings from research. Research will be adapted and translated, given meaning within the local contexts of its use, rather than simply adopted. This might involve working collaboratively with researchers and other practitioners as well as teachers themselves undertaking research.

(2) A selective process

Teachers engage with research in individualised, subjective and idiosyncratic ways. Their response to research will vary, and their use of research reflects both their practical needs and their unique ways of thinking.

(3) A values-rich process

Teachers use research where it fits their own personal values and beliefs. Evidence alone is not enough: research use is often an emotional, not simply instrumental, process.

(4) A rewarding process

Teachers also use research to make sense of their own experiences, and view engaging with research as a learning process. They share and discuss research with colleagues as well, weighing up new results and new ideas.

(5) A developing process

Teachers may change the ways in which they use research across the course of their professional careers. Among newly qualified teachers, individualised appraisal of research is common. Mid-career, teachers extract research findings from their contexts in order to apply them. In the final, established phase of their careers, teachers are more likely to experiment with the findings from research.

Source: Adapted from Rickinson (2005)

Box 2.2 provides a way of thinking about practitioners' research use which complicates existing typologies and offers a more nuanced conceptualisation of uses of research. It suggests that practitioners do indeed use research in diverse ways – from simply applying research evidence to practice problems, through to much more educative and legitimising activities. Like Weiss' (1979) models, it draws attention to the processes through which practitioners use research and demonstrates the complexity inherent in research use. However, it is much less easy to fit such understandings of research use into neat and simple categories. Instead, it is clear that practitioners may use research in multiple and overlapping ways, and through instrumental, conceptual, strategic and process types of use simultaneously. Where conventional typologies highlight the contrasts between types of use, Rickinson's (2005) framing blurs the boundaries between them, and helps us begin to imagine how these different research use types may operate in parallel and even interact.

Box 2.2 also turns our attention to the active role that individual practitioners play in how research gets used. It emphasises the ways in which different needs and different ways of thinking lead to different forms of engagement with research and different kinds of use. Research use then represents an interaction between the ideas and findings contained in the research and the existing knowledge, experiences and attitudes of the practitioners themselves: a complex, varied and unique process. Yet at the same time, research use can also be a social process, involving interaction with other practitioners, so that the use of research may be jointly defined and enacted. Finally, Rickinson (2005) highlights the temporal dimension of research use, emphasising the ways in which practitioners' engagement with research is dynamic, and may change throughout the course of a professional career.

Weiss' (1979) seven models of research have, however, proved highly influential in the research use literature in both the policy and the practice arenas, and have been adapted and applied to studies of the use of research in a wide variety of contexts (see Box 2.3).

Box 2.3: Meanings of research use: applying Weiss' (1979) models to examine research use in policy and practice

The use of research in developing UK prison drugs policy

Duke (2001) has used Weiss' (1979) models of research use to analyse the role of research in developing UK prison drugs policy since 1980. Drawing on interviews and document analysis, she found that the relationship between research and policy making changed across the different stages of policy development. Initially, research contributed to the gradual

---

accumulation of knowledge about drugs in prisons, which both identified the problem and helped to place it on the policy agenda. This reflected Weiss' (1979) enlightenment model of research use. The interactive model was also relevant at this early stage, however. Research represented just one source of information for the policy process, alongside input from practitioners, bureaucrats, interest groups and the media.

During the policy development process, research was used in ways that better reflected Weiss' (1979) tactical model. For example, in the face of growing criticism of the emerging strategy on drugs in prisons, the Prison Service commissioned more research. This allowed it to delay its response, and helped to shift attention away from the strategy itself. Research was later used in ways that corresponded more to the political model, helping the Prison Service justify and reinforce its existing strategy on drug misuse rather than radically rethinking its approach. Finally, policy interest in and development around drugs in prisons in turn stimulated further research on the issue, reflecting the notion of research as 'part of the intellectual enterprise of society'. The relationship between research and policy in this case was both interactive and reflexive, influenced by and influencing wider social currents of thought on the issue of drugs in prisons (Duke, 2001).

Research use in Swedish social welfare agencies

Sunesson and Nilsson (1988) drew on Weiss' (1979) models of research use to explore the use of research by staff within Swedish social welfare agencies, including front-line social workers, administrative staff and agency directors. They found that, above all, research was used in 'enlightenment' ways, although political and interactive uses of research were important too. However, they also found that individuals might use research through more than one of Weiss' (1979) models at any given time. Further, the meanings given to research use varied among different settings and between different individuals and organisational groups. Sunesson and Nilsson (1988) concluded that the organisational contexts of the different welfare agencies studied had shaped these different uses of research. Complex issues of knowledge, power and control influenced the ways in which research was used by different staff within the agencies, and the overall use of research by an agency as a whole. For example, some agencies had an active and deliberate culture of drawing on research to address questions about the substance and development of services. Their members were more likely to report using research, and to use research through the political and enlightenment models (Sunesson and Nilsson, 1988).

The studies detailed in Box 2.3 have shown how the use of research may move through several different types or models over time, and suggest that we need to reconceptualise research use as a dynamic process that may not be readily 'boxed' into static typologies. For example, any single instance of research use may simultaneously involve several different types of use, while the same research may be used in different ways by different individuals within an organisation (for example, Sunesson and Nilsson, 1988). It may be that Weiss' (1979) models of research use then need to be conceived as potentially parallel processes, rather than contrasting 'types'.

From fixed typologies to fluidity and ambiguity in research use

Research use categories have occasionally proved difficult to apply empirically – in both policy and practice settings (for example, Sunesson and Nilsson, 1988; Greenberg and Mandell, 1991). Such studies have found that the boundaries between different types of use are often blurred, and the categories may not be mutually exclusive. Defining – and then identifying – every instance of 'use' is also problematic, and some – such as more concrete or instrumental uses of research – are more readily uncovered than others (Greenberg et al, 2003).

Other conceptualisations view research use as a continuum rather than in terms of static categories. Such frameworks better reflect the fact that there is movement and flow between different forms of research use. Whiteman (1985) describes a two-dimensional framework that includes many of the existing categories for defining research use, which Greenberg and Mandell (1991) have adapted, suggesting that each of the two dimensions effectively represents a continuum rather than a set of types of research use (see Table 2.1). The first of the

Table 2.1: Research use as a two-dimensional continuum

	Substantive	**Elaborative**	**Strategic**
Concrete	Research shapes the core of a decision or an issue	Peripheral use of research to further refine a position	Research is used to justify a position that has already been adopted
Conceptual	Research shapes a core orientation towards an issue or a basic understanding of the issue	Peripheral use of research to further refine an orientation or understanding	Research is used to confirm an orientation or an understanding that has already been adopted

Source: Adapted from Greenberg and Mandell (1991)

continua they describe is the concrete/conceptual dimension, ranging from the use of particular findings to make particular decisions, to the more intangible and conceptual influence of research on ways of thinking. The second dimension is the substantive/elaborative/strategic dimension, which defines the extent to which research outlines a position or decision, or serves to legitimate a position or decision once this has been adopted.

Placing types of research use along a spectrum in this way highlights the potential for flow and interaction between different kinds of use, so that research may contribute to policy decisions through multiple and indirect routes and forms of use. Greenberg and Mandell (1991) used their framework in a study of the use of social experiments by US policy makers, and found that there was much flow along the different dimensions of use. While concrete–substantive use of the experiments' findings was rare, multiple other forms of use emerged, and more conceptual or strategic forms of use might ultimately lead to more direct and instrumental applications of research (Greenberg and Mandell, 1991). Research use thus emerges as an iterative, fluid and non-linear process, which may progress through many different types of research use in sometimes unpredictable ways.

It is important to identify the multiple and varied ways in which research can be used. Crucially, this opens up a range of different ways of thinking about what is both possible and appropriate in terms of using research and developing strategies to promote research use. Further, as Weiss (1979) notes, it can also support more sophisticated empirical study of the field. However, on the whole, defining typologies of research use turns our attention away from the inherently dynamic nature of the research use process. Research use types represent a 'snapshot' in time (Sunesson and Nilsson, 1988), and so cannot easily capture the potential for flow through many different types in any given context. Frameworks that conceptualise research use as a series of stages begin to explore these ideas in more depth.

Research use as a series of stages

A different set of frameworks identifies types of research use as a series of stages, incorporating a more dynamic perspective which views the use of research as an ongoing process rather than a single event. Most simply, Oh (1996), working in the policy field, has distinguished the 'use' of research – in which research may simply have been read and understood – from research 'impact', when research influences a specific decision or choice. Similarly, Mulhall and le May (1999), examining research use by healthcare professionals, define:

- research dissemination: the simple communication of research to relevant parties;
- research utilisation: accessing and evaluating research, with the aim of increasing knowledge; and
- research implementation: changes in practice based on research.

Stage models have been used to define research use in both policy and practice contexts (see Boxes 2.4 and 2.5). Although developed to make sense of the use of research in contrasting arenas, broad similarities emerge between these different frameworks. Importantly, they break down the process of research use into a series of multiple steps or stages, from a broad awareness and understanding of research, through some translation of the findings to 'fit' the local policy or practice context, to the direct impact of research on policy outcomes and practice behaviours. In doing so, they highlight some of the complexity behind simple definitions of 'conceptual' or 'instrumental' use. They also draw our attention to the question of sustaining research use beyond a single policy or practice decision. Key to these models, however, is that they assume that instrumental uses of research are the ultimate goal. As such, they tend to underplay the importance and possibility of more conceptual uses of research, which are viewed as steps – albeit crucial steps – along the way to 'full' research use, rather than as an end in themselves. As we have seen, however, conceptual uses of research can be of considerable value in their own right, in both policy and practice settings.

Box 2.4: Knott and Wildavsky's 'standards' of research use among policy makers

Knott and Wildavsky's (1980) model is perhaps the best known of the different 'stage' approaches to defining the use of research. It identifies seven standards of research use by policy makers (although these could be applied in organisational and practice settings too). In effect these standards are seven different stages of research use, which represent key links in the 'chain of utilisation':

(1) Reception

Reception means simply that research has been received by an individual. Research is 'used' when it lands on their desk, even if they never read its findings.

(2) Cognition

The next stage occurs when research is both read and understood.

(3) Reference

When research changes ways of thinking – provokes a shift in an individual's 'frame of reference', for example in terms of defining key problems and priorities – the third standard of use has been reached.

(4) Effort

At the next stage, research has shaped action: some effort has been made to get the findings adopted, even if this is ultimately unsuccessful.

(5) Adoption

Adoption means that research has had a direct influence not just on the policy process but on the policy itself.

(6) Implementation

While research may have been used to develop policy, at this stage it has also been translated into practice on the ground.

(7) Impact

For Knott and Wildavsky (1980), full utilisation of research only takes place when an implemented policy is successful, and there are tangible, identifiable benefits to citizens.

Source: Adapted from Knott and Wildavsky (1980)

**Box 2.5: Glasziou and Haynes' 'Pipeline Model':
the different stages of practitioners' use of research**

Glasziou and Haynes' (2005) 'Pipeline Model', developed within the healthcare field, outlines seven different stages that define research use from a practitioner perspective:

- Practitioners are *aware* of findings from research.

- Practitioners *accept* the research findings.
- Practitioners view the research findings as locally *applicable*.
- Practitioners view the research findings as *doable* within the local context.
- Practitioners *act on* the research findings.
- Practitioners *adopt* the research findings.
- Practitioners (or patients) *adhere to* the research findings.

However, this 'pipeline' of research use is typically leaky, in that potentially useful research findings will be lost at each stage along the way.

Source: Adapted from Glasziou and Haynes (2005)

A number of studies have adapted these kinds of stage models to identify the nature and extent of research use among policy makers and practitioners (for example, Bullock et al, 1998; Landry et al, 2001a, 2001b; see Box 2.6). In general these studies reach the perhaps unsurprising conclusion that the amount of research use declines at each stage. Policy makers and practitioners are more likely to read and understand research, and to use research to think about their work in new ways, than to actually apply research directly to policy and practice decisions. This reflects the findings of studies of research use types: the emphasis is firmly on conceptual, not instrumental, uses of research.

Box 2.6: The use of Canadian social science research

Landry et al (2001a, 2001b) have assessed the use of research produced by social scientists in Canada using an adapted version of Knott and Wildavsky's (1980) stage model. They define a 'ladder' of research use with six key steps:

Stage 1   *Transmission:* the researcher has transmitted key findings to relevant policy makers and practitioners.

Stage 2   *Cognition:* the research findings were read and understood by their recipients.

Stage 3   *Reference:* the findings were cited in reports and action plans.

Stage 4   *Effort:* policy makers and practitioners made efforts to ensure the findings were adopted.

Stage 5: *Influence:* the findings influenced the decisions of policy makers and practitioners.

Stage 6: *Application:* the findings led to applications and extension within the policy or practice communities.

Landry et al's (2001a, 2001b) questionnaire survey found that nearly half of all researchers reported transmitting their findings to policy makers and practitioners. Nearly one third of findings, however, failed to reach even this first stage. Research use also decreased at each subsequent step up the ladder, although 16% of respondents said that their findings had led to some kind of policy or practice application.

Source: Adapted from Landry et al (2001a, 2001b)

These stage models suggest that different types of research use may build on each other and emerge over time. They turn our attention to the idea of research use as a cumulative process, in which conceptual uses of research may help support, or may even be required for, more instrumental uses of research. But they also have their limitations. They suggest, for example, that research use proceeds in a linear and logical fashion, and that the next 'stage' of use can only be reached when the previous one has been achieved. Other research has, however, highlighted the potential for research use to be much more iterative and non-linear than this suggests (for example, Sunesson and Nilsson, 1988). Stage models also fail to encompass the kinds of strategic uses of research which can in turn lead to more instrumental or end-stage uses (for example, Greenberg and Mandell, 1991). Finally, they present largely passive accounts of research use, which focus on individuals' use of research in the absence of contexts and systems developed for more active engagement with research. As such, they may fit best in environments where research and its use remain unmanaged.

In some ways, research use typologies and stage models of the use of research are simply variations on a theme. Where categories of research use provide static 'snapshots' of how research gets used, stage models offer a way of conceptualising research use as a process which flows between different types of use. They too, however, identify different types of research use which are essentially reducible to more conceptual and more instrumental forms of use: they then add the assumption that the latter proceeds from the former. As an alternative, we can locate conceptual and instrumental uses of research at either end of a continuum, ranging from simply raising awareness of research findings, through enhanced knowledge and understanding and shifts in attitudes and ideas, to direct changes in policy and practice (see Figure 2.1).

Figure 2.1: A continuum of research use

This continuum effectively combines typologies of research use with stage models of the research use process. Crucially, however, the continuum is seen as two-way rather than a simple linear flow from conceptual use to instrumental use, acknowledging the iterative and interactive nature of much research use.

The continuum is focused on the use of the findings from research, however, and omits those kinds of strategic and process uses of research for which the actual findings of the research may be less relevant. It aims to be of practical value in helping to develop effective strategies for improving the use of research, strategies which are primarily aimed at ensuring conceptual and instrumental research use (which we return to in Chapter Five). Such strategies can have an impact at any point along the research use continuum, and the continuum helps to define the kinds of outcomes that are desired or expected from such research use strategies. But both strategic and process uses of research are important too, and may in themselves lead to more instrumental end-stage uses. The implications of these should thus not be overlooked in thinking about how best to improve the use of research among policy makers and practitioners.

The 'misuse' of research

It is unlikely that those wishing to develop strategies to enhance the use of research will have political and tactical uses of research in mind as their goal. Indeed, Weiss (1979) has commented that researchers often dislike or disapprove of the use of research in more symbolic and strategic ways, for example to justify a decision that has already been made (see, for example, Patton, 1997; Shulha and Cousins, 1997). Practitioners too express concerns about the use of poor-quality findings, or that research may be misapplied and used to justify bad practice (for example, Sheldon and Chilvers, 2000). There are considerable debates within the field about whether more strategic uses of research are valid or legitimate. Weiss (1979) has argued strongly that research use is only illegitimate where findings are distorted or misinterpreted. In her view, supportive research can provide those who take up a particular political position with additional confidence, certainty, and 'an edge in the continuing debate' (1979, p 36). As such, if research finds 'ready-made partisans', it is more likely directly to influence the development of policy in instrumental ways.

This raises the question of what constitutes the 'proper' use of research. How the misuse of research is defined will inevitably vary among individuals and groups. In particular, these issues are less clear-cut when there is less agreement about the nature of evidence that should be used to support policy and practice, or where the focus is on conceptual rather than instrumental uses of research. Over-use may be an issue as well, where tentative findings or ideas are taken up too zealously, or become the latest fad or fashion and are implemented wholesale. The literature has mostly been focused on addressing the under-use of research, and far less attention has been paid to its potential for misuse.

One exception to this is in the field of evaluation. Patton (1997) makes a key distinction here between 'misevaluation', in which evaluation is conducted poorly or unethically, and 'misuse' of evaluation, where potential research users undermine the evaluation in ways that skew the results or the study itself. Yet, as Patton (1997) argues, the use and misuse of research are not opposite ends of the same spectrum. Patton suggests that we need to imagine instead two continua: one that leads from the non-use of research to its use, and a second that leads from the non-use of research to misuse. The two are related, however, so that 'as use increases, misuse will also increase' (Patton, 1997, p 360). This is a key issue: as research use is increasingly encouraged – as with the EBPP movement in the UK – then the misuse of research also becomes more likely.

Reviewing the field, Shulha and Cousins (1997) differentiate a more complex set of ideas about evaluation misuse:

- the 'justified non-use' of findings – where good-quality findings are deliberately not used (for example because they raise ethical dilemmas);

- 'mischievous use', or misuse, of evaluation – undermining the process or outcomes of a study;
- 'misevaluation', when the findings that are used are poor quality; and
- 'abuse', the suppression of potentially useful and high-quality findings.

Crucially, however, the misuse of research is situationally defined (Patton, 1997). What is regarded as misuse in one context may be viewed as justified non-use in another (Shulha and Cousins, 1997). For example, while it may seem self-evident that poor-quality findings should not be used, there is still considerable debate in many sectors and disciplines about what constitutes good or adequate evidence for policy and practice. Defining misuse in the here-and-now may also be problematic when questions about the use of research for wider social benefit are considered (Shulha and Cousins, 1997). Definitions of the misuse of research are thus contested and often ambiguous. More pertinently, as Shulha and Cousins (1997) note, it is very difficult to study the misuse of research in any systematic way.

Further, neither the use nor the misuse of research need be intentional. Tyden (1993) has made a distinction between intended and unintended uses of research. While some changes are clearly intended when using research, other changes may emerge which are neither intended nor visible (Tyden, 1993). Research may thus be used in ways that are beyond the control of those who conducted the study; and such use may be negative or harmful as well as positive (Walter et al, 2004a). Questions of power will, however, play a key role in shaping whether research gets used, in what ways, and by whom (for example, Watkins, 1994) – issues we return to in Chapter Four. Researchers may then need to be clear about their own roles not only in producing knowledge – research is not a 'value-free' activity – but in influencing its use as well (Weiss, 1998).

Research use as replication or innovation

One reason why research use is such an uncertain and ambiguous process is that the nature of research evidence is itself far from being fixed and uncontested. Instead, research knowledge is a product of its context of creation, and will likely be reinterpreted within the context of its use. This raises some key questions for potential research users in terms of how they understand and apply any piece of research. Research findings rarely 'speak for themselves' but will be given meaning and validated by policy makers and practitioners within the specific contexts of their use.

For some, 'using' research means faithfully replicating its findings in different contexts. Their key concern is with fidelity – ensuring that research findings or research-based programmes are implemented precisely according to the original study (see Box 2.7).

Box 2.7: Ensuring fidelity in research-based programmes

Mihalic et al (2004a) outline five key components to programme fidelity:

(1) *Adherence:* whether the programme is being delivered as it was designed, for example using the correct protocols and tools and with appropriately trained staff.

(2) *Exposure:* for example the number of sessions delivered, their length and frequency.

(3) *Quality of programme delivery:* the ways in which staff deliver a programme, including issues of skills and attitude.

(4) *Participant responsiveness:* the extent to which participants are engaged in the programme.

(5) *Programme differentiation:* defining the key elements of different programmes that can be reliably differentiated from one another.

Source: Adapted from Mihalic et al (2004a)

Fidelity is primarily a concern for those aiming for instrumental forms of research use. It is critical where it is assumed that 'the effectiveness of an intervention is dependent upon the rigour with which that intervention is conducted' (Hollin, 1995, p 196; see also Mihalic et al, 2004a). A wide range of studies has shown that the higher the quality of implementation fidelity, the more effective a programme is likely to be (Mihalic et al, 2004a). Hollin (1995), writing from a criminal justice perspective, suggests that paying attention to programme fidelity not only supports effective outcomes, but can also address ethical issues in working with offenders and help set and meet quality standards in practice. Using research in ways that support fidelity to the original findings may thus bring added benefits. Those who advocate for programme fidelity propose that this is best achieved through some form of monitoring and evaluation of the programme's implementation (for example, Hollin, 1995; Mihalic et al, 2004a).

There are, however, a number of potential threats to maintaining fidelity to the original findings from research. For example, it is difficult to maintain strict fidelity outside the controlled environments of the trials in which research-based programmes are typically developed, and programmes are likely to be modified simply in the process of their dissemination (Mihalic et al, 2004a). Further, programme implementers are often keen to adapt programmes in ways that support local community needs and help establish a sense of ownership (Mihalic et al, 2004a). This raises further questions about what it means to 'use' research. For example, some commentators have argued that any modifications to the original research may undermine the mechanisms through which the programme achieved success (for example, Denton et al, 2003; Mihalic et al, 2004a). Box 2.8 describes an initiative in which using research means maintaining high levels of programme fidelity, in order to secure effective outcomes.

Box 2.8: The Blueprints for Violence Prevention Initiative

The Blueprints for Violence Prevention Initiative is based in the US and focuses on identifying and implementing effective violence and drug prevention programmes. The initiative is supported by the US Office of Juvenile Justice and Delinquency Prevention (OJJDP) and has two main goals:

- to identify effective, research-based violence and drug prevention programmes; and
- to replicate these programmes through a national dissemination project.

The dissemination of effective programmes takes place through a structured process in which the Blueprints initiative provides training and skills to support sites in implementing programmes. The initiative also provides an assessment of and feedback on sites' progress.

Key to this initiative is the emphasis placed on maintaining fidelity to the original programme designs. The original programme designers themselves provide technical assistance in implementing interventions, and Blueprints staff conduct detailed evaluations to monitor the quality of replication at each site. The initiative also disseminates information about factors known to improve the quality and fidelity of implementation. Blueprints' evaluations have shown that, contrary to expectations, it is possible to secure both high fidelity to a programme and local satisfaction with implementation.

Source: Adapted from Mihalic et al (2004a, 2004b)

Others, however, see the use of research in much less rigid terms, and argue that some degree of adaptation is still possible – and may even be essential – for research to be used effectively. Crucially, no social context for applying research will ever be exactly the same as the one in which the original research was conducted: 'strict' replication is impossible (Tilley, 1993). Context is key to scientific realist perspectives on what 'using' research should mean (see, for example, Tilley, 1993). The focus in this view is no longer on precisely replicating a study, but on identifying those links between mechanisms, contexts and outcomes that produced the original findings. Any outcomes are assumed to emerge from the activation of one or more underlying causal mechanisms. The operation of such mechanisms is, however, context-dependent. Using research then means both developing theories that specify the mechanisms and contexts which lead to particular outcomes; and then reproducing the features of the context that will trigger the mechanisms needed for change (Tilley, 1993).

As Gomm (2000) notes, however, it is often not feasible or possible to restructure policy and practice contexts so that they match or are sufficiently similar to the conditions under which the original research was conducted. At the same time, implementing research needs to be balanced against other objectives, demands and commitments within policy and practice settings, which may mean doing something very different from the original study (Gomm, 2000). Using research will thus involve a degree of adaptation of the research itself. Yet if research becomes transformed in its application, can we still talk about 'using research' – or is something else going on?

In practice, using research is likely to mean finding a balance between strict forms of replication, and the need to adapt research-based knowledge and programmes to particular contexts. Ekblom (2002) notes that this will necessitate a trade-off between more local and more generic knowledge, and proposes that this can be achieved by developing overarching 'what works' principles which are field tested and adjusted locally as required. Hargreaves (1998) makes a similar point when he suggests that teachers should 'tinker' with research findings to adapt them to local classroom contexts so that they can be used more widely. This perspective on what it means to use research is some distance from demands for careful replication of the original findings. It does, however, allow for greater innovation and local adaptation in developing interventions, which may be stifled by demands for more strict adherence to specific research findings or research-based programmes. Box 2.9 describes how the 'Communities that Care' (CTC) initiative reflects this approach, where broad evidence about 'what works' is combined with local evidence to develop effective interventions adapted to meet local needs.

Box 2.9: Communities that Care: a community-oriented approach to implementing research

Crow et al (2004) describe a series of UK demonstration projects based on 'Communities that Care' (CTC), an international initiative providing an early intervention programme for children considered to be at risk of developing social problems. The CTC approach is underpinned by research findings which demonstrate that certain future problem behaviours can be traced back to specific risk factors in children's local communities. It is focused on mobilising local communities to develop services that can address key risk factors. The initiative places strong emphasis on research-based approaches to addressing these risks. Research tools are used to identify local risk levels; the initiative provides research findings about promising interventions to tackle risk; and all projects are encouraged to conduct evaluations whose findings are fed back into the process.

CTC does not directly deliver services, but aims instead to facilitate and bring about change. It stimulates the involvement of the local community as partners with local professionals in the process of identifying risk and protection factors, and in designing programmes to address these. Action Plans are developed that match local risks and resources with the services to be developed. This may involve adapting pre-existing local services as well as implementing programmes that have been shown to work well elsewhere. While they follow the broad overall CTC methodology, local projects differ in terms of how they engage in the process and how they interpret its guidance and advice. Rather than demanding strict adherence to research-based programmes, the emphasis is on adapting research findings to local circumstances.

Source: Adapted from Crow et al (2004)

Local reinvention of research findings can support adaptation to specific contexts and reduces the likelihood of local resistance to implementation (Nutley and Davies, 2000). It also enhances the possibilities for more conceptual, and not just instrumental, uses of research. However, 'tinkering' with research findings in this way represents a very different process of research use from straightforward replication, one which is likely to involve multiple forms of knowledge and evidence – such as practice wisdom or locally collected data – alongside research, as well as considerable refinement of the original findings. And there can be dangers in taking this 'tinkering' too far. For example, it raises the possibility that untested innovations will be disseminated, adapted and adopted (Nutley and Davies, 2000). More generally, where reinvention is too high, the effectiveness demonstrated by the original research may be undermined (Nutley et al, 2003b). Ekblom (2002) proposes that replication and innovation be viewed as opposite ends of a spectrum, which ranges from implementing initiatives shown to be successful elsewhere, to trying out something completely new. This means that we need to be aware that at some point, adapting the findings from research may reach such levels of reinvention that it is no longer appropriate to talk about 'research use' at all.

Concluding remarks

The use of research is a varied and complex phenomenon, and what it means to use research can be defined in many different ways. Identifying different models or types of research use highlights the multiple and often subtle ways in which research can be used. They broaden our understanding of what research use means and the possible ways it might be enacted. Key distinctions emerge between conceptual and instrumental uses of research, and between these kinds of research influence and the more symbolic, strategic or process forms of use that are less concerned with the content of the research and may emerge from conducting the research itself. Attempts to apply research use typologies have demonstrated, however, that the use of research is ultimately a fluid and dynamic process rather than a single event. Different types of research use will interact and build on one another, sometimes in a relatively predictable and linear fashion but also in more complex, unpredictable and iterative ways.

Identifying different types of research use raises questions about what kinds of research use may be seen as legitimate, as well as the potential for research to be used in unintended ways. However, defining what constitutes the 'misuse' of research is likely to vary among different settings and groups and is closely linked to questions about what constitutes good or appropriate evidence for a particular policy or practice field. Further, research and its use are not 'value-free' activities, but are inherently linked with the power relations at play in different social contexts. These issues in turn shape our definitions of what counts as appropriate use of research, as well as research misuse.

Finally, a common assumption exists that research use involves a simple one-to-one replication of findings in new contexts. In reality, transferring and translating research into new contexts is a highly complex process, which is likely to require at least some refinement and adaptation of the original research. Issues of replication and innovation in using research are complex and are intimately linked to the epistemologies that underpin both the original research and strategies for its implementation. Crucially, though, research knowledge is likely to be actively interpreted and negotiated within the contexts of its use. Research use may thus be more about transformation than straightforward application. There may, however, come a point where such refinements are so extensive that it is no longer legitimate to refer to this process as 'research use' at all.

THREE

What shapes the use of research?

In Chapter Two we identified the many different ways in which the policy and practice communities can make use of research. This chapter begins to examine in more detail the processes through which research enters policy and practice, and the kinds of conditions and circumstances that seem to support the use of research. We begin by exploring the channels through which research may travel into the policy and practice arenas. Identifying these routes for research starts to highlight the sorts of processes through which research gets used, as well as the points at which the flow of research may be impeded or stimulated in its journey among researchers, policy makers and practitioners.

An extensive empirical literature exists on the kinds of factors that seem to shape the use of research, and on the barriers and enablers to the flow of research into policy and practice. This work provides our starting point for examining what we know about when and why research might get used. However, closer probing of this literature suggests that we know less about some barriers and enablers than others. The ways in which such factors may interact is also less clear. In concluding, we examine some of the implications of these issues for our understanding of the use of research, as well as more recent research findings that begin to address these questions.

The routes through which research enters policy and practice

Research can enter policy and practice through diverse channels and some understanding of these routes offers a first step to understanding the process of research use more generally. Identifying the routes through which policy makers and practitioners learn about research also offers some initial pointers about how to improve their access to and use of such research.

Surveys of policy makers and practitioners have asked them about the sources through which they obtain information about research, and these kinds of study dominate the empirical evidence we have about this issue. When asked, policy makers and practitioners describe a wide array of sources through which they access research-based information. Such access may be passive – where research findings land on a policy maker's or practitioner's desk – or much more active, when individuals seek out findings from research to help support their work. The extent to which policy makers and practitioners actively do search for research findings is unclear, however. Among practitioners, as few as a quarter may be 'active seekers' of research (Bergmark and Lundstrom, 2002). However, this is likely to vary considerably between different professions and contexts.

How policy makers and practitioners access research

Written materials are an important source of information about research for both policy makers and practitioners. Research can enter the policy and practice communities in diverse formats – journal articles and research reports, but also summaries and briefings, books, professional organisational literatures and newsletters, for example. It is rare, however, for either group to turn to the traditional, academic, peer-reviewed literature. Policy makers are more likely to rely on reports produced by research, government and specialist organisations (for example, Percy-Smith et al, 2002; Wilson et al, 2003). In contrast, practitioners tend to read about research in professional journals and magazines and books (for example, Sheldon and Chilvers, 2000; Hemsley–Brown and Sharp, 2003; Rickinson, 2005), although this will differ across disciplines. For example, surgeons are much more likely than teachers to read academic research journals, and this probably reflects the fact that surgeons are both exposed to research as part of their professional training and are also more likely to carry out research themselves in the course of their careers (Hannan et al, 1998).

Forms of dissemination to and within an organisation will shape the routes through which written research materials enter policy and practice, as well as what kinds of research findings make it into an organisation and who gets to see them. Mail-outs from research organisations or intermediary brokering agencies are an oft-used approach here. These may involve scattergun tactics or can target key individuals, either those holding research-related posts or more senior members of an organisation (for example, Percy-Smith et al, 2002). The nature and extent of any internal dissemination systems will also determine whether and how this research is accessed by an organisation's members. In their study of UK local government, Percy-Smith et al (2002) found that dissemination of research within policy organisations was often *ad hoc* and informal, and depended heavily on the initiative of individuals to circulate research to those who might find it of value. This process might mean pushing research findings up to more senior levels but was more often about filtering research down through the organisation. Local or central resource centres also actively distributed research, sometimes in an abridged format such as a newsletter (Percy-Smith et al, 2002). For practitioners, too, local information services are important for getting hold of research (for example, Williams et al, 1997; Sheldon and Chilvers, 2000).

However, both policy makers and practitioners also describe a range of sources of research information other than traditionally published written materials. Increasingly, the internet is used by both groups to access the latest findings from research (for example, Percy-Smith et al, 2002; Rickinson, 2005). Policy makers who have used the internet to access research state, however, that information overload is a problem, and this may lead to bias in what kinds of research gets considered (Feldman et al, 2001; Willinsky, 2003). For practitioners, access to online sources of research is often limited (for example, Sheldon and Chilvers, 2000; Wye and McClenahan, 2000). Conferences, seminars, workshops and other forums for presenting research are also mentioned by both policy makers and practitioners as a means of picking up on the latest findings in their field, although opportunities to attend such events may be more limited for front-line practitioners (for example, Williams et al, 1997; Sheldon and Chilvers, 2000; Feldman et al, 2001; Percy-Smith et al, 2002). The media – newspapers, popular magazines, radio and television – are also a source of information about research for both groups (for example, Bullock et al, 1998; Weiss, 1999; Rickinson, 2005).

In the policy field, knowledge brokers – whether individuals or agencies – are an important route through which research reaches those who might use it. Knowledge brokers mediate between research providers and research users by filtering and disseminating the findings from research. They effectively construct a bridge between the research and policy communities (see Box 3.1).

Box 3.1: Knowledge brokers

Examining the policy field of long-term care at US state level, Feldman et al (2001) found a very wide range of research brokers, including charitable foundations, different kinds of research centre, government agencies, bridging organisations, professional organisations and individual researchers. These brokers differed considerably in terms of their constituencies and target audiences, their issues of concern, the kinds of research and other information they dealt in, the resources available for brokering work, and the activities used to communicate research to policy makers. Such activities typically involved a wide range of written materials but also included websites, e-mails and one-to-one communication. Crucially, however, Feldman et al (2001) concluded that this brokering environment was highly disjointed and that both brokering work and its funding were irregular and inconsistent. Their study highlights the diverse, complex and erratic routes through which research can enter the policy community.

Source: Adapted from Feldman et al (2001)

In the UK, knowledge brokers are emerging to support the practice community too. For example, the social care field is well served by an array of agencies that aim to support better use of research by practitioners, such as Research in Practice (www.rip.org.uk) and Making Research Count (for example through the Universities of East Anglia and Warwick). These convey research to practitioners through a variety of routes and activities, ranging from dissemination of written and interactive materials (such as CD ROMs) to websites, seminars, workshops and training sessions.

Research funders can also act as knowledge brokers, for the policy and practice communities alike. For example, the UK NHS Service Delivery and Organisation Research & Development (R&D) programme has developed a communication strategy for its research that adopts an active approach to tailoring findings for its key target audiences. This involves developing an array of communication formats, from traditional reports through to briefings and workshops. On occasion, it also means using specialist editors and communicators, rather than academics, to draw together and disseminate key messages from the bodies of research to emerge from this research funding stream (www.sdo.lshtm.ac.uk).

Finally, for practitioners in particular, training and professional development activities represent an important method for keeping abreast of the latest findings in their field. In-service training can update practitioners on the relevant research in their disciplines and how this might relate to their day-to-day work (for example, Booth et al, 2003; Wilson et al, 2003; Rickinson, 2005). Practitioners themselves often feel that this route could be used more effectively and extensively to encourage research-informed practice (for example, Sheldon and Chilvers, 2000). More rarely, research might be considered in supervision sessions or in wider departmental meetings (for example, Bullock et al, 1998; Sheldon and Chilvers, 2000).

Despite all this activity, however, what emerges from studies of the field is that, above all, personal contacts are the most important source of information about research. This is true for policy makers and practitioners alike. For both groups, finding out about research often means talking to their colleagues (for example, Feldman et al, 2001; Rickinson, 2005). This suggests that social learning through peers may be an important process through which policy makers and practitioners access and use research – and that research use may be a collective, not just individual, process. For policy makers more specifically, a range of other interpersonal contacts are also important for finding out about research. For example, research will flow through formal and informal networks within the policy arena, such as interest groups and issue networks, and these provide an important channel for findings to reach policy makers (for example, Court and Young, 2003). We look at such policy networks in more depth in Chapter Four. Policy makers also typically rely on one-to-one contacts with individual researchers in their field to keep up to date with the latest findings, and may develop their own resource of such experts on whom they call as and when required (for example, Percy-Smith et al, 2002; Willinsky, 2003). Of course, while this may filter the vast amount of research information available, it can also bias the kinds of research that policy makers get to know about (Willinsky, 2003). Overall, however, interpersonal interactions with both experts and peers seem to be key to the flow and uptake of research in both policy and practice environments.

Indirect channels for using research

Studies that directly ask policy makers and practitioners how they get to know about research have their flaws, however, and can only present a limited picture of the routes through which research may enter policy and practice. For example, they assume that individuals are necessarily aware of the ways in which they come to learn about the findings from research. Yet as we have seen in Chapter Two, research may also have a broad and 'enlightenment' role, in which knowledge from research accumulates and accretes, filtering into the policy and practice communities through subtle and indirect routes, and only gradually contributing to shifts in ways of thinking and acting (Weiss, 1979). In such circumstances, policy makers and practitioners may simply not know that their particular approach or point of view is derived, in small or large part, from research (Weiss, 1979). In other contexts, individuals may be unaware that the guidance and protocols they follow are based on research. These may, however, be a key route for research to enter day-to-day practice (for example, Fisher, 1997; Bullock et al, 1998). Halladay and Bero (2000) note that research may enter policy and practice at the levels of the organisation and the wider system, as well as through individuals. Surveys of individual policy makers and practitioners often fail to capture these broader routes to research use.

On the whole, we know less about these kinds of indirect routes, largely because studies of the field have often focused on surveying individuals. However, case study approaches offer a wider view of the channels through which research can flow. For example, 'payback' approaches to assessing the use of research define three key routes through which research may have an influence (developed in more detail in Chapter Nine):

- *Knowledge:* the products from research, including journal articles and other publications and written reports and briefings.
- *Research:* the conduct of the research itself, including the development of staff and skills, which might involve capacity building in the policy and practice communities as well as among researchers.
- *Policy and products:* the use of research to define new protocols, policies or practice tools, which are then applied (Wooding et al, 2004).

Other key diffusion channels for research that have been identified include the movement of research staff between different posts, both within and outside the research community; and researchers acting as consultants to user communities (Molas-Gallart et al, 2000). Routes through which research has an influence may thus be much broader than those identified by policy makers and practitioners alone.

Factors shaping the use of research

Identifying the routes through which research may feed into the policy and practice communities provides some initial understanding of when and why research is most likely to be used. This section examines whether we can also identify specific factors that support the use of research. A substantial body of knowledge has emerged in response to this question – the 'factors affecting' literature (Oh, 1997). We now know a good deal about the kinds of barriers and enablers to the use of research within both policy and practice contexts.

A wide range of studies has contributed to building this evidence base. Most often, studies have focused on the 'user' side of the equation – policy makers' and practitioners' perceptions of what supports and what inhibits their use of research. On the whole, less attention has been paid to the barriers and enablers perceived by researchers themselves. Many studies have relied on quantitative surveys to gather information on factors affecting the use of research, but more in-depth, qualitative approaches, using interviews and sometimes documentary analysis, have also been employed. Yet despite this methodological diversity, some remarkably consistent findings come to light about the kinds of factors that seem to shape the use of research in policy and practice. These findings also generally hold true across a range of different contexts – education, health care, criminal justice and social care.

On the whole, however, this evidence does not allow us to examine whether different factors support different types of research use. This is mainly because studies often fail to define what they mean by the 'use' of research. Yet as we have seen in Chapter Two, the nature of research use is a varied, complex and dynamic process. Some studies identify specific 'instances' of use; others rely on policy makers' and practitioners' own definitions of what research use means to them. Studies' measures of research use are thus highly diverse. For a few, the fact that research is read may be enough to tick the 'research use' box. Others focus solely on instrumental uses of research (identifiable changes to policy and practice). Measures of research use have included:

- whether research has been accessed and considered;
- the presence of research citations in documents;
- changes in knowledge, understanding and attitudes;
- direct applications of research in policy or practice;
- changes in ultimate outcomes for service users.

Most often, subjective assessments of the use of research have been used – for example, policy makers' and practitioners' own accounts of whether or not they draw on research in their day-to-day work. Pooling research use studies as we do here thus means pooling many different definitions and measures of the use of research. This caveat should be borne in mind when reading the evidence presented later.

Four issues emerge from the 'factors affecting' literature as key to understanding whether and how research gets used:

(1) the nature of the research to be applied;
(2) the personal characteristics of both researchers and potential research users;
(3) the links between research and its users;
(4) the context for the use of research.

Each of these is now considered in more depth.

(1) The nature of the research to be applied

Policy makers and practitioners give surprisingly similar accounts of what they want from research. The quality of the research in particular is a key factor in shaping whether or not potential users say it will be used. Policy makers and practitioners say they are much more likely to pay attention to research that is seen as high quality (for example, Bemelmans-Videc, 1989; Weiss, 1995; Innvaer et al, 2002; Wilson et al, 2003; McKenna et al, 2004). Conversely, a key reason they give for not using research is doubt about its methodological adequacy (for example, Funk et al, 1995; Sheldon and Chilvers, 2000). However, the relationship between the quality of research and its use is not straightforward, and often depends on how such 'quality' gets defined. Policy makers and practitioners may rate the quality of research using very different criteria and standards from those applied by researchers themselves (for example, Weiss, 1995). For example, Simons et al (2003) describe how teachers judge the value of research for their practice both socially and situationally, drawing on other teachers' assessments of the research and its usefulness and not always on traditional research-driven notions of validity. For policy makers, however, the ability of a piece of research to withstand wider political critique may be more important (Weiss, 1995). The relevance of a piece of research for policy makers' and practitioners' day-to-day work may also take precedence over issues of technical quality. A large-scale study of the use of findings from US social policy experiments concluded that the relevance and timeliness of the findings were more important to uptake than their perceived generalisability (Greenberg et al, 2003).

Questions about the quality of research are also linked to questions about what counts as good, or appropriate, or acceptable evidence in different sectors and settings. It is often assumed, for example, that policy makers prefer quantitative research that offers statistical, objective data and 'hard' facts. Some studies support this view (for example, Barker, 1994; Landry et al, 2001a). Others have suggested, however, that the reverse is true (Oh, 1997). In the developing world, policy makers often favour participatory approaches to research (Court and Young, 2003). Different sectors and disciplines also value different forms of research in different ways. Within the healthcare field, an established 'hierarchy of evidence' promotes evidence from systematic reviews and experimental studies, particularly around 'what works' questions, reflecting a strongly positivistic paradigm that effectively excludes alternative approaches (Davies et al, 2000a). Conversely, qualitative research is likely to be given a more sympathetic hearing in fields such as social care (see, for example, Webb, 2001). In many sectors, unresolved issues about what should count as (good) evidence for practice can itself be a barrier to using research (for example, Drummond and Weatherly, 2000; Sheldon and Chilvers, 2000; Barratt, 2003). More generally, research is less likely to be used where its findings are contested or unclear (for example, Court and Young, 2003; Drummond and Weatherly, 2000).

The credibility of research is important too. Research is more likely to be accessed and used when it comes from a credible and trusted individual or organisation, or else where it is supported by experts in the field (for example, Court and Young, 2003; Hemsley-Brown and Sharp, 2003). Credibility in this sense may be more important than the technical quality of the research. Often, the reputation of the source of the research is key. For example, Percy-Smith et al (2002) found that UK local government officials were more likely to draw on research from authoritative sources, such as central government. Other sources, which were viewed as overly political or commercially driven, were viewed as less trustworthy. The credibility of a piece of research is also judged in terms of its fit with professional or practice wisdom. In Zeuli's (1994) study, many teachers only viewed as credible those research findings that matched their personal experience. Whether or not policy makers and practitioners 'trust' the findings from research may thus be as much about whether they fit with existing knowledge and experience (Rickinson, 2005). For example, where findings challenge a strongly held viewpoint, issues of technical quality become more important in judging research (Weiss, 1995). Policy makers and practitioners may also be less willing to use research where it excludes other standpoints, such as those of service users (for example, Sheldon and Chilvers, 2000). In general, questions about the quality and credibility of research need to be considered in the context of wider questions about the relationship between research and other forms of knowledge, including practice wisdom, expert opinion and the views of service users, in any given sector and settings.

We might also expect that deliberately commissioned research would be more likely to be used (for example, Percy-Smith et al, 2002). Such research aims to meet a specific need – and relevance is key to the uptake of research among both policy makers and practitioners (for example, Funk et al, 1995; Weiss, 1995; Percy-Smith et al, 2002; Booth et al, 2003; Hemsley-Brown and Sharp, 2003). Commissioned research is developed and conducted in line with contractors' demands; dissemination can be carefully tailored to their requirements and they are more likely to take notice of the findings. Court and Young (2003) suggest that where policy makers have commissioned the research, they may well find it hard to ignore the results. Again, however, the relationship between commissioning research and its use is not always straightforward. For example, Selby Smith and Selby Smith (2002) found that commissioning research developed and strengthened policy makers' links with researchers, which in turn enhanced the uptake of research more widely. However, in their study policy decisions were made before the commissioned research was completed and reported, so that the findings themselves were not used. Further, while commissioning research tends to support its use, the reverse can also hold true: independent research may be viewed as more credible because it is detached and therefore more likely to be seen as unbiased (Percy-Smith et al, 2002). On the whole, however, where policy makers have directly requested the research, or there is support for research at a senior level, it is more likely to be on the agenda and hence used (Court and Young, 2003). More generally, research conducted locally – within the context of its future use – stands more chance of being taken up. Such research is typically closely aligned with local priorities and needs, and ownership of the findings among policy makers and practitioners may also be strong (for example, Feldman et al, 2001; Percy-Smith et al, 2002). Research carried out elsewhere may be seen as irrelevant to local contexts, while many potential users of research are nervous about the validity of transferring findings across different settings (for example, Williams et al, 1997; Sheldon and Chilvers, 2000; Percy-Smith et al, 2002).

Research findings also need to be timely if they are to be used. This is particularly important among policy makers who typically work to tight timescales and need information at short notice. Research, however, usually reports over much longer timescales, and this mismatch is often identified as a key barrier to policy makers' use of research (for example, Granados et al, 1997; Innvaer et al, 2002; Percy-Smith et al, 2002). The speed of policy change may mean that the agenda has moved on even before explicitly commissioned research has had a chance to report (for example, Selby Smith and Selby Smith, 2002).

But in practice contexts, too, there are complaints that research is not timely for users' needs (for example, Funk et al, 1995; Hemsley-Brown and Sharp, 2003; McKenna et al, 2004).

Questions about the timeliness of research are in large part concerned with whether the findings from research are relevant – here and now – to policy makers' and practitioners' requirements. Potential users complain that, in general, research is not sufficiently linked to their day-to-day needs (for example, Sheldon and Chilvers, 2000; Booth et al, 2003; McKenna et al, 2004). In some instances, research may just not exist to answer the questions that policy makers and practitioners confront in their working contexts. In others, research fails to provide the kind of practical, action-oriented results that its users demand (for example, Weiss, 1995; Booth et al, 2003; Hemsley-Brown and Sharp, 2003). Policy makers and practitioners often want research to give definitive answers, firm recommendations, clear directions for action (for example, Weiss, 1995; Hemsley-Brown and Sharp, 2003; Wilson et al, 2003). They complain that research is often inconclusive or else offers no practical guidance for applying findings in their daily work. For their part, researchers are often at pains to point out the uncertainty that surrounds their results and their potential for multiple readings. They are cautious in reporting their findings and are reluctant to give direct and unambiguous advice (Granados et al, 1997; Drummond and Weatherly, 2000). Weiss (1987) suggests that this is a particular problem for the use of social science research, which 'tends not to simplify problems but reveal new complexities. Its evidence comes from the past and extrapolations to the future are always problematic. So it cannot claim to provide the definitive answer' (Weiss, 1987, p 277).

Policy makers and practitioners believe that at least some of these research-related issues could be addressed through better presentation of the findings from research. They are often put off by the academic style researchers use to report their work, and by the complex analyses that may accompany research findings (for example, Funk et al, 1995; Granados et al, 1997; Sheldon and Chilvers, 2000; Barratt, 2003; Rickinson, 2005). How research is packaged will influence its uptake (for example, Innvaer et al, 2002; Percy-Smith et al, 2002; Court and Young, 2003). The language used must be accessible and appropriate to its target audience, and any data need to be delivered in a comprehensible way. Presentation is key: research must be attractive, 'user-friendly' and visually appealing, concise and jargon-free (for example, Court and Young, 2003). In particular, policy makers and practitioners often say they want summaries of research, although views may vary about whether researchers should then spell out clear implications or recommendations for action (for example, Lavis et al, 2005). For policy makers to be swayed by research, it may also need to provide new narratives that are powerful enough to destabilise the existing discourses through which policy is enacted (Court and Young, 2003). Syntheses of research may be important too: policy makers and practitioners often say that the sheer volume of research that exists is a barrier to using it (for example, Hemsley-Brown and Sharp, 2003; Reid, 2003).

(2) The personal characteristics of both researchers and potential research users

Many studies have looked for the individual characteristics that seem to define those policy makers and practitioners who report the greatest use of research. Perhaps predictably, there is some evidence that those with higher levels of education or qualification – especially where this has involved some engagement with research issues – are more likely to use research (or example, Light and Newman, 1992; Booth et al, 2003; Rickinson, 2005). This may reflect differences in both values and skills. These individuals may have greater familiarity with and understanding of research, but may also have a more generally positive attitude towards research and its significance for their work. Similarly, other regular research users are those practitioners and policy makers with an interest in or some experience of research (for example, Tyden, 1994; Williams et al, 1997; Rickinson, 2005). This kind of experience may well differ across sectors: for example, physicians are much more likely than teachers to have undertaken some research during their professional careers, and are also more likely to consult the research literature (Hannan et al, 1998). Research use may also vary across the biography of a practitioner's career, with more limited research use among newly qualified professionals, and greater application of research once professional practice has become established or at more senior levels (Rickinson, 2005).

An oft-reported barrier to the use of research is that policy makers and practitioners have trouble understanding and interpreting research findings for their day-to-day work (for example, Funk et al, 1995; Sheldon and Chilvers, 2000; Percy-Smith et al, 2002). Individuals who have some experience of or training in research are more likely to possess these kinds of skills. However, actually applying research to practice requires more specialist skills that are often poorly developed among policy makers and practitioners (for example, Drummond and Weatherly, 2000; Walter et al, 2004b). On the other side of the equation, researchers themselves report that they lack the knowledge and expertise to engage successfully in research use activities, such as tailoring research outputs to a target audience, or ensuring effective dissemination to policy makers and practitioners (for example, Tang and Sinclair, 2001).

Individuals' attitudes are also likely to influence their use of research. They may be unwilling to change current practice or to experiment with the new ideas research provides (Funk et al, 1995). There is also some evidence that individual policy makers and practitioners may harbour an aversion not just to using research, but to research more generally (for example, Funk et al, 1995; Walter et al, 2004b). They may not value research or may feel that research does not have anything to offer policy or practice, or else perceive research as a threat to the kinds of tacit knowledge and skills – practice wisdom – that they bring to their work (for example, Booth et al, 2003). Individual ideas and understandings about how research should be used will also be important. For example, in Zeuli's (1994) study, some teachers saw research use in wholly instrumental terms and so judged research according to whether it could be directly translated into classroom practice, while others felt that research could have a more indirect impact, for example by improving their knowledge and perceptions of a key issue.

On the whole, however, the search for individual characteristics that might shape the use of research has borne limited fruit. For example, a systematic review of the kinds of personal factors thought to influence nurses' use of research failed to find conclusive overall evidence of a link between research use and any of the following: involvement in research activities; information-seeking behaviours; education; professional characteristics; or socioeconomic factors (Estabrooks et al, 2003). Attitude towards research emerged alone as significant in shaping whether or not any individual nurse might use research.

(3) The links between research and its users

Lack of physical access to research is regularly reported by both policy makers and practitioners as a major barrier to their use of research (for example, Sheldon and Chilvers, 2000; Percy-Smith et al, 2002; Booth et al, 2003). They describe, for example, limited access to libraries, to research databases, or to web-based sources of research. Where resources exist, their quality is not always perceived as good (Sheldon and Chilvers, 2000). Poor dissemination within and between organisations can also prevent research ever reaching the people who might use it.

Percy-Smith et al (2002) found that dissemination of research within UK local government was typically *ad hoc* and often relied on informal networks and on the resourcefulness of individual officers. This meant that research might get 'stuck' at certain points within the organisation, and those at the frontline generally had less access to research than those at more senior levels. Effective dissemination often relied on a research 'champion' to support key findings, or more generally to call for greater use of research within the organisation (Percy-Smith et al, 2002).

Knowledge brokers – individuals and agencies who play an intermediary role between research and its potential users – can also help secure the use of research (for example, Feldman et al, 2001; Greenberg et al, 2003). As already described, such knowledge brokers act as a bridge between the research and user communities, and address some of the research-related barriers to research use. For example, they translate research accounts for policy maker and practitioner audiences, and can ensure that research findings are targeted at the right people, at the right time (for example, Williams et al, 1997; Feldman et al, 2001).

One of the best predictors of research use is, however, the extent and strength of linkages between researchers and policy makers or practitioners (for example, Granados et al, 1997; Innvaer et al, 2002). Personal contact is crucial, which may be informal and *ad hoc*, through e-mail exchanges or telephone conversations, or else more structured and formal, for example at scheduled meetings or shared workshops. As we have seen, individual policy makers often rely on a personal network of researchers to identify key findings and as a 'sounding board' for ideas (for example, Willinsky, 2003). These interpersonal routes for getting research into policy seem particularly effective. Court and Young (2003) have found that more generally, both formal and informal networks can support greater exchange and harmonisation of research knowledge among the research, policy and practice communities. These may be facilitated in a variety of ways, including through virtual as well as direct meetings. Above all, however, studies suggest that it is face-to-face interactions that are the most likely to encourage policy and practice use of research (for example, Weiss, 1995).

Where these kinds of linkages occur throughout the course of a study, research use is further enhanced. Ongoing interaction and dialogue, two-way communication and sustained efforts towards dissemination significantly increase the chances that research will be used (Huberman, 1990, 1993; Court and Young, 2003). Such engagement means that research is more likely to be relevant to users' needs, and helps develop ownership of research findings among potential users. It also establishes relationships of trust, which are important to support the use of research (Innvaer et al, 2002; Court and Young, 2003). In these ways, research–user linkages start to overcome some of the barriers to research use that arise from more traditional approaches to conducting, presenting and disseminating research. They imply that social interaction and social learning may be crucial to the use of research (an issue that is addressed further in Chapter Five).

(4) The context for the use of research

A fourth and crucial factor shaping the use of research has received increasing attention in the literature: the powerful role played by the context in which research use takes place. It is useful here to distinguish between issues that arise in macro- and meso-level policy contexts; in practice contexts; and in the contexts in which research itself is conducted.

Policy contexts

To examine the ways in which policy contexts might shape the uptake of research, we have found it helpful to draw on Weiss' 'four I's' framework (for example, Weiss, 1999). This identifies interests, ideology, information and institutions as key factors that shape public policy and the use of research within this process.

- *Interests* are first and foremost the self-interests of those engaged in the policy process, whether these are political (advancing a particular cause) or personal (advancing one's career).
- *Ideology* means the systems of beliefs, moral and ethical values and political orientations that guide policy makers' actions.
- *Information* represents the array of knowledge and ideas from multiple sources that crowd for attention in the policy field and that are used by policy makers to make sense of current issues and problems.
- *Institutions* are the organisations within which policy makers act, with their own histories, cultures and constraints, and that in turn will shape how policy makers define their interests, ideologies and information, and the ways in which decisions are made (Weiss, 1999).

Each of these factors will interact in shaping a policy context. For example, information will be used to shape interests and ideologies and may change the practices and cultures of institutions (Weiss, 1999). The context created by these interactions will in turn shape the uptake of research. For example, Weiss (1995) suggests that ideology and interests are only weakly influenced by research; and that research is less likely to be used where there is already strong agreement between ideologies, interests and information from alternative sources.

In general, research will be used where its findings are aligned and compatible with the current ideological environment, with personal values and with individual and agency interests (Hutchinson, 1995; Weiss, 1998; Innvaer et al, 2002; Greenberg et al, 2003). Court and Young's (2003) analysis of 50 case studies from the developing world found that where research contradicted the interests of key political players, it was unlikely to be used; but also that, conversely, research sometimes influenced policy simply because there were no strong interest groups to argue against it. Research findings need to fit with existing ways of thinking within the policy context, or else must be sufficiently challenging and convincing to be able to overturn these (Court and Young, 2003). Research that simply confirms existing policy or requires only small-scale change is also more likely to be used (Weiss, 1998; Innvaer et al, 2002). Stable political contexts where there is little political contestation support the use of research; but policy makers will also turn to research for solutions in times of political crisis or where more radical or fundamental policy decisions are being made (Weiss, 1998; Court and Young, 2003). Research can also help generate a consensus in these kinds of contexts (for example, Selby Smith and Selby Smith, 2002; Court and Young, 2003). Court and Young (2003, p 15) conclude that when it comes to policy uses of research, 'policy change equals [research] demand minus contestation'.

In terms of information, a key issue is that research enters a policy arena which is already swamped with knowledge from a wide variety of sources: interest groups, the media, think tanks, consultants, working groups, experts, policy colleagues, personal experience, policy networks and so on (for example, Weiss, 1995, 1999; Drummond and Weatherly, 2000). Research findings must compete with these other sources of information and with existing and embedded knowledge and understandings if they are to influence policy. A range of studies has found that policy makers favour other forms of information over research, including that from planning committees, public consultation, interest groups and colleagues (for example, Light and Newman, 1992; Feldman et al, 2001; Greenberg et al, 2003). Policy makers also often say that they lack the time fully to interrogate the findings from research and find other sources of information more accessible for their needs (for example, Feldman et al, 2001; Reid, 2003). Research use is, however, more likely where findings dovetail rather than conflict with other sources of information in the policy environment (Weiss, 1999; Drummond and Weatherly, 2000).

The wider political institutions and structures within which policy is made will also shape the use of research (discussed further in Chapter Eight). Open political systems must be in place for research even to be considered in the policy process, and policy makers must trust the institution of research (Court and Young, 2003). Federal political structures will promote a more distributed and interactive policy-making process with continual shifts in power among different interest groups. Research is then likely to be used by these groups in more strategic than instrumental ways (Selby Smith and Selby Smith, 2002).

While local institutions are also likely to play a key role in shaping policy uses of research, empirical work on this issue has been more limited. Mechanisms and structures that bring together policy makers with their analytical counterparts do, however, seem to support greater use of research (for example, Nutley et al, 2002; Laycock and Farrell, 2003). This might involve co-locating researchers and policy makers within a single unit, permanently or through secondment, so that they work in tandem to take forward research-based policy development and implementation. Alternatively, intermediary forums and organisations may be important, such as advisory bodies that regularly bring together academics and policy makers, or knowledge brokering agencies that link the research and policy communities (for example, Feldman et al, 2001). In particular, quasi-policy bodies that are specialists in a particular policy domain and its associated evidence base seem to support the use of research within government (Nutley et al, 2002). High turnover of policy staff can, however, inhibit the establishment of links with researchers and hence the uptake of research (for example, Reid, 2003; Walter et al, 2004b).

Much of the research and debate around the role played by policy contexts in the uptake of research has focused on macro-level policy making. Less attention has been paid specifically to the influence of context at the meso or organisational policy level (in fact, studies have often collapsed the two in looking at the use of research, for example, Innvaer et al, 2002; Court and Young, 2003). Of course, the kinds of issues that will shape research use among policy makers at local levels will often be similar to those among national level policy makers. Issues of interests, ideologies, information and institutions still apply, albeit these will operate around local issues and with local stakeholder groups (for example, Percy-Smith et al, 2002). For example, Gabbay et al (2003) found that the agendas of powerful individuals could suppress the uptake of evidence in developing local policies for delivering health and social care. One of the central issues at the meso level of making policy is, however, the potential for tension between national policies and legislation, and local needs, priorities and agendas. Research uptake is likely to be shaped by the interplay between these local and national concerns. For example, Percy-Smith et al's (2002) study of research use in UK local government found that, on the whole, research that was broadly aligned with local policy was more likely to be taken up. However, where local research findings contradicted national policy, it was difficult to get them used.

It is institutions, however, that often hold the key to shaping the use of research among local policy makers. For example, at the meso level, organisational cultures are likely to play a central role in supporting or inhibiting the use of research (for example, Sunesson and Nilsson, 1988). A hostile or indifferent organisational attitude to research will limit evidence uptake among local policy makers (Percy-Smith et al, 2002). Box 3.2 provides an example of the complex ways in which local political and organisational issues are likely to play out in shaping meso-level policy makers' use of research.

Box 3.2: How organisational contexts shape policy uses of research

Lovell and Kalinich (1992) studied the use of research by senior administrators and programme managers within a US not-for-profit criminal justice organisation. The organisation had its own in-house research section, but Lovell and Kalinich (1992) found that nevertheless the organisation's policy makers made little use of research apart from some limited strategic use. They attributed this lack of research use in part to poor integration between researchers, administrators and programme managers within the organisation, alongside an ambiguous role for the research unit itself. The local culture was also generally hostile to the use of research. However, the uptake of research was most heavily influenced by personal and internal political concerns. For example, programme managers' criticisms of the research unit often reflected concerns about their own autonomy and status within the organisation. In contrast, senior administrators were more externally oriented and were doubtful about the value of research produced internally. It was the interaction of these multiple issues, played out within a particular organisational context, that served to shape (and ultimately inhibit) local policy makers' use of research.

Source: Adapted from Lovell and Kalinich (1992)

Practitioner contexts

The highly politicised environment in which policy making takes place means that context is particularly pertinent in shaping policy uses of research. However, local context has also been identified as a factor influencing practitioners' uptake of research. Many of the barriers practitioners report to using research are related to the wider organisational contexts in which they work. For example, lack of time to search for and read research is a commonly reported barrier to research use among practitioners across a wide range of settings and professions (for example, Funk et al, 1995; Sheldon and Chilvers, 2000; Rickinson, 2005). Funk et al (1995), reviewing studies of the barriers to nurses' use of research, conclude that organisational issues are the main factors inhibiting greater uptake of research. Nurses said that they had no time to read research or to implement or experiment with its findings. They also felt they lacked authority and autonomy to instigate research-based practice change, as well as any organisational, practical or personal support for this process (Funk et al, 1995). More generally, practitioners often describe contexts characterised by heavy workloads, competing pressures and continual demands for change, and research use takes a low priority in these kinds of circumstances or else is seen more as a burden than a benefit (for example, Sheldon and Chilvers, 2000; Wilson et al, 2003). Internal organisational politics can also inhibit the use of research (for example, Williams et al, 1997). Further, other factors may take precedence over research use. Limited budgets may restrict the development of research use projects (Rickinson, 2005), while new initiatives are typically implemented through policy mandate and little opportunity exists for practitioners and organisations to develop research-based practice themselves (for example, Wilson et al, 2003). Service user expectations or preferences may also be prioritised over the findings from research (for example, Granados et al, 1997).

Many of the barriers – and enablers – to the use of research in practitioners' contexts are linked to professional and cultural issues and so will vary across disciplinary and organisational boundaries. For example, physicians are far more likely than nurses to have the kind of professional authority needed to apply the findings from research in their day-to-day practice (for example, Funk et al, 1995). Conversely, they may be reluctant to comply with research-based protocols that limit their autonomy (Drummond and Weatherly, 2000). Some social workers report a 'blame culture' within their profession that inhibits questioning and experimentation in applying the ideas from research to practice (Barratt, 2003; Booth et al, 2003). There can also be local cultural resistance to research and its use, among practitioner groups and within practitioner organisations (for example, Walter et al, 2004b; Rickinson, 2005). These kinds of cultural barriers to the use of research may be particularly strong where less agreement exists about the nature of evidence for practice and the value of research for improving service delivery and outcomes. More generally, where engaging with research is not viewed as an integral part of professional practice, there will be limited encouragement for practitioners to use research (for example, Sheldon and Chilvers, 2000; Wilson et al, 2003). Practitioners often suggest that better organisational support would increase their use of research. This might involve dedicated study time for reading research; training to develop skills in searching for and interpreting research; and administrative and financial support for implementing research-based change (for example, Sheldon and Chilvers, 2000). Another approach is the use of active facilitation to encourage skill development and enhanced engagement with research, such as senior nurse practitioner roles. However, as well as changing structures, it may be as important to develop an organisational culture that encourages practitioners to question and evaluate current practice, and to develop innovative approaches based on research (for example, Funk et al, 1995; Wilson et al, 2003).

Research contexts

It is worth bearing in mind that the contexts within which researchers themselves operate can also have a powerful influence on the use of their research by policy makers and practitioners. In the UK in particular, the environment in which academic researchers work has often served actively to inhibit the flow of research from universities to policy and practice communities. For example, the Research Assessment Exercise (RAE) gives credence to traditional academic forms of dissemination, particularly peer-reviewed journal articles, at the expense of other forms of publication and of engagement with non-academic audiences (for example, Granados et al, 1997; Drummond and Weatherly, 2000; Tang and Sinclair, 2001). Yet we know that many policy makers and practitioners rarely turn to these kinds of sources to find out about research. More generally, there are few incentives or rewards within academic institutions and career structures even for disseminating research to policy makers and practitioners, much less for engaging in a broader array of activities aimed at increasing research uptake. Research funding structures can also inhibit wider uses of research. Typically, minimal resources are allocated for dissemination and user engagement activities, both during and at the end of a research project (Tang and Sinclair, 2001). Researchers themselves say they rarely have the time to engage in disseminating their work (Tang and Sinclair, 2001), and in any case often lack the skills to do so effectively.

Among researchers, too, there may be some cultural resistance to the use of research beyond the immediate research community. Tang and Sinclair (2001), interviewing UK social science academics, identified two core attitudes towards the exploitation of research. One was broadly supportive, taking the view that exploitation is an inherent part of academic research. Members of this group saw diverse benefits from disseminating their research and recognised the wider value of engaging in research use activities. They themselves were more likely to disseminate their work extensively and to undertake research projects jointly with potential users. The second set of attitudes was much more sceptical about the value of engaging in research use activities that do not support career development or enhance RAE ratings. Researchers subscribing to this view limited their activities to traditional academic methods of dissemination and were concerned about media 'dumbing down' of research. They believed that universities were for teaching, education and generating ideas and that wider research exploitation was not part of their remit (Tang and Sinclair, 2001).

Research use realities

The empirical literature thus identifies a wide range of barriers and enablers to the use of research, and these are summarised in Box 3.3. As we have seen, however, the relationship between research use and these different barriers and enablers is not always a simple one.

Box 3.3: Barriers and enablers to the use of research

The nature of the research

Research is more likely to be used that:
- is high quality and comes from a credible source;
- provides clear and uncontested findings;
- has been commissioned, or carries high-level political support;
- is aligned with local priorities, needs and contexts;

- is timely and relevant to policy makers' and practitioners' requirements;
- is presented in a 'user-friendly' way – concise, jargon-free and visually appealing.

The personal characteristics of researchers and potential research users

- Policy makers and practitioners with higher levels of education or some experience of research are more likely to be research users.
- Lack of skills to interpret and appraise research can inhibit research use.
- Some individuals may be hostile towards the use of research, or to research more generally.
- Researchers may lack the knowledge and skills to engage effectively in dissemination and research use activities.

The links between research and its users

- Research use may be inhibited where policy makers and practitioners have limited access to research.
- Knowledge brokers – both individuals and agencies – can play an effective 'bridging' role between research and its potential users.
- Direct links between researchers and policy makers or practitioners also support research use. Face-to-face interactions and two-way exchanges of information are most likely to encourage the use of research.

The context for the use of research

Context plays a key role in shaping the uptake of research.
- In policy contexts, research is more likely to be used where:
  - it is aligned with current ideology and individual and agency interests;
  - its findings fit with existing ways of thinking or acting or with other information within the policy environment;
  - open political systems exist;
  - institutions and structures bring researchers and policy makers into contact;
  - at a local level, an organisational culture exists that is broadly supportive of evidence use.
- In practice contexts, local organisational, structural and cultural issues may limit the use of research, for example:
  - lack of time to read research;
  - lack of autonomy to implement the findings from research;

- lack of support – financial, administrative and personal – to develop research-based practice change;
- local cultural resistance to research and its use.
- In research contexts, a number of barriers inhibit the flow of findings to policy makers and practitioners:
  - lack of incentive or reward for engaging in dissemination and research use activities;
  - high value placed on traditional academic journal publications at the expense of 'user-friendly' research outputs;
  - lack of time and financial resources for research use activities;
  - a set of attitudes among some academic researchers that dissemination is not part of their role.

Further, while many factors seem to be important, merely defining these says little about their relative significance, or the ways in which different factors might interact. For example, simply presenting findings in a more 'user-friendly' way may be a first step to research use, but is unlikely to overcome the kinds of political barriers research faces when it enters the policy-making arena.

Integrated causal models begin to address these issues. Such models combine the different variables that have been shown to be important in research use, and begin to assess the role each plays in supporting – or inhibiting – the use of research. For example, the path model developed by Oh (1997), which examines when and how policy makers use research to make decisions, integrates variables concerned with:

- the characteristics of the research or information, including its source, quantity, type and format, and the interaction between researchers and policy makers;
- policy makers' characteristics, such as their perceptions of the policy process and their attitudes towards research, as well as age and education levels; and
- organisational characteristics, including norms, structures and incentives, and policy makers' positions within an organisation.

Oh's (1997) model also specifies detailed causal linkages between the different variables and the impact of research. It was tested using data from more than 500 federal, state and local mental health policy makers in 18 US states, who were either generalists (concerned with service delivery) or specialists (dealing with financial issues). Its findings suggest that multiple factors, and the relationships between them, need to be taken into account more fully to explain the use of research. The most important variables were policy makers' perceptions of the policy process and the source of the information used. However, factors explaining the use of research differed markedly between the two policy areas (Oh, 1997). Context was critical in determining whether and how research was used.

Other quantitative causal models of the research use process have reached similar conclusions. They highlight the importance of interactions between different variables in shaping the use of research, but above all assert that context is the key to understanding the use of research (for example, Webber, 1986; Landry et al, 2001a). Landry et al (2001a) conclude that research use processes are far more complex than the existing literature allows. They suggest that contingent factors, which are difficult to integrate into a comprehensive model, are often critical to whether or not research gets used. These findings alert us to the fact that there is no simple, one-way relationship between particular 'factors affecting' and the use of research. Instead, such variables will interact in complex ways, and these interactions will themselves be shaped by the context within which research is being used.

There are some limitations to the broader empirical literature on which such quantitative models are based. For example, simple surveys of the factors affecting research use are unable to grapple with the complex interactions between these different elements that characterise the research use process. Weiss (1998) has argued that the dynamic and interactive nature of research use means its elements cannot be reduced to a set of quantitative variables. She maintains that a growing recognition of the complexity of research use processes has meant that studies aiming to isolate the main determinants of research use have gone out of fashion (Weiss, 1998). However, such studies seem to have enjoyed a recent resurgence in the 'barriers and enablers' literature that has accompanied the growth of the evidence-based policy and practice (EBPP) agenda (for example, Everton et al, 2000; Sheldon and Chilvers, 2000).

These 'barriers and enablers' studies, while offering some important insights into the research use process, are also somewhat limited by the assumptions they often make about the ways in which research gets used. Typically they focus on policy makers' and practitioners' definitions of the barriers and enablers to their use of research, but in doing so implicitly subscribe to a view that research use is – or should be – primarily an individualised process. The assumption is that research is mainly used by policy makers and practitioners individually, and involves them deliberatively accessing and applying research in the course of their day-to-day work. This focus on individuals making use of research is a key feature of much of the EBPP agenda. As Sheldon and Chilvers (2000, p 42) put it, 'evidence-based practice ultimately depends on readers'. The barriers to emerge from studies underpinned by this view inevitably focus on those that exist at the individual level, such as lack of time to read research, lack of skills to interpret research, and lack of autonomy or authority to apply research. The same is true where enablers to research use are identified, for example the need for personal contact between researchers and research users, or better organisational support for individuals to engage in research use activities. The question of whether research use *should* be an individualised process is a moot point, which is taken up in later chapters, although it is perhaps worth noting that practitioners often feel that the use of research should be as much an organisational as an individual responsibility (for example, Walter et al, 2004b). Our concern here, however, is to recognise the limitations of the literature on the barriers and enablers to research use and the ways in which they shape our understandings of how research gets used in these individualised terms. In particular, we need to be wary about how we might use these findings to develop specific strategies to support greater use of research. For example, we know much less about how research might be used at the wider organisational and system levels and what the barriers and enablers to these levels of research use might be. Strategies to improve research use may be important at these levels too, however, and may not be most appropriately focused at the individual level. We return to this issue in Chapter Seven.

In summary, then, despite the variety of approaches used to date in trying to understand what shapes the use of research, much of the complexity of research use processes, and the important influence of local contexts, remain relatively unexplored. What is needed are more qualitative, in-depth accounts of the use of research in policy and practice contexts. More recent studies, based on documentary analysis and direct observation as well as surveys of key players in the field, have used a case study approach to begin to open up the 'black box' of the research use process. Box 3.4 presents an example of one such study. It highlights how those factors that shape the use of research interact in complex and contingent ways within a continually shifting context.

Box 3.4: The use of research in Australian educational policy

Selby Smith and Selby Smith (2002) studied the use of research in developing a 'user choice' policy in the provision of vocational education and training (VET) in Australia. A 'user choice' approach meant that funds for VET flowed directly to the training provider chosen by the firm or employer. The decision to adopt a user choice policy was based on an accumulation of knowledge about the topic to which research had contributed. Five research reports were prepared for policy makers about the issue, which both drew on existing research and provided new information and new insights on user choice. As such, research played a key role in getting user choice onto the policy agenda. Further research, to evaluate policy pilots of the planned approach, was additionally commissioned by the policy makers to support their work. As part of this process, researchers played an increasingly consultative role in relation to the policy community.

Research had the greatest influence at the early stages of the policy-making process. The fact that this was a novel policy area, with no substantial pre-existing body of knowledge or opinion, meant that the research findings met with little opposition or contradictory evidence in these initial stages. In fact, research was welcomed as a means of developing a policy framework and to give the policy some material content. Selby Smith and Selby Smith (2002) found that the research enhanced policy makers' knowledge of user choice issues and helped them to reach a common definition of the problem. It supported the development of clear policy objectives and identified the issues that would need to be addressed to implement a user choice approach.

The fact that research was commissioned also helped support policy use of research. The purpose and audience for the research were both clear, and the commissioning process developed strong linkages between policy makers and researchers. There were ongoing interactions between the two groups, which were characterised by a process of 'mutual adjustment' that enabled them to adapt to each others' timelines and needs and supported greater use of research (Selby Smith and Selby Smith, 2002).

Over time, however, the detailed implications of adopting a user choice policy became apparent, and this in turn made the policy less appealing to certain stakeholders. Selby Smith and Selby Smith (2002) point out that in a federal government context such as Australia, policy responsibility is distributed and policy making takes a highly engaged and interactive form. In this kind of setting, different stakeholders viewed and used the research on user choice in different ways. During the course of policy development, shifts in power among these different stakeholders then supported or restricted the use of research. Research also became ammunition in the political debate. For example, those opposed to the user choice policy could argue that the findings from the policy pilots were not generalisable and so were invalid. While this might appear to reflect a rejection of research on the basis of inadequate quality, Selby Smith and Selby Smith (2002) suggest that because the research went against their interests, it was used strategically rather than conceptually or instrumentally.

During the process of policy development, research was cited in policy documents and speeches by ministers. It clearly had some kind of conceptual impact on the policy-making process (Selby Smith and Selby Smith, 2002). Yet there was little evidence that research had a direct influence in changing the national VET system. Further, the policy was rolled out before the first stage of the commissioned research evaluating the policy pilots had even reported.

Selby Smith and Selby Smith (2002) conclude from this case study that the process of using research is both cumulative and interactive, with ongoing and iterative feedback between the research and policy worlds. They also believe that:

It is likely that no single participant knew the complete story, wholly, however closely involved in policy development, however senior or central to one aspect of the process. If so, estimates of research use and impact on decision making are almost always subjective. (p 78)

Source: Adapted from Selby Smith and Selby Smith (2002)

The case study in Box 3.4 highlights the complex, iterative and dynamic nature of the research use process, in which different 'factors affecting' interact both with each other and with the shifting context in which they are played out. It also emphasises the methodological difficulties of achieving a complete and objective account of how and why research gets used. Work by Levitt (2003) and Gabbay et al (2003) in policy and practice settings has similarly found that using research represents a complex, interactive and dynamic set of behaviours that cannot be captured by simply delineating the factors that seem to be important in this process. Their studies suggest that the use of research is a haphazard and contingent affair, dependent on shifting power relations and agendas, and best understood through the ways in which key stakeholders attach different values and significance to different pieces of research. Further, they demonstrate how evidence itself becomes transformed and reconstructed in the process of its use, and its meaning is continually renegotiated. Levitt (2003, p 31) concludes that questions of process and content, which 'reveal the beliefs, values and perceptions, as well as the facts, on which actions are based', are key to analysing and understanding the use of research. What is clear is that more of these kinds of in-depth and qualitative studies are needed if we are to better understand what shapes the use of research in different policy and practice contexts.

Concluding remarks

A substantial body of empirical work has highlighted the multiple routes and channels through which research may enter policy and practice. Such routes emerge as highly varied, ranging from the simple dissemination of written materials, to the use of intermediary 'knowledge brokers' and formal and informal networks linking researchers, policy makers and practitioners. The diversity of channels through which research may spread and flow reflects the complexity of the research use process, which we highlighted in Chapter Two. While studies rarely consider the different types of research use that emerge as part of this process, such different routes are likely to encourage different ways of thinking about and using research. For example, simply distributing written research findings to policy and practice organisations involves a one-way flow of evidence from the research to the user community, which assumes that if the research is good enough, it will simply be applied. In contrast, other channels for research use, such as individual communications with researchers or within knowledge-based networks, support greater dialogue and exchange around research evidence between researchers and potential research users in the process of using research. However, personal contact – whether with other policy or practice colleagues or with researchers themselves – seems to be the most important route for research to enter policy and practice. This suggests that research use may above all be a social process, involving interaction among individuals and the joint (re)construction of research evidence through ongoing debate, interplay and exchange.

Surveys of the factors affecting research use have been similarly extensive. These demonstrate that such factors cluster around four key areas: the extent to which the research itself is relevant, credible and meets users' needs; the extent to which policy makers and practitioners are willing and able to use research; the degree of linkages between research and the policy and practice communities; and the context in which research use takes place. Above all, however, it is the latter factor – context – that seems to be the key to whether and how research gets used. Research use emerges as a highly contingent process, which varies both across different settings and over time. This picture of research use as fluid and context-dependent reflects our conclusions from Chapter Two and suggests that research use is not likely to be readily pinned down and amenable to manipulation through two or three key variables. Simple surveys of what seems to support or inhibit the use of research can only take our understanding of the research use process so far. This means that we need to attend in more depth to the ways in which these different 'factors affecting' interact, in complex and dynamic ways, in complex and dynamic contexts.

Crucially, however, studies both of the routes through which research enters policy and practice and of the 'factors affecting' research use have focused on the individual – how individuals access research (or research reaches individuals), and individuals' views on what enables or inhibits their use of research. They are underpinned by a model of research use that assumes that using research primarily involves individual policy makers and practitioners keeping up to date with research and applying relevant findings to their day-to-day work. Much less attention has been paid to research use at organisational and system levels and what supports the use of research in these arenas; forms of use of which individual policy makers and practitioners are often unaware. More studies are needed of research use at these levels. Further, there is a danger in relying on existing evidence to develop strategies to enhance the use of research, as the kinds of solutions suggested – such as providing policy makers with the time, skills and resources to access and interpret research – inevitably tend to be focused on individuals. The issue of designing activities to improve research use that address the organisational and system levels as well as the individual level is developed further in Chapter Seven.

What is clear from both Chapter Two and this chapter is that research use is a complex phenomenon, which needs to be seen as a shifting and ongoing process rather than a single event. In the next chapter, we set out to identify some key models of this process of research use that can begin to give shape to the complexities encountered when we look at the use of research in real-world settings; and which can provide some clear frameworks for understanding and enhancing the use of research.

FOUR

Descriptive models of the research impact process

In this chapter we examine the different ways in which relationships between research and policy and research and practice have been conceptualised. Such models provide different frameworks for thinking about and understanding the research use process. As such, they capture some of the complexities that forms of research use take, which we discussed in Chapter Two; and they highlight some of the assumptions that underpin the different studies of the use of research encountered in Chapter Three. At the same time, these models also help us begin to think about the ways in which we might improve the use of research. Explicit theoretical development in the research use field has been relatively limited (for example, Wingens, 1990; Marteau et al, 2002), and to some extent this is reflected in the nature of the models we consider. Despite this, we can identify a range of conceptual frameworks for understanding the processes through which research enters the policy and practice arenas.

Models of the relationship between research and policy and between research and practice are considered separately in this discussion. Although the practice–policy divide may be viewed as a somewhat artificial distinction (see Chapter One), research use models in the literature are typically considered in terms of either policy or practice. They tend to focus on the relationship between research and macro-level policy (typically at a national or federal level) or the relationship between research and front-line practice. Models of the process of research use specifically within meso-policy contexts, including organisational decision making, are less clear, and our own focus in this chapter reflects this. Some key contrasts between the policy and practice arenas also emerge when examining the role research may play within each, and these are elaborated in the concluding section to the chapter.

Despite the distinctions made between policy and practice in modelling research use, there have been very similar developments in terms of thinking and ideas around the use of research in both these fields. Broadly, early models tend to specify a relatively rational, linear and one-way relationship between research and policy/practice. These models have subsequently been critiqued and elaborated through a growing recognition of the complexity of research use, and the development of multidimensional models that attend in more depth to the diversity of factors influencing the use of research. At the same time there has been a related shift in thinking, where research use is no longer seen as the simple transfer of knowledge to passive recipients. Instead, policy makers and practitioners are seen actively to engage with and translate research findings through their own perspectives and experiences and within the specific contexts of their use. Finally, more postmodern accounts of research utilisation have emerged, providing very different perspectives for understanding research–policy and research–practice relationships, in which analyses of power are brought to the fore. The discussion in this chapter is structured to reflect these developments in research–policy and research–practice models.

Models of the research–policy relationship

Weiss' (1979) seven models of the ways in which policy makers use research have already provided us with some initial insight into the relationship between research and policy (see Chapter Two). In this section we examine other models of the research–policy relationship, which probe the processes of both policy making and the use of research in more depth. Detailed frameworks that aim specifically to understand the research–policy interface are relatively few and far between in the literature. Such frameworks will, however, be shaped by the ways in which we conceptualise the policy process itself, and the role that research and other evidence might then play within policy making. In this section our focus is thus primarily on models of the policy process which may be useful for understanding how research and policy can interconnect. We also examine how such policy models are linked with more specific models of the research–policy relationship where these have been elaborated.

Traditional models of the research–policy relationship

The traditional model of policy making pictures the process as a cycle. This represents a relatively simple and descriptive model of the policy process, in which policy making is seen to progress through a series of key stages (for example, Stone, 2001; Bridgman and Davis, 2003). Typically, four such stages are delineated, ranging from initial problem identification through to policy evaluation and subsequent feedback into the beginning of the cycle, although these four stages have sometimes been elaborated and extended (for example, Howard, 2003). The role of research and other evidence will then vary at each stage.

(1) *Problem identification and agenda setting*

At this initial stage the key problems to be addressed by policy makers are identified. Research can be important to help clarify the nature of the issues of concern, and to push such issues onto the policy agenda. Stone (2001) suggests that researchers can influence what kinds of knowledge are seen as relevant and valid for use within this process.

(2) *Decision making*

Once the policy agenda is in place, decisions must be made about the actions to be taken to address identified issues of concern. Research can play a central role at this stage of the policy-making process, defining alternatives for action or providing evidence about the likely outcomes of different decisions.

(3) *Policy implementation*

At implementation, policy is translated into practice on the ground. However, as Stone (2001) notes, there may be a gap between the original objectives of a policy and the way these are realised at the point of delivery, so that research that helped shaped policy development may get lost when policies are applied. Research can, however, play an important role in helping policy makers address problems with policy implementation (Stone, 2001).

(4) *Monitoring and evaluation*

Implemented policies are then monitored and evaluated. Research can make a substantial contribution at this stage. The findings are then fed back into the policy process and may be of value in developing new policies as well as refining those already in place.

The policy cycle model has, however, been widely critiqued for presenting an overly simplistic, linear and logical view of the policy process. Its neat stages fail to reflect the messy complexity that typically characterises policy making as it really occurs, and Colebatch (2005) suggests that it represents no more than a 'policy myth'. However, it has been argued that the principal value of the policy cycle model is as a heuristic device, 'an ideal type from which every reality will curve away' (Bridgman and Davis, 2003, p 100). Empirical work has found that looser interpretations of the model – which recognise, for example, that not all stages may be followed in order, and the potential for iterative flow between them – can be useful for defining the essential elements of the policy-making process (for example, Howard, 2003). As such the model may have some analytic value and can suggest the kinds of roles research might play at different stages of making policy (Neilson, 2001; Stone, 2001).

Other rational models of policy making present a similarly linear view of the policy process (see, for example, Dror, 1983; Bulmer, 1986; Stone, 2001). One such model identifies a series of steps in which all possible policy options are researched, evaluated and compared in arriving at a decision. The first step is to define the problem at hand and the goals to be achieved. Different solutions are then identified and the consequences of each of these are assessed. Finally, a decision is made that optimises overall benefit (Bulmer, 1986; Albaek, 1995). In this model, research can play a key role in identifying alternative courses of action and their likely policy outcomes. As Stone (2001) notes, this process demands widespread consultation and expert involvement, and so places research at the heart of policy making.

Such rational-linear models of the policy process broadly correspond with Weiss' (1979) models of research use as a knowledge-driven or problem-solving process (see Chapter Two). This model has, however, been subject to substantive critique. In particular, doubt has been cast as to whether policy makers do – or even can – act in 'rational' ways. Herbert Simon first drew attention to the limits on our ability to behave in line with models of simple rationality (Simon, 1957). He argued that human rationality is 'bounded'. We are simply unable – individually or collectively – to deal with complex problems in ways that meet the demands of objective rationality, for example to imagine and assess all the possible alternatives to any given problem. More pragmatically, he suggested that policy makers typically lack both access to the extensive information needed to carry out such comprehensive analyses, and the time to do so. Limits to rationality are thus further shaped by the constraints of local organisational contexts (Simon, 1957). Simon (1957) argued instead that rather than aiming to maximise benefits, people will 'satisfice': in other words, they will focus on solutions to problems which are 'good enough'. In line with such analysis, it has been argued that policy makers tend to make pragmatic decisions and to focus on short-term outcomes rather than longer-term social goals (for example, Dror, 1983; Lomas, 1997).

Lindblom (1968) drew on Simon's notion of 'satisficing' to develop an alternative 'incremental' model of the policy process. He argued that rational models of policy making are impossible to fulfil, because conclusive investigation of policy alternatives is beyond policy makers' analytic competence, and policy goals and values are always contested.

He also suggested that such models fail to reflect everyday policy-making realities. Lindblom (1968) argued that, in practice, what is politically feasible typically involves only small-scale, incremental policy change. He suggested that focusing on marginal policy change then brings particular advantages. For example, it enables policy makers to draw on their existing knowledge and experience, and reduces both the number of policy alternatives to be considered and the overall complexity of the policy process. The 'piecemealing, remedial incrementalist' is thus a 'shrewd, resourceful problem-solver' (Lindblom, 1968, p 27). In Lindblom's (1968) view, policy making involves a wide range of players – not only traditional policy elites, but also interest groups, the media and citizens themselves. It has no clear beginning or end and no clear boundaries. The policy process instead represents a series of complex interactions among these stakeholders that aim towards cooperation and consensus (Lindblom, 1968). As part of this pluralist process, research and policy analysis will play a role as a key bargaining tool for persuading others to cooperate (Lindblom, 1968). Within the incremental model, research may thus interact with the policy process at multiple points and through multiple players. It therefore envisages a much more diffuse role for research than rational-linear frameworks (Nutley and Webb, 2000). Research is still used in 'rational' ways, but primarily as a means of exerting power over others (Albaek, 1995; Bulmer, 1986). This reflects Weiss' (1979) definitions of more political and tactical uses of research (see Chapter Two).

The incremental model of the policy process suggests that the use of research in policy making may well be modest. Comprehensive research to inform policy change is unlikely, and while evidence may still inform policy choices, it will no longer be centre stage as in the rational-linear model. Research may be used in predominantly tactical ways, to advance particular positions rather than adjudicate among competing stances. Questions of research quality may be downplayed in this process. Albaek (1995) notes that the incremental model reintroduces values as a key component of policy making – defining a policy process that involves negotiation among different individuals and groups with different preferences and interests – which can help explain why research use will be less than the 'optimal' defined by the rational-linear model. In fact, Dror (1983) has suggested that incremental approaches to making policy may actively limit the role of social research in the policy process. For example, new knowledge that creates new policy opportunities and solutions may be ignored in favour of continuing to make incremental change to existing policies.

Inertia becomes the norm, so that policy makers have little motivation to seek out and use knowledge from research (Dror, 1983). Dror (1983) argues that this can in turn encourage social scientists themselves to restrict their research to incremental solutions and conservative viewpoints. Innovative research gets stifled, and the knowledge available for making policy becomes less useful (Dror, 1983). Research is also inhibited from playing more contentious and paradigm-challenging roles in the policy arena (see Chapter One). More generally, the incremental model cannot encompass the kinds of radical policy change needed where past policies have failed or completely new problems emerge, and where, in fact, research often has a key role to play (for example, Dror, 1983; Bulmer, 1986; Haas, 1992).

A more radical critique of rational frameworks for understanding the policy process is embodied in the 'garbage can' model of policy making (Cohen et al, 1972; March and Olsen, 1976). This presents a picture of the policy process as dynamic, unpredictable, chaotic and often fundamentally *irrational*. In this model, solutions need not follow from the analysis of policy problems, but may instead pre-date them – seeking a problem to which they can become attached. Policy problems and solutions get 'dumped' in a metaphorical garbage can, and become joined together when opportunities arise to make new policy decisions. In this way, 'existing proposals ... can be passed off as solutions to new problems' (Stone, 2001, p 11). The dynamics of this process are contingent and uncontrollable, and it may not be appropriate to think about 'decisions' being made at all (Albaek, 1995). Social and economic structures and cultural values will, however, play a role in shaping who participates in these decision-making opportunities and the possible outcomes that are available (Nutley and Webb, 2000). Kingdon (1984) has refined the garbage can framework to develop his 'multiple streams' model, which is primarily concerned with understanding the agenda-setting stage of the policy process (see Box 4.1).

Box 4.1: Kingdon's 'policy streams' model

Kingdon (1984) proposes that policy making involves three separate streams running through the policy arena. It is when these three streams join together that the greatest agenda change occurs.

(1) The *problem stream*, where problems come to the attention of policy makers and are recognised as important. This can happen in response to systematic indicators, key events or crises, or feedback about existing policies. Activists can also play a substantial role in this process.

(2) The *policy stream*, a 'primeval soup' in which policy ideas and proposals are generated and evaluated. Such alternatives emerge through an evolutionary process and must be both politically and technically feasible to survive. Specialists, including researchers, are the main players in this process.

(3) The *political stream*, through which problems and solutions reach the decision agenda. This stream comprises such elements as national mood, organised political forces (such as interest group pressures), shifts in public opinion and election results. It has its own dynamics and rules and can have a powerful effect on the policy agenda.

Researchers may be involved in any of the three streams, but are most active in the policy stream. All three streams mainly operate in isolation: for example, policy solutions may develop independently of any problem. Unlike the garbage can model, however, Kingdon (1984) argues that these processes are not solely random, but that some patterns emerge.

The key to understanding agenda and policy change lies in the 'coupling' of the three streams. Problems are combined with solutions and enter the political stream. This happens when 'policy windows' open, because particular problems become pressing, or as a result of a shift in the political stream (such as a change in administration). Policy windows open relatively rarely, and do not stay open for long. At such times, policy entrepreneurs – individuals advocating certain policy ideas or proposals – play a key role in coupling solutions to problems and political opportunities. Policy entrepreneurs represent an important route for research to enter policy, for example by championing a set of findings that supports their position (Neilson, 2001; see below, pp 108-9).

Source: Adapted from Kingdon (1984) and Neilson (2001)

It is difficult to see a clear place for research within the chaos of the garbage can model, although the more structured policy streams model more readily admits such a role. Nonetheless, such dynamic, irrational and unpredictable models of the policy-making process suggest that research is unlikely to be used through any simple or logical process of dissemination and application. Instead, research may enter policy through diverse and indirect routes and from a variety of different sources. It will most likely contribute in a gradual way to shifts in perceptions and ways of thinking, reflecting Weiss' (1979) 'enlightenment' model of the use of research (Albaek, 1995).

These different models of the policy process suggest a range of possible roles for research in making policy. Rational–linear models place research at the heart of the policy process, but these have been subject to widespread critique, and in practice it is hard to find examples where policy decisions have been made in this way (Albaek, 1995). Despite this, such models continue to hold sway in many contexts. For example, in the UK the Cabinet Office Centre for Management and Policy Studies (CMPS) (now the National School of Government) has taught a textbook example of this approach to policy making, which involves:

• setting manageable objectives;
• developing ways of meeting these goals; and
• comparing these options to find the best solution (Reid, 2003).

While rational–linear approaches can be helpful as exemplary models against which policy realities can be compared, their value in understanding the research–policy relationship is more limited. They fail to reflect the complexity of the policy-making process and the intricate interactions that occur between the research and policy communities. They focus on the instrumental use of research at the expense of more subtle and less tangible impacts, which may in fact be more important in the policy arena (Albaek, 1995). Finally, they suggest that research provides neutral 'facts' which help policy makers weigh up the pros and cons of any course of action – an assumption that denies both the value-laden nature of research, and the key role that values play in the policy-making process itself. These latter problems are, of course, particularly acute when it comes to using social research in making policy.

Alternative, less rational–linear models of the policy process (incremental models, policy streams and the garbage can model) suggest a much weaker and more indirect role for research. The 'two communities thesis', described in the next section, also suggests that research use by policy makers is limited, but provides a different account of the reasons behind this.

The 'two communities' thesis and related models

The two communities thesis has had a powerful influence on the ways in which the relationship between research and policy has been understood. First elaborated by Caplan (1979), the thesis borrows from C.P. Snow's conceptualisation of the humanities and the hard sciences as two different cultures (Caplan, 1979; Wingens, 1990). It assumes that a fundamental gap exists between research and policy which is held to be the result of cultural differences between these two communities. Researchers and policy makers 'live in separate worlds, with different and often conflicting values, different rewards systems, and different languages' (Caplan, 1979, p 459).

The central premise of the two communities thesis is that policy makers rarely use research. This non-use of research is understood as a problem of communication between researchers and policy makers who exist in foreign worlds and cultures. Greater interaction between the two groups – enhancing the communication between them – then becomes the main solution to bridging the research–policy gap (Caplan, 1979). According to the two communities thesis, interaction can help researchers and policy makers to better understand each others' worlds. It can begin to translate the different languages that each group speaks, and thereby encourages knowledge exchange between these apparently 'estranged' communities (Gibson, 2003). More and better contact between researchers and policy makers will thus, under this model, enhance the use of research. However, Caplan (1979) did not suggest that simply bringing the two groups together is somehow a panacea. He argued that effective interaction 'necessarily involves value and ideological dimensions as well as technical ones' (p 461) and so may be difficult to achieve. He also believed that different forms of interaction may be required in different circumstances, for example for different types of research or policy decisions (Caplan, 1979).

The two communities thesis has an intuitive appeal and has provided the basis for much subsequent thinking and action around the research–policy relationship. Gibson (2003) believes its popularity may be in large part because it so well captures the experiences of many policy makers and researchers. However, as an explanatory framework, it has some limitations. In particular, it presents a relatively simplistic model that is mainly concerned with the interaction (or non-interaction) between policy makers and practitioners. As several commentators have noted, its focus is then on *individual* policy makers and researchers and as such the model tends to downplay the wider political and organisational contexts that shape and constrain such individuals' actions (Wingens, 1990; Gibson, 2003). The thesis also minimises the diversity among researchers and policy makers and the likely overlap between the two groups, as well as neglecting other key players in the research–policy relationship (such as individual and organisational knowledge brokers) (Wingens, 1990; Lomas, 1997). Finally, its focus on the *non-use* of research deflects our concern from the ways in which research is actually incorporated into the policy-making process (Wingens, 1990).

From a cogent critique of the two communities thesis, Wingens (1990) has elaborated a 'general utilisation theory' based on a systems approach. Wingens sees the two communities framework as little more than a metaphor, and attributes its development to the particular historical moment of its conception, rooted in an *'exaggerated negative assessment'* (Wingens, 1990, p 30; emphasis in original) of the relationship between research and policy at the time. He suggests that the differences between researchers and policy makers are functional rather than cultural: that each represents a functionally differentiated social system or subsystem. Wingens (1990) argues that research use occurs when the systems interact, which happens when there is a contextual change within the wider social system such as a change in policy issues. This contextual change enables the political system to integrate knowledge from research. But according to Wingens (1990), research knowledge cannot simply be adopted by the political system: instead it needs to be adapted, recreated and transformed before it can be used by policy makers. This model thereby integrates constructionist theories of learning, which propose that any new knowledge will be filtered through and shaped by pre-existing frameworks and experiences in the process of its use (Wingens, 1990).

The more recent 'linkage and exchange' model of the research–policy relationship (CHSRF, 2000; Lomas, 2000) also has its roots in the two communities thesis. It too focuses on communication and interaction as the key to policy uses of research. However, it offers a much more complex and contextualised theorisation of the connections between research and policy. The model is underpinned by work by Lomas (1997), which reconceptualises both research and policy as processes, rather than products. This opens up multiple opportunities for mutual influence between them, beyond interactions that hinge on a particular research product or policy decision. Lomas (1997) also highlights the influence of the institutional and political context on policy uses of research, suggesting that three interrelated spheres are key:

- information: research and other forms of evidence, including experience and anecdote, and the different 'knowledge purveyors', including think tanks, interest groups and the media;

- the institutional structure for decision making: its format, those able to speak within it, interest groups and the rules of conduct;
- values that shape a decision, which emerge from the interaction of interests, ideologies and beliefs.

Lomas (1997) concludes that within such an arena, policy decisions are likely to be pragmatic and shaped by their political and institutional circumstances rather than rational and determined by research.

The linkage and exchange model recognises the wide variety of groups and individuals engaged in connecting policy and research. Two groups in addition to policy makers and researchers are seen as key: research funders and knowledge purveyors. And all these groups are not seen as homogeneous, but as diverse – for example, researchers may comprise in-house employees, management consultants, stand-alone centres, applied research institutes and academics (see Figure 4.1). The main focus of the model is, then, on the interfaces between these four groups (see Figures 4.1 to 4.4). Policy makers ask researchers about pressing problems, and researchers aim to supply policy makers with appropriate solutions. Research funders consult with policy makers around key problems, issues and priorities, and then translate these into funded programmes for research. Finally, through knowledge purveyors such as think tanks, conferences, journals and the media, findings from research (together with other forms of evidence) become ideas, best practices and interventions to be fed directly to policy makers.

This model suggests that research use will happen when the links between all four groups are both mutual and strong (CHSRF, 2000; Lomas, 2000). It represents a 'virtuous cycle', in which any weak link in these relationships may inhibit the uptake of research within the policy community (CHSRF, 2000). Crucially, the model re-imagines the use of research as a sophisticated process that involves multiple steps and multiple actors operating within a wider political context, rather than single, simple interactions between policy makers and researchers. It does, however, tend to place a stronger focus on instrumental rather than conceptual uses of research.

Figure 4.1: Evidence-based decision making: is this enough?

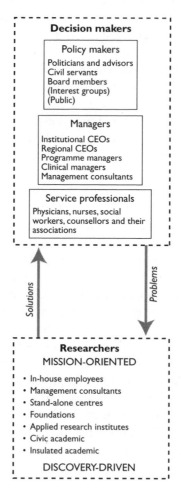

Source: Reproduced from CHSRF (2000)

Figure 4.2: Evidence-based decision making: the role of research funders

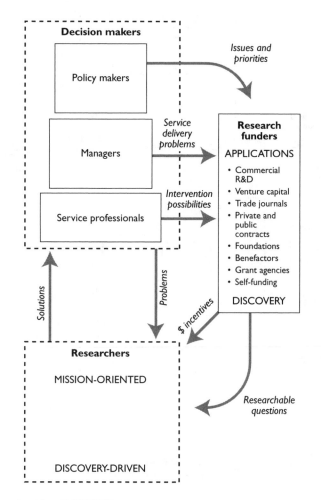

Source: Reproduced from CHSRF (2000)

Figure 4.3: Evidence-based decision making: the influence of knowledge purveyors

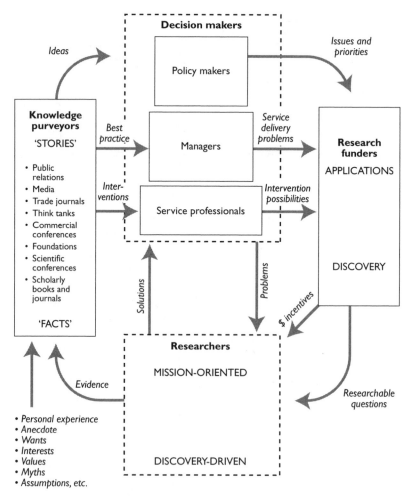

Source: Reproduced from CHSRF (2000)

Figure 4.4: Evidence-based decision making: where to focus for improvement

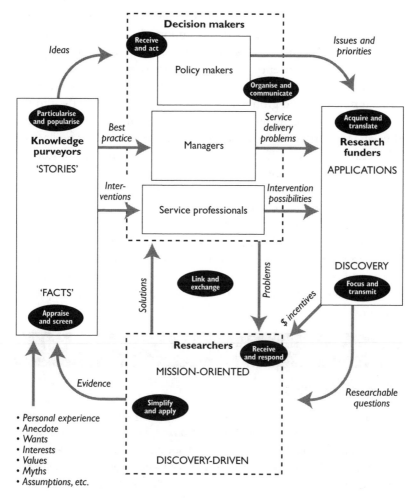

Source: Reproduced from CHSRF (2000)

Policy network approaches

Pluralist approaches to understanding the policy process suggest that decision making may be diffuse rather than centralised, operating outside formal channels and emerging through pressure from different groups who are themselves involved in setting agendas and developing policy solutions (for example, Haas, 1992). They highlight the role of policy networks in shaping how research and policy connect. For example, interest groups are a key channel for the flow of evidence and analysis and so may provide an important route for research to enter the policy process (Weiss, 1987). Similarly, networks can sometimes broker the entry of new ideas into official decision-making processes (Haas, 1992). In fact, researchers may themselves be members of such networks and groups, and thereby feed more directly into the policy-making process. Ideas about policy networks and communities thus offer a framework for conceptualising the context for policy uses of research, by identifying the patterns of formal and informal interactions that shape how a policy agenda is defined and how decisions are made (Nutley and Webb, 2000).

A variety of network approaches have been theorised and four key types are detailed in Box 4.2. Policy networks and communities differ in terms of their level of integration and the basis for their membership. They will vary across policy sectors and between states, and their different forms will affect policy development and implementation, and the ways in which research is accessed and considered as part of this process.

Box 4.2: Policy network approaches

Policy communities

Policy communities are made up of specialists in any given policy area (Kingdon, 1984). Their members come from a range of backgrounds, both within and outside government, and will include academics and analysts. They are well integrated with the policy-making process and coalesce around specific policy fields and institutions (Stone, 2001). They may have diverse orientations and interests, but all share specialist knowledge and experience of a particular policy domain (Kingdon, 1984). Kingdon (1984) suggests that policy communities play a key role in developing, testing out, selecting and refining those policy ideas and proposals that make it onto the policy agenda. This process will involve the exchange of information and the dissemination of research in developing shared perspectives on a policy problem. Policy communities may be more or less integrated but tend to be resistant to change, and operate independently of the wider political sphere (Kingdon, 1984).

Advocacy coalitions

Originally developed by Sabatier and Jenkins-Smith (1991), the advocacy coalition framework (ACF) rests on a systems approach to policy analysis in which the policy process is made up of policy 'subsystems', 'those institutions and actors that are directly involved in the policymaking process in a specialized policy area' (Jenkins-Smith et al, 1991, p 852). These actors and groups coalesce to form discrete and competing advocacy coalitions, with two to four such coalitions at any given time (Jenkins-Smith et al, 1991; Sabatier, 1998). Advocacy coalitions comprise varied policy actors from different levels within government as well as academics, representatives from business and from interest groups, the media and other key stakeholders. They develop on the basis of shared normative and causal beliefs (Sabatier, 1998; Sabatier and Pelkey, 1987).

The ACF envisages that research gets used primarily through Weiss' (1979) 'enlightenment' model (see Chapter Two), and so takes a long-term approach to understanding the full influence of information on policy change (Jenkins-Smith and Sabatier, 1994; Sabatier, 1998). New information such as research may lead to a shift in coalitions' beliefs or in the strategies they use to influence policy making, but in general this will happen cumulatively over time (Sabatier, 1998). Further, coalitions are likely to resist any research evidence that runs counter to their core beliefs, while developing analyses themselves that support these beliefs or else challenge the stance of opponents (Sabatier, 1998). Political and tactical uses of research are thus to the fore. However, information alone is not sufficient for policy change: this emerges in response to factors external to the policy subsystem – such as socioeconomic conditions or decisions made in other subsystems (Sabatier, 1998).

Epistemic communities

The concept of epistemic communities has been advanced by Haas (1992), who defines such groups as a 'network of professionals with recognized expertise and competence in a particular domain and an authoritative claim to policy-relevant knowledge within that domain' (Haas, 1992, p 3). While their members are often researchers, they also come from a wide range of disciplines and backgrounds. They share beliefs and are committed to a common policy enterprise, but what binds them together is their faith in the legitimacy and value of particular forms and bodies of knowledge (Haas, 1992). Such epistemic communities can operate at both national and transnational levels and support the diffusion of knowledge and wider learning from research. Stone (2001) suggests that they may be both long-standing and stable, or else *ad hoc*, emerging in response to a specific issue. Through the legitimacy given by their professional training and claims to expertise, members of epistemic communities can secure unique access to and influence on the political system: knowledge is their main source of power (Haas, 1992). In fact, in situations of uncertainty and complexity, which require substantial technical or scientific understanding, policy makers may themselves turn to epistemic communities for advice (Haas, 1992). Haas (1992) suggests that epistemic communities can then both shed light on the problem at hand, and play a role in developing policy themselves.

Issue networks

Issue networks tend to be the most fluid and least stable form of policy networks and communities. Originally proposed by Heclo (1978), their membership tends to be large and continually shifts as people join and leave the network all the time. The boundary between the issue network and its surrounding environment is thus blurred. Moreover, although participants need not have a strong commitment to other network members, they do share a common knowledge base (Heclo, 1978). However, it is above all the issue that drives and binds this kind of network. Heclo (1978) proposes that such issues are not defined by members' interests, but rather the issues themselves become their interests. Expertise in issue networks arises primarily through knowledge of a policy debate, rather than (as in epistemic communities) their technical proficiency (Heclo, 1978). Research has a central role to play in issue networks, where information represents a key 'currency of exchange' (Weiss, 1995).

Kingdon's (1984) 'policy entrepreneurs' – those individuals who advocate certain policy proposals or ideas – are key players in policy networks. Like their business equivalents, policy entrepreneurs are defined in terms of their 'willingness to invest their resources – time, energy, reputation, and sometimes money – in the hope of a future return' (Kingdon, 1984, p 129). They may be motivated by self-interest – the opportunity for heightened status or career advance – or else by the chance to shape public policy in line with their concerns (Kingdon, 1984). Policy entrepreneurs can often be a key route for research to enter the policy process (Neilson, 2001), and may indeed be researchers themselves. To be successful, they need to have a claim to a hearing, for example on the basis of their expertise or authority to speak for others; excellent political connections; and above all the persistence to pursue their goals (Kingdon, 1984). They may act as 'champions' for research where this supports their cause and enhances their own credibility. They both 'soften up' the system to their own ideas and proposals and act as brokers, negotiating among key stakeholders (Kingdon, 1984).

A focus on policy networks means that the research–policy interface is no longer directly between researchers and policy makers (Gibson, 2003). Research can play a key role in the policy process, especially where individual researchers and analysts – or research organisations and think tanks – are network participants. Policy impact will be enhanced where policy makers are themselves active network members, but even where this is not the case, networks can be vital in shaping both policy opinion and public discourse (Stone, 2001). Stone (2001) suggests that researchers can feed information and analysis into networks as well as develop supportive network infrastructures, for example by holding conferences and setting up databases. At the same time, researchers can provide a network's 'conceptual language', and 'help create common ideas and arguments that educate network participants into the values or consensus of the network' (Stone, 2001, p 16). Above all, network approaches begin to emphasise the role of politics and power in shaping how research and policy interact (Gibson, 2003).

Context, evidence, links: an integrated model of the research–policy relationship

The context, evidence and links model (Crewe and Young, 2002) integrates many of the models already described within a broad-based framework for examining the research–policy relationship, originally intended to extend analysis of this field into the developing world. It draws on a wide range of theories, discourses and disciplines and highlights the importance of context, the nature of the research and the linkages between key players in modelling when and how research is used in the policy-making process.

Crewe and Young (2002) believe that policy making is 'structured by a complex interplay between political interests, competing discourses and the agency of multiple actors' (p 3). This process will vary across contexts, for example in terms of the kinds of policy networks at play and the kinds of knowledge regarded as useful or legitimate. Based on a synthesis of previous literature in the field, they propose a three-dimensional framework for understanding the research–policy relationship. Policy uptake of research is viewed as a function of the interaction of all these three factors (what follows is adapted from Crewe and Young, 2002).

(1) *Context*

Policy uses of research will be shaped by the political and institutional structures of the broader policy context and by the shifting play of power among these. The interests and roles of both policy makers and researchers are important too, as are the organisational cultures and pressures within which they act. Different types of policy decision will further affect the use of research – for example, more radical change requires more extensive debate. Finally, research use will be shaped by the ways in which policy is ultimately implemented on the ground.

(2) *Evidence*

The credibility of the research and its communication will affect its uptake by policy makers. The quality of the research, its source, and the way it is packaged are all significant. However, research and policy become integrated through a variety of processes and routes. This may involve direct links between researchers and their policy counterparts, but more indirect channels for impact are important as well, as research evidence accumulates and permeates into the policy arena over time. The role of different processes and channels for impact will then vary across different contexts. This model assumes that policy makers actively engage with research (rather than being merely its passive recipients), and in line with constructionist theories of learning suggests that evidence from research will be shaped through policy makers' pre-existing knowledge, values and experiences.

(3) *Links*

The model proposes that the use of research will be greater where researchers and policy makers 'forge close personal links, with appropriate chains of legitimacy to those they represent' (Crewe and Young, 2002, p 16). Policy networks may shape these research–policy links, and policy entrepreneurs are likely to play a key role in integrating policy and research. Research use will also be influenced by how 'experts' are defined in any given policy domain. For example, intellectual expertise may not be enough for researchers to call for policy change: they may need to establish 'chains of legitimacy' with research participants as well (Crewe and Young, 2002).

This model builds on and integrates much previous work in the field to provide a more sophisticated framework that moves our understanding of research–policy relationships beyond unidimensional rational-linear models and simplistic 'two communities' approaches. Crucially, it focuses on the interaction between the multiple facets of research use identified in the literature (see Chapter Three). It thereby represents the use of research as a dynamic, complex and mediated process, which is shaped by formal and informal structures, by multiple actors and bodies of knowledge, and by the relationships and play of politics and power that run through the wider policy context. Its focus on the contingent and contextual factors that shape policy uses of research builds from and reflects the growing body of knowledge that we have about what influences the uptake of research (see Chapter Three).

Models of the research–practice relationship

In much of the preceding discussion, our focus has largely been on general models of the policy process and the role these specify for research, where much of the work on the research–policy relationship has been directed. By contrast, the literature on practice uses of research has more often concentrated on specific models of the research–practice relationship, while paying comparatively less attention to the wider models of practice within which such interactions are embedded. In broad terms, however, development of research–practice models has reflected similar shifts in thinking to those identified earlier, from more simple, linear models of the flow of research into practice, to models that recognise the complexity and contextual nature of the use of research in practice settings.

Linear models of research into practice

Traditional models of the research–practice relationship are again linear and unidimensional, emphasising the flow of knowledge from the research community into the practice arena. These models tend to view research and practice as distinct and separate entities: knowledge is produced by researchers, then transferred through dissemination processes to practitioners who apply it. In such models, knowledge from research is usually seen as factual, unambiguous and discrete, able to be straightforwardly applied to practice decisions (Tyden, 1993). Typically, the focus of these linear-rational models is on instrumental rather than conceptual uses of research. At the same time, a rational process of research use is assumed: in other words, if the findings are relevant and useful, practitioners will adopt them (NCDDR, 1996).

Huberman (1994) sets out a classic model of this form (see Figure 4.5). The research community first produces knowledge, then disseminates this knowledge to the practice community, where it is used. Subsequently, a fourth element has been added to this model in the form of a feedback link from practitioners to researchers, enabling research users to convey their knowledge needs and supporting more practice-relevant research (Huberman, 1994). The separation of research and practice in this model reflects the 'two communities' characterisation of the research and policy arenas described earlier.

A number of variations on this model have been defined. 'Spread' represents the one-way diffusion of information, with proactive approaches to transmitting research and strategies that aim to make practitioners aware of the evidence (Klein and Gwaltney, 1991). 'Producer-push' models (for example, Landry et al, 2001a, 2001b) also focus on the process of transmitting research findings to practitioners. They maintain that the supply of research is the main factor shaping its use. These kinds of model assume that we need good research and effective dissemination if practitioners are to make use of research, and that evidence will thereby diffuse among potential users to narrow the research–practice gap (Cousins and Simon, 1996). Such models

Figure 4.5: A classic model of using research in practice contexts

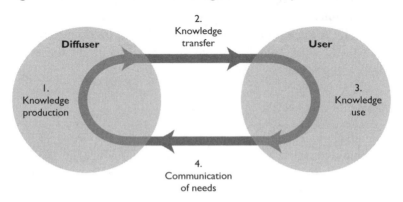

view practitioners as 'targets' for research – blank slates on which research evidence can simply be inscribed (NCDDR, 1996).

Kitson et al (1996) have outlined an example of a rational-linear model of research use which has been employed in the healthcare field. This model places heavy store on the creation of rigorous research knowledge for practice, for example through systematic reviews. It assumes that when good-quality findings are made accessible, and when support is provided to locate and apply them, practitioners will want to use research. The research use process is then evaluated, and the evaluation findings are fed back into the production of knowledge for practice (Kitson et al, 1996; see Figure 4.6).

However, Kitson et al (1996) suggest two main problems with this approach. The first concerns the availability of research. They argue that on the ground, relevant and robust research findings that can be applied to practice problems are often few and far between. The second concerns the impact of the wider practice context within which research gets used. Kitson et al (1996) propose that factors over and above the individual practitioner will shape and constrain the use of research, particularly organisational issues and other contextual influences on the practice environment.

Rational-linear models of the use of research in practice are firmly grounded in a positivist and objectivist epistemology (Watkins, 1994). Huberman (1994) has accused them of being 'hyper-rational' because such models assume that knowledge from research is uncontested,

Figure 4.6: A rational-linear model of research use

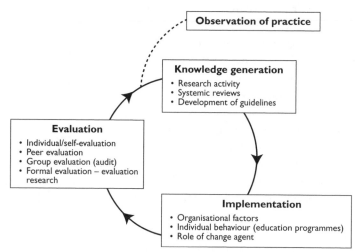

Source: Reproduced by permission of Blackwell Publishing from Kitson et al (1996)

and that increasing practitioners' use of research merely requires an increase in research dissemination. These models thus ignore the complex and contingent nature of the research use process (Huberman, 1994; Cousins and Simon, 1996). Despite such critiques, however, Louis (1998) has noted that traditional models of the research–practice relationship are not as simplistic as has sometimes been imagined, and that early work within this framework identified important barriers and facilitators to the use of research.

Rational-linear models of practitioners' research use are intuitively attractive, and have underpinned much of the thinking – and also action – within the evidence-based policy and practice agenda. This may in part be precisely because they specify such a key role for research. While simplistic, they can act as a useful normative model to examine how and why research use diverges from a rational and linear approach. However, more recent conceptualisations of research use as a learning process highlight some of the limitations of these models for a full understanding of the research use process within practice communities. These context-focused models of the use of research are considered in the next section.

Context-focused models of the use of research

Subsequent work on the research–practice relationship has recognised that research use is a complex process, which is strongly influenced by the context in which it takes place (for example, Huberman, 1993, 1994; Cousins and Simon, 1996; see Chapter Three). These accounts acknowledge that research is only one of many factors that will influence practice, and that will in turn shape practitioners' use of research. For example, in the education field, issues of accountability, regulation and teaching cultures will mediate teachers' practice alongside knowledge from research and other sources (Desforges, 2000). Desforges (2000) notes how such influences will have differential power and so will differentially constrain and enable the use of research: for example, accountability systems often take precedence over any other influence in shaping teachers' practices and may in turn stifle experiment and innovation based on research. Research knowledge may emerge from or, indeed, have an impact on, any of these influences, but will always be interpreted within the context they create (Desforges, 2000).

A range of models exist that entail a similar shift in focus from the production and dissemination of research to the research users themselves and the contexts in which they act. For example, the 'choice' model of research use focuses on helping research users actively search for and acquire research evidence (Klein and Gwaltney, 1991). Similarly, 'user-pull' models focus on practitioners' research needs, and on the organisational and political contexts that shape their uptake of research (Landry et al, 2001a, 2001b; Lavis et al, 2003). The idea that practitioners may be active – not just passive – in engaging with research, and that their research use depends at least in part on the wider contexts in which they work, begins to challenge the assumption that there is a simple and direct correlation between research availability and its use (Tyden, 1993).

In the healthcare field, Kitson et al (1998) have introduced a conceptual framework for understanding the research-to-practice process to encompass the multiple contextual influences that shape practitioners' use of research. The model takes the form:

$$SI=f(E, C, F)$$

in which successful implementation of research (SI) is a function (f) of the nature of the evidence (E), the local context for its use (C), and the ways in which research use is facilitated (F). Evidence is defined as knowledge from research combined with clinical expertise and patient preferences. Context represents the local environment for research use, including its culture, leadership and monitoring systems. Facilitation refers to a specific change management strategy, in which a single individual works closely with other practitioners to help them understand how to achieve their goals. Kitson et al (1998) suggest that in any research-to-practice setting, each of these three factors can be located along a continuum, from low to high, and they argue that when all three are high, research use is most likely to occur. Kitson et al's (1998) own research does, however, suggest that facilitation may be the most important factor in securing practitioner use of research.

Landry et al (2001a, 2001b) note that while such user-pull models shift attention to research consumers and the local contexts in which they operate, they still embed a linear and instrumental framing of the research use process. For Desforges (2000), however, understanding research use means more than simply identifying those contextual factors that will shape research uptake; it means understanding too how practitioners conceptualise practice problems in relation to their own experience and expertise. Research is not simply transferred to practitioners, but is 'transformed' in the process of its use (Desforges, 2000). When practitioners engage with research, they will translate, adapt and renegotiate new findings and ideas in order to make sense of them within the contexts of their day-to-day work (Huberman, 1993; NCDDR, 1996). Desforges (2000) thus defines research use as 'a knowledge-led, problem-constrained learning process' (p 4). Rethinking research use as a process of learning reflects interpretivist frameworks for understanding how research gets used (Cousins and Simon, 1996). It derives from constructionist theories of learning, which propose that any new knowledge will be filtered through and shaped by pre-existing knowledge, perspectives and experience (for example, Huberman, 1987; NCDDR, 1996). Hargreaves (1998) describes this process as 'tinkering', which not only blends explicit knowledge from research with tacit 'craft' knowledge or practice wisdom, but also creates new knowledge as part of this process.

Such interpretivist frameworks for understanding the use of research undermine linear-rational models which view research use as simply a mechanical process of transferring research evidence from one place to another. The use of research emerges instead as a complex and non-linear process, contingent on the values, knowledge and contexts of those practitioners who engage with research. It represents a process of change, in which practitioners have to 'unlearn' – let go of old ways of thinking – before they can take on new ideas from research (NCDDR, 1996; Rushmer and Davies, 2004). Research is thus actively adapted, not just adopted, by practitioners, reconstructed through being combined with and subordinated to a range of other influences and forms of knowledge (Tyden, 1993).

Interactive models of research use

Interpretivist frameworks are helpful for understanding the complex and contextual nature of research use in practice settings. However, in its most extreme form, interpretivism destabilises the very premise of research use. It views knowledge – including knowledge from research – as socially constructed, given meaning in different ways by different individuals and groups. From this standpoint, the meaning of research is always contingent, and no external criteria exist that would allow any group's interpretation to be privileged over that of any other (for example, Cousins and Simon, 1996). The apparent 'truth' of research findings is merely a social construction: research can no longer claim to provide superior knowledge for practice, and so the very project of using research is undermined (Huberman, 1994).

In response, many theorists have established more moderate ground for understanding research and its use. These 'revised modernist perspectives' aim to balance and combine more traditional, positivist approaches with interpretivist accounts of the constructed nature of knowledge (Huberman, 1994; Cousins and Simon, 1996). They assert the possibility that research can be communicated to practitioners, but suggest that such research must be interpreted if it is to be 'usable knowledge' (Louis, 1998).

In the education field, Huberman (1994) has adopted this perspective to try to define a model of research use that draws simultaneously on positivist and interpretivist framings. He outlines a 'dissemination effort' model that details the diverse and linked influences that shape whether and how research gets used (see Box 4.3). While this model retains elements of more linear, rational and instrumental models for research use, Huberman's (1994) focus is on the linkages between researchers and research users. He argues that such linkages hold the key to understanding the use of research in the form of 'sustained interactivity'. Sustained interactivity involves ongoing, interpersonal and two-way links between researchers and practitioners, that take place across the whole duration of a research project and not simply at its end (Huberman, 1994). This dialogue and exchange supports joint interpretive processes of negotiating and reconstructing research findings within the contexts of their use. The emphasis is on mutual exchange rather than the one-way flow of knowledge from researchers to practitioners, with both groups 'laying claims to conceptual power and replicability' (Huberman, 1994, p 23; see also Simons et al, 2003). The underlying process reflects constructionist accounts of learning, in which practitioners frame the findings and concepts from research in the light of pre-existing experience and understandings. But at the same time, researchers are themselves reconstructing their own knowledge, frameworks and ideas: the effects are 'reciprocal' (Huberman, 1993, 1994). Huberman (1994) maintains that sustained interactivity thus provides a situation of 'relative symmetry' between researchers and practitioners in the research use process. He further claims that where these kinds of linkages are maintained beyond the lifespan of a single study, future uses of research may also be enhanced (Huberman, 1990).

Box 4.3: Huberman's (1994) 'dissemination effort' model

Huberman's (1994) 'dissemination effort' model outlines a range of interconnected influences on the use of research:

- *researcher context*, for example, study characteristics, investment in dissemination, user relevance of the research;

- *user context*, for example, the perceived value of the study, commitment of local leaders, credibility of the research team;
- *linkage mechanisms*, for example, formal and informal contacts between researchers and users during the study and the presence of boundary spanners;
- *predictors of local use*, for example, users' understanding of the findings and organisational investment in their use;
- *dissemination effort*, for example, in terms of the quality, competence and intensity of its implementation and the quality of any written products.

Source: Adapted from Huberman (1994)

A similar interactive model, that of 'synthesis pedagogics', has been outlined by Tyden (1993, 1996). It derives from the notion of dialectic pedagogics (Tyden, 1993), and emphasises interplay and dialogue among all the participants in the research use process. Opposing perspectives are surfaced, and researchers and practitioners actively engage with each other's standpoints. Each brings their own values and perspectives: knowledge and ideas are jointly shared and then blended to create something qualitatively new (Tyden, 1993). During this process, the 'senders' and 'receivers' continually swap places in co-producing knowledge, and both researchers and practitioners participate actively and equally in the process of using research (Tyden, 1993).

These kinds of interactive frameworks for understanding the research use process are currently to the fore in conceptual discussions of practitioner uses of research. For example, Landry et al (2001b) detail the emergence of an 'interaction model', while Klein and Gwaltney (1991) use the term 'exchange'. Such models define research use as a messy and dynamic set of interactions between researchers and research users, rather than a linear, rational flow from one to the other. The focus is on mutual exchange between the research and practice communities. Interactive models provide a better frame for understanding the complex, contingent and multifaceted process of research use, as well as beginning to suggest what might be required if we want to improve the use of research in practice settings.

Understanding research use – the importance of interaction

In both the policy and practice fields, then, a set of similar models has emerged that attends to the complex and context-bound nature of research use, the importance of links and interactions among researchers and research users as part of this process, and the role of actors and communities beyond 'research', 'policy' and 'practice', such as research funders, interest groups and networks. In the policy arena, the linkage and exchange model and the context, evidence and links model propose that research use involves multiple actors and multiple exchanges, and is contingent on both the nature of the research itself and on the context for its use. Frameworks that understand research use as a learning process or as the result of 'sustained interactivity' focus on similar issues within the practice community.

These interactive models of research use offer powerful frameworks for understanding the process through which research gets used. They integrate our best current knowledge about the kinds of factors that seem to support the use of research (for example, Huberman, 1994; Lomas, 1997; Crewe and Young, 2002; see Chapter Three). For example, the context, evidence and links model is based on studies of the key variables that shape policy uses of research. Crucially, however, these variables are not considered in isolation, but in terms of the complex and dynamic ways in which they interact. As we saw in Chapter Three, it is these kinds of interaction that have emerged as key to our understanding of the use of research (for example, Landry et al, 2001b). Interactive models reconceptualise the use of research as dynamic and unpredictable – a process, rather than a single event.

Further, unlike more linear models of research use, interactive models do not assume that research will always, or even often, be used in rational ways. They highlight the role of a complex range of contextual factors – cultural, organisational, personal and political – in shaping whether and how research gets used, above and beyond the efficiency and effectiveness of any attempts at dissemination. They also reject the notion that research offers neutral 'facts' that can be simply applied, and instead see research use as a socially mediated process. Research is not merely adopted: it is adapted, blended with other forms of knowledge, and integrated with the contexts of its use.

Interactive models thus offer a more nuanced understanding of the ways in which research is taken up by policy makers and practitioners. They show how knowledge from research will be shaped and reconstructed through policy makers' and practitioners' pre-existing frameworks and understandings – which may be collectively, not just individually, held (for example, Huberman, 1993; Crewe and Young, 2002). As such, where linear models tend to downplay or deny the role of research users' own, often tacit, knowledge and experience, interactive models begin to incorporate these. At the same time, interactive models focus on mutual exchanges between researchers and research users, proposing a relation potentially of greater equality between those who produce and those who use research (Huberman, 1994).

Postmodern accounts of the research use process have, however, provided some critique of these 'revised modernist perspectives'. They suggest that interactive models still retain researchers in a dominant position of power in the research use relationship, and fail fully to take account of the local knowledges at play in research use contexts (Watkins, 1994; Cousins and Simon, 1996). Postmodern currents of thought provide a very different take on what research use might mean and how it might be understood. The challenges they offer force us to take a more careful and reflective stance in developing our thinking about the ways in which research is used, and how such use might be improved.

Postmodern accounts of research use

There is much to be gained from examining and reflecting on the challenges presented by postmodern approaches to the research use field. However, such approaches vary widely, and in this section we aim to outline just some of the key features and ideas that emerge from this work that can enhance our understanding of the use of research.

Postmodern readings of research use turn our attention first of all to the idea that knowledge from research represents a fundamental 'truth'. They argue instead that research is socially constructed through relations of power to give an appearance of truth (Gibson, 2003). This has two key consequences for the ways in which we think about the use of research. The first is that it draws our attention to the play of power within the process of research use. The second is that it alerts us to the ways in which alternative forms of knowing and knowledge may be suppressed in the use of research.

As Gibson (2003) notes, being able to assert that research is 'true' reflects relations of power inherent in the structures through which such knowledge gets produced. Power thus runs through any claim by researchers to have useful knowledge for policy or practice. Watkins'

(1994) critical theory of research use is focused on recognising and surfacing these power relations within the research use process. His starting point lies with interactive models that simultaneously frame the use of research through the dual lenses of positivism and interpretivism. However, he adds to these a third, critical, lens, which can examine the issues of power, influence and ideology implicit in the use of research. This framing highlights questions about the value and appropriateness of using research in any given context. In practical terms, it suggests a range of strategies that might be taken to help surface these issues, for example developing researcher–practitioner groups in which individual interests are made transparent (Watkins, 1994). Conceptually, it can stimulate analyses of the inherent play of power in attempts to secure the use of research (Gibson, 2003; see Box 4.4).

Box 4.4: The Effective Practice Initiative – issues of power in using research in probation practice

Robinson (2001) has drawn on Foucault's concept of 'knowledge/power' to analyse the use of 'what works' knowledge in probation practice in England and Wales. The 'Effective Practice Initiative' (EPI) aimed to bring probation practice in England and Wales in line with research evidence on what works to reduce reoffending. Robinson's (2001) analysis demonstrates the ways in which this process was shot through by relations of power, and how this power operated in ways that were both productive and repressive. For example, appropriation and control of the 'what works' body of knowledge enhanced the professional status of probation staff. It gave them greater credibility, as well as the opportunity to demonstrate their effectiveness in the criminal justice system. However, it simultaneously undermined their professional status in other ways. For example, it provoked the development of more routinised, research-based practices and practice tools. This meant that probation practice became increasingly focused on the technical application of these research-based procedures, at the expense of practitioners' specialist and 'craft' knowledge and professional judgement.

Source: Adapted from Robinson (2001)

Giving weight to research as a fundamental 'truth' also denies or suppresses alternative forms of knowledge. Postmodern accounts of the use of research alert us to the fact that research – as detached, theoretical and generalisable knowledge – is typically privileged over more local, specific and contingent forms of knowledge that exist within the policy and practice communities (Watkins, 1994; Wood et al, 1998). These forms of 'craft' knowledge or practice wisdom are thereby delegitimised in the research use process. However, postmodern accounts aim to break down the dualities between research and policy, or research and practice. In doing so, they also aim to negate the imbalance of power between them (see, for example, Wood et al, 1998).

But removing the distinction between research and policy or research and practice means that we can no longer talk about getting research 'into' policy or practice at all (for example, Wood et al, 1998). From a postmodern perspective, different forms of knowledge (as opposed to information) are 'not disseminable *per se*' (Watkins, 1994, p 65). They only make sense – and can only be used – within the local contexts of their production (Watkins, 1994). Postmodern perspectives thereby highlight the importance of situated, local knowledges in the research use process. They give greater privilege to the experiential and tacit forms of knowledge held by policy makers and practitioners than traditional accounts of the use of research, and highlight the ways in which research must be 'reconnected' with these forms of knowledge if we are to think about its 'use' (Wood et al, 1998).

Postmodern accounts of research use encourage us to take a more reflexive and critical view in thinking about and modelling the research use process. We need not, however, as Weiss (1998, p 29) puts it, 'throw out the baby with the bathwater', and assume that research cannot be disseminated at all. In fact, Louis (1998) has argued that many of the propositions of postmodern theories on research use fit well with contemporary ways of understanding the process: for example, the view that knowledge is always contested and provisional, and the idea that knowledge will always need to be adapted within the local contexts of its use. She further notes that people do still seek out knowledge from research, that they are able to understand such knowledge, and that they go on to apply this knowledge in ways that lead to change on the ground. Weiss concludes that: 'Conditions and interpretations differ, but there is enough commonality across people, programs, and organizations to make a functioning social world possible' (Weiss, 1998, p 30).

Concluding remarks

Ways of thinking about the use of research in both policy and practice have followed similar trajectories. Traditional linear and rational models have largely been rejected in favour of more interactive approaches that draw on interpretivist accounts of the social construction of knowledge in the process of its use. Postmodern frameworks provide an additional, critical edge to these analyses, focusing on the play of power in any attempt to conceptualise or undertake research use activities.

Underpinning these developments are shifts in the ways in which research knowledge itself is conceptualised. In early models, research is seen to provide discrete, unambiguous, factual accounts that can straightforwardly be transferred and applied to policy or practice. Interactive models also view knowledge from research as isolatable and transferable, but emphasise the ways in which such knowledge will be negotiated, adapted and reconstructed within the contexts of its use, in a process which integrates research knowledge with local 'craft' knowledge. The emphasis is on joint processes of knowledge production. By contrast, postmodern accounts reject the conceptual separation of research from policy or practice. This means that it makes no sense to view research knowledge as something distinct from practice or policy knowledge. For example, Wood et al (1998) conceive of knowledge as something fluid, continually in flux, produced through interactions between research and policy or research and practice, but which may become temporarily stabilised in ways that give the appearance of a body of research knowledge. Postmodern accounts privilege instead local 'situated knowledges', and pay attention to the processes through which different forms of knowledge are defined and accepted as legitimate in different contexts (Wood et al, 1998). Different models of the research use process are thus embedded in very different ontological and epistemological perspectives.

While clear parallels can be drawn between research–policy and research–practice models, it is also important to distinguish the ways in which they differ. In particular, models of the use of research in policy need to embrace the highly politicised context in which this process takes place. Similarly, they pay greater attention to issues of values, beliefs and ideologies than models of the use of research in practice contexts. On the whole, ways of thinking about the research–policy relationship have relied to a greater extent on existing models of the policy process. In contrast, specific models of the use of research in practice are more abundant but seem often to have been developed in isolation from models of the process of practice within the contexts to which they refer. Crucially, however, the ways in which research–policy and research–practice relationships are framed and understood will shape the kinds of strategies that are developed and deployed to try to enhance these relationships. Such strategies form the focus of Chapter Five.

FIVE

Improving the use of research: what's been tried and what might work?

Chapter Four identified the principal models that we have for understanding the relationships between research and policy and research and practice. This chapter examines the different strategies that have been used to attempt to improve research use in relation to these different models. Research use improvement strategies are underpinned – explicitly or implicitly – by different frameworks for conceptualising both the nature of research use and the research use process. These different ways of thinking shape the kinds of research use initiatives that are put in place. In this chapter, we focus in particular on the putative mechanisms that seem to underpin different strategies for improving the use of research. Teasing out these mechanisms allows us to see both what is common across seemingly diverse strategies, as well as clarifying the wider theories that these mechanisms draw upon.

A wide range of initiatives exist, in the UK and beyond, that aim to improve policy and practice use of research (see, for example, *Effective Health Care Bulletin*, 1999; Hemsley-Brown and Sharp, 2003; Walter et al, 2004b). Many of these have been initiated in the context of the evidence-based policy and practice agenda outlined and discussed in Chapter One. This chapter explores some of the key strategies and activities that have been used to try to improve the use of research, and examines the evidence that exists about their effectiveness. Its main aim is to identify broad and cross-sector lessons from the health, education, criminal justice and social care fields about 'what works' to improve the use of research in policy and in practice. Inevitably, there will be far more research use initiatives on the ground than have been subject to formal evaluation. The first section of this chapter thus considers the diversity of research use strategies and activities by looking at the kinds of categorisations and taxonomies that have been developed to try to rationalise these.

Taxonomies of strategies to improve the use of research

An enormous variety of approaches have been taken to try to improve the use of research. Strategies vary according to the scale of the project, the nature of intended impact from research and their context for implementation, as well as the kinds of research evidence whose uptake is being promoted. In line with the models presented in Chapter Four, we can also distinguish strategies that focus on 'pushing' research findings out to policy makers and practitioners; strategies undertaken in policy and practice contexts to 'pull' in research; and interactive strategies, concerned with developing better links between researchers and potential research users. Establishing some kind of categorisation of these diverse activities can help systematise current thinking and understanding about improving the use of research.

In the healthcare field, the Effective Practice and Organisation of Care (EPOC) group within the Cochrane Collaboration has developed a widely used taxonomy of interventions to promote practice change (see Box 5.1). This categorisation closely reflects the healthcare context in which it was developed and focuses more generally on change in practice, rather than specifically on the use of research.

Box 5.1: The EPOC taxonomy of interventions to achieve practice change

Professional interventions

- Distribution of educational materials
- Educational meetings
- Local consensus processes
- Educational outreach visits
- Local opinion leaders
- Patient-mediated interventions
- Audit and feedback
- Reminders
- Marketing
- Mass media.

Financial interventions

- Provider interventions
- Patient interventions.

Organisation interventions

- Revision of professional roles
- Multidisciplinary teams
- Formal integration of services
- Skill mix changes
- Continuity of care
- Interventions to boost morale
- Communication and case discussion.

Patient-oriented interventions

- Consumer participation in governance of healthcare organisation
- Mail order pharmacies
- Mechanisms for dealing with patient suggestions and complaints.

Structural interventions

- Changes to site/setting of service delivery
- Changes to physical structure
- Changes in medical records systems
- Changes in scope and nature of benefits of services
- Presence and organisation of quality monitoring
- Ownership of hospitals and other facilities
- Staff organisation.

Regulatory interventions

- Changes in medical liability
- Management of patient complaints
- Peer review
- Licensure.

Source: **Reproduced from Davies et al (2000a)**

The EPOC taxonomy defines the different types of intervention that have been used to promote practice change according to the form that they take and the context in which they operate. It is particularly useful for highlighting the different levels – individual, organisational, structural, system and even service user – at which interventions may be made.

A recent review of research use in the UK social care field identified a very wide range of initiatives on the ground to try to improve the use of research among practitioners, and categorised these according to their primary purpose (Walter et al, 2004b; see Box 5.2).

Box 5.2: Types of research use strategies in the UK social care field

(1) *Ensuring a relevant research base*

This can involve commissioning new research, synthesising existing research, or involving staff in the development and conduct of individual studies.

(2) *Ensuring access to research*

This might mean providing better library services or enabling access to research databases and the internet. It also involves improving the circulation of research materials between and within organisations.

(3) *Making research comprehensible*

This might include producing 'user-friendly' accounts of research, as well as activities to improve users' abilities to interpret study findings such as critical appraisal skills training, journal clubs and practitioner-led research.

(4) *Drawing out the practice implications of research*

This typically involves the production of research-based guidelines, tools and protocols.

(5) *Developing best practice models*

This might mean developing pilot or demonstration projects based on findings from research, usually supported at local levels through training, project management and individual supervision.

(6) *Requiring research-informed practice*

This can involve writing research use into job descriptions, including it in staff appraisals, or embedding it in national standards for practice.

(7) *Developing a culture that supports research use*

These kinds of activities might include developing appropriate leadership and management practices; collaborations between researchers and research users; the creation of specific research brokering posts; and membership of intermediary organisations that aim to get research into practice.

Source: Adapted from Walter et al (2004b)

The activities described in Box 5.2 involve different levels of engagement with and adaptation of research evidence in the process of its use. For example, developing research-based guidelines and practice tools begins to redefine the findings from research in practice terms, while developing best practice models requires a close integration of research and practice. Further, while most are concerned to facilitate research use, some activities – such as requiring research-informed practice – are more coercive in their approach. Finally, those activities that support a more 'research-minded' culture within social care focus less on ensuring that specific research gets used, and more on selling the overall idea of research use.

While developed in the social care field, it is easy to see parallels between those activities described in Box 5.2 and those in other areas of public service delivery, especially health care and education, so that this taxonomy may have value beyond social care contexts alone. Identifying the purpose of an intervention offers a useful way of framing different methods for promoting evidence uptake in both practical and conceptual terms. However, it is important to note that similar activities may be used for a number of different purposes. For example, networks and collaborations are likely to have multiple objectives that may emerge over time. Equally, different activities are likely to be combined within wider strategies to enhance the use of research. However, this set of categories gives a useful indication of the very wide range of research use activities that are likely to be taking place on the ground in different sectors. They also turn our attention to the fact that research use activities need not be focused solely on achieving instrumental gains but can also address the broader conceptual and enlightenment impacts of research.

Within the Research Unit for Research Utilisation (RURU) (www.ruru.ac.uk), we have developed a cross-sector taxonomy of research use interventions based on an extensive review of the literature in the health care, social care, education and criminal justice fields (Walter et al, 2003b). The taxonomy takes a two-stage approach, classifying research use strategies (such as workshops, journal clubs or collaborative research) according to:

(1) *intervention type* – grouping interventions that are similar in form and content, for example, written materials (including journal articles, research reports and evidence briefings) or boundary spanners (such as knowledge brokers or practitioner-researchers);

(2) *underlying mechanism* – grouping interventions according to their underlying mechanism(s), for example, dissemination (presenting or circulating research findings to a target audience) or interaction (developing stronger dialogue and links between researchers and potential research users).

A key feature of this taxonomy is that these two forms of categorisation exist in parallel, rather than as a hierarchy. In other words, any single intervention type may draw on one or more different mechanisms, and the categories are not mutually exclusive groupings. For example, seminars that involve presenting research to policy makers or practitioners are generally underpinned by dissemination mechanisms – the circulation of findings to a target audience. However, where such seminars allow for considerable discussion between researchers and their audience, which begins to translate research into its policy and practice implications, dissemination shades into a more interactive approach.

In its focus on underlying mechanisms rather than the format of the intervention, our taxonomy recognises that it is not the interventions themselves that lead to change, but the underlying reasons or resources that they offer (Pawson, 2002). The mechanisms specified by the taxonomy are drawn from the social and behavioural literatures. Research use strategies rarely have an explicitly specified theoretical base, but theories from the social, organisational and behavioural sciences can offer valuable insight into their successful development and implementation (Moulding et al, 1999; Grimshaw et al, 2002). Through such theories, we can begin to hypothesise the underlying mechanisms for research use strategies to help us understand which approaches are likely to be effective in different circumstances. We can also begin to explore what 'effectiveness' means (Grimshaw et al, 2004). In the next section, we therefore begin to consider evidence for the effectiveness of different research use strategies in relation to the key mechanisms that seem to underpin their development.

What works? Evidence on the effectiveness of different strategies and mechanisms for promoting the use of research

In examining the success of different research use strategies, we necessarily rely on the existing evaluation literature in this field, which has tended to focus on strategies deployed in practice rather than policy contexts. The evidence we have about 'what works' to improve research use in the policy arena is both more limited and less robust. It is also likely that evaluated approaches will represent only a very small proportion of existing research use initiatives, and that these may also be less diverse and less innovative than current activities on the ground.

Our evidence about effective research use strategies is drawn from the four key sectors that form the focus of this book – health care, education, social care and criminal justice. Our focus is primarily on the UK, although we draw on findings from international contexts too. However, much of the best evidence that we have about effective research use strategies comes from the healthcare field. In fact, as a first route to engaging with research use issues, other sectors have often focused on whether approaches used within health care can be successfully transferred to other settings (for example, Hargreaves, 1997; Hughes et al, 2000; Gira et al, 2004). The question of whether effective research use strategies can be diffused across contexts is a complex one, however, and one to which we briefly return in the concluding section of this chapter.

Evaluations of research use strategies within the healthcare field provide particular forms of evidence. They have tended to focus on objective measures of the process or outcomes of care, and usually fail to consider more conceptual forms of research use. How research use is theorised, defined and measured (see Chapter Two) will clearly shape the ways in which 'effectiveness' is then understood. Yet, as with other research use studies, it is relatively rare for evaluations of research use strategies – in any sector – explicitly to address or theorise what they mean by the 'use' of research (see Chapter Three). Instead they have used a very wide range of measures of research use, including changes in access to research, changes in knowledge and understanding, changes in attitudes and beliefs and changes in behaviour or in outcomes for service users. The methods used to assess research use have been similarly diverse and have included both qualitative and quantitative measures of effectiveness. These issues should be borne in mind when considering the evidence presented in the remainder of this chapter. It is also important to note that evaluations from the healthcare field may have involved studies of the use of more clinical and not just social research, but these can offer valuable insight in the absence of a strong body of evidence elsewhere.

Strategies and mechanisms for effective research use

In this chapter, we have pulled together evidence about the effectiveness of different research use strategies according to the key mechanisms that seem to underpin them. In identifying these mechanisms, we have drawn on the RURU taxonomy of research use interventions (Walter et al, 2003b) as well as on the kinds of theories that seem to drive different approaches to improving the use of research. Five mechanisms emerge as prevalent and important:

- *dissemination:* circulating or presenting research findings to potential users, in formats that may be more or less tailored to their target audience;
- *interaction:* developing stronger links and collaborations between the research and policy or practice communities;
- *social influence:* relying on influential others, such as experts and peers, to inform individuals about research and to persuade them of its value;
- *facilitation:* enabling the use of research, through technical, financial, organisational and emotional support;
- *incentives and reinforcement:* using rewards and other forms of control to reinforce appropriate behaviour.

While it is analytically useful to distinguish between these different mechanisms, in reality many strategies will draw on more than one of these in order to encourage better use of research. Different mechanisms may also overlap: for example, feedback that presents information on the performance of practitioners' peers involves not only reinforcement but also social influence (for example, Balas et al, 1996b). What follows thus represents a broad narrative review of the evidence about the success or otherwise of different strategies and mechanisms in increasing research use and impact.

Dissemination

Dissemination simply means distributing and circulating findings from research to policy makers and practitioners. A range of different formats have been used to disseminate research, from written materials to audiotapes, videos and interactive CD ROMs, as well as oral presentations at conferences, workshops and seminars. These approaches tend to emphasise the role of the disseminator in adapting and targeting research findings to potential users. They typically assume a one-way flow of information from research to policy or practice, and view research consumers as relatively passive recipients of evidence (Philip et al, 2003). Such strategies reflect 'spread' or 'producer-push' models of the research use process described in Chapter Four. They tend to assume that research use is a linear and rational process: in other words, where relevant, useful and high-quality research is effectively disseminated, it will be used (Tyden, 1994; NCDDR, 1996; Landry et al, 2001a, 2001b).

The simple distribution of written research findings is perhaps the most straightforward and most common form of dissemination. Evidence from healthcare settings suggests, however, that the provision of written materials alone is not usually sufficient to change practice (for example, *Effective Health Care Bulletin*, 1999; Palmer and Fenner, 1999; Grimshaw et al, 2001; Freemantle et al, 2002). However, there is some evidence that this approach can raise awareness of research findings and begin to change individuals' attitudes as a prelude to future practice change (for example, Lomas, 1991).

The same holds true even for guidelines, which actively translate research findings and detail their implications for policy or practice contexts. Reviews of attempts to implement guidelines have usually concluded that simply disseminating them is not enough, at least to encourage practice change (for example, *Effective Health Care Bulletin*, 1994, 1999; Thomas et al, 1998, 1999, 2002; Grol and Grimshaw, 1999; Smith, 2000). However, Grimshaw et al's (2004) more recent review concluded that disseminating guidelines can lead to modest practice improvements, and so may represent a cost-effective approach to supporting research-based practice. Crucially, guideline compliance increases when the guidelines are carefully tailored to their target audience, and both the characteristics of a guideline and its quality will influence its chances of adoption (Grilli and Lomas, 1994; Smith, 2000).

Much attention has been paid to tailoring and targeting other research-based materials in ways that might enhance their uptake. These methods typically draw on marketing, innovation and communication theories (Rogers, 1995; Grol and Grimshaw, 1999). The US National Center for the Dissemination of Disability Research (NCDDR) has outlined four key elements that need to be considered for effective dissemination: the source of the information; its content or key message; the medium through which it is disseminated; and the potential user (see Box 5.3). These kinds of approach begin to address some of the barriers identified by policy makers and practitioners in relation to using research, for example the language used and the way in which research is 'packaged' (see Chapter Three).

Box 5.3: Issues in effective dissemination

Source   Credibility of the researcher, in terms of experience, motive and competence

Researchers' existing relationships with users

Researchers' orientation towards dissemination and use

Content   Quality of the research

Relevance and usefulness of the research

Research methods used

Competing knowledge or products

Medium   Physical capacity to reach users

Timeliness

Accessibility and user-friendliness

Flexibility and reliability

Clarity and attractiveness of the information 'package'

User   Perceived relevance to needs

Readiness to change

Nature of information needed

Preferred dissemination media and information sources

Capacity to use information or product

Source: Adapted from NCDDR (1996)

Dissemination of written materials is often supported by oral presentations, for example at conferences, seminars or targeted workshops. Such presentations have been shown to have a small additive impact on practice change in healthcare settings (Freemantle et al, 2002). Weyts et al (2000) studied the use of the UK Department of Health *Blue Book* (Department of Health, 1995), a tailored overview of research findings on child protection whose dissemination was supported by regional seminars. They found that many professionals, including managers and front-line practitioners from social care and health care, believed that the publication had raised their awareness of research and had changed both their knowledge and their practice. However, the conclusions of a UK review of the use of research about teacher induction are less optimistic (Bolam, 1994). Bolam (1994) found that although the research findings were extensively disseminated through a variety of means, including conferences, summary publications and handbooks, and were indeed widely accepted, actual change in practice was only patchy.

Alternative media have also been used to disseminate research. Hagell and Spencer (2004) studied the use of audiotapes to keep social care staff up to date with the latest findings from research. The tapes summarised existing research in key areas and proved an accessible and cost-effective method of disseminating research-based information. They supported greater awareness and knowledge of research, and there was some limited evidence of influence on policy and practice as well (Hagell and Spencer, 2004). Price et al (2006) evaluated the use of a combination of video CDs and targeted leaflets to disseminate messages from the literature on fostering to a range of stakeholders – practitioners, but also foster carers and young people in foster care. Surveys found that this *Fostering Voices* pack was widely used in many different ways, including training, support and staff development, and had supported changes in knowledge and ways of thinking (Price et al, 2006). Using the mass media can also be an effective approach: it has proved successful in changing behaviour across different contexts within health care (Grilli et al, 2002).

Finally, seminars or workshops that enable some discussion of research findings with their potential users, or which adopt a more collaborative approach, seem to be the most effective method of dissemination for both policy makers and practitioners (for example, Shanley et al, 1996; Bogenschneider et al, 2000; Norman, 2004; see Box 5.4).

Box 5.4: Using seminars to disseminate research findings to policy makers

Bogenschneider et al (2000) describe how Family Impact Seminars have successfully disseminated research findings to state-level policy makers in Wisconsin, USA. These provided an ongoing series of seminars, briefing reports and follow-up activities directly targeted to the unique information needs, work culture and preferences of their audience. Credibility was provided by a high-level advisory board and respected academic speakers. A quarter of the seminar time was devoted to discussion, and there were opportunities for follow-up dialogue too. An evaluation of the seminars drew on questionnaires and follow-up interviews to assess their effectiveness. Seminars were rated highly by participants, and policy makers reported using the information they obtained in diverse ways, for example to develop pilot programmes (Bogenschneider et al, 2000).

Norman (2004) details a series of seminars convened by the UK National Education Research Forum (NERF) that aimed to provide opportunities for researchers and policy makers to explore research findings and to discuss how such evidence might be used in policy development. The seminars were designed to enhance interaction between researchers and policy makers. A number of key features for success were identified by their evaluation, including a seminar leader who understands the contexts of both policy and practice, and a collaborative design and approach to all aspects of the events (Norman, 2004).

Critiques of the kinds of rational and linear models of research use that underpin most dissemination strategies have been extensive (for example, Wood et al, 1998; Woolgar, 2000; and see Chapter Four), and so it is perhaps unsurprising that simply disseminating research has not been widely effective in promoting policy and practice uptake of research. However, dissemination can help increase awareness and knowledge of research. It does seem to support conceptual impacts from research. Further, where research products are more tailored and targeted to their intended audience, they are more likely to be used, and to be used in more instrumental ways. In particular, though, enabling some discussion of findings between researchers and potential users as part of the dissemination process seems to lead to more success. These approaches draw additionally on interactive mechanisms for improving the use of research.

Interaction

Interactive approaches to improving the use of research aim to strengthen the links between the research, policy and practice communities. They encourage two-way flows of information between researchers and potential research users. Through this process, research users gain better knowledge of and access to the latest research, while researchers are better able to orient their work to users' needs and perspectives. Interactive strategies are typically enacted through developing partnerships or collaborations between researchers, policy makers and practitioners. They are closely linked to action and participatory research traditions (Denis and Lomas, 2003). They reflect more interactive models of the research use process, including 'two communities' approaches (see Chapter Four). As such they are underpinned by constructionist theories of learning, which imply that any new knowledge from research will be shaped and filtered by users' pre-existing experiences and perspectives (for example, Cousins and Simon, 1996). Simply providing research findings to policy makers and practitioners, as in the dissemination model, is in this view unlikely to lead to change. Research users need to adapt and negotiate findings within the contexts of their use.

A number of interactive strategies have focused on promoting the development of partnerships between researchers and potential research users as a means to encourage research use. Studies of these kinds of initiative in Canada and Switzerland have found that policy-induced partnerships between researchers and practitioners can be effective in supporting research use – particularly conceptual research use (Huberman, 1990, 1993; Cousins and Simon, 1996). Research use was found to be strongly correlated with ongoing or increased linkages between researchers and practitioners during the course of a study. Further, such linkages may support research use even in an initially antagonistic environment (Huberman, 1990, 1993). Antil et al (2003) found that the success of such programmes to promote researcher–research user partnerships seemed to depend on a number of key factors: strong leadership and coherence within the programme; a supportive political and social context; and the programme's responsiveness to the needs of both researchers and user organisations.

In the UK, the School-Based Research Consortium Initiative provides an example of a successful partnership approach within the education sector. The initiative established partnerships between schools, local education authorities and universities with the aim of supporting teachers to engage in and with research. Evaluations of individual projects and of the initiative as a whole reported improvements in teachers' skills and capacities, gains for pupils, and school-wide changes in knowledge and attitudes as a result of engaging with research. They also suggested that to use research in more instrumental ways, teachers needed to negotiate its meaning within their own classroom contexts (Cordingley and Bell, undated; Cordingley et al, 2002; Simons et al, 2003). Other studies offer further support for the effectiveness of teacher–researcher partnerships which enable practitioners to test out the findings from research and encourage collaborative reflection on this process. Both conceptual and instrumental uses of research are reported (for example, De Corte, 2000; Jaworski, 2000; McGuinness, 2000; Abbott et al, 2002; Greenwood et al, 2003). While these kinds of collaboration focus on the joint production of knowledge between researchers and research users, they have also sometimes encouraged practitioners themselves to undertake research, for example through the UK Teacher Training

Agency (TTA) 'Best Practice Research Scholarships' scheme (see Cordingley et al, 2002; Wilson et al, 2003; Wood, 2003).

Interactive approaches have additionally been developed to try to enhance the use of research in policy settings. Initiatives may generate closer collaboration between researchers and policy makers on a project-by-project basis, by involving key stakeholders in the research-planning process or on project steering groups (Eagar et al, 2003). Alternatively, more formal and long-standing partnership arrangements may be established between policy makers and researchers (see Box 5.5). Ross et al (2003) suggest three models of policy-maker involvement in research:

(1) *Formal support*

In this model, policy makers provide explicit support for the research but are not involved in the research process at all. This can give a research project credibility and provide access to additional resources.

(2) *Responsive audience*

Here policy makers respond more actively to researchers' efforts at interaction, although policy makers typically get involved through the initiative of researchers rather than vice versa. Such involvement may range from informal, *ad hoc* exchanges to formal organised meetings. Policy makers may offer advice, ideas and information, and may play a role in any strategies to ensure the use of the research.

(3) *Integral partner*

As integral partners, policy makers act as close collaborators in the research process. Interaction with researchers typically takes place at the initiative of policy makers themselves, and policy makers are much more actively involved in influencing the research process and in getting the research used.

Ross et al's (2003) research found that policy makers were more likely to be actively involved in research where this required minimal investment of time, where they felt they would gain in some way from being involved, and where their expertise closely matched the project's requirements.

Box 5.5: A tiered approach to partnership working between researchers and policy makers

Goering et al (2003) describe a formal partnership arrangement between the Health Systems Research and Consulting Unit (HSRCU) and the Mental Health Rehabilitation and Reform Branch (MHRRB) of the Ontario Ministry of Health and Long-term Care in Canada. The partnership aimed to improve the 'linkage and exchange' between research, policy development and service provision and comprised four key tiers:

(1) *Partnership*

The first tier involved the development of a formal partnership arrangement between the two organisations, which included clarifying the terms of engagement and drawing up a shared work plan.

(2) *Research*

The second tier comprised interactions around a specific research project on mental health systems integration. At this tier, the researchers had to develop a more 'arm's length' relationship with policy makers to ensure the research remained independent and objective. This was achieved by creating an advisory committee of key stakeholders, which included policy makers.

(3) *Policy forum*

The third tier involved the dissemination of the research. Researchers and policy staff were jointly involved in presenting the findings to local taskforces. A policy forum was also held by the partners, enabling large-scale consultation with stakeholders around the issues raised by the research.

(4) *Policy direction*

The policy forum helped establish a common language around the issues raised by the research and was viewed as a success by participants. However, while the researchers had anticipated that the forum would lead to some clear guidance for policy at this fourth tier, the Ministry had viewed it as an opportunity to highlight an existing policy mandate to those in the field. Through subsequent exchange, the researchers came to understand that the Ministry's approach reflected a need to manage stakeholder tensions.

Goering et al (2003) suggest that these kinds of formal organisational arrangements can secure partnerships between researchers and policy makers that increase opportunities for interaction and can ultimately enhance the dissemination and use of research at tiers 3 and 4.

Source: Adapted from Goering et al (2003)

Establishing partnership working across professional groups creates both tensions and challenges, and those between researchers, policy makers and practitioners are no exception. Some key features of success can, however, be identified from studies in this field:

- Successful collaborative working involves considerable investment of resources – in terms of time, energy, finances and underpinning support (for example, Huberman, 1993; Goering et al, 2003; Ross et al, 2003). Denis and Lomas (2003) suggest that good leadership and a commitment to partnership working are, however, key to success – in other words, the people involved may be as important as creating new structures for working.
- Differences in goals, timescales, power, information needs, reward systems and language can all create barriers to effective interaction. Success depends on participants' ability to appreciate and understand each others' cultures and ways of working (for example, Huberman, 1993; Goering et al, 2003; Golden-Biddle et al, 2003).
- It can be difficult to balance the competing agendas of partnerships and organisations. Collaborative approaches benefit from clear definition of objectives and roles and open channels for communication (for example, Huberman, 1993; Goering et al, 2003; Ross et al, 2003).
- Trust between researchers and research users is core to successful collaboration, and this is best developed by creating a wide range of opportunities for interaction (for example, Denis and Lomas, 2003; Golden-Biddle et al, 2003; Ross et al, 2003).

Despite these challenges, those who engage in interactive approaches to improving research use describe a wide range of benefits to participation. Policy makers, practitioners and researchers all report gains in skills, knowledge and understanding, and for many these outweigh the costs involved in developing effective partnership ways of working (for example, Huberman, 1990, 1993; Cousins and Simon, 1996; Cordingley et al, 2002; Ross et al, 2003).

Interactive approaches to improving the use of research have gained increasing currency in recent years, especially in the policy field (see, for example, the special issue of *Journal of Health Services Research & Policy*, Vol 8, October 2003; and also Chapter Four, this volume). These kinds of strategy can be both costly and intensive, but can be flexibly applied: at local or national levels, and both more informally – for example through existing networks – as well as through formalised partnership arrangements. They seem to be effective in promoting both conceptual and instrumental impacts from research; and may also stimulate process uses of research through much closer engagement of policy makers and practitioners with the conduct of research itself. However, concerns are sometimes voiced about the threat raised to researcher independence by greater interaction with practitioners and policy makers, or that researchers may be 'captured' by policy-led partnerships. Conversely, postmodern critiques of interactive approaches suggest that these may be prey to researcher dominance (for example, Watkins, 1994). Such strategies thus need to pay careful attention to managing the power relationships that play out within researcher–research user partnerships.

Social influence

Social influence approaches to improving research use rely on influential others, such as colleagues and role models, peer leaders and research champions, to inform individuals about research and to persuade them of its value. As we saw in Chapter Three, practitioners and policy makers will turn to their colleagues as a key source of knowledge to inform their day-to-day work (for example, Bullock et al, 1998; Feldman et al, 2001; Innvaer et al, 2002; see Chapter Three). Social influence strategies thus focus on interactions within policy and practice contexts, rather than with researchers *per se*, to improve research use. They draw on social influence and social learning theories, which propose that our actions may be changed by the attitudes and behaviours of significant others (Grol and Grimshaw, 1999; see Chapter Six). For example, the chance to discuss with colleagues new information such as that from research provides the opportunity for social influence to be exerted or for a consensus to develop through 'social processing' (Cousins and Leithwood, 1993). The aim is to alter local values and norms as a means to secure research-based policy and practice.

Both peers and experts can play a role in this process. A systematic review by Yano et al (1995) found that expert review was effective in changing practice within healthcare settings. Again within health care, educational interventions that involve discussion with colleagues or practice experts appear to be more effective than other formats (Davis et al, 1999; Palmer and Fenner, 1999). Those that draw on social influence theories have similarly been successful in promoting research-based practice (Bradley et al, 2005). Such interventions are characterised by interactive and participatory teaching approaches; guidance and feedback on developing new practices; the inclusion of local experts; informal learning; and the use of role models (Bradley et al, 2005).

A study by Cousins and Leithwood (1993) found that the social processing of information through discussion with colleagues was a key factor in teachers' use of research and this suggests that social influence approaches may have some relevance in sectors beyond health care too (see also Simons et al, 2003).

Opinion leaders can be defined as individuals with a specific influence on the beliefs and actions of their colleagues (Locock et al, 2001). They represent a key tool in social influence strategies to improve the use of research. Systematic reviews of studies of the effectiveness of opinion leaders in healthcare settings report mixed findings (for example, Bero et al, 1998; *Effective Health Care Bulletin*, 1999; Grol and Grimshaw, 1999; Grimshaw et al, 2001). However, evaluations of large-scale programmes to develop research-based practice in the healthcare and criminal justice fields suggest that opinion leaders may play a critical role in getting research used, both conceptually and instrumentally (Musson, undated; Dopson et al, 2001; Locock et al, 2001; Mihalic et al, 2004a). Despite this, opinion leader support alone may not be sufficient to effect research-based practice change. Conversely, hostile or ambivalent opinion leaders can create a barrier to change (Dopson et al, 2001; Locock et al, 2001; Mihalic et al, 2004a).

As Locock et al (2001) note, the definition of opinion leaders is problematic, and opinion leaders may also differ within and between groups. Such nuances may not be captured by aggregative systematic reviews. The evaluation of the PACE (Promoting Action on Clinical Effectiveness) initiative found that expert (academic or clinician) opinion leaders were important in the early stages of projects, to help endorse research-based innovation, while peer opinion leaders played a more influential role in mainstream implementation (Locock et al, 2001). However, findings from the education field suggest that using expert opinion leaders can encourage research use to be perceived by practitioners as a coercive rather than a negotiated process (Wikeley, 1998).

A rather different social influence approach is to target research to service users, with a view to changing practitioner or policy behaviour indirectly. In health care, patient-mediated interventions have provided patients rather than experts or peers with research-based information to try to influence practitioner behaviour. Such approaches have proved generally effective (for example, Oxman et al, 1995; *Effective Health Care Bulletin*, 1999; Grol and Grimshaw, 1999). Patient-mediated interventions have also proved successful in implementing guidelines (for example, *Effective Health Care Bulletin*, 1994; Davis and Taylor-Vaisey, 1997; Bero et al, 1998). Grassroots activists have also drawn on research to try to achieve policy and practice change. For example, the UK National Childbirth Trust (NCT) is a parent-focused organisation which plays an active campaigning role and draws on research to try to influence policy and practice change, for example through its own evidence-based briefings (www.nctpregnancyandbabycare.com/).

Social influence strategies have mainly focused on changing the minds and actions of practitioners rather than policy makers. They appear to offer a promising approach, however, with examples of both conceptual and instrumental impact, and given that policy makers often rely on colleagues as a source of information (see Chapter Three), they may be of value within the policy arena as well. Tapping into policy networks and policy entrepreneurs may be important here (see Chapter Four). Identifying key groups or individuals who might influence the take-up and use of research is critical to the success of social influence approaches. Studies from the healthcare field suggest, however, that this is rarely a straightforward process (for example, Locock et al, 2001).

Facilitation

Facilitative strategies provide various forms of support – technical, financial, organisational and even emotional – to try to improve policy makers' and practitioners' uptake of research. They focus on creating a context that can facilitate the use of research. Facilitative strategies thus reflect 'user-pull' models of the research use process, where research users and their local contexts hold the key to the use of research. Such strategies might involve professional development activities to equip people with the willingness and expertise to use research themselves; or they might target structural and organisational conditions that support or inhibit the use of research. Facilitative approaches derive from change management theories, which emphasise the importance of enabling strategies giving practical assistance for individuals and groups to change. Learning theories also emphasise the importance of facilitation in achieving change – the degree to which an intervention provides the resources to take action and/or removes the barriers to change (Granados et al, 1997).

One facilitative approach has been to try to enhance individuals' skills and motivation to access, interpret and apply research. In effect, such strategies provide the complement to dissemination approaches, aiming to develop a willing and able 'market' for research. The Front-Line Evidence-Based Medicine Project in the NHS North Thames region aimed to facilitate hospital clinicians to use research in their day-to-day practice by providing them with access to electronic research databases and by training staff in critical appraisal skills. Outcomes from the project varied, however: specific institutional and historical barriers limited the use of research, and the project's evaluation concluded that substantial training and resources were required to ensure that practitioners drew on the databases to support their practice (Cumbers and Donald, 1998; Donald, 1998). Critical appraisal skills workshops have also been held with staff from English social services departments to help practitioners assess and interpret research. Participants felt the workshops were useful, and their self-reported knowledge also increased (Spittlehouse et al, 2000). However, a review of interventions to teach critical appraisal skills to healthcare practitioners found that this approach was generally ineffective (Shannon and Norman, 1995).

In the healthcare field, facilitative strategies have often involved educational interventions to teach individuals about new research-based practices. Systematic reviews of such interventions have found them to be broadly successful (for example, Davis et al, 1999; Grol and Grimshaw, 1999; Smith, 2000). A review of 160 educational interventions found that two-thirds were effective in changing practice, and where three or more educational interventions were combined, success was demonstrated in 80% of cases (Davis, 1998). However, passive and didactic approaches, and interventions of one day or less, were consistently found to have little or no effect in changing practice (Davis, 1998). Successful educational initiatives have been identified as those that have clear objectives; that identify and target barriers to learning; and that offer an informal, participatory approach, for example through locally adapted workshops (Bradley et al, 2005). Other reviews have found individual instruction and educational outreach to be effective approaches among healthcare practitioners: and where these interventions included an interactive element, gave supportive materials or provided the opportunity to discuss cases or test new practice, they were more likely to change practitioners' behaviour (for example, Davis et al, 1999; *Effective Health Care Bulletin*, 1999; Grol and Grimshaw, 1999; Palmer and Fenner, 1999; Smith, 2000; O'Brien et al, 2002a). Educational outreach has additionally met with success in implementing guidelines (Gross and Pujat, 2001).

Other facilitative strategies have focused on developing and implementing research-based programmes, protocols and tools. In the healthcare field, using computers to support the implementation of research-based practice, including guidelines, has on the whole produced positive results (Johnston et al, 1994; Balas et al, 1996a; Gross and Pujat, 2001; although see Hunt et al, 1998). Office tools such as stickers and wall charts can also support research-based practice change (Dickey et al, 1999). In social care, similar initiatives have involved developing and implementing a range of research-based practice tools, such as checklists and assessment frameworks. Typically, staff training is used to support their implementation. This approach has often proved to be effective in changing practice, and may also change practitioners' knowledge and attitudes (Bullock et al, 1998; Qureshi and Nicholas, 2001; Nicholas, 2003).

Another facilitative approach involves providing support for implementing wider research-based social programmes. Evaluations of both large- and small-scale initiatives in the social care, education and criminal justice fields have identified some key features of success for this kind of strategy (for example, Ward, 1995; Bullock et al, 1998; Mukherjee et al, 1999; Sprague et al, 2001; Little and Houston, 2003; Qureshi and Nicholas, 2001; Mihalic et al, 2004a; Vaughn and Coleman, 2004; see also Box 5.6):

- providing adequate resources and support, in terms of training, skilled staff, administrative support, money, materials, time and ongoing supervision;
- leadership, commitment and support at a sufficiently high level within local contexts;
- buy-in, motivation and a sense of ownership among front-line staff; and
- agency stability and good vertical and horizontal communication.

Box 5.6: Implementing a research-based key worker service for families with disabled children

Mukherjee et al (1999) and Sloper et al (1999) compared the approaches taken by two English social services departments to implement a research-based 'key worker' service for families with disabled children. Implementation strategies differed between the sites, as did levels of success. Both sites provided an initial training or information event. Follow-up support was given through meetings, supervision and steering group feedback, but was accessed to a different degree at different sites. Findings from an evaluation of the programme's implementation found that success was supported by:

- a dedicated project coordinator;
- adequate initial training;

- high-level commitment to developing the service; and
- a small-scale, reflective, learning approach.

Source: Adapted from Mukherjee et al (1999) and Sloper et al (1999)

However, such success factors may relate to more general issues in project or programme implementation, and not specifically to the use of research. A key question is whether the fact that projects and programmes are based on research provides an additional positive, or even negative, impact on their uptake. Findings from existing studies provide little evidence about this issue. Enabling some discussion of research findings in order to adapt programmes or programme choice to local contexts may, however, support the implementation of research-based programmes (Sloper et al, 1999; Qureshi and Nicholas, 2001; Mihalic et al, 2004a).

Providing the right kinds of practical and emotional input can successfully secure research-based change across a range of practice settings. Most studies of these facilitative strategies have examined instrumental impact – direct changes in practice – but there is some evidence that research-based practice tools can be used to support more conceptual impacts too. Although facilitative strategies have been used among policy makers as well – for example by providing training in appraising and interpreting research – these have not been widely evaluated. Evidence from practice contexts suggests, however, that higher levels of investment in resources such as training and administrative support generally improve the chances of success. However, to be successful, facilitative strategies may require a level of ideological buy-in as well (for example, Bullock et al, 1998; Mihalic et al, 2004a).

Incentives and reinforcement

The final key strategy we identify is the use of incentives or other kinds of reinforcement to secure better use of research. This means developing 'reinforcers' – which may be positive or negative – to influence the actions of policy makers, practitioners and researchers. Strategies might provide some kind of reward or encouragement for using research or for engaging in research use activities (such as disseminating research). In the healthcare field, a common approach has been to use audit and feedback and reminders in order to implement and sustain research-based practice. These kinds of strategy are underpinned by learning theories, which assert that behaviour can be influenced by controlling external stimuli. According to such theories, the chances of acting in a particular way increase when the behaviour is followed by positive consequences and decrease when it is followed by negative consequences. Both rewards and feedback are important in this process (Granados et al, 1997).

One strategy has been to provide funding incentives to encourage greater exploitation of research. For example, the Swiss National Research Council developed a funding programme in which researchers were required to submit comprehensive dissemination plans, and 10% of funds were deliberately set aside for dissemination work outside the academic community. All the projects funded under this programme engaged in research exploitation activities to some degree, which in turn enhanced the use of research among the practitioners targeted (Huberman, 1990, 1993). Other initiatives have tried to promote the development of partnerships between researchers and potential research users with a view thereby to improving the use of research. One such programme, established by the Canadian Social Sciences and Humanities Research Council (SSHRC), offered partnership development grants, and funding decisions gave greater weight to research proposals with strong evidence of partnership development. These incentives stimulated partnership growth, and projects with partnerships in place had the greatest impact on practitioners (Cousins and Simon, 1996).

A different strategy has been to provide competitive funding for research-based social programmes within service delivery organisations. Monies are made available through a competitive bidding process and programmes with an explicit research base are favoured in funding decisions. This approach has been adopted in the UK for a wide range of social programmes, but has not always met with success. Coote et al (2004), evaluating a range of such initiatives, found that despite policy rhetoric to the contrary, programmes were not always well supported by research. There was also a potential gap between the research-based policy design of the programmes, and the way they were actually implemented on the ground (Coote et al, 2004). Such initiatives have the potential to encourage innovation in developing research-based practice (see Chapter Two). They can, however, be complex to develop, manage and apply (see Box 5.7).

Box 5.7: The Crime Reduction Programme: encouraging the development and implementation of research-based programmes

The UK Home Office's Crime Reduction Programme (CRP) aimed both to realise a sustained reduction in crime and to mainstream knowledge of best practice in the field. This was to be achieved by pulling together research-based evidence on 'what works' to reduce crime and developing a portfolio of viable initiatives. At the local level, the design and delivery of CRP projects was mainly to be achieved by inviting local agencies to submit competitive bids for programme funds. Projects were to be evaluated and refined during implementation, with learning from the initial three-year phase disseminated more widely. Over time, successful initiatives would move into mainstream funding and ineffective projects would be withdrawn.

The CRP's aims were ambitious – to implement and evaluate a complex assortment of initiatives; to assess the best combination of such initiatives for achieving crime reduction; and to learn about how such initiatives might be mainstreamed and their impact sustained over time. In doing so, it faced a range of implementation challenges. In particular, there were difficulties translating the research evidence into programmes and projects on the ground. No seed money was available for initial development work, and access to research findings at local level was sometimes limited. As a result, fewer bids were received than originally anticipated and these were not always of high quality. In response, the CRP commissioned researchers and other facilitators to help translate the evidence into projects on the ground, and also provided a high level of central specification about what was required. However, while increased central direction for projects generally meant a stronger evidence base, in some cases it stifled the development of more innovatory initiatives.

Source: Adapted from Nutley and Homel (2006)

Among physicians, explicit financial incentives have been used to encourage them to follow research-based practice. This approach does seem to have a positive influence on guideline use (for example, *Effective Health Care Bulletin*, 1994), although initial successes may not persist over time (Palmer and Fenner, 1999). Moreover, summaries of the effects of more general 'pay for performance' schemes in health care again suggest that financial incentives can indeed play an important role in changing physician behaviour but they also caution that incentives require very careful design to elicit the desired response (Conrad and Christianson, 2004; Chassin, 2006; Petersen et al, 2006).

Other incentive-based strategies involve writing the use of research into individuals' job descriptions or staff appraisal systems. For example, the UK Department of Health's requirements for social work training embed the use of research as part of the national occupational standards for social work (Walter et al, 2004b). Similarly, performance management and scrutiny mechanisms can be deployed to support the use of research. Laycock and Farrell (2003) describe the wide range of approaches used to disseminate research on repeat victimisation to police services in England and Wales, but suggest that core to the use of this research was the adoption by the Home Secretary of repeat victimisation as a national performance indicator. Examining a range of case studies of the use of research in education, Bolam (1994) concludes that policy mandates that make research-based practice to all intents compulsory are the key to ensuring that research gets used.

The success of reminders and of audit and feedback in healthcare settings has been examined through a range of systematic reviews. Prompts and reminders are widely reported to be effective, as a single strategy and for a range of behaviours (for example, Davis, 1998; *Effective Health Care Bulletin*, 1999; Grol and Grimshaw, 1999; Smith, 2000; Grimshaw et al, 2001). Significant benefit can be obtained when computer reminders are used in addition to manual reminders, but both were also found to be individually effective (Balas et al, 1996b). Reminders have also been successful in implementing guidelines (for example, *Effective Health Care Bulletin*, 1994, 1999; Davis and Taylor-Vaisey, 1997; Thomas et al, 1998, 1999, 2002). Findings regarding audit and feedback are more mixed, however. It seems to be a useful approach for some behaviours (for example, Gill et al, 1999; Hulscher et al, 2002), but not all (for example, Davis, 1998; Grimshaw et al, 2001; Freemantle et al, 2002; O'Brien et al, 2002b, 2002c). Mixed results are also reported from studies comparing shorter- and longer-term effects, and any positive changes demonstrated in practice or outcomes tend to be moderate (O'Brien et al, 2002c). Audit and feedback does, however, appear to be effective in implementing guidelines (for example, *Effective Health Care Bulletin*, 1994; Oxman et al, 1995; Davis and Taylor-Vaisey, 1997). Feedback that involves peer comparisons also seems to be effective in changing practice (for example, *Effective Health Care Bulletin*, 1999). This approach combines a reinforcement strategy with a social influence approach.

Overall, we have mixed and often limited evidence about whether reinforcement and incentive strategies are successful in improving the use of research. Some promising approaches have been tried, but more evaluations are needed before we can be clear about effective ways forward. Further, studies of audit and feedback and reminders have been limited to healthcare contexts, and these approaches may not readily lend themselves to other sectors and settings. It is also worth noting that these kinds of strategy often represent more coercive approaches than the other methods detailed in this chapter, and are very much geared to instrumental, rather than conceptual, impacts from research. They thus fit poorly with our understandings of the use of research as an iterative, contingent process that involves the active (re)construction of findings from research by research users in a dynamic and often collective way.

Concluding remarks

This chapter highlights the wide range of strategies that can be used – often with a good deal of success – to improve the use of research. Some differences in approach do emerge across sectors. For example, the education field seems to have adopted more collaborative and interactive approaches to improving the use of research; health care has been much more focused on dissemination, feedback and incentives; and the criminal justice field is characterised by more facilitative approaches. The kinds of research use strategies adopted within any sector will, of course, be shaped by the nature of the relevant evidence base and by the form its service delivery takes. However, it is worth bearing in mind that evaluated strategies are likely to comprise only a small proportion of all initiatives taking place on the ground to improve the use of research. The picture this chapter paints is thus unlikely to be a representative one. That said, it does seem that research use strategies as yet fail fully to capitalise on current, more subtle understandings of research use described in preceding chapters. They often neglect the complex, multifaceted nature of research use – as something more than instrumental research impact alone; and relatively few draw on the contingent, dynamic and interpretive models that seem to offer our best insights into how research is used on the ground.

Our findings do suggest, however, that many research use strategies can be successfully transferred across different contexts and countries. For example, interactive strategies have been used effectively in healthcare, social care and education settings and across a range of national contexts. Facilitative approaches to implementing research-based programmes have also been used within a wide range of settings both in the UK and beyond. For other strategies, the potential for transfer may, however, be more limited. For example, encouraging service users to exert pressure on practitioners to adopt research-based behaviour is unlikely to be appropriate in the education field, where service delivery takes a more collective than individualised form. Similarly, reminders alerting healthcare practitioners to specific research-based treatments at the point of care delivery will not be relevant in many social care or education settings. The transfer of effective approaches to improving the use of research beyond the settings in which they were developed may perhaps be best achieved through a focus on the mechanisms that underpin them, rather than the details of the research use strategies themselves, together with a careful analysis of their contexts for implementation.

A number of the strategies described in this chapter begin to address those barriers to the use of research identified in Chapter Three. For example, enhanced dissemination strategies tackle the issues policy makers and practitioners often raise about the nature and presentation of research. Other strategies – particularly social influence strategies such as using opinion leaders or participatory educational workshops – go some way to developing individual (and organisational) attitudes that are less hostile to research and its use. The need for better links between researchers and potential research users is addressed through interactive strategies, by developing informal networks or more formal partnership arrangements. Finally, both facilitative strategies and the use of incentives and reinforcement are important for creating contexts that support better uptake of research.

It is, however, somewhat artificial to suggest this kind of one-to-one relationship between strategies and barriers. Any research use strategy or activity is likely to tackle a range of barriers to research use simultaneously. For instance, several of the strategies outlined in this chapter will play a more general role in developing a culture – among researchers as well as in the policy and practice communities – that supports better use of research. This kind of outcome is less tangible but is nevertheless important for improving the chances of success of research use initiatives. Different strategies and activities, both locally induced and more 'top-down', are thus likely to interact in complex ways. The evidence suggests though that the key to getting research used, especially by practitioners, is to identify those barriers and enablers to research use that exist within the local context, and to target these in developing any research use strategy (for example, Dopson et al, 2001).

Identifying the key mechanisms that underpin any strategy to improve the use of research is an important part of this approach. A focus on mechanisms helps manage some of the complexity of attempting to encourage the use of research in real-world contexts. It forces us to be clear about why it is that we believe any given approach will be successful in any given circumstances. The mechanisms and theories that underlie different approaches to improving research use are often implicit. The aim of this chapter has been to unearth some of these theories and mechanisms as a means to support the development of more successful research use strategies.

At the same time, we have explored 'what works' to promote the use of research, both in terms of individual activities and initiatives and in relation to their underpinning mechanisms. Some good evidence exists about the success of different research use strategies, but drawing wider conclusions about the effectiveness of mechanisms they deploy is at the moment a more tentative exercise. Further, the evidence that we have comes mainly from practice contexts: we know much less about what works to improve the use of research among policy makers. Overall, however, interactive approaches currently seem to show most promise in improving the use of research. Interactive strategies may range from simply enabling greater discussion of findings by policy makers and practitioners at presentations, through local collaborations between researchers and research users to test out the findings from research, to formal, ongoing, large-scale partnerships that support better connections between research, policy and practice over the longer term. Strategies based on social influence theories, and adequately resourced facilitative approaches to implement research-based programmes and tools, also seem to offer hopeful ways forward. Tailored dissemination efforts may additionally support more conceptual uses of research. More evidence is needed, however, about interventions that rely on incentives or reinforcement.

These conclusions reflect those of Chapter Four, which identified interactive models as our best guide to understanding the processes through which research gets used, as well as the important role of social mediation in using research. But the conclusions of Chapter Four also suggested that the use of research is both complex and context-dependent. It is likely that a range of strategies, drawing on multiple mechanisms, will be needed if we are successfully to support better use of research. Grimshaw et al (2004) have proposed that multifaceted strategies, built from an assessment of barriers to change and underpinned by a clear theoretical framework, may be more effective than stand-alone strategies. Further research is needed, however, to develop the theoretical bases of research use strategies, and to evaluate these. The next chapter attempts to fill in some of these gaps by examining a set of related literatures – on learning, knowledge management and the diffusion of innovations – to explore what their theoretical bases might have to offer in developing more sophisticated and effective research use strategies.

SIX

What can we learn from the literature on learning, knowledge management and the diffusion of innovations?

There is an emerging view that strategies and interventions aimed at promoting research use are most effective when underpinned by an appropriate theoretical framework. The previous chapter identified what some of these may be and summarised some of the evidence for their effects from research studies of research use. However, theorising in this area is not yet well developed. This chapter considers three additional bodies of theory and evidence that can inform the design of strategies to promote research use but which have not yet been widely applied in this area. These are learning, knowledge management and the diffusion of innovations.

Considering research use from a learning perspective encourages us to think carefully about processes of knowledge acquisition within individuals and across groups and organisations. Alternatively, if knowledge management is our perspective then attention is drawn to the ways in which knowledge is captured and shared within organisations. Finally, a diffusion of innovations perspective focuses attention on the spread and adoption of ideas across populations of individuals and organisations. Learning, knowledge management and the diffusion of innovations are then all concerned to a greater or lesser extent with understanding the acquisition, spread and enactment of ideas and knowledge, concerns that are central to understanding research use. Of course there are other bodies of theory and evidence with the potential to offer further insights into strategies for improving research use, such as the literature on marketing and communication, which could also be explored. However, we concentrate on learning, knowledge management and the diffusion of innovations because they seem particularly relevant to understanding the complex, dynamic and interactive nature of research use.

Our purpose is to broaden and deepen our understanding of research use by connecting it with a wider social science literature in each of the three areas. We examine the potential insights offered by this literature and highlight its implications for strategies to promote research use. Our overview is relatively brief and necessarily selective. Nevertheless, we draw on a diverse range of theoretical and empirical studies, which emanate from a number of disciplinary perspectives (for example, psychology, organisational sociology, information science and cultural anthropology). Some studies have been conducted in a public sector context but many, particularly in the organisational learning and knowledge management areas, report on private sector practice. The studies also adopt different ontological and epistemological standpoints. Inevitably this means that our overview is eclectic and broad brush. The conclusions that we draw are therefore tentative and suggestive, and of differential application to policy and practice settings.

Learning: individual and organisational

Learning can be defined as 'the process of gaining knowledge and/or expertise' (Knowles et al, 2005, p 17), and as research use can helpfully be viewed as an individual and/or organisational learning issue it is appropriate to consider this body of literature first. When research use is viewed as an individual learning issue, the assumption is that use is a matter of individual practitioners, service managers or policy makers acquiring and applying new knowledge and expertise from research. When research use is viewed as an organisational learning issue it is assumed that there is a need to look beyond individual learning in order to consider how organisations acquire and deploy new knowledge and expertise. But how does learning occur and what can be done to encourage individual and organisational learning? Much of the literature relevant to addressing these questions focuses on the acquisition of knowledge by individuals and we consider this first. We then discuss the literature on organisational learning. There is a further literature on the nature and facilitation of interorganisational learning, but as this is concerned with how ideas, knowledge and innovations are shared across organisational and professional boundaries, it is discussed with the literature on the diffusion of innovations.

Individual learning

Explanations of individual learning processes are rooted in three main schools of thought:

- *Behavioural theory*, which assumes that much of what we learn can be understood as the formation of new associations or the strengthening or weakening of existing associations; that is, learning occurs through the association of stimuli.
- *Cognitive theory*, which assumes that the internal representations that people develop in order to understand the world around them lie at the heart of learning.
- *Social-cognitive theory*, which argues that we learn by observing others and modelling their behaviour.

Although the assumptions of behavioural theory may underpin the design of incentives and rewards for learning, it is cognitive and social-cognitive theories that have been particularly influential in explaining and shaping adult learning activities, and that is where we shall focus our attention.

Key aspects of a cognitive approach to learning are summarised in Box 6.1. A cognitive perspective eschews the notion of learning as the simple transfer of information from one person or context to another. Instead, learning is seen as a process by which individuals revise their internal representations of the world (their schema) in the light of new information. Incorporating new experiences and knowledge into one's cognitive schema is a recursive process, whereby information and knowledge are transformed rather than simply transferred. This complex process is heavily influenced by the context in which it takes place (Brown, 1995). It is the basis of constructionist theories of learning, which (as we discussed in Chapters Four and Five) have been used to model and shape research use as a learning process.

Box 6.1: Key aspects of a cognitive approach to learning – schema theory

- Schemas are patterns of internal representation that people develop in order to understand the world around them.
- A schema will always have limitations and new experiences may challenge existing schemas.
- Learning consists of revising the schema in the light of new information.
- Learning does not take place if the effort needed to restructure is not made. A non-learner may choose to ignore conflicting experiences, select only those aspects of an experience that can be readily assimilated or live with cognitive conflict.

Source: Abstracted from Brown (1995)

Much of the literature on cognitive learning focuses on how children learn and develop. However, children and adults tend to learn differently, and adult learning is generally viewed as a more individualised process (Knowles et al, 2005). The analytical framework outlined in Box 6.2 has been developed in order to understand the key factors that impact on this process, and this is likely to be of relevance in understanding the process of encouraging greater individual use of research.

Box 6.2: A framework for understanding and designing adult learning processes

Consider the learner's:
- *need to know* – why and what they need to know;
- *self-concept*, particularly the extent to which they are autonomous and self-directing;
- *prior experience of learning*, including the mental models they have developed as a result of this;
- *readiness for learning*, which may be life-related or task-related;
- *orientation to learning*, which is often assumed to be problem-centred and context-related;
- *motivation for learning*, particularly the perceived personal payoff.

And consider the context within which learning takes place, particularly the learning situation and the goals and purposes of learning.

Source: Adapted from Knowles et al (2005)

Despite the view that there are individual differences in how adults learn, there are some reasonably well-supported generic lessons about the best strategies for enhancing adult learning and development. Such learning appears to be most effective when learning opportunities are face to face and when they enable learners to interact with one another (Stroot et al, 1998). An experiential approach, which encourages processing experiences through reflection, analysis and critical examination, is also well supported (Knowles et al, 2005). Such findings sit well with the evidence presented in Chapter Five supporting interaction and social influence as important mechanisms for encouraging research use.

Although researchers and learning theorists have not reached consensus on any single definition of 'reflection', there is general agreement about its importance in adult learning (Buysse et al, 2003).

Reflection requires practitioners to stand back from their work and this can be done in different ways. For example, Hatton and Smith (1995) describe four distinct forms of reflection:

- technical examination of one's immediate skills and competencies in specific settings;
- descriptive analysis of one's performance in a professional role;
- dialogic exploration of alternative ways to solve problems in a professional situation;
- critical thinking about the effects on others of one's actions.

The different levels of sophistication involved in these four forms of reflection imply that in so far as there is engagement with research in each of these situations it will be very different, although in each situation the emphasis is on learning within the local context.

Situated learning theory, a particular brand of cognitive theory, sees learning as knowledge obtained from and applied to everyday situations. It not only emphasises the importance of learning from experience but also views learning as a sociocultural phenomenon, rather than as an isolated activity (Barab and Duffy, 2000). This shifts the emphasis away from an individual's learning context to focus on what it means to be a member of a community of learners (Barab and Duffy, 2000). Learning is thus viewed as the result of social processes that require negotiation and problem solving with others (Stein, 1998). Again, this sits well with social influence approaches to increasing research use.

Learning and development programmes for professionals frequently draw on the ideas of experiential learning, problem solving and reflective practice. For example, Davies (1999) comments that a central feature of the Oxford Programme in Evidence-Based Health Care is that students learn by attempting to solve problems that they bring to the course. There is evidence to suggest that such approaches are effective, especially when they involve collaborative learning – learning with others (General Teaching Council for England, 2004, 2005). For example, learning opportunities for teachers seem to be most effective when:

- individuals identify their own learning focus and starting points;
- individuals receive support from their peers and have access to specialist expertise;
- there are processes to encourage dialogue, reflection and change;
- learning opportunities are sustained over time. (See Box 6.3.)

Box 6.3: Collaborative learning for teachers

Three linked reviews of Continuing Professional Development (CPD) in the education field found that collaborative CPD (where teachers receive support from other teachers from either their own school or other schools) was a more effective learning strategy than individually oriented CPD (which does not use collaboration). The characteristics of CPD found to have positive outcomes were:

- the use of specialist expertise linked to school-based activity;
- peer support or coaching, including observation, to provide a safe environment for experimentation;
- scope for participants to identify their own CPD focus and starting points;
- processes to encourage, extend and structure professional dialogue, reflection and change;
- processes for sustaining CPD over time.

These core areas of CPD included a wide range of associated activities such as, observation and interpretation of shared experiences, joint planning and curriculum design.

Source: Adapted from General Teaching Council for England (2004, 2005)

The emphasis on situated, experiential learning and reflective practice is taken further by constructionist theories of learning, which stress the importance of understanding how individuals construct personal meaning from their learning experiences (Ausubel et al, 1986; Brumner, 1990; Novak, 1998). Box 6.4 outlines a study into how new knowledge from formal education programmes becomes meaningful in professional practice. It found that meaning-making processes are framed by the nature of professional work and by client interactions. The study also provides some support for a more cultural approach to understanding the process by which knowledge and experience become meaningful. This locates the processes of cognition in the interaction between individuals and their culture (in this case their professional culture) rather than primarily within the individual themselves (John-Steiner and Souberman, 1978). This view is reinforced by studies of communities of practice (see interorganisational networks later), which suggest that individuals share ideas informally through collaboration and it is in these contexts that a shared way of interpreting complex activity is constructed. This process of constructing meaning provides organisational members with identity and cohesion (Newell et al, 2001).

Box 6.4: How knowledge becomes meaningful in professional practice

Daley (2001) interviewed social workers, lawyers, adult educators and nurses (80 people in total) who had attended continuing education programmes in the previous 9-24 months. She asked them about their learning subsequent to an education programme. Across all the professional groups she found that new information learned in an education programme was added to a professional's knowledge through a complex process of thinking about, acting on and identifying their feelings about new information. Information was assimilated and integrated with previous experience such that the nature and character of both the new and the old information changed.

Each of the professions used slightly different meaning-making processes, which appeared to arise from differences in the way they viewed their professional work. For example, social workers emphasised their advocacy role in defending clients' interests, and the importance of combining new information with their experience in professional practice in order to further clients' interests. Lawyers, on the other hand, described how logical thinking processes prevailed in their work, and the updated information from education programmes helped foster these processes.

The professionals also indicated how client interaction affected their meaning-making processes. In many cases the professionals described a practice event that forced them to examine their own beliefs and their previous learning.

Source: Adapted from Daley (2001)

Cognitive and social-cognitive perspectives on learning therefore fit well with interactive models of the research use process. They also reinforce Chapter Four's criticisms of models that view research use as a process of transferring knowledge from one place or person to another. Adult learning theories generally view knowledge acquisition as an experience-led and socially constrained process, which can be stimulated through exposing individuals to new experiences and providing them with opportunities for critical reflection. Studies of adult learning suggest that if individual learning is the goal, research use strategies and interventions should adopt a user perspective and encourage dialogue, reflection and local experimentation. They emphasise the potential importance of local collaborations between researchers and research users, particularly collaborations that focus on users' needs and are sustained over time.

Learning may not always be a conscious process; it may be intentional and explicit but is also often incidental and implicit (Reber, 1993). So while research use strategies may emphasise explicit learning opportunities, the importance of incidental learning – through, say, the unconscious modelling of peer behaviour – should not be underestimated. In addition, individuals are not simply vessels that need to be 'topped up' with new knowledge: they already know much that is outdated, partial or of dubious effectiveness. Thus, any strategy that focuses on individual learning will also need to pay attention to the often neglected ideas of 'unlearning' (Rushmer and Davies, 2004).

Organisational learning

The importance of collaborative learning, and concepts such as a 'community of learners' (Barab and Duffy, 2000), highlight the need to think beyond individual learning. If service benefits are to flow from individual learning, that learning needs to be deployed within organisations and shared with others. Furthermore, if the processes by which knowledge and experience become meaningful are as much to do with social context and collective cultural values as they are to do with individual processes of cognition, we need to pay attention to these. In a work context, organisational arrangements can foster or inhibit the process of adult learning. Organisational structures and cultures appear to shape the way in which individuals engage individually and collaboratively with learning opportunities (Nutley and Davies, 2001). Moreover, they influence whether and how the organisation harnesses the learning achieved by individual members, that is, the organisation itself learns (Senge, 1990; Argyris and Schon, 1996).

The phrase 'organisational learning' inevitably raises an important philosophical question about whether an organisation can be deemed to learn. If an organisation is just a collection of individuals, then organisational learning could be seen as merely the sum of individual learning. However, an organisation as a whole may, on some matters, know less than the individuals who comprise it. Conversely, the organisation can also be viewed as more than the sum of its parts.

Individuals come and go, but the organisation endures. Some of the accumulated knowledge of those who have left remains within the organisation – embedded in its work structures, routines and norms (Hedberg, 1981).

Organisational learning is an emergent field of study and there is as yet no overall agreement about what it is, let alone how it can be facilitated. However, in general it refers to the way organisations build and organise knowledge and routines, and use the broad skills of their workforce to improve organisational performance (Dodgson, 1993, p 377). In this way it builds on past knowledge and experience and thus depends on organisational mechanisms for retaining and deploying knowledge. Organisations that deliberately seek to develop organisational learning are often referred to as learning organisations.

Learning is not always about the acquisition of new knowledge. As with individuals, much organisational activity is based on custom and practice and there may be a strong case in some situations for 'unlearning' previously established ways of doing things. Organisations may need to identify, evaluate and change whole service routines that have become embedded in organisational customs.

One aspect of the organisational learning literature that seems particularly relevant to understanding research use in public services is that which highlights the different learning routines found within organisations. Of particular importance is the distinction between adaptive (single-loop) learning and generative (double-loop) learning (Argyris and Schon, 1996). Adaptive learning routines can be thought of as those mechanisms that help organisations to follow pre-set pathways. Generative learning, in contrast, involves forging new paths. Both sorts of learning are said to be essential for organisational fitness, but by far the most common practices found in organisations are those that are associated with adaptive learning.

Adaptive (single-loop) learning

The core insight from early work on cybernetics (a technique for designing self-regulating systems) was that a system's ability to engage in self-regulating behaviour depends upon building information flows that enable negative feedback. It is the negative feedback loops within a system that allow it to detect when it veers away from a desired course and this in turn triggers corrective behaviours to bring it back on course. This basic level of detection and correction of error is referred to as single-loop (or adaptive) learning. Inspection activities within many service areas provide a good example of such a learning routine.

Generative (double-loop) learning

The self-regulating behaviour resulting from adaptive learning is determined by the operating norms or standards that guide it. This works well so long as the action defined by these guidelines remains appropriate. When this ceases to be the case the system becomes dysfunctional. This has led modern cyberneticians to consider the design of more complex learning systems. For example, Argyris and Schon (1996) argue that beyond basic error correction, a more sophisticated learning is possible: that which changes fundamental assumptions about the organisation and may lead to a redefinition of the organisation's goals, norms, policies, procedures or even structures. This is referred to as double-loop (or generative) learning, as it calls into question the very nature of the course plotted and the feedback loops used to maintain that course.

Learning about learning (meta-learning)

One further, usually underdeveloped, aspect of learning is the ability of organisations to learn about the contexts of their learning – when they are able to identify when and how they learn and when and how they do not, and then adapt accordingly. This can be thought of as 'learning about learning' (or meta-learning). These three forms of learning are illustrated in Box 6.5.

Box 6.5: Learning routines: a healthcare example

Single-loop (or adaptive) learning

A hospital examines its obstetric services. Through clinical audit, it finds various gaps between actual practice and established standards (derived from evidence-based guidelines). Meetings are held to discuss the guidelines, changes are made to working procedures, and reporting and feedback on practice are enhanced. These changes increase the proportion of users receiving appropriate and timely care (that is, in compliance with the guidelines).

Double-loop (or generative) learning

In examining its obstetric care, some users are interviewed at length. From this it emerges that the issues that are bothering women have more to do with continuity of care, convenience of access, quality of information and the interpersonal aspects of the user–professional interaction. In the light of this, obstetric care is dramatically reconfigured to a system of midwife-led teams in order to prioritise these issues. The standards as laid down in the evidence-based guidelines are not abandoned but are woven into a new pattern of interactions and values.

Meta-learning

The experience of refocusing obstetric services better to meet user needs and expectations is not lost on the hospital. Through its structure and culture, the organisation encourages the transfer of these valuable lessons. The factors that assisted the reconfiguring (and those that impeded it) are analysed, described and communicated within the organisation. This is not done through formal written reports but through informal communications, temporary work placements and the development of teams working across services. Thus, the obstetric service is able to share with other hospital services the lessons learned about learning to reconfigure.

Source: Reproduced from Davies and Nutley (2000)
(2000) *British Medical Journal*, vol 320, pp 998-1001,
reproduced with permission from the BMJ Publishing Group

The prominence of adaptive learning routines is reflected in the research use literature. The use of dissemination, facilitation and reinforcement mechanisms are all likely to promote adaptive rather than more generative forms of learning. However, it is possible that more interactive approaches to research use promote generative learning, especially where this is combined with an approach that encourages local experimentation and analysis. Indeed, some of the research–practice partnerships highlighted in Chapter Five are promising in this regard.

More generally, what can an organisation do to improve its capacity for organisational learning? Those attempting to answer this question will find a ready supply of advice in the learning organisations literature. This includes specification of the conditions that facilitate learning (Megginson and Pedlar, 1992), outlines of the characteristics of the learning organisation (Pedlar et al, 1997), models of the strategic architecture of a learning organisation, and lists of activities which encourage organisational learning (Goh, 1998). All such lists need to be treated with caution as the learning organisation probably has to be realised from within, rather than imposed as a given architecture from outside (Pedlar and Aspinwall, 1998). However, we reproduce two lists in Boxes 6.6 and 6.7. The first summarises Senge's (1990) advice about the five disciplines to be mastered by learning organisations, and the second outlines the cultural values that appear to facilitate organisational learning.

Box 6.6: The five key disciplines of learning organisations

- *Improving individual capabilities* – Individuals need to be encouraged constantly to improve their own personal proficiencies. Initiatives such as problem-based learning fit well with the development of organisational learning as long as these do not overly promote a culture of individualism.
- *Team learning* – The ability to work collaboratively in teams is essential because it is largely through teams that organisations achieve their objectives. Activities that focus on developing whole teams rather than *ad hoc* groups of individuals in isolation are crucial.
- *Updating mental models* – Day-to-day practice is shaped, largely unconsciously, by embedded mental models consisting of deeply held assumptions and generalisations. They shape, for example, how causes and effects are linked conceptually and thus constrain what individuals see as possible within the organisation. Surfacing, challenging and updating these mental models are essential if organisations are to learn to do things differently.
- *A cohesive vision* – Learning organisations constantly seek ways to remove unnecessary hierarchy and constraints on individuals and teams. Such empowerment has to be counterbalanced by providing clear strategic direction and articulating a coherent set of values that can guide individual and team action.
- *Open systems thinking* – Underpinning everything else is the need to move away from a parochial and fragmented view of the world. Systems thinking seeks to see things as wholes and not just as parts – whole services provided to whole people. This integration needs to stretch beyond internal departmental boundaries, and even beyond the boundaries of the organisation itself, to encompass other services.

Source: Adapted from Senge (1990) and reproduced
from Davies and Nutley (2000)
(2000) *British Medical Journal*, vol 320, pp 998-1001,
reproduced with permission from the BMJ Publishing Group

Box 6.7: Cultural values that facilitate organisational learning

- *Celebration of success* – Existing values often promote the avoidance of failure and to break out of this, success needs to be celebrated.
- *Absence of complacency* – Learning organisations search constantly for new ways of delivering products and services. Thus, innovation and change are valued within the organisation.
- *Tolerance of mistakes* – Incidents of failure are inevitable in innovative and learning organisations. Learning requires a culture that tolerates failure rather than naming and blaming the perpetrators. (This does not, however, imply a tolerance of routinely poor or mediocre performance from which no lessons are learned.)
- *Belief in human potential* – It is people who drive success in organisations – using their knowledge, skills, creativity and energy. Therefore the culture within a learning organisation values people, and fosters their professional and personal development.
- *Recognition of tacit knowledge* – Learning organisations recognise that those individuals closest to processes have the best and most intimate knowledge of their potential and their flaws. Therefore, the learning culture values tacit knowledge and shows a belief in empowerment (the systematic enlargement of discretion, responsibility and competence).
- *Prioritising the immeasurable* – Learning organisations recognise the dangers of focusing on what can be measured. In order to avoid the tyranny of numbers, judgements based on qualitative understandings of performance need to be prioritised.
- *Openness* – An open sharing of knowledge throughout the organisation is crucial in developing learning capacity. This sharing tends to be achieved more by informal channels and personal contacts than by written reporting procedures.
- *Trust* – A culture of mutual trust between staff and managers best suits organisational learning. Without trust, learning is a faltering process.
- *Outward looking* – Learning organisations are engaged with the world outside as a rich source of learning opportunities. They look to their competitors for insights into their own operations and are focused on obtaining a deep understanding of clients' needs.

Source: Adapted from Schein (1996) and Mintzberg et al (1998)

The literature on organisational learning can enrich our understanding of how organisations at times facilitate and at other times inhibit individuals' use of research evidence and other forms of knowledge. It also cautions us against assuming that individual learning is enough to improve organisational performance.

As we have noted in earlier chapters, the research use literature tends to define research users as individuals rather than as organisations, yet more sophisticated understandings of research use in both policy and practice settings have emphasised the importance of local cultures and contexts. The organisational learning literature highlights the importance of focusing more attention at the organisational level, and it also outlines the cultural values associated with organisational learning cultures (Box 6.7). Although such lists are necessarily tentative, they nevertheless suggest where interventions aimed at improving the organisational 'pull' for research might focus. The organisational learning literature also cautions us against an uncritical use of reinforcement mechanisms, such as audit and feedback, to improve research use because they tend to focus attention on error correction rather than on more generative forms of learning.

A key limitation of the organisational learning literature is that it is emergent, largely speculative and highly contested. It also tends to paint a fairly rosy picture of organisations, where issues of power, politics and conflict are relegated to the sidelines (Coopey, 1995). This is likely to be an unrealistic scenario for many public services. This does not mean that organisational learning is an unobtainable ideal; politics and conflict can play a central role in providing positive learning experiences but this aspect of the organisational learning literature is not as yet well developed (Coopey and Burgoyne, 2000).

Knowledge management

Consideration of how learning is built and shared within organisations links directly with an allied body of literature on knowledge management. However, while the knowledge management literature covers similar ground to that covered by organisational learning, it has different disciplinary origins. Studies of organisational learning are rooted in social science, particularly organisational sociology and cultural anthropology. In contrast, much of the early knowledge management literature originated in information science and its main models and concerns reflect this.

Knowledge management has been defined as 'any process or practice of creating, acquiring, capturing, sharing and using knowledge, wherever it resides, to enhance learning and performance in organisations' (Scarborough et al, 1999, p 1). As research use is also concerned with the generation and uptake of knowledge, there are clear parallels between the two, which have to some extent been explored by others (for example, Fennessy, 2001; Dopson and Fitzgerald, 2005).

In this overview of knowledge management, a brief introduction to the literature is followed by an outline of push and pull approaches to knowledge management. We then consider models of the interplay between tacit and explicit knowledge, and studies of the barriers to and enablers of knowledge management.

Endeavour within the knowledge management field has been shaped by how people view the nature of knowledge and, in particular, whether knowledge is seen as an object or as a process. When knowledge is seen as an object (primarily explicit knowledge), knowledge management tends to focus on building and managing knowledge stocks. Resulting knowledge management strategies tend to be computer-centred; knowledge is carefully codified and stored in databases and then accessed and used by staff. Conversely, if knowledge is seen as a process of accessing and applying expertise (largely tacit knowledge), then there is recognition that knowledge is closely tied to the person who develops it. Resulting strategies seek to develop enhanced opportunities for sharing knowledge, often through person-to-person contact. The role of information and communication technology in the latter scenario is to help people communicate knowledge, not to store it (Hansen et al, 1999). Early research within the knowledge management field tended to focus on knowledge as an object. More recently, an increased emphasis on the process of knowing has been noted (Blackler et al, 1998). Indeed, the more critical literature on knowledge management has sought to challenge the reification of knowledge by highlighting how it is situated within social and politicised systems of meaning (Swan and Scarborough, 2001; and see Chapter Four on the postmodern perspective).

Knowledge push versus knowledge pull

Two main approaches to managing knowledge have been highlighted – knowledge push and knowledge pull – both of which tend to treat knowledge as an object. Knowledge-push approaches assume that the fundamental problem for knowledge management is the limited flow of knowledge and information into and within an organisation. They aim to increase that flow by capturing, codifying and transmitting knowledge. Conversely, knowledge-pull approaches are concerned with the problems of engaging employees in the process of sharing and searching for knowledge. Consequently, they focus on reward systems and other mechanisms to encourage employees to share, search for and apply knowledge. Both knowledge-push and knowledge-pull approaches tend to have a technological component, although the use of such technologies differs (see Table 6.1). Clearly parallels can be drawn here with the 'producer-push' and 'user-pull' models of research use outlined in Chapter Four.

The knowledge management literature suggests that where service delivery is concerned with standardised and mature services or products, which rely on the successful application of explicit knowledge, knowledge-push and codification approaches may work well (for example, Box 6.8 outlines the implementation of a decision support system in health care). However, the knowledge management literature increasingly points to the limitations of knowledge push, and argues that more attention should be devoted to developing knowledge pull.

Box 6.8: The application of expert and decision support systems

Davenport and Glaser (2002) argue that it is possible to 'bake knowledge' into the work processes of 'high-end professionals' such as physicians. They describe an initiative which linked up-to-date medical knowledge with a medical record system in creating an order-entry system for hospital physicians in the US. This order-entry system forces physicians to engage with queries or recommendations as they order tests, medications or other forms of treatment. For example, it alerts physicians to potential drug reactions or interactions based on running their orders through a series of checks and decision rules.

The conclusion from their evaluation of this initiative is that decision support systems are best suited to fields with low levels of ambiguity, a well-established external knowledge base, and a relatively low number of possible choices facing decision makers. Furthermore, they argue that to implement such a system you need the right information, good IT people, and an organisational culture of measurement. You also need to leave the final decision to the experts – it must always be possible to override the system.

Source: Adapted from Davenport and Glaser (2002)

Table 6.1: Some differences between push and pull technologies

	Push	Pull
Objective	Information capture	Navigation
User	Passive	Active
Technology	Always active	Active only when used
Best for	Continuing knowledge needs Time-dependent information Creating awareness of what can be pulled (notification)	One-time knowledge needs Conducting research Detailed information
Main advantage	Brings important material to users' attention	Allows users to access information at point of need
Main disadvantage	Can overload users since they do not control it	Requires time on the part of users (to both master the technology and to deploy it)
Examples	Search agents E-mail	Search engines Browsers Directories, frameworks

Source: Reproduced with permission from Bukowitz and Williams, *The Knowledge Management Fieldbook* (Pearson Education Ltd), p 54. Copyright © Pearson Education Ltd 1999.

There have been a number of surveys aimed at identifying best practices in knowledge management (Hildebrand, 1999; Heisig and Vorbeck, 2001; Kluge et al, 2001). A survey by Kluge et al (2001) suggests that top performing companies tend to use knowledge-pull rather than knowledge-push techniques (see Box 6.9). However, a danger of such surveys is that they assume that successful knowledge management practices can be separated out from the context within which they work. Other studies conclude that success is far more contingent than this (Hansen et al, 1999; Armistead and Meakins, 2002).

Box 6.9: Successful practices in knowledge management

Kluge et al (2001) surveyed 40 leading companies in Europe, the US and Japan. At least eight people in each company were asked about their use of a basic set of 139 knowledge management techniques. The financial and process performance of each company was assessed and correlation analysis was used to see if certain types of knowledge management were associated with superior performance. The analysis focused on the top 15 and bottom 15 performers and found that these two groups did indeed use different knowledge management techniques. The top-performing companies used more knowledge-pull techniques than the other companies, including setting ambitious targets that could not be reached single-handedly and linking incentives to the use of external knowledge.

Source: Adapted from Kluge et al (2001)

Hansen et al (1999) reviewed the knowledge management practices of consulting firms and found that they adopted either a codification approach (the construction of databases) or a personalisation approach (enabling person-to-person contact). They found that the choice between these two strategies is far from arbitrary – it depends on a number of factors:

- The extent of provision of standardised services and products: the more standardised, the more appropriate is a codification strategy; the more that services and products are bespoke the more that personalisation may be better.
- The extent to which services and products are mature or innovative: for more mature service lines codification may be possible, whereas innovative services may need a personalisation approach.
- The extent to which an organisation relies on explicit or tacit knowledge to solve problems: the more that explicit knowledge is used, the more appropriate is codification; tacit knowledge is better communicated interpersonally.

While it may be tempting to go for a blend of codification and personalisation approaches, the authors argue that there are tensions and that it is necessary to make a choice. They claim that it is only possible for the approaches to coexist in a corporation where business units operate like stand-alone companies (Hansen et al, 1999).

The debates about the relative merits of push and pull approaches to knowledge management echo similar debates within the research use literature (see Chapters Two to Four). Many of the dissemination activities associated with improving research use are based on a knowledge-push approach. However, the creation of online databases of studies and the synthesis of research findings in the form of systematic reviews may also underpin a knowledge-pull approach. While the knowledge management literature suggests that the creation of such databases and research syntheses are unlikely to be sufficient for effective knowledge sharing and use, they may be a necessary component of a research use strategy. For example, it seems that many UK government departments have poor knowledge management systems for capturing the findings of project and programme evaluations (Homel et al, 2004; Boaz, 2006). Making research and evaluation studies available beyond the lifetime of a project, by placing them on a relevant database, is an important way of ensuring that their findings are accessible in the future.

The central issue of whether different approaches to knowledge management can be blended, and if so how, also has potential implications for research use. It is tempting to argue that strategies aimed at improving research use should use a judicious mix of push and pull approaches, of approaches that support codification where possible and collaboration both as a means and as an end in itself. However, there is enough doubt shed on this as a strategy by the knowledge management literature to suggest that caution is appropriate. At the very least a contingent approach may be necessary, with strategies varying in emphasis as a function of both knowledge type and service context.

The interplay between tacit and codified knowledge

Modelling the interplay between tacit and codified knowledge is fundamental to understanding knowledge creation and use. In discussing this interplay, much of the knowledge management literature draws upon the work of Nonaka and Takeuchi (1995), who argue that organisational knowledge is created by human interaction among individuals. Such interactions, they suggest, produce four modes of knowledge conversion:

- *socialisation* – where individual tacit knowledge is converted to group tacit knowledge to produce sympathetic knowledge;
- *externalisation* – where tacit knowledge is converted to explicit knowledge to produce conceptual knowledge;
- *internalisation* – where explicit knowledge is converted to tacit knowledge to produce operational knowledge;
- *combination* – where separate explicit knowledge is combined to produce systemic knowledge.

Organisational knowledge creation is thus seen as a continuous and dynamic interaction between tacit and explicit knowledge, which Nonaka and Takeuchi (1995) describe as a knowledge spiral. They argue that several triggers induce these four modes of knowledge conversion:

- *Socialisation* starts with building a field of interaction.

- *Externalisation* is triggered by 'meaningful dialogue' or 'collective reflection'.
- *Internalisation* is triggered by 'learning-by-doing'.
- *Combination* is triggered by networking.

Many of these triggers mirror the features of effective individual learning processes outlined at the beginning of this chapter. This is hardly surprising given that individual learning is also fundamentally concerned with the interplay between explicit and tacit knowledge. However, the above references to 'meaningful dialogue' and 'collective reflection' are a far cry from knowledge management models based on the management of corporate digital information. They represent a shift in emphasis to a model of knowledge management that is concerned with the sensitive management of social relations (Swan and Scarborough, 2001; Dopson and Fitzgerald, 2005), where knowledge is intrinsically linked to the social and learning processes within an organisation (McAdam and Reid, 2001).

Despite the widespread appeal of Nonaka and Takeuchi's (1995) knowledge spiral, their work has also received sustained criticism. It is said to provide a shaky foundation for knowledge management because of two fallacies (Little and Ray, 2005): first, the possibility of converting tacit to explicit knowledge; and second, the advisability of abstracting knowledge management practices from Japanese companies and transporting them elsewhere, which ignores the deeply embedded nature of these practices.

That said, a core issue for both knowledge management and research use is the need to develop a better understanding of the interplay between tacit and explicit knowledge. This may require us to move away from definitions of tacit and explicit knowledge that treat them as separate categories, towards understanding them as 'two sides of the same coin' (Tsoukas, 2005, p 122). Much of the analysis within the knowledge management literature has tended to view knowledge as a fixed and abstract entity but an alternative view is that knowledge cannot be separated from action. Knowledge is thus defined as 'situated action' (Tsoukas and Vladimirou, 2001) which occurs within local networks and communities of practice (see 'interorganisational learning networks' on p 185). This raises the question about whether there is a role for 'management' at all: at best the role might be to facilitate the development of communities of practice (Bate and Robert, 2002), which are discussed further later. Here again, this problematising of the nature of knowledge mirrors debates in the research use field on the extent to which research findings can be seen as fixed or whether they only make sense when situated in practitioner actions.

Barriers and enablers

As in the research use literature, lists of challenges, barriers and enablers abound within the knowledge management literature. Many of these suggest that the main challenges are culture- and people-related, regardless of whether the knowledge management approach is based on 'push' or 'pull', or whether it emphasises codification or collaboration (Liebowitz, 2000). The knowledge management literature increasingly emphasises the importance of developing an organisational culture that both values knowledge and recognises the importance of knowledge sharing within the organisation. The critical literature is, however, quick to point out that focusing on cultural factors runs the danger of ignoring the way in which 'knowledge work' and 'knowledge management' are intimately bound up with social and politicised systems of meaning (Swan and Scarborough, 2001), again reflecting the postmodernist critique outlined in Chapter Four.

Pfeffer and Sutton (2000) argue that the main barriers to knowledge use relate more to a knowing–doing gap than to knowledge sharing problems. Addressing this gap requires not only cultural but also system changes. Worryingly, they suggest that typical knowledge management practices tend to make the knowing–doing gap worse. Overall their analysis presents a tall order for any organisation intent on improving its management of knowledge so that what employees and managers know is translated into action (see Box 6.10). A similar cautionary note is sounded by McKinlay (2005, p 255) who argues that 'the introduction of a knowledge management system can disrupt rather than extend existing grass roots networks of experts and reduce the likely success of the formal system'.

Box 6.10: The knowing–doing gap

Employees and managers in organisations know much about how to improve organisational performance, yet they work in ways that they know will undermine performance. Based on multiple case study analysis, Pfeffer and Sutton (2000) argue that the knowing–doing gap is not a problem of individual psychology but is due more to organisational practices. Typical knowledge management practices make the knowing–doing gap worse because they:

- emphasise technology and the transfer of codified knowledge;
- treat knowledge as a tangible 'thing' – an object that can be separated from the use of that object;
- do not recognise that formal systems cannot easily store or transfer tacit knowledge;
- make people who do not understand the actual work being documented responsible for transferring and implementing knowledge;
- focus on specific knowledge practices and ignore the importance of overall philosophy.

Addressing the knowing–doing gap requires action to overcome the following main barriers:

- talk as a substitute for actions;
- memory as a substitute for thinking – doing what has always been done without reflecting;
- fear, which prevents people from acting on knowledge;
- measurement, which often obstructs good judgement;
- internal competition, which turns friends into enemies.

Source: Adapted from Pfeffer and Sutton (2000)

The knowledge management literature thus reinforces earlier comments about the importance of organisational culture in understanding how knowledge is created, acquired, shared and used in organisations. It also provides some insights into why individuals within organisations do not always act on the basis of their knowledge. Overall it reinforces our earlier conclusion about the limits of understanding research use as an individual learning issue and the consequent need to focus more attention on how organisations 'manage' knowledge, encourage individual and collective learning, and promote new modes of behaviour as a consequence of that learning.

Diffusion of innovations

The diffusion of innovations literature is concerned with understanding the spread of ideas, technologies and practices among individuals and organisations. As the research use literature is also concerned with the spread of research ideas and research-based technologies and practices, it is not surprising that several researchers have already used the diffusion literature to make sense of research use (for example, Sobell, 1996; Lia-Hoagberg et al, 1999; Dopson and Fitzgerald, 2005). This literature can help us understand not only the diffusion of research-based technologies and practices, but also the organisational reconfigurations that might support better research use. Indeed, the diffusion of innovations literature can also help us understand that the very ideology of evidence use needs to be diffused.

In this brief overview of the literature we first consider the ways in which the diffusion process has been modelled and then go on to discuss the key factors found to affect the spread of innovations: the nature of the innovation itself; adopter characteristics; communication and implementation processes; context; and the role of opinion leaders and change agents. We conclude this section by considering the literature on interorganisational learning networks, which have risen in prominence as a potential mechanism for diffusing knowledge and innovations.

Models of the diffusion process

The classic model of the diffusion process views it as a decision process which passes through a series of stages that are very similar to the linear research–into–practice models of research use outlined in Chapter Four (see Box 6.11). As in the research use literature, there has been much criticism of this linear view of the diffusion process. The whole process has been characterised as far more messy than this model implies (Van de Ven et al, 1999). For example, evidence-based innovations appear to go through a lengthy period of negotiation among potential adopters, through which their meaning is discussed, contested and reframed (Greenhalgh et al, 2004).

Box 6.11: The innovation-decision process

Rogers (2003, p 169) argues that there are five main stages in the innovation-decision process:

(1) *Knowledge* – the individual (or decision-making unit) is exposed to the innovation's existence and gains some understanding of how it functions.
(2) *Persuasion* – the potential adopter forms a favourable or unfavourable attitude toward the innovation. This may involve, for example, a matching of the innovation to a perceived problem, and some kind of appraisal of the costs and benefits of adoption.

> (3) *Decision* – the potential adopter engages in activities that lead to a choice to adopt or reject the innovation. This may include interaction with forces of support or opposition that influence the process.
>
> (4) *Implementation* – the adopter puts an innovation into use.
>
> (5) *Confirmation* – the adopter seeks reinforcement for an innovation-decision already made, but may reverse this decision if exposed to conflicting messages about the innovation.
>
> *Source:* Adapted from Rogers (2003)

The prescriptive model for diffusing an innovation used to be a relatively centralised one: a central authority decides which innovations to diffuse, to whom and by what means. Diffusion was thus thought to flow from the top down, from experts to users, from the centre outward. Several decades ago, Schon (1967, 1971) challenged the adequacy of this centre-periphery model. He argued that, in practice, there is often no clear centre and that the diffusion process is frequently more decentralised and iterative in nature (innovations evolve as they are diffused).

It is now recognised that the process of diffusion can range on a continuum from highly centralised to highly decentralised (Rogers, 2003). In a highly centralised system there is central (often government) control of decisions about which innovations should be diffused, a top-down diffusion of the innovation from experts to users, and a low degree of adaptation of the innovation when adopted by users. In comparison, in a highly decentralised system there is wide sharing of power and control among members of the diffusion system, peer diffusion of innovations through horizontal networks, and a high degree of local adaptation as innovations diffuse among adopters.

We shall return to the issue of centralised versus decentralised approaches to diffusing research-based intervention programmes in Chapter Seven, but we note here that the diffusion of innovations literature indicates that there are advantages and disadvantages associated with both centralised and decentralised systems of diffusion (see Box 6.12). Furthermore, Greenhalgh et al (2004) found that horizontal networks are more effective for spreading peer influence and supporting the construction and reframing of meaning, while vertical networks are more effective in cascading codified information and passing on authoritative evidence.

> ## Box 6.12: Centralised versus decentralised diffusion systems
>
> ### Centralised systems
> - Provide central quality control over which innovations to diffuse
> - Can diffuse innovations for which there is as yet no felt need
>
> But:
> - Can encounter user resistance to central control
> - May result in inappropriate adoption because of low adaptation to local circumstances
>
> ### Decentralised systems
> - Users tend to like such a system
> - Promote a closer fit between innovations and user needs and problems
>
> But:
> - Ineffective innovations may be diffused due to lack of quality control
> - Depend on local users having knowledge about other users' problems and about whether the innovations available could solve them
> - Are likely to involve site visits to observe an innovation in use and this may create an overload problem for the site(s) visited.
>
> *Source:* Adapted from Rogers (2003)

Rogers (2003) offers the tentative conclusion that decentralised systems are most appropriate when innovations do not require a high level of newly acquired technical expertise and when users are relatively heterogeneous. He adds that the potential for users to run their own diffusion system is greatest when the users are highly educated and technically competent practitioners. It seems that a decentralised approach to diffusing innovations is likely to encounter less user resistance than a centralised approach. It is also likely to result in a greater level of reinvention – although whether this is desirable will in turn depend on both the nature of the innovation and the knowledge/capabilities of the reinventors. Rogers (2003) suggests that the most likely scenario is a hybrid diffusion system, which, for example, may combine a central coordinating role with decentralised decision making about which innovations should be diffused. These debates about the balance between centralised versus decentralised decision making have clear parallels with similar debates about the degree of centralisation required to diffuse evidence-based innovations (for example, see Chapter Seven for its discussion of 'embedded research' versus 'research-based practitioner' or 'organisational excellence' approaches to practice-based change).

The nature of innovation

The perceived characteristics of an innovation are considered to have an important influence that may affect adoption. Five innovation attributes are typically identified as being important for rapid diffusion: relative advantage, compatibility, complexity, trialability and observability (see Box 6.13). Greenhalgh et al's (2004) review of the diffusion of innovations literature found strong evidence to support the importance of each of these attributes. Other attributes have also been identified as being potentially important. These include the adaptability of the innovation, its centrality and relevance to the day-to-day work of the organisation, the extent to which its adoption would require additional visible resources, and the complexity of its implementation in the organisational context (Wolfe, 1994; Greenhalgh et al, 2004).

Box 6.13: Innovation attributes associated with rapid diffusion

- *Relative advantage* – the extent to which the innovation is perceived to have significant advantages over current alternatives.
- *Compatibility* – the degree to which the innovation is seen as being consistent with past practices, current values and existing needs.
- *Complexity* – the extent to which the innovation can readily be understood and easily implemented.
- *Trialability* – new ideas that can be tried out at low costs before wholesale adoption are more likely to be taken up.
- *Observability* – the degree to which the use and benefits of the innovation are visible to others, and therefore act as a further stimulus to uptake by others.

Source: Adapted from Rogers (2003)

These factors are potentially very relevant to the design of strategies aimed at promoting research use. They suggest that such strategies should seek to highlight the relative advantage of research-based innovations as well as aiming to reduce perceptions of their complexity. 'Relative advantage' is, however, an ambiguous concept. Several studies suggest that the strength of evidence on whether adoption would indeed lead to improved effectiveness is not a key factor influencing adoption decisions (Stocking, 1985; Westphal et al, 1997) – it is perceptions that are important (Greenhalgh et al, 2004). This may have relevance for understanding research use. However, the PACE (Promoting Action on Clinical Effectiveness) study in health care (Dopson et al, 2001 – see Chapter 7) found that the strength of evidence *was* an important factor in explaining research uptake, albeit one that might be overridden by other concerns.

The adopters and adoption decisions

Adopter categories have been developed which are classifications of members of a social system on the basis of their tendency to be innovative – that is, the extent to which an individual or other unit of adoption is relatively early in adopting new ideas. Five categories of adopters have been identified: innovators, early adopters, early majority, late majority and laggards (Rogers, 2003). Following this, there have been attempts to identify the factors associated with each of these categories, such as the socioeconomic status of the adopter (Rogers, 2003). However, these are rather value-laden terms and it is claimed that they do not pay sufficient attention to the ways in which adopters interact purposively and creatively with an innovation (Greenhalgh et al, 2004).

Adoption of an innovation by an individual seems to be more likely if they are similar (in terms of socioeconomic, educational, professional and cultural background) to current users of an innovation. Greenhalgh et al (2004) also found strong evidence to suggest that adoption and continued use of an innovation were more likely when:

- the intended adopter has sufficient information about an innovation and its implications for them;
- the adopter has continuing access to information about the innovation and sufficient training and support on task issues;
- there is adequate feedback on consequences of the innovation.

These findings have several implications for the design of strategies for promoting research use. They reinforce earlier comments about the importance of peer influence and the modelling of peer behaviour. They also suggest how dissemination materials might be tailored and targeted (on user implications) and where facilitative and reinforcement interventions might be focused (on training support and feedback).

However, there is a danger that this summary of the findings presents a picture of adoption as a relatively ordered and rational decision-making process. This is countered by other findings that indicate that organisational choices about whether to adopt or not can relate more to the institutional pressures associated with certain fads or fashions. While early adoption of an innovation may be due to the prospect of improved performance, as the innovation gains acceptance others may adopt more in order to seek legitimacy (DiMaggio and Powell, 1983; Westphal et al, 1997, O'Neill et al, 1998). This pattern of behaviour is heightened during times of high uncertainty, when organisations are more likely to imitate other organisations, especially those deemed to be norm setters (DiMaggio and Powell, 1983). Such observations suggest opportunities for new strategies aimed at increasing research use that utilise 'beacon' or 'exemplar' sites as potential trendsetters (of which more later under 'interorganisational learning networks').

Communication and implementation processes

The diffusion literature suggests that the rate of adoption is also influenced by the communication channels involved – that is, the means by which messages get from one individual to another. A distinction is generally made between interpersonal and mass media channels of communication, with interpersonal influence through social networks operating as the dominant mechanism for promoting adoption of innovations (Rogers, 2003). This reinforces the finding in Chapter Three that of the multiple channels by which research travels, it is social influence and social networks that appear to be prominent routes.

One of the issues raised in the diffusion literature, which is of particular relevance for understanding and promoting research use, is whether the adoption of an innovation involves significant adaptation, amounting to reinvention. Some of the drivers of reinvention are summarised in Box 6.14. In some cases, the process of reinvention reflects a partial utilisation of knowledge, in others innovation knowledge is changed or augmented. The diffusion literature suggests that reinvention not only increases the likelihood of adoption (Greenhalgh et al, 2004) but also reduces the likelihood of discontinuance (Berman and Pauley, 1975). Indeed the very concept of replicating an innovation may be misguided (Rogers, 2003) as an element of reinvention is inevitable. However, some studies within education suggest that when the level of reinvention is quite high it can mean that the *status quo* engulfs the innovation, such that the service changes very little and the innovation changes substantially (Berman and Pauley, 1975; Berman and McLaughlin, 1978).

These issues are central to debates about how to promote the effective use of research-based intervention programmes, and relate to the issues of programme fidelity first raised in Chapter Two. The diffusion of innovations literature can thus help us to understand why and when substantial reinvention may be appropriate.

Box 6.14: The drivers of reinvention

- Reinvention can occur because of adopters' lack of full knowledge about the innovation.
- Relatively complex innovations are more likely to be reinvented and simplified.
- An innovation that is an abstract concept or a tool with many possible applications is more likely to be reinvented.
- When an innovation is implemented in order to solve a wide range of problems, reinvention is more likely to occur.
- Local pride of ownership may be a cause of reinvention.
- Reinvention may be encouraged by a change agency.
- The adaptation of an innovation to the structure of that which is adopting it may lead to reinvention.
- Reinvention may occur as later adopters learn from the experiences of earlier adopters.

Source: Adapted from Rogers (2003, pp 186-7)

Context

The organisational context within which adoption decisions are made also shapes the rate of adoption. Contextual factors found to be associated with an organisation's readiness for a particular innovation are summarised in Box 6.15. These highlight the importance of both the internal organisational context and outer contextual factors, including the policy environment. In relation to public services, the latter set of factors reinforces Chapter Four's messages about the importance of policy networks and policy streams in understanding research use. Overall, the factors highlight those issues that need to be considered when planning research use strategies and interventions, and they have the potential to inform the design of diagnostic tools aimed at understanding receptivity to research-based ideas and innovations.

Box 6.15: Contextual factors associated with readiness for innovation adoption in organisations

Organisational readiness

- *Tension for change* – a perception that the present situation is intolerable.
- *Innovation-system fit* – extent of fit with existing values, norms, strategies, goals, skill mix, technologies and ways of working.
- *Assessment of implications* – full assessment of the implications of an innovation (including its knock-on effects).
- *Support and advocacy* – extent to which supporters outweigh opponents.
- *Dedicated time and resources* – the allocation of adequate resources.
- *Capacity to evaluate the innovation* – rapid and tight feedback on the impact of an innovation increases the likelihood that it will be assimilated and sustained.

Outer context factors

- *Informal interorganisational networks* – these serve to promote an innovation once it is perceived as the norm, otherwise they may act as a barrier to adoption.
- *Intentional spread strategies* – formal networking, such as quality improvement collaboratives, may promote adoption but success of these strategies is variable.
- *Wider environment* – environmental uncertainty may promote adoption.
- *Political directives* – may increase the predisposition but not the capacity of an organisation to adopt an innovation.
- *Policy streams* – the congruence of an innovation with prevailing values and perceived problems may increase the likelihood of adoption (see Chapter Four. this volume).

Source: Abstracted from Greenhalgh et al (2004)

Role of intermediaries

Finally, intermediaries are considered to play an important role in convincing others to adopt an innovation. They are considered to be crucial because innovators (such as inventors and academics) are usually dissimilar to the broad mass of potential adopters and therefore have communication and credibility problems. Two categories of intermediary are identified:

- *Opinion leaders* who are near–peers play an important role in persuading others to adopt (or not adopt) an innovation. Opinion leaders influence the beliefs and action of their colleagues both positively and negatively (Greenhalgh et al, 2004; Dopson and Fitzgerald, 2005). Greenhalgh et al (2004) distinguish between expert opinion leaders, who influence through their authority and status, and peer opinion leaders, who influence by virtue of representativeness and credibility. It seems to be important to identify true opinion leaders and distinguish between those who are only influential for a particular innovation and those who have influence across a wide range of innovations.
- *Change agents* work proactively to expedite and widen innovation. They create demand for the innovation by reducing barriers to adoption, persuading adopters and supporting adoption decisions. The literature emphasises that since change agents act as bridges between technical experts and their clients, without being a member of either group, their ability to work effectively with both is critical. It is argued that they are most effective when they work in partnership with opinion leaders (Rogers, 2003). Greenhalgh et al (2004) point to the importance of champions and boundary spanners (those who have significant social ties both within and outside the organisation).

We noted in Chapter Five that opinion leaders have already been identified as an important source of social influence in promoting research use. The diffusion of innovations literature can enrich our understanding of different types of opinion leader and how they work. Change agents, by contrast, work to facilitate the adoption of innovations, and the diffusion literature also has the potential to inform our understanding of their 'bridging' role. As we noted in Chapter Three, such boundary-spanning roles seem to be key in understanding research use.

Interorganisational learning networks

There has been substantial interest in recent years in the potential for learning networks to facilitate the sharing of ideas, knowledge and innovations across organisational and professional boundaries, both in the private sector (Bessant et al, 2003) and in the public sector (Currie, 2006). Reviewing these may also offer insights to those interested in increasing the uptake of research-based knowledge.

Learning networks may take many forms and serve a range of purposes (see Table 6.2). They may also be formal (officially organised)

Table 6.2: A typology of learning networks

Type	Learning target	Examples
Profession	Increased professional knowledge and skill	Professional institutions
Sector-based	Improved competence in some aspect of competitive performance	Trade associations Sector-based research organisations
Topic-based	Improved awareness/knowledge of a particular field	Best practice clubs
Region-based	Improved knowledge around themes of regional interest	Clusters and local learning cooperatives
Supplier or value-stream-based	Learning to achieve standards of best practice in, for example, quality delivery	Particular firms supplying to a major customer or members of a shared value stream
Government-promoted networks	National or regional initiatives to provide upgrades in capacity	Regional development agencies
Task support networks	Similar to professional networks, aimed at sharing and developing knowledge about how to do a particular task	Practitioner networks

Source: Adapted from Bessant et al (2003, p 24)

or informal and emergent. Many professional networks start through informal, self-organisation but then become more formalised over time.

The effectiveness of learning networks is often viewed in terms of their success in enhancing the individual learning of participants, although most studies of learning networks have not really grappled with the issue of how to measure their benefits (Armfield et al, 2002). From a private sector study, Bessant et al (2003) have identified eight core network processes, and the effectiveness of a learning network is said to vary according to the way these processes are handled (see Table 6.3).

Table 6.3: Eight core network processes

Processes	Underlying questions
Network creation	How the members of the network are defined and maintained
Decision making	How (where, when, and by whom) decisions get taken
Conflict resolution	How (and if) conflicts are resolved
Information processing	How information flows and is managed
Knowledge capture	How knowledge is articulated and captured to be available for the whole network
Motivation/commitment	How members are motivated to join/remain in the network
Risk/benefit sharing	How the risks and benefits are shared
Integration	How relationships are built and maintained between individual representatives in the network

Source: Reproduced from Bessant et al (2003, p 36)

Within public services, there have been various initiatives aimed at sharing knowledge and innovations across professional and organisational boundaries. These include collaboratives and managed clinical networks in health care and beacon award schemes in education and local government (see Box 6.16). Reviews of these initiatives identify a number of key problems limiting the extent of knowledge sharing: the contested nature of knowledge; differences in interests in and between organisations; and the stickiness of knowledge – professional knowledge is difficult to share because it is tacit and difficult to articulate to others (Hartley and Benington, 2006). Dopson and Fitzgerald (2005) argue that the educational and socialisation regimes of the different healthcare professions create epistemic cultures that are not shared between the professions. These often act as barriers to a common, shared understanding of knowledge. In addition, the knowledge sharing objectives of such initiatives are often overtaken by other concerns. For example, the primary focus of the managed clinical networks studied by Ferlie and Addicott became structural reconfiguration rather than knowledge sharing and learning (Ferlie and Addicott, 2004; Addicott et al, 2006).

Box 6.16: Examples of knowledge sharing initiatives

Healthcare quality improvement 'collaboratives'

Drawing on work from the Institute for Healthcare Improvement (www.ihi.org) in Boston, USA, healthcare collaboratives involve developing quality improvement work and shared learning across organisations. Sometimes described as a 'temporary learning organisation' whose purpose is to test and implement a programme of change quickly across many settings (Øvretveit, 2002), collaboratives use rapid cycles of action learning or PDSA cycles (Plan-Do-Study-Act) to share localised learning across larger groups of service providers. Although the structures developed in support of collaboratives are temporary, the thinking behind the approach is that they should facilitate a culture of improvement that continues beyond the life of the initiative itself. A review of the approach suggested that there was some evidence that quality collaboratives can help some teams to make significant improvements quickly if the collaborative is carefully planned and managed, and if the team has the right conditions. However, it is also noted that such approaches are costly (Øvretveit, 2002).

Managed clinical networks

Managed clinical networks are defined as 'linked groups of health professionals and organisations from primary, secondary, and tertiary care, working in a coordinated manner that is not constrained by existing organisational or professional boundaries to ensure equitable provision of high quality, clinically effective care' (Baker and Lorimer, 2000, p 1152). Networks may cover, for example, a specific disease, such as diabetes or cancer; a specific specialty, such as neurology; or a specific function, such as emergency medical admissions. The concept as applied in health care is very flexible, but most managed clinical networks have as a major preoccupation the development and sharing of explicit knowledge (underpinned by evidence) on, for example, care pathways, treatment protocols and shared record keeping.

Networked Learning Communities in Education

The National College for School Leadership (NCSL) has facilitated and evaluated the NCSL Networked Learning Communities Programme in Education, a programme that aims to develop professional knowledge creation and sharing, resulting in changed practice and ultimately in an impact on pupil learning engagement and success. An ongoing evaluation of this initiative has identified seven key features of learning networks that appear to be significant: an explicit statement of purpose and focus; learning relationships based on trust, a commitment to shared goals, and social norms; active collaboration in the development of practice; systematic inquiry, which draws on research experts and each other in support of problem solving; farsighted but dispersed and pragmatic leadership; mutual accountability for the activities of the network and the quality of the work that ensues; planned strategies for building capacity for change and improvement within and between schools (NCSL, 2005a, 2005b).

Beacon schemes

Beacon schemes have been set up in a number of public service areas including local government, schools and police services. They aim to reward good practice and to share knowledge about that practice with others in the same service area. For example, the beacon scheme in UK local government was introduced in 1999 to identify centres of excellence from which others can learn. Authorities are appointed as beacons on the strength of assessed excellence in the delivery of specified services, supported by good overall performance and effective plans for dissemination (www.communities.gov.uk).

The wider context within which these initiatives operate has also served to undermine knowledge sharing goals. For example, the beacon award schemes have been inhibited by a much larger investment in audit and inspection, which has focused on compliance with national standards rather than local learning and knowledge sharing (Downe and Martin, 2005; Hartley et al, 2005). However, the remedy does not seem to be a simple matter of reducing oversight and comparative performance assessment, as explicit comparison with other organisations in the sector (and outside) has been identified as an important element of improvement and learning both within and between organisations (Hartley and Benington, 2006).

Interorganisational knowledge sharing initiatives tend to focus their attention on the exchange of explicit knowledge, sometimes relying on information communication technologies (such as websites) as the main medium of communication. This contrasts with what the practitioners involved in these schemes valued most: the opportunities to gain tacit knowledge through site visits, close working and active dialogue with their counterparts. This is important because knowledge exchange often involves knowledge generation due to the importance of context and tacit understandings.

A key issue for knowledge sharing initiatives such as healthcare collaboratives, managed clinical networks and beacon award schemes (Box 6.16) is that they all tend to be contrived networks rather than emergent communities of practice. The concept of 'communities of practice' (Wenger, 1998) has been influential in understanding how knowledge is generated, communicated and applied in practice contexts – contexts that may cross organisational and professional boundaries but which frequently do not. Communities of practice can be defined as a group of professionals and other stakeholders who are informally bound by common interests, and who interact through interdependent tasks guided by a common purpose (Davenport, 2001; Buysse et al, 2003). Through this interaction they develop shared understandings of practice issues (Buysse et al, 2003). The central tenets of a community of practice are said to be that knowledge is situated in experience, and experience is understood through critical reflection with others who share this experience (Buysse et al, 2003). Barab and Duffy (2000) identify three essential characteristics of a community of practice:

- They share a common culture and historical heritage, which inculcates goals and meanings that go beyond meeting for a specific period of time to address a particular need.
- They are situated within an interdependent system in which individuals are part of or are connected to something larger.
- They have the ability to regenerate themselves as members leave and new members enter the community.

The literature on communities of practice highlights the importance of tacit knowledge, situated learning and situated action in understanding how knowledge and expertise are nurtured in practice contexts. Communities of practice are seen as a powerful medium for enhancing learning both within and across organisations. However, opinion differs about the extent to which such approaches can be harnessed and whether communities of practice can be deliberately created and managed (Bate and Robert, 2002; Wenger et al, 2002).

The concepts of interorganisational learning networks and communities of practice have direct relevance for understanding research use and designing strategies aimed at promoting research use. For example, learning networks have been employed to disseminate the lessons of public health research (see Box 6.17). Strategies have also sought to encourage research use by ensuring that research enters into the discussions of communities of practice. However, to date these initiatives have met with mixed results. For example, research on two multi-agency communities of practice found that personal knowledge and experience are the main influences on collective decision making, even when relevant research evidence is brought to the attention of participants (Gabbay et al, 2003), although again these were contrived rather than naturally occurring communities of practice.

Box 6.17: Learning networks in public health

In 2002 the Scottish Executive funded the establishment of three national learning networks on heart health, the sexual health and wellbeing of young people, and early years child health. They aim to develop and share the evidence base for action in each of these areas in order to develop stakeholders' ability to translate these policy priorities into practice and inform future developments across Scotland.

The functions of these networks are to sift, collate, analyse and share the existing evidence base, practice and experiences; to cultivate links with other relevant learning networks; and to identify implications for future practice and come forward with relevant strategies/plans. It was anticipated that the networks would engage with and bring together a wide range of stakeholders.

A review of the networks (Percy-Smith et al, 2006) found that each of the networks had developed in different ways. Their main impact seemed to be on increasing awareness, knowledge and understanding of research and other evidence on the part of individual members of the networks. Concerns were raised about whether the networks really operated as networks, and the review recommended either re-designating them as contact databases for distributing information or re-emphasising their role in shared learning as part of an enhanced programme of activities intended to support practice change.

Source: Adapted from Percy-Smith et al (2006)

Studies of communities of practice suggest that there is a need to develop a clearer understanding of the processes of collective sense-making in order to understand how to encourage the more systematic use of relevant research knowledge in collective decision making. Research suggests that it is important to focus attention on naturally occurring communities of practice rather than contrived networks, but the identification of these is not likely to be straightforward (Bate and Robert, 2002).

Concluding remarks

Due to the diverse nature of the literature reviewed in this chapter, and the dangers of assuming that there is a direct read across to the issues of research use, our conclusions are necessarily provisional and suggestive. Nevertheless, this literature appears to provide a rich source of theories and evidence that can be mined to inform strategies for promoting research use. It appears to have most relevance to understanding the instrumental use of research in practice contexts; it offers fewer insights into understanding the conceptual use of research, or how research is used in policy contexts.

Although the literature on learning, knowledge management and the diffusion of innovations considers the issues of knowledge generation, sharing and enactment from different perspectives, current thinking in each of the fields reinforces comments in earlier chapters about the limits of a research/knowledge-push approach. The three fields of literature also provide insights into what a user-pull approach might entail. They enrich our understanding of how knowledge is filtered and shaped by existing experience and understandings, and the role of collaborative learning in shaping these understandings. The importance of focusing on organisational culture is also highlighted and the literature on organisational learning, in particular, offers insights into the cultural values that may need to be developed to facilitate knowledge sharing and individual and organisational learning.

The literature reviewed suggests that strategies for promoting research use should focus, in particular, on three of the mechanisms outlined in Chapter Five: interaction, social influence and facilitation. It also offers insights into the potential operation of these mechanisms. We have already mentioned, for example, the need to address organisational culture issues in facilitative strategies; in addition, the literature on learning emphasises the importance of designing collaborative training and development opportunities, which are experience-led and problem-focused. These activities are most likely to be effective when they encourage dialogue, reflection and local experimentation.

Interventions to promote research use are often employed in combination and a key question is what combinations work best. We consider this issue in more detail in Chapter Seven, but we note here that the three bodies of literature suggest that careful analysis should precede combined interventions. The knowledge management literature highlights that choices may need to be made between push and pull approaches rather than trying to blend them together. Similarly, the diffusion of innovations literature suggests that circumstances will dictate whether a centralised, decentralised or hybrid approach to diffusion is the most appropriate strategy when the aim is to promote the instrumental use of research-based innovations. The contingent factors to consider include the extent to which services are standardised and well established, the heterogeneity of the target audience (for example, their level of education) and the technical sophistication of the innovation.

A key implication of the literature on organisational learning and knowledge management is the need to pay particular attention to the ways in which organisations facilitate or hinder research use. As we have already noted in earlier chapters, strategies for promoting research use have tended to assume that the target audience is individual practitioners or individuals in policy roles. Organisations are assumed to play a subsidiary and intermediary role in constraining or facilitating individual learning and action. However, the literature reviewed here highlights the importance of developing a better understanding of collective sense-making, collective action, shared memory and supportive systems. It suggests that strategies to promote research use need to pay more attention to how research use can be encouraged at the team, organisational and interorganisational levels. The literature on learning networks and communities of practice can deepen our understanding of the processes of collective sense-making, but it is as yet far from clear as to how greater research use can be encouraged within these communities.

There are limitations to the literature reviewed in this chapter, which have implications for the design of research use strategies. We have already mentioned its somewhat limited focus on the instrumental use of knowledge. The knowledge management literature, in particular, is preoccupied with the instrumental use of existing knowledge. In addition, lack of knowledge use is seen as the core problem and hence the literature has far less to say about how to avoid the utilisation of outdated knowledge or the too rapid deployment of tentative new findings. This is despite the fact that it has long been recognised that:'The greatest difficulty lies not in persuading people to accept new ideas, but in persuading them to abandon old ones' (Maynard Keynes, cited in Bukowitz and Williams, 1999, p 321).

There is also a pro-innovation bias within the diffusion of innovations literature, which leads to the assumption that a good diffusion system is one that results in swift and widespread adoption of an innovation. This literature too has less to say about discontinuing ineffective practices (unlearning), or slowing the uptake of inappropriate technologies. In a similar vein, the individual and organisational learning literature offers some insights into the processes of 'unlearning', but this tends to be the least developed aspect of this literature.

Another limitation of the literature is the scant attention paid to issues of power and conflict. Although the phrase 'knowledge is power' has almost reached the status of a truism, little of the mainstream literature in any of the fields reviewed here devotes much attention to the implications of this. Within each of the areas, there are, however, critiques from a postmodern perspective, which highlight the ways in which knowledge and learning are intimately tied up with social and politicised systems of meaning.

The overall thrust of the literature is that learning, knowledge sharing and innovation diffusion are complex, socially contingent and context-dependent processes. They suggest that strategies to improve research use will need to be equally nuanced and sensitive to context. In the same way that strategies to improve learning, knowledge management and the diffusion of innovations need to be underpinned by a coherent view of the main approaches and their relevance to different situations, so strategies to improve research use need to be embedded in a coherent view of the main approaches to research use and their appropriateness. This is the focus of Chapters Seven and Eight.

SEVEN

Improving research use in practice contexts

As will be evident from much of the discussion to this point, we believe that research can play a positive role in informing the development of public services. Thus, encouraging and enabling research use in practice settings seems to us to be a laudable aim, especially if *use* is defined broadly to encompass the conceptual as well as the instrumental uses of research, and other forms of knowledge are respected and drawn upon in the process of encouraging that use. But how should we seek to encourage research use? In Chapter Five we discussed what we know about the effectiveness of the main mechanisms and interventions that have been employed to improve the use of research. We noted that many initiatives to increase research use draw on several mechanisms in combination. Chapter Six in turn explored what might be learned from a reconnection with the wider social science literature on learning, knowledge management and the diffusion of innovations. But the question remains of how best to develop a composite and coherent approach to improving research use that draws on this wide range of insights.

In this chapter we outline three broad ways of thinking about and developing research-informed practice (the following chapter, Chapter Eight, addresses how policy processes may be helped to be more evidence informed). These three ways of thinking – drawn inductively – reflect what seem to us to be the main differences in approach to improving research use in practice contexts, drawing especially on work carried out in the UK. These differences are often implicit rather than explicit and our aim is to surface and highlight their characteristics and implications by encapsulating them in three composite models of research-informed practice. We use the insights from previous chapters to tease out the key characteristics of each of these models, focusing in particular on their assumptions about what research use means and how it is best achieved. We also explore what each model implies for the design of coherent approaches to improving research use. After discussing the models we reflect on possible roles for government in encouraging research use in practice settings and how these roles link to our models. Before introducing the models, however, we discuss the findings of studies which have evaluated the effectiveness of initiatives that have sought to develop a multifaceted approach to improving research use, arguing that these initiatives need to be underpinned by a clearer articulation of the models of research-informed practice that are being invoked.

Multifaceted initiatives: combining different mechanisms to promote research use

Many initiatives aimed at promoting better use of research rely on a combination of the five main mechanisms outlined in Chapter Five (dissemination, interaction, social influence, facilitation, and incentives/reinforcement), rather than on one alone. For example, initiatives that have focused on developing *facilitative* research-based programmes and tools may also use *interaction* to ensure that these programmes and tools are developed collaboratively by researchers and practitioners. Indeed, combining facilitative and interactive mechanisms in this way may enhance the success of research-based programmes and tools when they are rolled out for wider implementation (Buntinx et al, 1993; Qureshi and Nicholas, 2001; Nicholas, 2003).

Reviews of studies in the healthcare field overwhelmingly conclude that multifaceted strategies to promote research use are more likely to be successful than stand-alone interventions (for example, Bero et al, 1998; *Effective Healthcare Bulletin*, 1999; Grimshaw et al, 2001; Gross and Pujat, 2001; Hulscher et al, 2002). Yet the additional effects reported with each extra intervention employed are often moderate. It is unclear whether combining strategies simply provides an additive effect or whether the elements within different combinations interact in particular and synergistic ways. There are also indications that some combinations may not be beneficial – for example, in relation to implementing guidelines, Grimshaw et al (2004) found no evidence that multifaceted strategies were necessarily more effective than single interventions. What we know about the research use process from earlier chapters would suggest that the different components of these multifaceted strategies are likely to interact in non-linear and surprising ways.

Case studies of large-scale interventions to implement research-based practice offer more mixed findings about the success of multifaceted approaches. The examples described in Boxes 7.1 and 7.2 begin to provide some insight into the ways in which such interventions might operate. Whereas systematic reviews (for example, those cited earlier) are generally confident about the effectiveness of multifaceted approaches to implementing evidence-based practice, these case studies are more circumspect. In general they support the need for a multifaceted approach but they also highlight the importance of tailoring approaches to specific circumstances.

Box 7.1: Case studies of multifaceted interventions to implement research-based practice in health care

The North Thames Purchaser-Led Implementation Projects Programme comprised 17 small-scale initiatives, each using different multifaceted approaches to support research-based changes in healthcare provision. Only three projects were able to demonstrate practice change after 18 months. However, most projects reported improvements in skills, knowledge, systems and services, and in the development of new networks and relationships. The evaluation of the programme argues that four main features supported the relative effectiveness of different projects:

- sufficient resources, in terms of time, money and appropriate skills;
- providing benefits of interest to front-line staff, to ensure motivation;
- involving all key stakeholders from the start of the project; and
- an interactive approach that linked research clearly to current practice.

The project evaluation also identifies the importance of context in understanding how and why particular mechanisms are successful in some contexts but not in others (Wye and McClenahan, 2000).

The PACE (Promoting Action on Clinical Effectiveness) programme sought to implement clinically effective practice in 16 local health services, with each site using a different multifaceted approach. Half of the projects achieved substantial levels of both learning and clinical change. A review of PACE identifies the key success factors as good project management, a strong evidence base, supportive opinion leaders and the integration of new activities within a committed organisation. Even where evidence was strong, however, successful use depended on local adaptation and ownership. Prior analysis of context, piloting approaches and developing clear communication strategies also enhanced the chances of success (Dopson et al, 2001; Locock et al, 2001).

Box 7.2: Case study of the implementation of a research-based drug treatment programme

Liddle et al (2002) describe a project to transfer a research-based drug treatment programme into community practice, which focuses on analysing and targeting the context for implementation. The project is based on a clear model of change and draws on mechanisms that specifically address barriers to implementation to encourage uptake of the programme. It is founded on a collaborative approach that partners researchers with treatment providers and specifically aims to avoid the perception that expert researchers become involved in programmes to impose external mandates on practice. Training and ongoing supervision of programme staff facilitate treatment implementation, which is underpinned by a social learning framework and a stage model of change. Initial findings from the project's evaluation suggest that staff view the programme positively, and demonstrate small but significant changes in practice.

Source: Adapted from Liddle et al (2002)

These case studies suggest that models for planning change can support the development of multifaceted interventions. For example, the PRECEDE-PROCEED framework (Box 7.3) aims to identify predisposing, enabling and reinforcing factors for change (Green and Kreuter, 1992). Predisposing factors provide the motivation for change, and interventions may seek to alter beliefs, attitudes and perceptions, for example through dissemination or social influence activities. Enabling factors allow change to be realised and facilitative interventions may target these. Finally, reinforcing factors encourage change and ensure that it is sustained, and incentives or feedback activities may serve to achieve this.

Box 7.3: PRECEDE-PROCEED framework

Green and Kreuter (1992) developed the PRECEDE-PROCEED model as a framework for planning health promotion activity. The framework consists of two elements or phases:

- an assessment phase, which considers the Predisposing, Reinforcing and Enabling Constructs in Educational/Ecological Diagnosis and Evaluation (PRECEDE);
- a development phase, which addresses the Policy, Regulatory and Organisational Constraints in Educational and Environmental Development (PROCEED).

Source: Adapted from Green and Kreuter (1992)

Understanding what mechanisms to combine and when to combine them is important, but while our knowledge about which mechanisms are most appropriate in which contexts, and how different mechanisms interact, is growing, it remains incomplete. General models for planning change, such as the PRECEDE-PROCEED framework, may be helpful in developing detailed research use strategies but a vital element is missing from our discussion thus far: what is the vision of research-informed practice that underpins any strategy aimed at promoting research use? For example, are conceptual as well as instrumental uses of research envisaged (Chapter Two)? To what extent do strategies assume that the process of research use is broadly linear and rational or are they based on a more interactive process model (Chapter Four)? Do strategies assume that individual policy makers and practitioners rather than teams, organisations and systems are the main users of research (Chapter Three)? It is to these issues that we now turn.

Ways of thinking about and developing research-informed practice

The design of multifaceted approaches to improving research use needs to be rooted in an understanding of the research use process and how this can be improved. In Chapter Four we discussed descriptive models of the research impact process; here we seek to capture how and in what ways these have been translated into initiatives for developing research-informed practice. Our starting point is an outline of three contrasting initiatives aimed at improving research use.

There have been many initiatives aimed at promoting the use of research within and across the fields of education, health care, social care and criminal justice services (see Chapter Five). The three examples drawn from the UK and outlined in Box 7.4 highlight some of the key ways in which these initiatives contrast with one another. In the first example, the Centre for Evidence-Based Social Services (CEBSS) sought to enable social workers and social services departments to make better use of research by improving the supply of research and enhancing users' capacity to understand research and incorporate it into their decision making. In the Probation Service example, the emphasis was on ensuring that evidence from systematic reviews of what works in supervising offenders was used to design and deliver both the offender programmes offered by local probation services and the broader offender management system within which these programmes are situated. The approach was highly centralised: the centre specified what was to be delivered and put control mechanisms in place to ensure that central plans were implemented. This example illustrates how research use in practice settings may largely be driven through policy action, and thus also serves to highlight that there may be no neat and easy distinction that can be drawn between practice and policy initiatives around evidence. In the final example – the School-Based Research Consortia – it was local autonomy and experimentation that was emphasised. This initiative was also as much about enabling teachers to conduct new research as it was about encouraging them to engage with the existing research literature.

Box 7.4: Three contrasting initiatives aimed at improving research use

Centre for Evidence-Based Social Services (CEBSS)

CEBSS was established in 1997 as a partnership between UK local authority social services departments, the Department of Health and the University of Exeter. The Centre was one of the early pioneers of evidence-based practice in social services, which it defined as 'the conscientious, explicit and judicious use of current best evidence in making decisions regarding the welfare of those in need of social services' (Sheldon, 1998, p 16). It sought to improve the supply of research evidence by conducting systematic reviews and overviews of evidence and by disseminating research findings to services. Practitioners (mainly social workers) were trained to access, appraise and apply research evidence to their practice. Managers were advised on how to encourage research use by ensuring that findings were discussed in team meetings and service reviews. CEBSS ceased operations in 2004 but a successor organisation has been established: research in practice for adults (www.ripfa.org.uk).

The Effective Practice Initiative in the Probation Service

In 1998 the UK government launched the Effective Practice Initiative, a bold plan to introduce systematic change in the Probation Service so that its practices are based on evidence of what works with offenders. A new research-based offender assessment tool was designed, piloted and rolled out to all probation services. Probation services were required to use this tool as a means of assessing the risks posed by offenders and their supervision needs. The output from the assessment shaped the supervision plan for each offender, including an assessment of which probation programmes, if any, the offender should attend. The central thrust of the

Effective Practice Initiative was that these programmes (which focus on issues such as drug and alcohol misuse and challenging offending behaviour) ought to be evidence-based. A central accreditation panel was set up to approve and accredit probation programmes, to ensure that they comply with 'what works' principles. To ensure fidelity in programme delivery, service delivery requirements were set out in the accreditation criteria and the audit of service delivery was based on these (Furniss and Nutley, 2000).

School-Based Research Consortia

From 1998 to 2001 the UK Teacher Training Agency and the Centre for British Teachers funded the establishment of four School-Based Research Consortia. Each consortium comprised a three-way collaboration between local primary or secondary schools, their local education authority/ies and higher education institutions. Their aim was to develop evidence-informed teaching and learning by enabling teachers to conduct their own research and to 'test out' research findings within a supportive collaboration of schools, universities and local education policy teams. Approaches varied among the four consortia involved but included 'linked pairs' of teachers and academics, individual school research coordinators, thinking lunches, action- and other research projects, and developing new teaching practices (Cordingley et al, 2002).

These three examples highlight at least *six factors* which seem to distinguish different approaches to improving research use in practice settings. While we explain these factors separately, we also note their somewhat overlapping nature and that they are strongly interlinked:

- *The emphasis placed on different types of knowledge.* Initiatives vary according to the extent to which they focus on particular types of knowledge, including the respective roles of research-based knowledge and practice wisdom, and the emphasis placed on 'know about, know what, know how, know who and know why' types of knowledge (see Chapter One). For example in the CEBSS and School Consortia examples it is anticipated that research-based knowledge will be blended with practice wisdom in developing practice, whereas in the Probation Service example, research-based knowledge is to the fore. 'What works' knowledge tends to be emphasised in all the initiatives, most strongly so in the Probation Service example.

- *The emphasis on instrumental uses of research.* Many initiatives to increase research use focus on the instrumental uses of research in changing practice. However, we know that research in general is more likely to have a conceptual or enlightenment impact. Initiatives such as CEBSS and the School Consortia seem to be more likely to facilitate these broader conceptual impacts than the more focused Probation Service example where instrumental use is prioritised.
- *The assumptions made about the importance of local context in appraising the relevance of research.* For example, an approach to improving research use may be firmly rooted in the assumed benefits of an accumulated, 'global' body of research evidence (the CEBSS and Probation Service examples) or place as much, and maybe even greater, emphasis on local, 'situated' knowledge (the School Consortia example).
- *The extent to which research production and research use are seen as separate activities.* Where they are seen as separate, this tends to result in research use being approached as a fairly linear process of accessing, appraising and applying research, which is reflected in both the CEBSS and Probation Service examples. In contrast, in the School Consortia initiative researchers and practitioners work together not only to access existing research but also to investigate its local application. They also jointly conduct new research. This has implications for what counts as knowledge and the assumptions made about generalisable versus locally situated knowledge.
- *The emphasis placed on local context in developing strategies for 'applying' research findings.* An initiative may pay only limited attention to local context issues in promoting widespread application of research findings (the Probation Service example) or view application issues as the domain of local decision makers who are able to take local contextual factors into account in their decision making (the CEBSS and School Consortia examples).
- *Who or what is seen as the main target for research use activities.* This can range from assuming that the individual practitioner is the main target (CEBSS), through focusing on organisations as the key to research use (Schools Consortia), to a predominant concern with the design of overall service systems (Probation Service).

As the examples in Box 7.4 illustrate, initiatives aimed at improving the use of research make different assumptions in relation to each of the above six factors. But are there particular combinations of assumptions that characterise the predominant approaches to improving research use? In a review of activities designed to promote research use in UK social care, together with colleagues we identified three broad ways of thinking about and developing research–informed practice (Walter et al, 2004b). These different approaches are encapsulated in three models:

- the *research-based practitioner model*, where research use is the responsibility of individual practitioners;
- the *embedded research model*, where research use is achieved by embedding research in the systems and processes of service delivery; thus it is the service managers and policy makers who play a key role;
- the *organisational excellence model*, where the key to successful research use lies in the development of appropriate structures, processes and cultures within local service delivery organisations.

These three approaches are summarised in Box 7.5 and elaborated in subsequent sections.

Box 7.5: Three models of research use

Research-based practitioner model

In this model:
- It is largely the role and responsibility of the individual practitioner to keep abreast of research and ensure that it is used to inform day-to-day practice.
- The use of research is most often seen as a linear process of accessing, appraising and applying research in largely instrumental ways.
- Practitioners usually have high levels of professional autonomy to change practice based on their interpretation of research findings.
- Professional education and training are seen as the key factors in enabling research use.
- Access provisions to knowledge resources are a common preoccupation.

Embedded research model

In this model:
- Research use is largely achieved by embedding research in the systems and processes of practice, by way of standards, policies, procedures and tools.
- Responsibility for ensuring research use lies primarily with policy makers (national, regional and local) and local service delivery managers.

- The use of research is largely seen as both a linear and an instrumental process: research is translated directly into planned practice change.
- Funding, performance management and regulatory regimes are used to encourage or coerce the use of research-based guidance and tools.

Organisational excellence model

In this model:
- The key to successful research use largely rests with local service delivery organisations: their leadership, management and organisational arrangements.
- Research use is supported by developing an organisational culture that is 'research-minded'.
- There will usually be significant local adaptation of research findings and ongoing learning within teams and local organisations.
- Partnerships with local universities and intermediary organisations may be used to facilitate both the creation and use of research knowledge.
- The nature of the research considered may be much wider than instrumental 'what works' findings.

The three models were initially developed to capture what was happening on the ground to promote research use in UK social care, but our cross-sector work and international experience suggests that they also resonate with much of what is happening to promote research use in the health care, education and criminal justice fields in many different countries and settings. Indeed the initiatives outlined in Box 7.4 broadly reflect the three models: CEBSS (the research-based practitioner model); Probation Service (the embedded model); School-Based Research Consortia (the organisational excellence model).

Next, we explore each of the models by considering further their underpinning assumptions, and the key activities associated with them. These activities are not value-free, but contain particular ideas about what research-informed practice means and how it is best achieved. Our models help surface these ideas. They also highlight the implications of adopting any one approach to promoting the use of research: for example, who is viewed as responsible for this activity, and where funds and actions will be focused. Throughout, we draw on the findings reported in Chapters Three and Five to highlight any specific barriers to the development of each of the models, and to note whether there is evidence to support their usefulness in achieving a greater degree of research use.

Of course the models that we present are *archetypes*. That is, they have been cast so as to accentuate differences from each other because we believe that this is useful in enabling us to tease out divergence in their underlying assumptions and preoccupations. On the ground, however, there will not always be clear delineation between specific implementations of the models, and one model may shade into another or borrow some of its key elements. Certainly, multiple variants and hybrids of the models may co-exist in any one setting, raising questions about coherence, interference, dissonance and synergy. We hope that drawing the models quite starkly as we have done is not seen as advocating any particular exemplification, but will instead help clarify thinking around the design of better approaches to research uptake strategies in practice settings.

The research-based practitioner model

The key feature of this model is that it is seen as the role and responsibility of the individual practitioner (for example, doctors, nurses, teachers and social workers) to seek out and keep abreast of the latest research, which then informs his or her day-to-day practice and decision making. Thus the model reflects the general assumption of individualised research use noted in Chapter Three. Practitioners identify best practice by integrating research knowledge with their own practitioner or 'craft' knowledge. Research knowledge is thus applied in combination with practitioner knowledge, a process whereby service users' preferences and views may also be taken into account.

The model assumes that staff have relatively high levels of autonomy in conducting their day-to-day practice. It is also underpinned by a fairly linear view of research use: existing research findings are accessed and appraised by practitioners, and then applied to the specific problem in hand. The opportunities for active dialogue with researchers are likely to be limited. However, as we noted in Chapter Four, Hargreaves (1998) has argued that the integration of research knowledge and craft knowledge occurs as practitioners 'tinker' with practice issues and problems, a process that contributes to the ongoing creation of knowledge itself. 'Tinkering' is likely to involve reflection and possibly local experimentation, activities that have been associated with effective learning processes (Chapter Six).

The type of research use envisaged by the model is predominantly instrumental; research is used to inform practitioners' day-to-day decisions about the services/care to be provided. However the very act of keeping abreast of research is likely to lead to a more general awareness and understanding of research – conceptual use. The type of research privileged in the model is knowledge about the nature of problems and the effectiveness of specific interventions. The focus is very much on the use of research findings rather than the 'process use' of research, where practitioner involvement in the conduct of research is as important as the findings themselves (see Chapter Two). However, critical appraisal skills training, an activity associated with the model, may have a more general 'process' effect on ways of thinking and behaving.

The assumptions and approach of the research-based practitioner model appear to have their origins in the concept of evidence-based medicine, which describes research-informed practice as:

> the conscientious, explicit and judicious use of current best evidence in making decisions about the care of individual patients.... It requires a bottom up approach that integrates the best external evidence with individual clinical expertise and patients' choice. (Sackett et al, 1996, p 71)

It has been argued by some that the evidence-based medicine approach is equally applicable in education (Hargreaves, 1997, 1998; Davies, 1999) and in social care (Macdonald, 2000; Sheldon and Chilvers, 2002). As we shall discuss, others are more sceptical about the transferability of the model (for example, Hammersley, 2001). Its practicality in a medical setting has also been questioned (for example, Dawson et al, 1998), sometimes quite aggressively (Miles et al, 2002; Holmes et al, 2006).

The activities and strategies associated with the research-based practitioner model tend to focus on both enabling practitioners to access good-quality research evidence and on developing their ability to critically appraise this evidence. Initiatives to improve research availability include the development of electronic databases, such as Social Care Online (www.scie-socialcareonline.org.uk), and the development of 'user-friendly' research findings aimed at practitioners, such as the Joseph Rowntree Foundation (JRF) *Findings* series (www.jrf.org.uk). Initial professional training is seen to play a key role in developing practitioners' understanding of research and this is reflected in the training requirements for doctors, teachers and social workers. Professional registration requirements also make individuals responsible for their ongoing professional development, including keeping up to date with research-based developments in their field. Organisations such as CEBSS (see Box 7.4) have provided specific training to develop practitioners' critical appraisal skills for assessing the relevance and quality of research for making decisions. There are also some (fairly heroic) step-by-step guides for practitioners intent on ensuring that research evidence is an integral part of their decision making (see, for example, Box 7.6). So overall, the research-based practitioner model emphasises the dissemination and facilitation mechanisms highlighted in Chapter Five.

Box 7.6: Five steps for integrating research evidence into practice

(1) Clearly identify the problem faced.
(2) Gather information from research studies about this problem.
(3) Ensure that you have adequate knowledge to read and critically analyse the research studies.
(4) Decide if a research article or review is relevant to the problem in which you are interested.
(5) Summarise the information so that it can be easily used in your practice.

Source: Adapted from Law (2000)

On the face of it, the research-based practitioner model fits well with notions of professional responsibility and thus may in theory be an appropriate model in situations where public service delivery involves a one-to-one relationship between the professional and the client. The doctor–client relationship has been seen as the epitome of this but even in this context there have been mixed reactions to the model. The medical profession largely drove the development of evidence-based medicine in its early stages, and there appears to have been widespread initial support for Sackett's ideas about what this entailed (Dopson et al, 2005). However, support seems to have ebbed over time, partly due to practicalities – 'nice in principle but difficult to do in practice' (a clinician quoted in Dawson et al, 1998 and cited in Dopson et al, 2005, p 39) – but also due to growing concerns about the negative effects on professional autonomy (Davies and Harrison, 2003; Dopson et al, 2005). Critics have also questioned whether evidence-based medicine is worth it, that is, whether it leads to better healthcare outcomes. Despite strong support for the principle from some quarters (for example, Chalmers, 2005), others have concluded that there is no evidence for the superior clinical effectiveness of evidence-based medicine (Miles et al, 2003). There is a suggestion that where there has been continued support for the idea of evidence-based practice this has been based on medical practitioners reinterpreting it as a need to draw on practice-based evidence and knowledge (Fairhurst and Huby, 1998).

Other professions tend to have fairly positive attitudes to the general idea of using research to inform practice but again the practicalities of the research-based practitioner model have been questioned. There is the question of whether it is practical to use research to inform decisions when practitioners make so many decisions in a single day – it has been suggested, for example, that a primary school teacher makes a thousand decisions a day (Jackson, 1971). In addition, there is the issue of whether practitioners have time to keep abreast of new and emerging research, or the time to search for findings relevant to key areas of their practice; there is also the issue of whether it is inefficient for lots of individual practitioners to be doing this. Some professionals also seem unconvinced that research use is an individual responsibility. For example, many studies report that social care staff tend to view the development of research-informed practice as a joint responsibility between individual staff and departments, rather than the responsibility of the practitioner alone (for example, Sheldon and Chilvers, 2000; Barratt, 2003; Hodson, 2003). We noted the importance of attitudes to research as a factor shaping its use in Chapter Three, and these attitudes seem to vary considerably. Some studies report pockets of a 'culture of antipathy' to research within service organisations that runs counter to the culture and attitudes required to underpin the research-based practitioner model (Tozer and Ray, 1999; Walter et al, 2004b).

In terms of the likely success of the activities associated with the research-based practitioner model – improving the supply of research findings and practitioners' ability to access, appraise and apply them – there are only limited grounds for optimism. Despite efforts to improve the availability of tailored research findings, studies continue to identify the lack of access to 'user-friendly' findings as a barrier to the implementation of research-based practice (see Chapter Two). Given the limited amount of time that many practitioners say they are able to devote to reading research (Chapter Three), it is doubtful whether improving the accessibility of research will have much impact on its use. Similarly, although many practitioners report the lack of expertise to interpret research (Chapter Three), training practitioners in critical appraisal skills may be of limited help. As we noted in Chapter Five, a review of interventions to teach critical appraisal skills to healthcare practitioners found that this approach was generally ineffective (Shannon and Norman, 1995). The effectiveness of the model is also likely to depend as much on practitioners 'unlearning' some customs and practices as on the acquisition of new knowledge (Rushmer and Davies, 2004). However, many of the current activities associated with the research-based practitioner model pay scant attention to this broad range of obstacles. Reflecting this, although its focus is on using research in group discussions rather than simply acting as independent practitioners, the study detailed in Box 7.7 provides some additional insight into the workings – and potential failings – of the research-based practitioner model.

Box 7.7: Improving services for the over-fifties

Research by Gabbay et al (2003) brought together two local multi-stakeholder groups and charged them with formulating policies to improve local services for the over-fifties. Individual members were expected to locate and bring relevant information to the group, including research findings. The groups' librarians also passed on the results of literature searches requested by the groups.

The study found that research use by both groups failed to match the linear process assumed by the research-based practitioner model. Instead, certain forms of knowledge became accepted currency, primarily knowledge based on professional and personal experience rather than research knowledge. Some existing relevant research was never accessed by the groups and on occasions robust research findings presented at meetings were devalued. Although members possessed both critical appraisal skills and tools with which to assess the quality of new information brought to the groups, these were rarely used. Research was re-presented and 'transformed' through individuals' experiences or agendas or through synthesis with other forms of knowledge such as experience. Overall, this study demonstrates that even with training and resources being made available for literature searches, people tend not to critically appraise research and often experience and power override research evidence.

Source: Adapted from Gabbay et al (2003)

In conclusion, and as we noted in Chapter Two, there only appear to be relatively isolated groups of practitioners who regularly seek out research and use it in their day-to-day work. This leads us to question the widespread appropriateness and applicability of the research-based practitioner model. It may be a relevant model for some individuals such as those with practice development roles, who would not only have the role of applying research to their own practice problems, but also in developing practice across groups of staff. Furthermore, the literature reviewed in Chapter Six suggests that activities to promote research use need to pay more attention to the ways in which organisations constrain practitioner behaviour than is reflected in the research-based practitioner model, and particularly to the role of organisational culture and the processes of collective sense-making.

The embedded research model

In the embedded research model, practitioners rarely engage directly with findings from research. Research enters practice by becoming embedded in service systems and processes, through mechanisms such as standards of care, inspection frameworks, national and local policies and procedures, intervention programmes and practice tools. Research knowledge enters practitioner knowledge indirectly through its translation into practice activities by those in national and/or local policy and service management roles. However, other forms of knowledge may also influence the guidance and practice tools that are produced, particularly the tacit and experiential knowledge of both expert practitioners and service users.

In this model, the key link is thus not directly between research and practice, but indirectly between research and policy/service management, and thence on to practice change. The responsibility for developing and ensuring research-informed practice thus lies with local and national policy makers and service delivery managers, who translate key messages from research into governance frameworks, guidance and practice tools. The underlying view of research use is again a fairly linear one, where existing research is accessed and used instrumentally in the design of processes and practices. Thus, the type of research use envisaged is overwhelmingly instrumental: getting research to have a direct impact on practice decisions and actions. Again the emphasis is on using research findings rather than the process use of research use, and the type of research privileged by the embedded model is again that relating to 'what works' bodies of knowledge. The embedded research model does not, however, require high levels of practice autonomy, and in fact may restrict this. To be effective, the model's approach depends on widespread adoption of research-informed guidance and tools. Adoption may be encouraged or demanded by, for example, performance measurement, audit, inspection and appraisal regimes.

The guidelines movement in health care to some extent reflects the embedded research model. The guidelines approach has been adopted by the Royal Colleges, government-sponsored bodies and many professional special interest groups. In the late 1990s the Labour government set up the National Institute for Clinical Excellence (NICE) to help formalise and accelerate the production of guidelines for practice. However, there are concerns about the extent to which many guidelines are truly evidence-based: a concern that is often difficult to judge because of the lack of transparency surrounding the production of many guidelines (Miles et al, 2003). As a means of embedding research in practice, guidelines may also be of limited effectiveness due to partial uptake and poor implementation. As we noted in Chapter Five, there is substantial evidence, primarily from the healthcare field, that guidance alone rarely changes practice and needs to be supported by additional activities such as training, which, to be fair, is usually recognised within an embedded research approach.

Despite such concerns, the production of guidelines and research-based practice tools, such as checklists and assessment frameworks, continues apace in many public service areas. In social care, the Social Care Institute for Excellence (SCIE) produces resource guides for practice. Research-based practice tools and protocols have also been developed in local contexts, for example the 'Ten Pitfalls' practice booklet and accompanying referral chart developed from Department of Health research on child protection (Cleaver et al, 1998). In criminal justice, the Home Office has developed over 20 toolkits in areas such as vehicle crime, domestic burglary, alcohol-related crime, and safer hospitals and schools. Each toolkit brings together information on the latest developments, research findings, and promising approaches to reducing specific crime and disorder problems. The toolkits include tools for identifying problems, developing responses and monitoring progress, and each highlights practical measures to make communities safer (see www.crimereduction.gov.uk/toolkits/index.htm).

In terms of the likely effectiveness of guidelines and practice tools, there is some evidence that the senior officials who tend to develop them have better access to research than practitioners (Barratt, 2003; and Chapter Three), and more support is available to this group for appraising and interpreting the research. Where research is embedded in policies and guidance, the barriers that practitioners face in accessing and understanding research are no longer relevant, although some individual policy makers may still face these barriers. The embedded research approach may also minimise problems created by negative attitudes to research, as practitioners need not necessarily be aware that policies and guidance are informed by research. There is some evidence that developing and implementing research-based guidelines and practice tools can be effective in changing practice and may also change practitioner knowledge and attitudes (see Chapter Five). The knowledge management literature (Chapter Six) suggests that the potential to 'bake' research knowledge into practice systems and tools will depend on the extent to which service delivery is already standardised and routinised: the greater the standardisation, the greater the potential for research-based practice tools. However, many such tools are designed to support practice, rather than determine it, with final decisions about what action to take in a particular case left to the individual practitioner. In this way, strategies for promoting research use may include elements of both the embedded research and research-based practitioner models.

We noted in Chapter Five that the ownership of the research by potential users, through processes of interaction and local adaptation, seems to be important in developing research-informed practice. However, ownership, interaction and local adaptation are all somewhat sidelined in the embedded research model. Practitioners do not necessarily engage directly with the research or its development into guidance and tools, although studies of initiatives to develop research-based practice tools suggest that practitioner engagement with research can occur at the development stage (see Box 7.8). Furthermore, the ways in which some tools are designed encourages some engagement with the research that underpins them (for example, the Home Office crime reduction toolkits referred to earlier), again an example of the embedded research model shading into the research-based practitioner model.

Box 7.8: Research-based checklists for looked-after children

Bullock et al (1998) report on the way practice-based checklists were developed and implemented for looked-after children. These checklists were developed from the Unit's 'going home' research. The checklists were introduced to nine local authority social services departments. They were initially developed through a consultation process with some of the potential checklist users, but most authorities took them 'blind', without being involved in their development. Implementation was supported by varying levels of training.

An evaluation of the implementation of the checklists found that they had been completed for half of the relevant cases in nine authorities, but there was much variation. Use of checklists also declined over time. In general, more intensive models of intervention gave higher completion rates, but there were exceptions. The majority of those who completed the checklist booklets found them useful, and felt they had increased knowledge of the issues around looked-after children.

Source: Bullock et al (1998)

Although research may become embedded in guidelines, intervention programmes and practice tools, it only becomes embedded in service delivery if these guidelines, programmes and tools are adopted. For the most part, adoption is simply encouraged but there are also examples where government has played a more coercive role. The Probation Service example (Box 7.4) is a prime example of this. In the education field as well, the centrally defined national curriculum has provided a vehicle for requiring adoption of certain research-based practices, for example the use of a 'phonics' approach to teaching reading and writing, although the research evidence in this case is seen as promising rather than conclusive (*The Economist*, 2006a, pp 36 and 41).

Overall the embedded research model tends to emphasise the facilitation and incentives/reinforcement mechanisms highlighted in Chapter Five. In doing so it addresses some of the shortcomings of the research-based practitioner model, particularly the latter's assumption that practitioners will have the time and inclination to engage with research, the skills to make sense of what they find and the autonomy to act upon any findings. There is some evidence to support the effectiveness of the embedded research model in achieving practice change but implementation of a centrally driven embedded research approach encounters at least two related problems: how to avoid a 'one-size-fits-all' approach and how to deal with practitioner resistance to more coercive forms of the model. It seems that successful research-based tools and programmes are often those that have been refined to fit local practice contexts (Quereshi and Nicholas, 2001) but paradoxically more coercive forms of the model often emphasise the need for implementation fidelity (see discussion in Chapter Two). The embedded research model may therefore be most effective when it is developed locally by service managers, although this raises questions about efficiency given the likely development of multiple guidelines. There may be circumstances when widespread roll-out of a particular research-based intervention programme or practice tool is justified on the basis of the strength of evidence about its effectiveness in a range of contexts (Crane, 1998).

The organisational excellence model

In the organisational excellence model, the key to developing research-informed practice lies not with individual practitioners or national policy makers, but with service delivery organisations: their leadership, management and organisation. This approach recognises that the actions of individual practitioners, even those who are professionally qualified, are shaped and constrained by local management and service structures, and by the policies, procedures and culture(s) of the organisation (Davies and Nutley, 2000; Davies et al, 2000a). Initiatives to promote research use within this model focus on changing the culture and context of the organisation, as embodied in the ways service delivery organisations are led and managed. As such they draw heavily on the lessons from Chapter Six.

The organisational excellence model focuses on the need to reflect local circumstances and priorities when learning from research, and it emphasises that this is best done at the organisational level. The organisation is not seen as merely a conduit for getting externally generated research findings to impact on practice, as might be seen in the embedded research model. Instead, organisational learning is foregrounded, through local experimentation, evaluation and practice development based on research. Research knowledge thus becomes integrated with other types of local knowledge including routine monitoring data, experiential knowledge and practitioners' tacit understandings. To facilitate this, partnerships are often forged with local universities and with other intermediary research organisations.

The view of research use underpinning the organisational excellence model is thus more interactive and iterative rather than strictly linear. The focus is on local adaptation of research findings and the approach is often collaborative, with joint production of knowledge between researchers and practitioners. Research knowledge becomes integrated with other knowledge sources in a much more dynamic and interactive process, through testing out research findings and shaping them to local contexts and experience. 'Use' of research is part of, not separate from, this broader process of knowledge creation.

While the focus, as in the other two models, is on using research findings, service organisations are not limited to considering 'what works' types of research knowledge. Although this may be a priority, they are also likely to be concerned with understanding the nature of local problems and why these have arisen. The process of testing out findings may involve local pilots and evaluations. Thus there is the potential for using the research process as a means of reshaping ways of thinking and acting. Research is also likely to be used conceptually in reshaping understandings and attitudes as well as more instrumentally in influencing decisions and behaviour. Practitioner interaction with researchers in research–practice collaborations and partnerships also mean that it is not only research findings that are used but also the tacit knowledge held by researchers themselves.

Some of the activities to facilitate research use associated with the organisational excellence model, such as better facilities to access research and the creation of new 'boundary-spanning' research-practice posts, also reflect the research-based practitioner model. However, whereas the research-based practitioner model is mainly about individuals and their needs, the organisational excellence model tries to develop collective structures that not only support individuals but also foster a greater degree of local interaction, debate and exchange as a means of fostering a research-minded culture.

Many of the collaborative initiatives aimed at promoting research use in education, particularly in the UK, reflect the organisational excellence model, and we have already outlined the School-Based Research Consortia initiative, which fits well with the model (Box 7.4). Initiatives such as this encourage a process of collaborative reflection, whereby practitioners stand back from their work and critically examine with others current and past practice in the light of broader bodies of knowledge, including research. Collaborative initiatives have wider aims than simply encouraging the uptake of specific pieces of research. Instead they seek to bring about broader and deeper changes in local culture, aiming to develop policy and practice environments that are both more reflexive and more receptive to research evidence. Such approaches recognise, therefore, not only that research uptake happens through dialogic processes but also that local 'absorptive capacity' for new information is key and can be nurtured (Cohen and Levinthal, 1990).

A further example of an initiative which reflects the organisational excellence model is provided in Box 7.9. This example illustrates a rather different approach to developing research-informed practice in the Probation Service than that represented by the Effective Practice Initiative (Box 7.4) which it pre-dated.

Box 7.9: Integrating research within programme development in the Probation Service

Harry et al (1997/98) describe the way in which the Research and Policy Unit (RPU) within Mid Glamorgan Probation Service worked in partnership with probation officers in the field in the early 1990s to develop, deliver and evaluate effective groupwork programmes for people being supervised by the Probation Service. Programme development took place within the structure of Programme Action Groups (PAGs), which were established for each specific area of programme activity, such as work with sex offenders, women offenders and violent and aggressive offenders. Each PAG involved staff from the RPU and at least one probation officer from each of the fieldwork teams. The PAGs were responsible for developing groupwork programmes drawing on the best knowledge about what works in community sentences. They were also central to the delivery and evaluation of these programmes. The evaluation programme was integrated with service delivery and drew on existing information systems and practitioners' and service users' own evaluations of the effectiveness of the programme delivery. The RPU's role was to facilitate and coordinate evaluative work so that it was integrated with practice rather than being seen as an added extra. The findings from the monitoring and evaluation activities were fed back via the PAGs into practice development and local policy formulation. The aim was to enable practitioners and managers to build upon successes, mistakes and lessons learned. The RPU also sought to contribute to more exploratory initiatives by providing overviews and informed critiques on key themes between and across programmes.

Overall the approach was credited with encouraging a 'culture of curiosity' within Mid Glamorgan Probation Service. In large measure, practitioner evaluation of programmes, facilitated via PAGs, became an ongoing and routine activity within the service, encouraging reflection and learning.

Source: Adapted from Harry et al (1997/98)

The organisational excellence model is a good reflection of the complexities of research use uncovered in earlier chapters. In addition, the evidence on strategies for promoting research use presented in Chapter Five offers support for developing research-informed practice in line with the organisational excellence model. It fits well with the widely reported view among practitioners that ensuring research feeds into service delivery processes is a joint responsibility between organisations and individuals. It also reflects many of the tenets of organisational learning outlined in Chapter Six. Evaluations of research–practice partnerships generally conclude that collaborative approaches have proved successful (Walter et al, 2003c), and a key element in their success seems to be the facilitation of personal contacts between researchers and research users. However, such partnerships are costly and time-consuming to both establish and maintain and they may also be prey to researcher dominance (Chapter Five). Working in partnership requires specific skills that are often new to those involved (Huberman, 1993; Cousins and Simons, 1996; Jaworski, 2000). Those participating in partnerships have often found it hard to balance the competing agendas of partnerships and their local organisations, and high levels of staff turnover have been seen to destabilise otherwise successful partnerships (Cordingley and Bell, undated; Cousins and Simons, 1996). Their development may be hindered by a 'blame culture' in service organisations (for example, see Barratt, 2003), as such a culture may inhibit the experimentation and innovation that underpins the organisational excellence model.

Collaboration between researchers and practitioners can be encouraged not just for research uptake purposes but also as part of research production processes. There is support for involving practitioners in research in a variety of ways – as advisors, co-investigators or even as active data collectors. Practitioners involved in this way are likely to be more receptive to the findings emerging from such research (see Chapter Five). Going further still, reviews have found that internally conducted and commissioned research is more likely to be seen as relevant by potential users (Nutley et al, 2003a; Walter et al, 2005). While such an approach may have merits in terms of building a local 'research culture', the cost of commissioning research locally may present a significant barrier (Sinclair and Jacobs, 1994) and may lead to an accumulation of small-scale and potentially parochial research studies that do not offer cumulative messages. Such worries should not detract from the main message that partnership and dialogue between researchers and practitioners, and a deeper engagement of practitioners with the practice of research, seem to be important elements of the organisational excellence model.

Overall the organisational excellence model emphasises the interaction and social influence mechanisms outlined in Chapter Five and it fits well with our conclusions to Chapters Four and Five, that interactive models are our best guide to understanding the processes of research use and that interactive approaches currently seem to show most promise in improving the use of research. However, the model is unlikely to be a panacea. As we have noted, it often involves collaborations or partnerships with local universities or other intermediary research organisations and these are costly and time-consuming and difficult to maintain over time. Where they have been established they tend to be small-scale and of limited reach. 'Scaling up' such activity so that it encompasses the majority of service delivery organisations across a range of sectors is likely to prove challenging, if not impractical. It may also be an inappropriate approach to pursue in all circumstances, an issue to which we now turn.

Hybrids and archetypes

The three models outlined are useful because they help clarify the different ways in which research-informed practice is being approached, and the assumptions and implications that underlie different approaches. However, the picture on the ground is inevitably less straightforward than these archetypes might imply. The models are not mutually exclusive; there is some blurring at the boundaries and initiatives and recommendations may combine the ideas of more than one model. Furthermore, the models were derived from a review of the social care field and although they seem to reflect much of what is happening in other sectors as well, specific reviews of those sectors may identify additional or alternative models.

It is not clear whether approaches based on a combination of all three models will provide synergies, or whether there are tensions and contradictions between them that may work against this. An analysis of the assumptions underpinning the models suggests that there are likely to be tensions between:

- the assumption of professional autonomy which underpins the research-based practitioner model, and the constraints placed on individual practitioners which may result from the embedded research model;
- an approach that emphasises a rather linear view of research use (the research-based practitioner and embedded research models) and a collaborative interactive approach to the creation and use of research knowledge (the organisational excellence model);
- an approach that views the role of evidence as largely immutable (the embedded research model) and one that views evidence as pliable and context dependent (the organisational excellence model).

These tensions may be felt most acutely at the practice level. However, they are also likely to permeate into the dilemmas faced by regulatory organisations when designing audit and inspection systems, and affect how training organisations develop training strategies and learning opportunities.

It may be that different models are best suited to different circumstances. For example, different models might be relevant:

- depending on whether staff have professional qualifications;
- at different stages of a research, development and implementation cycle;
- for different research questions/findings;
- in different service areas;
- in different local contexts;
- for different aspirations for the types of research use, for example conceptual versus instrumental use.

In relation to the first of these issues, it might seem that the research-based practitioner approach is best suited to professionally qualified staff and the embedded research model to non-professionally qualified staff. However, the research-based practitioner model not only seems inappropriate for non-professionally qualified staff, but it also seems to be rejected by many professionally qualified staff as well. Insofar as it provides a relevant model, it may need to be applied more selectively. An adapted version of the model may be a more relevant model for those involved in service design (at national and local levels) than for every practitioner. Or, at the practice level, it may need to be embedded in more supportive contexts and cultures, so that it edges closer to the organisational excellence model. The embedded research model may be suited to both professionally qualified and non-professionally qualified staff in certain circumstances, such as where there is strong evidence for a particular practice or where practice tools can be tailored to local context, but such circumstances may turn out to be rather limited in extent given the difficulties surrounding the interpretation of evidence that have been alluded to throughout this book.

Certain models may be better suited to different stages of a research, development and implementation cycle (see Box 7.10) but there is insufficient evidence to support the idea that models should be separated and labelled as either development or implementation models. The relationship between, for example, the embedded research model and organisational excellence model is likely to be more iterative than that.

Box 7.10: Carer assessment and review

Nicholas (2003) describes a project that used findings from initial research with service users, carers, practitioners and managers within two local authority social services departments to implement an outcomes approach to carer assessment and review. Planning for the project and briefing and training events were undertaken collaboratively and included service users. Fourteen staff in one local authority piloted the assessment forms.

On evaluation, practitioners said they found the assessment forms useful in supporting practice and in helping raise awareness and understanding of relevant issues. They also reported improvements in practice, which were supported by written records. Carers made a number of positive comments about the new assessment process but also identified some room for improvement.

Although this project broadly represents an example of an 'organisational excellence' approach to developing research-informed practice, the assessment forms it developed reflect a more 'embedded research' approach, in which individual practitioners using the tools need not engage with their underpinning research base.

Source: Adapted from Nicholas (2003)

On the face of it, different models of research use would appear to be relevant for different research questions/findings. Some research questions and projects, such as those that address the effectiveness of various policing practices, translate more readily into practice lessons. In all three models there are ways that such research can be used. Other research questions and findings, such as those that focus on understanding the source and nature of client problems, may not lend themselves to being used in such an instrumental way. In this case, research use relates more generally to reshaping understandings. This can be accommodated within the research-based practitioner and organisational excellence models, but it may be more difficult for the embedded research model to address the more conceptual use of such research.

Finally, although examples of all three models are found in each of the four service areas reviewed (health care, education, social care and criminal justice services), at least in the UK there seems to be a tendency for different combinations of models to predominate in each area. In criminal justice the dominant approach seems to reflect the embedded model. In education many initiatives reflect the organisational excellence model, sometimes in combination with the research-based practitioner model. In social care, the research-based practitioner model is often the explicit model of choice but activity on the ground is also underpinned by a combination of the organisational excellence and embedded models. In UK health care there are clear examples of all three models. Each model seems to reflect the dominant approach in health care at different points in time: emphasis was first placed on the research-based practitioner model (evidence-based medicine); then on the embedded model (with the rise of the guidelines movement and the establishment of National Service Frameworks); and more recently the focus is on the organisational excellence model (with, for example, the development of healthcare collaboratives – see Chapter 6, Box 6.16).

The role of government in promoting research use in practice contexts

We have already highlighted some of the ways in which government can play a role in promoting research use, particularly through the promotion of the embedded research model. In this section we discuss this role in more detail by focusing on the actions of the UK government. Of course, in drawing wider lessons from the UK, one needs to be mindful of two defining features within the UK context: the unitary government structure; and the central role of government in funding public services and setting their overall policy direction. Both of these have seen significant changes over the past few years, with recent devolutionary arrangements in particular giving more control over the funding and direction of local services to the assemblies for Wales and Northern Ireland and the Scottish Parliament. These changes have introduced significant new complexity and have allowed for some distinctive policy flavours and/or service configurations to emerge in each of the four constituent parts of the UK. Nonetheless, there is much 'borrowing' of policy initiatives from across the UK and a degree of commonality of approach remains.

Government initiatives in the UK have at various times served to support and promote each of the three models previously described, and we now exemplify some of these supporting activities. We also discuss the coherence of the government's actions, and the relationship of these actions to the wider public service reform agenda.

The government has directly promoted and indirectly supported the research-based practitioner model. In particular it has sought to improve the supply of research, both by encouraging more practice-oriented research, and by funding or establishing bodies to assemble, disseminate and communicate research findings to practitioners (for example by establishing SCIE for social care and NICE for health care). It has also sought to influence practitioners' demand for research by emphasising the importance of evidence-based practice. It has worked with those bodies that set occupational standards and regulate the workforce (for example the General Teaching Council for England) to promote research use as standard practice.

Alongside these actions the government has also played a more directive role in support of the embedded research model. In this situation, central government has played a lead role in distilling research evidence, particularly in relation to 'what works'. It has then acted to roll out its findings into practice contexts via the setting of service standards (such as the National Service Frameworks in health care) and the regulation and inspection of services to ensure that they achieve the expected standards of service delivery. The Effective Practice Initiative in the Probation Service, outlined at the beginning of this chapter, is a good example of the directive role played by government. In other situations it has acted to support the embedded model without being quite so directive. For example, it has supported the development of guidelines and research-based tools that have advisory rather than required status.

Finally the government has played a broadly enabling role in support of the organisational excellence model, sometimes supporting activities directly and sometimes indirectly through the activities of various arm's-length agencies. Broadly, government has sought to incentivise collaborative working, and has funded a range of networks, partnerships and collaboratives, particularly in health care and education (see, for example, the initiatives outlined in Box 6.16). Although these collaborative initiatives have not been exclusively focused on improving the use of research, this has usually been one of their major aims. Government has also sought to develop the capability of public service leaders and the capacity of service delivery organisations through its support of leadership development programmes and broader training and organisational development initiatives. The use of evidence, and the ability to shape a learning culture, have often been prominent themes in such development initiatives.

As these examples indicate, government action has had multiple strands involving both directing and enabling research use in practice contexts. In order to understand such diversity of approach, it is useful to examine these actions in the wider context of the government's public service reform agenda. Public service reform in the UK has been characterised as combining 'pressure from government (top-down performance management); pressure from citizens (choice-and-voice); competitive provision; and measures to build the capability and capacity of civil and public servants' (Prime Minister's Strategy Unit, 2006, p 5 – see Figure 7.1). The relative emphasis placed on top-down performance management, on the one hand, and on capability and capacity building, on the other, appears to be particularly important in understanding the role of government in encouraging research use. The former suggests a directive role while the latter is more likely to be associated with an enabling one.

Although the four elements of public service reform are meant to be complementary rather than alternatives, there are tensions between them and the government has to date placed most emphasis on top-down performance management. Thus it is not surprising that the way the government has worked with others to promote research use has often been characterised as predominantly centrally directed and top down, that is, in line with the embedded research model. For example, the overall character of its initiatives in health care has been described as essentially top down and formalised:

> UK research policy has sought to increase the number of patients enrolled in randomised controlled trials (RCTs); new synthesising institutions (such as the National Institute for Clinical Excellence) have been set up to distil the knowledge base and make recommendations as to whether new treatments are clinically and cost effective and UK national service frameworks have facilitated nationally-consistent sets of guidelines. (Dopson, 2006, p 85)

While central direction may be a tempting response to the lack of research uptake, there are concerns about its effectiveness in the face of front-line resistance (Dopson and Fitzgerald, 2005; Dopson, 2006). There are also doubts about the very idea of central direction when this involves rolling out a standardised programme or intervention. Indeed, the most sensible approach in the face of complex social issues may be 'piecemeal engineering' because of the problems of addressing complex, multidimensional problems by simply scaling up interventions that have been shown to be effective in just one or two specific contexts (Albaek, 1995; Parsons, 2002, 2004). The best overall approach may be to promote a collection of micro-solutions tailored to local circumstances (Gorman, 2005). This emphasises the need for more,

Figure 7.1: The UK government's approach to public service reform

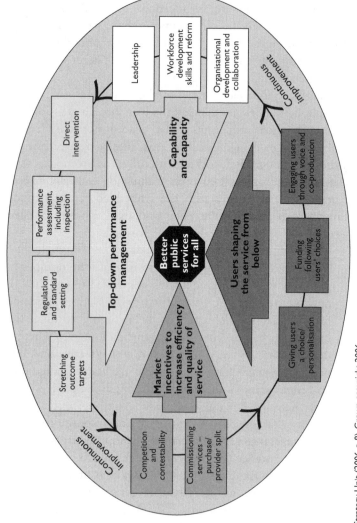

Source: Prime Minister's Strategy Unit (2006, p 8). Crown copyright 2006.

not less, local autonomy to enable services to adapt ideas from elsewhere and then develop their own innovations – a shift from the embedded research model towards one based on organisational excellence.

More recently the government has stated that it intends to rebalance its approach to public service reform by focusing more on outcomes and less on detailed top-down performance management. On the face of it, its stated intention to set performance targets as outcomes that are to be achieved, leaving professionals free to select the most appropriate means of delivering those outcomes, suggests a shift away from the embedded research model to the research-based practitioner and/or the organisational excellence models. However, other aspects of the public service reform agenda may disable rather than enable the development of the latter models. For example, in relation to the organisational excellence model, it is not only top-down directives and performance assessment that can stifle innovation and local experimentation: increased competition (which is often used as an alternative to top-down control) may discourage collaboration and information sharing.

Developing a coherent approach to promoting research use is not straightforward. At times it seems that too much hope has been invested in the research-based practitioner model as evidenced by the extent to which research supply has been emphasised. At other times, central direction and the embedded research model seem to have been overemphasised (see Box 7.11 for an example of this in relation to the funding of social programmes).

Box 7.11: The funding of social programmes in the UK

The UK government has used its funding of social programmes both as a means of generating new evidence and as a way of getting practice to engage with research. As we discussed in Chapter Five, central government funding of social programmes (such as the Crime Reduction Programme and Sure Start) has often been made available through a competitive bidding process. The intention has been that this bidding process would encourage practitioners to engage with research due to government statements that bids underpinned by an explicit and robust research base would be favoured when funding decisions were made. However, the theory has not translated well into practice and evaluations of several social programmes have found that many successful bids are not well supported by research (Coote et al, 2004; Maguire, 2004), despite prior action by government to review and distil the evidence base (for example, Goldblatt and Lewis, 1998). The government response to such a finding in the initial stages of the Crime Reduction Programme was mainly to develop more detailed central specification of the types of projects and bids that would secure programme funding (Homel et al, 2004; Nutley and Homel, 2006).

It is clear that no single approach to improving research use is likely to be suited to all circumstances. Just as the government's model of public service reform needs to be carefully tailored to the characteristics of different services, so does the relative emphasis placed upon the research-based practitioner, embedded research and organisational excellence models. Given the tendency for government action to emphasise central direction and the embedded research model there is a question about whether it is best placed to take on the role of promoting research use or whether this might better be left to others such as professional bodies and service provider associations. Certainly the local autonomy implied by the research-based practitioner and organisational excellence models suggests that at most the government should play an enabling role in relation to these models, particularly focused on addressing barriers to their operation.

Finally, although we have focused on the way in which government influences the context for service providers we should also note that it influences the context for researchers. Traditional measures of academic performance may work against researchers becoming involved in more practice-oriented research, and can tend to penalise their participation in dissemination activities beyond publication of peer-reviewed journal articles. We discuss this further in the next chapter.

Concluding remarks

Multifaceted interventions that combine several different mechanisms have been a mainstay of efforts to increase the use of research evidence in practice settings. However, 'multifaceted' has too often equated with 'scattergun', in combined approaches that have lacked coherence or any clear understanding of the mechanisms by which change is intended to be brought about. There is a need therefore for more carefully assembled packages, underpinned by a coherent view of the research use process and proposed mechanisms of change, designed in a way that is contingent on the types of evidence of predominant interest and the local contexts of use.

The three models or archetypes presented here have been used to tease out the set of assumptions that may underpin different approaches to increasing research use in practice settings. Because they were derived inductively, they form descriptive categories rather than prescriptions for action. No doubt, with further study, additional models or more clearly articulated and delineated hybrids may be identified, elaborated and applied. We believe that clarity over models such as these can help us not only in devising more appropriate research uptake strategies, but also in driving more focused research and evaluation in this area in the future.

None of the models offers any general solution; each has its own set of assumptions and difficulties. The research-based practitioner model has attracted significant critical debate in many areas and has persistent implementation issues, yet often it appears to underpin thinking around the evidence-based policy and practice agenda. The embedded research model can be effective in bringing about evidence-based change, but does tend to favour unproblematic instrumental research findings over wider considerations of research use. In turn, while the organisational excellence model is much broader and more adaptable in terms of the types of research that can get incorporated, and is certainly more in tune with many of the ideas developed in earlier chapters (interactivity, situated knowledge, organisational focus, learning through action), it too poses significant implementation issues. Culture change of the type envisaged in this model is far from easy (some would go further), and the sort of 'scaling up' required from demonstration projects to large-scale adoption is daunting indeed. In practice, a comprehensive approach to research use in practitioner settings may involve aspects of all these models, for example, specialist research-based practitioners being used as change agents in an overall organisational excellence approach, with embedded research where this is feasible and negotiable. The framework for evidence-based policing developed by Bullock et al (2006) is a possible example of how the strands of our three models might be blended to inform improvements in policing (Box 7.12). The exact nature of such balanced packages – and how the challenges of tensions, resourcing and scaling issues are to be addressed – is something that will play out differently in each of the public service areas, and government action to support and promote research use needs to recognise this.

Box 7.12: A framework for evidence-based problem-oriented policing

Problem-oriented policing aspires to identify families of similar issues or incidents that require the attention of police and their partners. Evidence plays an important role in problem-oriented policing. It is used to identify the problems arising from these incidents, to analyse them, to select responses and to assess the effects of these responses. The full implementation of problem-oriented policing principles is, however, relatively rare (Bullock et al, 2006).

In developing evidence-based policing, problem-oriented policing needs to sit alongside the more usual activities of problem solving and routine practice. In the light of this, Bullock et al (2006) present a framework suggesting how this might be achieved. This envisages differing kinds of activity at different levels, involving different agencies and individuals – summarised in the following figure:

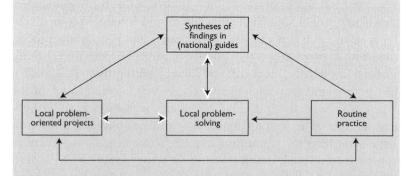

An important 'higher level' activity within this framework is the syntheses of research and evaluation findings in problem-oriented guides for police (such as the Home Office crime reduction toolkits referred to earlier in the chapter). These should inform specific local problem-oriented projects (whose activities resonate with our organisational excellence model), more general problem solving (which in part reflects the activities of our research-based practitioner model) and routine practice (through embedding guidelines within local protocols as per our embedded research model). In principle, at the local level, problem-oriented policing projects should feed into (and feed on) more general problem-solving activities. In addition, these projects should also inform (and draw knowledge from) routine practice.

At present the traffic between the activities reflected in the boxes in the figure is described as 'largely a matter of luck' (Bullock et al, 2006, p 182). However, the authors argue that there is scope for improvements in the linkages and balance between these activities.

Source: Adapted from Bullock et al (2006), ch 7

Chapter Six and the present chapter have focused our attention on research use predominantly in practitioner settings. While there are significant parallels at times between policy and practitioner concerns – and we believe there may in fact be some significant 'read across' from these practice-focused chapters to policy settings – we now turn our attention more directly to policy arenas. The next chapter considers what strategies and interventions can be applied to increase research use there.

EIGHT

Improving research use in policy contexts

In Chapter Seven we discussed the role played by government in promoting research use in practice settings. We now consider its own use of research in developing and implementing policy. In doing so, we aim to tease out the lessons from previous chapters about improving research use in government settings. We focus largely on national policy making, although we comment on the relevance of our analysis for regional and local policy settings towards the end of the chapter.

As we noted in Chapter Five, good empirical evidence about what works to improve research use in policy contexts is relatively thin on the ground, so this chapter not only draws on the documented and evaluated studies of research use summarised in Chapter Five, but also seeks to capture experiential knowledge about what has been tried and what seems to be effective. Since the mid 1990s we have been involved in a range of seminars, meetings and advisory groups centred on the core issue of improving research use; these have revealed a wealth of experiential knowledge on which we can draw. We know from these discussions that there has been a good deal of activity aimed at encouraging and increasing research use in policy making and in policy implementation, often driven by the twin aims of improving the availability of research and developing more evidence-based policy processes (see earlier discussion in Chapter One).

Similar to the situation in practice contexts (Chapter Seven), many of the initiatives to increase research use in policy settings draw on combinations of the mechanisms highlighted in Chapter Five (dissemination, interaction, social influence, facilitation and incentives/reinforcement). In order to understand the rationale for these combinations we need to surface the assumptions and frameworks that underpin them. We do this by highlighting first the roles envisaged for research and, within these broad roles, the frameworks that shape research enhancement activities. In discussing these frameworks we aim to capture the extent to which the various descriptive research–policy models outlined in Chapter Four have informed or supported prescriptions for developing research-informed policy.

In terms of the three roles for research outlined in Chapter One –

consensus supporting, contention rousing and paradigm challenging (see Box 1.1) – discussion of the research–policy relationship is often underpinned by an implicit assumption that it is the consensus-based use of research that needs to be improved. Here researchers work within the existing paradigm around the main issues of concern, aiming to consider how these should be addressed. In doing so, they provide policy makers with knowledge about how best to improve public service delivery and service outcomes. Thus, attention is focused on improving the instrumental uses of research (to inform policy directions and policy actions), although due acknowledgement is sometimes made of the broader and longer-term conceptual impacts of research on policy (see Chapter Two). In such a consensus-based view, an under-use of research is generally presumed, and there is also concern that when research is used, it is sometimes used as political ammunition, which tends to be construed as a form of misuse (see Chapter Two).

In the UK, a consensus-based role for research has often dominated the development of initiatives to enhance the use of research in policy making. In this chapter, we start by examining the ways in which such initiatives have typically used a 'supply-and-demand' framework to structure activities, focusing on how to improve research supply and how to increase policy demand for that research. Here, thinking about research use improvement activities implicitly draws on a market-based model of the research–policy relationship. We thus first describe and critique the initiatives associated with this framing of the issues, which assumes that there are two main communities to be considered – research producers and policy consumers of research – and that research use can be improved by facilitating the flow of knowledge between these two camps. There are clear overlaps between this framing of the issues and the producer-push and user-pull models and strategies outlined in Chapters Four and Five, which we draw upon to discuss the merits of the supply-and-demand approach to improving research use. We structure our discussion by considering first supply-side issues, then demand-side issues, before discussing the interplay between supply and demand, and noting the political implications of government taking the lead role in managing this process. Along the way we observe that UK initiatives to improve research use have largely adopted a somewhat bounded and conservative approach based on encouraging researchers and policy makers to do a little bit better, and only rarely have they been more radical in nature by seeking to establish fundamentally new relationships between research and policy.

We then discuss strategies for improving research use that draw on broader models of the policy process. As discussed in Chapter Four, more pluralistic perspectives on the policy process highlight the role of wider policy networks and policy communities in shaping how research and policy connect. Within such perspectives, interest groups provide a key route for research to enter the policy process and this opens up the possibility for more contentious and paradigm-challenging roles for research. It also moves the focus away from treating the research–policy relationship as solely a matter for the executive arm of government. In discussing this, we note the importance of scrutiny activities as one important way of bringing research evidence to the fore by supporting evidence-based challenges to policy.

Our discussion focuses on research use improvement activities within the UK policy arena. As such, while drawing broader lessons about these activities, it also demonstrates some of the ways in which such initiatives are necessarily shaped by the broader cultural and constitutional context in which national policy making is played out. For example, as we discuss later, the 'modernising government' and evidence-based policy and practice agendas (introduced in Chapter One) have provided the underlying framework for many of the UK initiatives to better connect research and policy. In the final section of this chapter, we explore this important issue of national context in considering what is possible and desirable when seeking to enhance the use of research in policy contexts. In particular, we discuss the potential significance of national differences in size; the machinery of government; the existing 'knowledge purveying infrastructure'; and the orientation of the media.

Research supply-side initiatives

As already noted, recent UK initiatives to enhance the research–policy relationship have often been framed in terms of 'supply and demand'. An emphasis on supply-side issues locates the 'problem' of research use in the lack of an appropriate flow of research into the policy process. It tends to presuppose a relatively unproblematic view of the nature of research findings – that research will provide objective, value-free facts – and an assumption that if the research is good enough, it will be used. Initiatives to address the supply of research have sought to build research capacity and have also targeted the way in which research is commissioned by, and communicated to, those in policy roles.

There has been significant government investment in the social research infrastructure of the UK since the mid 1990s, much of which has been focused on higher education institutions. For example, the government via the Economic and Social Research Council (ESRC) has ploughed significant funds into developing social sciences research methods and the capabilities of social scientists, particularly to address the perceived lack of expertise in quantitative research methods. The ESRC has also sought to fund the development of multidisciplinary centres of expertise in areas such as understanding social inequalities in health and developing knowledge about the social implications of new technologies. In Scotland, the Scottish Higher Education Funding Council (now the Scottish Funding Council) has worked with the Scottish Executive to address research capacity problems. A good example of this is the funding of the Scottish Centre for Criminal Justice Research, a cross-institution, multidisciplinary centre aimed at addressing the lack of capacity for criminal justice research in Scotland. Unsurprisingly, much of this investment has been welcomed by researchers, although there are concerns about potential threats to the independence of research and researchers, particularly when the emphasis on capacity building is coupled with changes to the way in which research is commissioned (Commission on the Social Sciences, 2003) – for example, more practitioner-led research can be felt by researchers to be constraining of both the types of problems that they are encouraged to investigate and the methods that are seen as acceptable for these enquiries.

The rationale underpinning a greater focus on research commissioning is that research use is hampered by a lack of good applied research that addresses key policy questions. For example, a review of school research in the UK by Hillage et al (1998) found that the field was dominated by small-scale, *ad hoc* studies, often diverse in approach, which did not contribute to a cumulative body of knowledge. The research agenda, they argued, seemed to be producer-driven rather than led by policy makers' or practitioners' needs. In response to such findings, attention has been paid to strategies for commissioning research and evaluation studies in order to ensure that they are robust, user-relevant and timely (see Box 8.1). This has not only affected the way in which government departments commission research and evaluation studies but has also had an impact on the approach of the research funding councils. For example, the ESRC now devotes much of its project funding to research programmes, which are designed to build research in areas where important current or future gaps in knowledge have been identified, rather than to response-mode funding, where researchers tend to set the agenda. Some of these research programmes, such as the ESRC's Teaching and Learning Research Programme, are a direct response to government concerns about the state of research in a particular area and specific additional funding has been received by the ESRC to focus on these areas.

Box 8.1: Revised strategies for commissioning applied research

Applied health services research programmes in both the UK (Service Delivery and Organisation [SDO] Programme; Health Technology Assessment [HTA] Programme) and Canada (Canadian Health Services Research Foundation [CHSRF]) have invested considerable effort in developing sophisticated prioritisation systems for the research that they then seek to commission. For example, the English HTA Programme uses four separate groups, each with a distinctive role, to identify priority technologies for assessment. Potential research users generate ideas; university researchers prepare briefing papers and background data; expert panels draw up initial priority lists; and, finally, multi-stakeholder groups apply priority-setting criteria in an interactive process of scoring and debate to finalise a ranked list. Building on this experience, the SDO Programme and the CHSRF have run extensive 'listening exercises' aimed at soliciting input from potential research users in the belief that this will lead to better-targeted work, of more direct relevance, and therefore more likely to meet potential research users' needs.

Source: Adapted from Lomas et al (2003)

Although the process of research funding has changed in the UK since the mid 1990s, just how significant an impact this has had on the shape and quality of the research produced is still uncertain. Social sciences research still tends to be a cottage industry with funding still mostly made available in relatively small packets (Commission on the Social Sciences, 2003). This may be changing but old habits seem to die hard. For example, a more recent review of social research commissioned by the Scottish Executive found a predominance of small *ad hoc* studies (cited by SHEFC/USS, 2005). Furthermore, while there may be general support for increased funding for social research, there are concerns that the associated emphasis on commissioning strategically focused, applied research threatens the independent status of university researchers and their ability to 'speak truth to power' (more of which later).

A further set of initiatives has sought to improve the quality of the research and evaluation studies commissioned by government departments. These have resulted in a series of Cabinet Office reports, for example: the *Adding it up* overview of analysis in government (Cabinet Office, 2000); *The Magenta book*'s guidance on policy evaluation and analysis (Cabinet Office, 2003a); guidelines on assessing qualitative research (Spencer et al, 2003); and the role and process of pilots in policy making (Cabinet Office, 2003b). The *Adding it up* report provided the foundation on which the others were built and it included the general advice that government departments should submit their internal research and analysis to external peer review in order to improve its robustness. Again we have little evidence about the effectiveness of such initiatives, although on the whole policy makers are more likely to use research that they perceive to be of high quality (see Chapter Three).

Emphasis has also been placed on making the evidence base of existing research and evaluative studies more accessible. Online databases of studies have been developed around a wide range of policy and practice issues, such as the social care online database encountered in Chapter Seven (www.scie-socialcareonline.org.uk). The UK government has also sought to improve the way in which it manages its own knowledge resources, including the accessibility of its large and accumulating stock of research and evaluation studies. There have been a range of knowledge management initiatives and recommendations, such as the 'knowledge pools' advocated by the former Cabinet Office Centre for Management and Policy Studies and the recommendation that a central electronic repository of pilot project reports should be set up to facilitate easy reference to past successes and failures (Cabinet Office, 2003b). Such initiatives appear to have had only limited success to date, which should come as little surprise given what we know from the knowledge management literature about the limitations of codification strategies based on the creation of online information resources (see Chapter Six).

Beyond the nature, quality and accessibility of individual research projects and programmes, supply-side approaches to improving research use in the UK have also sought to address the way in which a range of research is synthesised for policy users. The international Cochrane and Campbell collaborations (see Chapter One) have invested considerable energy in promoting and improving the methods of systematic review. The rationale for this is that policy makers need to consider where the balance of evidence lies on a particular issue, such as the effectiveness of screening technologies in health care, or the impacts of rehabilitation programmes for young offenders. It is known that the results of single studies can be misleading, and there is a limit to the extent to which policy makers can be expected to develop their own overviews of the evidence on a particular issue. Furthermore, idiosyncratic research reviews may be as misleading as single studies (Sheldon, 2005). Systematic review methodologies therefore aim to address these issues by ensuring that search strategies are comprehensive, fully documented and replicable, and that study selection and synthesis methods are robust and justifiable (see Box 8.2). A central preoccupation of supply-side initiatives is thus the development of these rigorous methods of research synthesis and communication.

Box 8.2: Key features of systematic reviews

Systematic reviews seek to identify all existing research studies relevant to a given evaluation issue, assess these for methodological quality and produce a synthesis based on the studies selected as relevant and robust. A distinctive feature of systematic reviews is that they are carried out to a set of pre-agreed standards. The main standards are as follows:

(1) Focusing on answering a specific question(s).
(2) Using protocols to guide the review process.
(3) Seeking to identify as much of the relevant research as possible.
(4) Appraising the quality of the research included in the review.
(5) Synthesising the research findings in the studies included.
(6) Updating in order to remain relevant.

Source: Adapted from Boaz et al (2002)

In the UK there has been a significant increase in the level of systematic review activity in recent years, not only in health care, where the approach has seen greatest attention, but also in other social policy areas. For example, the Evidence for Policy and Practice Information and Co-ordinating Centre (EPPI-Centre) has been established to support the conduct of rigorous reviews of social interventions, particularly in health care and education (http://eppi.ioe.ac.uk). Many see such work as a breakthrough in moving towards a robust, cumulative and synthesised knowledge base that can better inform policy and practice. However, there is little evidence to suggest, particularly outside of health care, that systematic review findings are used more than the findings of other forms of review activity or indeed the findings of single studies. It seems that the consumers of policy research have often not found the outputs of systematic reviews sufficiently relevant or useful (Lavis et al, 2005; Sheldon, 2005). Within the constraints of a supply-and-demand view of research use, this is often ascribed to the disappointing nature of the findings of many systematic reviews. Too often, it seems, expensive reviews conclude that there are very few robust studies relevant to the issue under consideration and that it is not possible to draw firm conclusions of the kind that policy makers demand (Young et al, 2002; and see Chapter Three).

There are hopes that this is a temporary problem that will improve as the number of robust primary research studies increases. Systematic review methodologies are also developing to enable synthesis of a broader range of study findings, so that they can address a wider range of policy and practice questions (Mays et al, 2005). For example, realist approaches to review activity hold out the hope of producing syntheses of research which directly address the key concerns of those in policy roles: not just whether a study found an intervention to have a certain effect but also why and how this might vary between settings (Pawson et al, 2005). Interviews with policy makers suggest that they would benefit from research reviews that provided further information relevant for their decision making, for example the context and factors that affect a review's local applicability and information about benefits, harms/risks and the costs of interventions (Lavis et al, 2005).

Finally, in addition to capacity building, research commissioning and systematic review activity, supply-side approaches to improving research use have focused on research communication activities, particularly the way in which research findings are presented and translated for policy audiences. Much of the activity here has concentrated on identifying the ways in which researchers can improve how they communicate (disseminate) their findings in policy contexts. Good practice guidelines abound (see Box 8.3 for one example), and these are supported to some extent by the evidence presented in Chapter Five, where we noted that the provision of targeted materials can raise awareness of research findings, and that seminars and workshops, which enable the discussion of findings, can encourage more direct use of research. Despite the strong focus on supply-side initiatives for improving the research–policy relationship, an issue that has not really been tackled is that of incentives for researchers to carry out such dissemination activities. As the Commission on the Social Sciences (2003, p 90) noted, researchers must be given inducements to engage in the 'sometimes fraught and time-consuming business of communication'. In fact, in the UK academic system there are few

---

incentives for academics to spend time on wider dissemination and communication activities.

Box 8.3: Improving dissemination: key recommendations

For research commissioners:
- Time research to deliver solutions at the right time to specific questions facing practitioners and policy makers.
- Ensure relevance to current policy agenda.
- Allocate dedicated dissemination and development resources within resource funding.
- Include a clear dissemination strategy at the outset.
- Involve professional researchers in the commissioning process.
- Involve service users in the research process.
- Commission research reviews to synthesise and evaluate research.

For researchers:
- Provide accessible summaries of research.
- Keep the research report brief and concise.
- Publish in journals or publications that are user-friendly.
- Use language and styles of presentation that engage interest.
- Target material to the needs of the audience.
- Extract the policy and practice implications of research.
- Tailor dissemination events to the target audience and evaluate them.
- Use a combination of dissemination methods.
- Use the media.
- Be proactive and contact relevant policy and delivery agencies.
- Understand the external factors likely to affect the uptake of research.

Source: Adapted from JRF *Findings* (2000)

Within the UK, therefore, there has been a heavy focus on initiatives to tackle 'supply-side' issues in the research–policy relationship. On the whole these seek to address those barriers to research use that relate to the nature of the research itself (see Chapter Three), by enhancing the relevance, availability, credibility and user-friendliness of research that is produced for policy consumption. Such initiatives may thereby increase the chances that such research gets seen, and even acted upon, by policy makers, but there is as yet little robust evaluation work to confirm this. However, supply-side approaches tend to rely on dissemination mechanisms, which assume a one-way flow of research into the policy community, and a relatively passive role for policy makers in the research use process. The rational, linear, 'producer-push' model that underpins these kinds of approach has been subject to sustained critique because it rarely reflects the way in which research actually gets used in policy contexts (discussed in detail in Chapter Four). Overall then, supply-side initiatives seem to have had only limited impact to date, something not unexpected given our understanding of the research–policy relationship (Chapter Four) and our analysis of knowledge-push strategies (Chapters Five and Six).

Such supply-side initiatives are, however, rarely implemented in isolation. In the UK, they have been coupled with a range of complementary activities aimed at the demand side of the equation, and it is to these issues that we now turn.

Research demand-side initiatives

As we noted in Chapter One, the demand for research evidence by policy makers has waxed and waned since the 1960s. In the UK, the call for more evidence-based policy processes in the late 1990s stimulated some of the research supply-side activities we have just outlined but in addition it focused particular attention on demand-side issues, perhaps in recognition that merely providing good research is not enough to ensure that policy makers will use it. Here the emphasis has been on reforming policy processes in order to inculcate more evidence-informed deliberations. Such reforms have gone under the banner of 'modernised' or 'better' policy making (Cabinet Office, 1999; Bullock et al, 2001). Government reports have outlined a number of initiatives and recommendations for increasing the demand for evidence, including: requiring evidence-based spending bids; making a commitment to publish the rationale and evidence for policy decisions; and training policy staff in evidence use (see Box 8.4). The Treasury-led Comprehensive Spending Review process in 1998 to some extent took on board the first of these recommendations and the 2000 Freedom of Information Act has been a spur to the second. A government agency that has taken the second recommendation to heart is the Food Standards Agency and it provides a good example of how open access to information can interact positively with evidence use (see Box 8.5). The Cabinet Office, through the Civil Service College (now the National School of Government), has acted on the third recommendation, about training staff in evidence use. Finally, the Cabinet Office has also taken the lead in calling for 'more and better use of pilots to test the impacts of policies before national roll-out' (Cabinet Office, 2000, p 6).

Box 8.4: Initiatives to increase the demand for evidence in the policy process

Such initiatives:

- require departmental spending bids to provide a supporting evidence base;
- require the publication of the evidence base for policy decisions;
- train staff in evidence use – thus improving their attitudes to evidence and their capacity to use it;
- encourage a greater use of evaluated pilots in developing and implementing policy.

Source: Cabinet Office (1999, 2000) and Bullock et al (2001)

Box 8.5: The Food Standards Agency

The UK Food Standards Agency (FSA) is explicit in publishing the evidence and rationale for its decisions. The Agency emerged in the aftermath of the BSE crisis, which was a key driver for its transparent approach (Phillips Report, 2000). The Agency aims to base its policies on 'the best evidence available' and draws on both in-house research and surveys, and external expertise, for example through its own network of scientific advisory committees. Guided by core values of openness and accessibility, the FSA makes available records of all its decisions and the evidence and interpretations on which these are based. Disclosure of information is the norm and all advice, information and research is published without political influence. The Agency also consults widely with its stakeholders, including consumers, and aims to make sure that all groups are able to understand how the Agency has used different sources of evidence in developing and implementing its decisions.

Source: Adapted from www.food.gov.uk

Whether such initiatives in reforming policy processes have had the desired effect is debatable. Although a UK government review – *Better policy making* (Bullock et al, 2001) – provides 130 examples of good practice from a diverse range of departments, initiatives and policy areas, these are not necessarily representative or evaluated. Instead the examples aim to illustrate interesting and innovative approaches to modernising policy making, such as holding research seminars for ministers; the use of external experts to advise on the development of new policy; using modelling and forecasting techniques; drawing on evidence from formal and informal stakeholder consultations and 'citizens' workshops'; creating policy advisory and steering groups involving researchers; and building in evaluations when new policies are implemented (Bullock et al, 2001). Such examples begin to show what might be possible but cannot really be seen as firm evidence of any sustained ramping-up of research use in policy making.

The call for more piloting of policies deserves specific attention. The *Trying it out* review of government pilots found that there has been a sharp growth in the number and scale of British pilots since 1997 (Cabinet Office, 2003b) although this practice is still less widespread and less large-scale than in the US. The review provides case study examples of pilots that have been conducted in the 'spirit of experimentation' to inform whether and how a policy should be rolled out. The actual influence of these pilots, however, is difficult to assess. A study of welfare policy trials in the US concluded that their main influence was on operational issues rather than on policy *per se* (Greenberg et al, 2003). In the UK, the *Trying it out* review noted that too often policy pilots had not been allowed to run their course and produce their findings before decisions on policy roll-outs were made, suggesting that here, too, pilots are more likely to feed into operational decisions about policy implementation rather than strategic choices about policy direction:

> Ministers and governments are usually reluctant to delay the implementation of a policy just so that (as they sometimes see it) the relatively ponderous course of rigorous social research may run its course....Their implicit position is effectively that evidence-based policy does not necessitate prior evidence when subsequent confirmation will do. (Cabinet Office, 2003b, p 27)

However, even when policy decisions seem to be made in advance of pilots running their course (so much so, that 'evaluation pilots' become 'pathfinder projects'), evaluation studies have still influenced policy direction and have even brought about U-turns in government policy (Box 8.6).

Box 8.6: The Connexions Card

The Connexions service, established by the UK Department for Education and Skills, aims to support young people through their transition to adulthood by providing independent guidance and advice on a range of key issues. In 2001 the Connexions Card was introduced across the UK, a 'loyalty card' system that provided young people who attended further education with access to discounted leisure facilities, equipment and books and to an information website. The card's principal aims were to encourage more young people to remain in learning, to reduce some of the financial barriers to learning, and to improve young people's career and life choices. Local demonstration projects, intended to be exploratory and experimental, were used to test out the idea of the Connexions Card as early as 1999, and were soon transformed into four extended 'pathfinder projects'. National roll-out of the card was based on interim rather than final evaluation results from these projects. Mixed but promising findings were reported, alongside a good deal of practical learning to help support wider implementation. A national evaluation of the scheme was subsequently commissioned and contributed to a shift in expectations of what the project might provide. However, the final evaluation report, published in 2005 (Rodger and Cowen, 2005), demonstrated that the card had generally failed to meet its key aims. A policy decision to abandon the card was made in 2006. This is an example where the policy choice to roll out the card had pretty much been made in advance of the pilots, although interim evidence from the pilots had some impact on the roll-out scheme. However, the eventual decision to abandon the card in 2006 was influenced by the negative findings of the national evaluation report.

Source: CRG (2001); NAO (2004); Rodger and Cowen (2005)

The aim of the policy reforms and initiatives discussed thus far has been to change the culture of policy making, including policy makers' attitudes to and understanding of evidence. By and large, for demand-side initiatives, this has meant introducing greater instrumental rationality into policy processes. While government documents note that the policy process does not consist of a neat set of stages, which are negotiated solely on the basis of rational argument, they nevertheless recommend a somewhat rational-linear model as something to aspire to (Reid, 2003; see also Chapter Three). Indeed, there is some support for the potential effectiveness of this approach from studies that suggest that research use is encouraged by a climate of rationality (Weiss, 1999; Nutley et al, 2002).

A good example of where this appears to have materialised is in the introduction of arrangements to institutionalise and systemise health technology assessments (HTAs). The broad aim of HTAs is to provide policy makers and clinicians with reliable and robust evidence on the clinical and cost-effectiveness of particular drugs, medical appliances or therapies (Sackett et al, 1996). In the UK, NICE was established by the government in 1999 to decide whether selected health technologies should be made available throughout the National Health Service in England and Wales. Since its establishment, NICE has assessed a wide range of health technologies and its decisions about many of these have received wide-spread attention – for example the media interest in the debate surrounding the availability of Herceptin (a drug for use in early stage breast cancer). Given the political sensitivity of many such decisions it would hardly be surprising if the decisions of NICE were shaped more by lobbying than by evidence and rational argument. However, a study of decision making in NICE found that while the appraisal process was not immune to lobbying, arguments based on quantitatively oriented, experimentally derived data held sway (Milewa and Barry, 2005). These data also took precedence over more subjective, experientially based perspectives. It is important to bear in mind, however, that this may in part reflect the fact that clinical rather than social evidence is to the fore in such decision-making processes. In other contexts – such as social care or education – where the nature of evidence is more contested, and there is less agreement about basing decisions primarily on empirical data, more 'rational' modes of argument may be harder to sustain.

In sum then, there has been a significant level of activity in the UK devoted to improving research use in policy settings by addressing both research supply and policy-based demand. Such initiatives have focused on coupling dissemination activities on the supply side with more facilitative and incentive-based approaches to enhance the demand for research (see Chapter Five). Very few of the resulting initiatives have been subject to independent evaluation, however, so we are not able to comment authoritatively on their relative success or failure. We have noted that the impact of the supply-side activities does seem to have been somewhat limited to date, but demand-side initiatives may have gone some way to engendering a more evidence-aware culture in policy making.

Assumptions embedded in supply and demand perspectives

It is likely that the particular 'bundling' of mechanisms for promoting policy uses of research through 'supply-and-demand' initiatives may be limited in impact because of the rational underpinnings intrinsic to the approach. 'Supply-and-demand' initiatives tend to be based on introducing greater instrumental rationality into policy, through reformed structures/processes and exhortation to key actors to strengthen rational deliberation. Yet both research use and the policy process itself rarely reflect this ideal. There are many factors that shape both policy processes and the uptake of research (see Chapter Three). For example, a detailed analysis of the design and implementation of 'evidence-based' policy programmes, such as the Crime Reduction Programme, demonstrates the many ways in which plans based on instrumental rationality are quickly disrupted by political imperatives, bureaucratic inconsistencies and limited capacity (for example, see Homel et al, 2004).

There may be some value in delineating a rational model of research use as an ideal to aspire to, as the examples of success detailed earlier testify (for example, HTAs and NICE). However, Weiss (1979) notes that the knowledge-driven and problem-solving models of research use – those that underpin supply-and-demand initiatives – are actually rather rare on the ground. An instrumental, problem-solving use of research seems most likely to occur where research findings are non-controversial, require only limited policy/service change and will be implemented within a supportive environment: in other words, when they do not significantly alter the current state of affairs (Weiss, 1998). There are thus likely to be a relatively limited range of circumstances in which supply-and-demand initiatives might be fully effective. Further, when these do occur, policy making is likely to be an incremental and inherently conservative process, hence the role that research can play may be quite restricted (Chapter Four).

Finally, the rationalist framing underpinning supply-and-demand initiatives assumes a particular view of evidence from research, a view of evidence as relatively uncontested, objective and value free. Research is seen to provide relatively straightforward facts that policy makers can use to weigh up a particular course of action. This suggests that supply-side and demand-side initiatives can best support a consensus-based role for research in the policy process, in which goals are already agreed and evidence is used to decide on how best to achieve them. These approaches are likely to be less supportive of more conceptual forms of research use; and offer no real possibilities for research to challenge or reframe the policy agenda itself.

That said, another set of initiatives – those that focus on improving the links between researchers and policy makers – have begun to establish new kinds of relationship between research and the policy process. In turn these may offer new roles for research within the policy arena. Such linking initiatives are discussed in the next section.

Between supply and demand

The language of supply and demand is suggestive of a market for research. If there were a well-functioning market in this area there would be little need to talk about initiatives to improve the linkages between supply and demand, as they would come together in a marketplace where the discipline of competition would ensure a balanced interaction between supply and demand. However, the research–policy 'market' exhibits many imperfections and seems prone to market failure. Indeed, the analogy of a market may not be the best way of reflecting the diversity of channels by which research flows into (and out of) the policy world (see Chapter Three). It is not surprising then that some research uptake initiatives in policy settings have sought to improve the linkages between supply and demand using network- rather than market-based approaches. This is partly fuelled by an alternative framing of the research use 'problem': that this does not relate primarily to supply or demand issues but to the lack of connection between the two. This assumption is not confined to the UK: 'it is not the modest supply of social science knowledge that blocks its influence in the United States, although it is modest; ... it is instead the location of our experts and intellectuals' (Wilensky, 1997, p 1254). In response, two forms of activity seem to be prevalent: activities to integrate researchers within the policy process; and initiatives to establish intermediary organisations and institutions to act as brokers between research supply and policy-user demand.

Integrating researchers into the policy process

Many of the initiatives aimed at improving the connection between supply and demand have focused on the location of researchers and their involvement in the policy process – be they internal (government) researchers or external researchers based in universities and other research organisations. Taking internal researchers first, in the UK there has been a good deal of discussion in recent years about the capacity and location of government researchers and their engagement with policy. In general, these researchers are viewed as key enablers of improved research use through their role in commissioning and managing research and evaluation projects, and in ensuring that the findings from these are summarised for and communicated to policy staff within government. In effect, social researchers are seen as internal brokers or, as one report phrased it, 'system-aware brokercrats' (Clark and Kelly, 2005, p 32). In recognition of their wider role, the number of social researchers employed by the UK government has more than doubled since 1997 and new social research units have been established in departments that had no previous history of social research (Government Social Research, 2002). A professional lead for these researchers has also been established through the appointment of a Chief Government Social Researcher.

Significant emphasis has been placed on ensuring that government social researchers are involved in the policy process from the earliest phases of problem identification right through to policy implementation and evaluation (see Box 8.7). One way of achieving this is to co-locate these researchers alongside their policy colleagues, but there is as yet only limited evidence about the effectiveness of such initiatives (Nutley et al, 2002; see also Chapter Five). Informal discussions with insiders do, however, suggest that government researchers are now more likely to be consulted earlier in the policy process than hitherto, especially when there is a clear decision to review and develop policy in a specific area. However, practice varies across departments and policy areas (Bullock et al, 2001) and it is not clear that early involvement necessarily leads to sustained interaction.

Box 8.7: Integration of government analysts into the policy process

The development of Scotland's Lifelong Learning Strategy (Scottish Executive, 2003) provides an example of the close integration of government analysts at all stages of the policy-making process. The Strategy was developed by the Enterprise and Lifelong Learning Department within the Scottish Executive and took a collegiate approach, rather than being directed by an overseeing steering committee. While the process overall was led by the policy division, analysts were a clear part of the team. Policy and analytic colleagues (including economists and social researchers) were brought together at an early stage in developing the Strategy in order to secure a wide range of perspectives. Over the course of policy development, policy makers, researchers and other stakeholders met to share information and expertise around key issues. The process was characterised by mutual adjustment through joint working across different disciplines, as those involved refined and tailored their ideas in response to each other's timescales, perspectives and needs. Early involvement of research staff in the process and this readiness to compromise were both felt to have helped build the mutual understanding and trust which contributed to the Strategy's success.

Source: Personal communication from Scottish Executive

Other initiatives have recognised the complexity of the research use process in terms of its diverse stakeholders and its interplay with other forms of evidence (see Chapter Four). In these kinds of framings, promoting better use of research is not as simple as bringing together two homogeneous groups, 'policy makers' on the one hand and 'researchers' on the other, as supply-and-demand initiatives often imply. In recent years departmental analytical service teams have been created within the UK government, incorporating economists, social researchers and statisticians (see, for example, Box 8.8). Such initiatives acknowledge the diversity of knowledge producers and providers for the policy process. They also address the issue of whether social research needs to be integrated with other forms of evidence for policy in order to have impact. However, again we are not aware of any systematic evidence on whether the creation of these teams has had an effect on the uptake and impact of social research.

Box 8.8: The Drugs and Alcohol Research Unit (DARU): an analytic service team in the UK Home Office

In 2002 the Drugs and Alcohol Research Unit in the UK government's Home Office deliberately drew together social researchers, economists and statisticians in examining the evidence around drug and alcohol misuse. Its staff aimed to integrate findings from research with other sources of data and information when discussing and transferring evidence to policy makers. They thus worked with a broad definition of what constitutes 'research', which included formal evaluation evidence, monitoring data, routine collection of statistics and findings from surveys. By contrast, in the UK Department of Health, those analysts dealing with the same drug misuse issues worked in separate divisions according to whether they were research managers, statisticians or economists.

Source: Adapted from Nutley et al (2002)

Turning to external researchers, there has been a range of initiatives targeted on the involvement of these researchers in the policy process. In general terms this has involved secondments of academic researchers into government to work in policy advisory roles and they have also become involved in the policy process through their *ad hoc* participation in advisory and consultation groups and in certain areas through their membership of Policy Action Teams (PATs) (see Box 8.9). In terms of specific research projects, the way in which research is commissioned from external researchers has in some circumstances changed from a client–contractor relationship to one where external researchers and their policy clients work more as partners, with interaction encouraged throughout the research project.

Evaluations of the effectiveness of these approaches for involving external researchers are thin on the ground, but as we discussed in Chapter Five, there is some evidence from both policy and practice settings about the benefits of developing sustained interaction between researchers and policy makers (Walter et al, 2003a). Furthermore, the government audit of PATs found them to be effective, although the extent to which this was due to the inclusion of researchers/experts is not clear (see Box 8.9). In general, however, the incentives for researchers to engage in such detailed policy work are not high, and there may be particular tensions that arise when they do. For example, those that give advice at the initial stage of developing a research agenda may then find themselves ineligible to contract for the subsequent research because of their prior involvement. There are also concerns about a potential loss of researcher independence (see later).

Box 8.9: Policy Action Teams (PATs)

In England the Social Exclusion Unit set up 18 PATs as part of its national strategy for neighbourhood renewal (SEU, 1998). The aim of each of the PATs was to bring a range of stakeholder knowledge and expertise together in developing policy, which was seen as an important departure from the usual model of government policy making (SEU and CMPS, 2002). Each PAT focused on a particular aspect of social exclusion, for example jobs (PAT1); neighbourhood management (PAT4); young people (PAT12); and financial services (PAT14). Each was chaired by a senior civil servant and had a lead department and champion minister. Membership consisted of between 20 and 46 people, incorporating a 'creative mix of practitioners, academics, researchers and policy makers' (SEU and CMPS, 2002, p 16). However, a research briefing for the Scottish Parliament notes that their membership has been criticised as being arbitrary (SPICE, 1999). In terms of impact, a PAT audit in 2000 found that 85% of the PATs' recommendations had been accepted by government (SEU, 2001). An evaluation of the PATs from the perspective of those involved describes the whole process of policy analysis and formation as evidence-based 'both through the extensive research gathering that preceded the establishment of the PATs and the continued research that was conducted by each individual PAT, including their fact-finding within local areas' (SEU and CMPS, 2002, p 9).

Developing intermediary broker organisations

The second major approach to bridging supply and demand involves initiatives to establish intermediary organisations and individuals to act as brokers between research and policy communities. In Chapter Three we commented that in policy settings, knowledge brokers – whether individuals or agencies – are an important route through which research reaches those who might use it. We have already mentioned the role played by internal government researchers as knowledge brokers. In addition there are a wide range of broker agencies within the UK, including specific government agencies, charitable foundations, think tanks and professional organisations. The role of non-governmental organisations will be explored a little later, but of particular note are the agencies established by government to undertake a three-way brokering role between research, policy and practice – agencies such as NICE, SCIE and the National Treatment Agency (NTA). We have discussed the role played by NICE and SCIE earlier in this and previous chapters, and in Box 8.10 we summarise the activities of the NTA. These agencies appear to have played an important brokering role between research, practice and meso-level policy decisions – that is, decisions about the provision of certain interventions/treatments by local service delivery organisations. The influence of organisations such as the NTA on broader questions of policy direction has been more limited (Nutley et al, 2002). This mainly reflects the way in which they were established to respond to the delivery agenda and provide guidance for service providers. In addition to national agencies, central government departments and local service providers have also contributed funds to the establishment of more local knowledge broker agencies and networks on specific areas of public service provision such as child protection and youth justice. However, as Feldman et al (2001) noted in relation to long-term care in the US, these brokering activities tend to be highly fragmented and subject to erratic funding, and similar problems are also reported in the UK (Commission on the Social Sciences, 2003).

Box 8.10 The National Treatment Agency (NTA)

The National Treatment Agency (NTA), established in 2001, is an example of a quasi-policy body that specialises in a particular policy domain, in this case drug misuse and its treatment, and feeds research into the policy process. It has the status of a special health authority but is a joint initiative between the UK Home Office and the Department of Health. The NTA oversees the delivery of drug treatment programmes in England and also aims to enhance the quality and availability of such programmes. To this end, its main role involves reviewing the evidence base relating to the effective treatment of drug misuse. The NTA produces summaries and briefings based on these reviews, which in turn feed into standards on commissioning and delivering treatment and also into training and development programmes.

Source: Adapted from Nutley et al (2002)

Linkage activities such as those we have just described, albeit officially sanctioned, suggest a somewhat different framing of the research use process, which is now envisaged as potentially more iterative and dynamic than conventional linear-rational models allow. They begin to acknowledge the complexity of the research–policy relationship, particularly its multi-streamed nature, and focus on interactions between policy makers and researchers as key to getting research used (Chapter Four). As such, they recognise that research evidence may not arrive as uncomplicated 'facts' to be weighed up in making policy decisions, but may be translated and reconstructed in the process of its use through ongoing dialogue with research producers (Chapter Four). Initiatives such as the PATs reflect this growing recognition that interaction between policy and research is important and helpful, although it is less clear how this may play out on a day-to-day level.

These kinds of interaction begin to open up the policy process to the influence of research. Whereas supply- and demand-side initiatives focus on making incremental changes on either side of the equation in order to enhance the use of research in policy, more interactive initiatives establish new, dynamic relationships between the two. Such relationships may in turn better support a more conceptual and perhaps even contentious role for research in the policy process than conventional supply-and-demand initiatives. The extent to which the influence of research can indeed move beyond a consensus-based role will, however, likely depend on the degree of independence researchers can secure and maintain in relation to the policy process. This is an issue to which we give more explicit attention in the next section.

On the whole, however, the government-driven initiatives discussed so far – on supply, demand, and the linkages between these – have generally envisaged a consensus-based role for research, where researchers work within rather than challenge existing ways of thinking about public service delivery. They have also focused on what happens within the executive arm of government, or at least on those activities sanctioned and supported by government. We will shortly broaden our view to consider initiatives that potentially challenge as well as support the *status quo*, and are aimed at stimulating research use in wider public debates about social policy, encompassing a broader range of actors than just researchers and policy makers. Before doing so, however, we will first elaborate on what are seen as the dangers of too cosy a relationship between research supply and policy demand.

Managing supply and demand, and the potential politicisation of research

The increased emphasis on managing the supply and use of applied research has raised serious questions about the politicisation of research (Walker, 2000). There has long been an argument about the need to ensure the separation of research and policy in order to protect the independence of research and its role in holding governments to account (for example, Campbell, 1969; Rein, 1976). The evidence-based policy and practice movement (Chapter One) is seen as a threat to this independence. For example, Hope (2004) has argued that as political life becomes 'scientised' through systematic evidence playing a greater role in shaping and governing social life, so the structures of authority in both policy and research settings lose their autonomy. Not only is science seen as a legitimate guide to politics but politics also has a say in science – what research is endorsed and supported, and even how this research is conducted: 'The value of science ceases to be derived from its methodology alone and is now also to be derived from its promises of applicability and utility' (Hope, 2004, p 291).

The desirability of developing more focused and applied research strategies has also been questioned due to the uncertainties about whether applied research is more impactful than basic research. Wilensky argues that we should resist the temptation to oversell the practical value of applied research:

The idea that applied research in the social sciences (as opposed to basic research) is more relevant to the public agenda and public policy is a mistake; it tends to divert money, talent, and attention away from the job of developing cumulative knowledge about culture, social structure, and politics ... good basic research deals with persistent problems of the human condition and is therefore public policy research in the broadest sense. (Wilensky, 1997, p 1242)

In the UK this question has arisen specifically in relation to the role of the ESRC, which is the lead funder of research on social and economic issues. In recent years some disagreement has surfaced over the purpose of the ESRC in relation to the balance of its funding between applied, policy-relevant research for government and research initiated by academics themselves. The Commission on the Social Sciences (2003) has noted that the ESRC is under pressure both from the UK government – to be able to demonstrate value for money and to provide evidence on which to base policy – and from the research community, in terms of its commitment to sponsor 'frontier research'. Debate on this issue has suggested that not only the independence but also the quality of the ESRC's research has suffered as a result of these joint pressures. The Commission on the Social Sciences has recommended that an explicit public discussion takes place around the ESRC's role in funding research in the UK (Commission on the Social Sciences, 2003).

The supply-and-demand initiatives described earlier raise precisely these kinds of concerns. For example, new processes for commissioning research mean that government defines not only *what* gets studied but *how* as well, including what counts as good-quality research. Further, where linkage initiatives have opened up the relationship between research and policy, for example by inviting independent researchers into policy deliberations, questions arise about whether researchers can *maintain* independence in this process, and the extent to which they may suffer from policy 'capture'.

The potential undermining of the researcher's traditional independence is a worry whenever researchers move into policy-influencing roles, but is of particular concern when researchers are actually co-opted into government business. Perhaps for this reason the past few decades have seen a proliferation of opportunities for researchers to work at arm's length from formal policy making while still having influence. It is this broader array of agencies and institutions, and their interactions with official policy-making machinery, that we now begin to explore.

Improving research use by drawing on broader models of policy influence

As we saw in Chapters Three and Four, research may influence policy indirectly as well as directly, through many non-official routes – such as policy-, issue- or advocacy-networks – that effectively limit the potential for government control of evidence, its interpretation and its use. Such routes may then offer opportunities for research to influence policy in more challenging ways, ways that go beyond a limited consensus-based and instrumental role for research. Moreover, much of the literature on the policy process outlined in Chapter Four has demonstrated the importance of looking beyond the executive arm of government in order to understand how policies are shaped and implemented. In line with both of these observations, we now begin to outline broader initiatives to improve the use of research in policy by first considering activities associated with the scrutiny function (which is one step removed from the executive) and then those activities associated with the operation of broader policy networks that encompass diverse and independent actors/agencies.

Scrutiny bodies as research advocates

The scrutiny of policy development and service delivery has grown substantially since the 1980s (Martin, 2002; Kelly, 2003). Public scrutiny is regarded as a means of increasing both the legitimacy and effectiveness of government (Centre for Public Scrutiny, 2005). It includes the activities of specialist scrutiny agencies (such as audit and inspection bodies), as well as the activities of lay scrutiny bodies such as the parliamentary select committees and local authority overview and scrutiny committees. The specialist audit and inspection bodies are both users and generators of research evidence – research is often used by them to underpin their standard setting, and their analyses of the performance of public services are an important stream of evidence feeding into the activities of lay scrutiny committees and beyond.

In the UK, parliamentary select committees in the House of Commons have long played an important role in scrutinising the activities of the executive. In this they are supported by parliamentary officers working in the Parliamentary Office of Science and Technology (POST) and the recently established Scrutiny Unit. Since 1997 there has been a select committee for each government department as well as several cross-cutting committees. The departmental select committees examine the expenditure, administration and policy of their department, and of any associated public bodies. They are free to choose the topics they wish to examine, which means that they can initiate debate rather than merely respond to policy proposed by the executive. Most of their review work involves taking oral and written evidence from a variety of sources. In recent years they have carved out a greater role in pre-legislative scrutiny (Centre for Public Scrutiny, 2005). There are also several select committees in the House of Lords. Members of the House of Lords are often perceived to be less politically partisan then their House of Commons counterparts and for this reason their scrutiny of the executive is sometimes considered to be more independent and deliberative (Centre for Public Scrutiny, 2005).

Since the 2000 Local Government Act there has also been a substantial development of the scrutiny function of local government. Under the Act, councils were required to put in place new arrangements designed to bring about a formal separation of roles between executive decision making and scrutiny of those decisions. In particular, they were required to establish one or more overview and scrutiny committees, comprising non-executive elected members (see Box 8.11). These committees are able to invite other people to attend their meetings in order to give their views or to submit evidence. Local authorities have varied widely in their implementation of this new overview and scrutiny power (Centre for Public Scrutiny, 2005). It is too early in their life to pass judgement on their effectiveness, however there are concerns that their potential will be undermined if they are under-resourced or unsupported. Evidence, including research-based evidence, is seen as an important resource, and evidence-based arguments are perceived by many participants to confer power and legitimacy to these committees (Centre for Public Scrutiny, 2006).

Box 8.11: Local authority overview and scrutiny committees

Overview and scrutiny committees are empowered to:

(1) Review or scrutinise decisions made, or other action taken by the executive or council.

(2) Undertake external reviews of other agencies, including (since 2001) local health service bodies, to ensure that services are properly provided for the inhabitants of a locality.

> (3) Consider broad issues of policy and development, and challenge assumptions, by undertaking detailed research on the delivery of particular services.
> (4) Initiate performance reviews by considering the performance of local authorities against targets (including Best Value requirements).
>
> *Source:* Adapted from Centre for Public Scrutiny (2005, p 21)

Scrutiny processes offer an alternative route through which research might be brought to bear on policy, but crucially in a more independent and challenging way than those approaches developed within, or driven by, the executive arm of government. They provide active opportunities for research to influence the policy process in ways that move beyond a conventional, consensus-based role for research. While they may sometimes focus on more traditional instrumental uses of research with which to contest policy development and delivery, scrutiny processes can also encompass a more conceptual role for research in holding policy makers to account, for example by providing greater understanding of issues at a local level. One example of this was work done by the Audit Commission on day case surgery in the 1990s, which was very influential in encouraging hospitals to pay more attention to the evidence supporting such an approach (Audit Commission, 1990). Scrutiny bodies can thus enable a wide range of research evidence to be drawn into the policy process and debated, including locally generated data and their own research findings. In particular, strong research evidence can provide scrutiny bodies with the legitimacy and power to challenge existing ways of doing things.

Paradoxically, however, scrutiny regimes may also limit research use. A target-driven approach, for example, can focus attention on the measured aspects of performance to the detriment of other areas of service (Bevan and Hood, 2006). By encouraging services to focus efforts on particular activities and outcomes, scrutiny can inhibit research-based experimentation and innovation both in policy and in service delivery. Thus, scrutiny agencies may encourage uptake of the evidence embedded in their view of the world but simultaneously inhibit a wider engagement with evidence that falls outside of this view.

Policy networks, knowledge purveyors and advocacy coalitions

Beyond the institutions of government there is an array of formal and informal relationships (policy networks across many organisational actors) that shape policy agendas and decision making. Around many major issues, organisations and networks, both formal and informal, have emerged which have long-term interests and knowledge in shaping policy. Some of these are charitable agencies with a strong research function and a clear advocacy remit; others are led by academics and researchers themselves. For example, in the UK, both the British Psychological Society and the Royal Economic Society have created specialist intermediary roles to help translate research for policy audiences, often well in advance of formal publication, and they are adept at using the media to secure better influence for research (Commission on the Social Sciences, 2003).

Think tanks and charities can have significant influence, although they vary widely in terms of their roles, staffing, funding and their relationships with both research and policy. Think tanks and charities may draw on existing research to develop policy analyses, carry out their own in-house research, or commission others to do so. They tend to be more flexible and innovative than other research commissioners, often seeking to bring research producers and research users together as part of the process. They are also very likely to make significant use of service users, clients or carers to ensure that these perspectives are reflected in campaigning activities, alongside those of professionals and other 'experts'. Typically, charities and think tanks use a wide range of routes for influence, including publications, conferences, policy briefings and other forms of dissemination, public meetings and lobbying (Commission on the Social Sciences, 2003; see Box 8.12 for an example of a successful, research-based think tank). Thus, one of the main ways by which research evidence becomes known and is discussed within policy networks is through the process of advocacy by a wide variety of think tanks, charities and other interest groups (Sabatier and Jenkins-Smith, 1993). These interest groups are important purveyors of data and analysis: 'it is not done in the interests of knowledge, but as a side effect of advocacy' (Weiss, 1987, p 278). Although research evidence used in this way can tend to be used for tactical advantage rather than for illumination, 'when research is available to all participants in the policy process, research as political ammunition can be a worthy model of utilisation' (Weiss, 1979, p 429).

Box 8.12: Think tanks: The Centre for Economic Policy Research

The Centre for Economic Policy Research (CEPR) is a successful think tank in the UK that claims impact on such key developments as the European Monetary System and the Single European Market. CEPR was established as a not-for-profit educational charity and raises funds from a variety of sources. It conducts a good deal of in-house research, which is disseminated widely through diverse routes, including publications, conferences, workshops and public meetings as well as briefings for government and for the press. As well as its own staff, CEPR supports an international network – a kind of virtual college – of more than 650 affiliates, primarily academics. Its core focus is on producing high-quality work through researchers based in both the UK and abroad, mainly Europe.

Source: Adapted from Commission on the Social Sciences (2003)

Agencies involved in research advocacy (such as think tanks, charities, research intermediaries and campaigning organisations) may devote considerable resources to exploiting and developing the evidence base, and they can be seen to deploy a number of strategies to increase the impact that their evidence-informed advocacy may have on policy (see Box 8.13 for an example). Informal analysis suggests at least three key areas of activity in getting the evidence heard. First, such agencies rarely take the policy context as a given, but seek instead actively to reshape that context. Publicity campaigns with persuasive, professionally produced material, often utilising the mainstream media, can begin to shape public opinion and change the climate within which policies are being made. More direct contact with ministers and policy makers is sought through specialist advisors and lobbying. In comparison to academic researchers, such activities are often pursued with great vigour, stamina and creativity by the sorts of 'policy entrepreneurs' that were introduced in Chapter Four. Such activists also often demonstrate a savvy-ness about the political process, with activities being fine-tuned to exploit windows of opportunity brought about by political cycles or propitious circumstance.

Second, independent evidence advocates often build alliances or networks with others of similar view, seeking synergies that are sometimes wide but relatively shallow (for example, marshalling the broadest array of support to campaign on a single common issue) and sometimes relatively narrow but deeper, more strategic and sustained.

Finally, some of these agencies have the resources to develop demonstration projects showing 'evidence in action'. Such working projects provide concrete exemplars that can be used to help persuade those engaged in the wider policy process. Demonstration projects can help allay fears about 'implementation failure' and can provide valuable knowledge about implementation processes that work. Examples of each of these strategies can be glimpsed in the Health Foundation's Safer Patients Initiative outlined in Box 8.13. Taken together, these strategies hint at the possibilities for development of a more substantial 'knowledge-purveying infrastructure' that goes far deeper and broader than individual researcher-led advocacy.

Box 8.13: Evidence as part of broader advocacy role

The Health Foundation (a major UK charity, www.health.org.uk) can be seen as an evidence advocate, particularly in its role around patient safety. The Foundation has been actively seeking to shape the debate around patient safety in a number of ways. First, it supports dialogue between policy makers, healthcare professionals and researchers, through roundtables and expert seminars, and has published a variety of briefing papers and research reports summarising or commenting on the evidence. Second, it has built alliances with other agencies both in the UK and abroad (most notably with the Institute for Healthcare Improvement in Boston, Massachusetts, a leading US evidence advocacy organisation – www.ihi.org). Third, it has invested considerable sums (circa £4.3 million) in supporting organisational efforts to improve quality and performance in health and healthcare services (the 'Safer Patients Initiative'). These investments are supporting demonstration projects clearly designed to have wider policy impacts. Stephen Thornton, Chief Executive of The Health Foundation said, 'Our vision is for the hospitals to act as shining examples of what works to improve patient safety, sharing their successes and experiences first locally and then further afield ... the findings will have important lessons for national policy development' (www.health.org.uk).

Source: www.health.org.uk

Focusing on agencies engaged in research advocacy, and their embedding in policy networks and policy communities, highlights the potential for a different vision of how the policy process might be improved to encourage greater research use. This shifts away from ideas of 'modernising' policy processes, with their emphasis on central control and rationality, to ideas of opening up or 'democratising' that process instead, so that a greater diversity of voices and views can be heard (Parsons, 2002; Sanderson, 2006). Indeed, political science has long been concerned to see how the institutions and mechanisms of government might be changed to facilitate more participative, deliberative and bottom-up approaches to policy analysis, and the growing interest in evidence advocacy is a part of that concern. Such reforms will likely involve shifts in power and authority as well as the design of new institutions, and Bell (2004) suggests that this might happen more easily locally and regionally, rather than nationally. The promise of 'opening up' policy processes to greater network and community engagement has been described as:

> ideally about inductive reasoning and learning. It is slower and more cumbersome than more centrist and deductive modes of knowledge for governance, but it does promise better knowledge and probably better legitimacy. (Bell, 2004, p 28)

Many of the initiatives highlighted earlier in the chapter, around establishing knowledge brokering bodies, facilitating service user consultations and making research summaries more readily available, may facilitate just such an opening up of evidence-informed policy debates. Initiatives such as the PATs and policy advocacy networks discussed earlier have also served to widen the range of people involved in policy development. If policy processes *are* democratised, then policy discussions are likely to contain a greater variety of voices: researchers of various hues; practitioners from sundry work backgrounds; and clients/users in all their diversity. But this approach is not without its challenges and will involve acknowledging that the use of research in such pluralistic discussions is an inherently messy and political process. Evidence from social research is contested, not fixed, and, like the policy process itself, is deeply infused with values. Albaek (1995) has argued that policy making and research (and, we would add, practice) involve values, choices and assumptions, and that such views and interests need to be engaged as part of the policy process, with interaction and learning among different stakeholders and fluid boundaries between scientific and political argumentation:

> Research contributes to the public reflection which grows up during a decision-making process in which opposing interests scrutinize the pros and cons of options and objectives. (Albaek, 1995, p 95)

It is important to note from this that there may therefore be significant tensions between evidence-based approaches to policy development and more inclusive and participative approaches (for example, see Quinn, 2002). Not least of the challenges is that the scope of what counts as evidence may be greatly enlarged and the primacy of research as privileged evidence is likely to see significant dissent. Dealing with these contentions in a positive and productive way may mean that we need to pay more attention to the features of good deliberations in decision making (see Box 8.14).

Box 8.14: Possible core features of a deliberative process

An international group of experts brought together by the Canadian Health Services Research Foundation (CHSRF) to discuss evidence use suggested that the core features of a deliberative process should include:

- presence of a strong chairperson;
- consideration of different types of evidence;
- engagement between the scientific and decision-maker communities;
- an explicit inclusion process;
- face-to-face discussions;
- an appropriate timeline for questions;
- a mechanism to elicit the values of the participants;
- a venue or process for minority views to be expressed and considered.

Source: CHSRF (2006)

Deliberative policy processes such as that outlined in Box 8.14 are usually seen as desirable when issues are open to considerable debate and interpretation. However, a potential limitation with formalised deliberative processes is that they often assume that discussions will be underpinned by some form of common interest (Culyer and Lomas, 2006), which may be far from the case when diverse interest groups come together for consultations. In fact, various vested parties may find it difficult to leave behind their sectional interests in pursuit of a common goal, and may revert instead to variants of Weiss' tactical uses of research (Weiss, 1979). Moreover, very little evidence is yet available as to whether formalised deliberative processes do actually result in better decision outcomes, although the use of such processes may be beneficial in their own right (Culyer and Lomas, 2006). In particular, the open and participative nature of deliberative processes can ensure that research has a voice which gets heard within the making of policy, and can also help respond to demands from postmodern critiques that the particular play of power inherent within different research use contexts is surfaced and made explicit (Chapter Four). But such deliberative processes may not be easy. The outcomes may be unpredictable and uncomfortable (at least to some), and there is little reason to presuppose that consensus about appropriate ways forward is more likely to emerge than fractious disagreement. While 'democratising' the policy process may be appealing, potentially 'anarchising' it may be less so. Nonetheless, such inclusive and pluralistic arrangements do emphasise the importance of research use as a process (leading to enlarged, reshaped, and sometimes shared, understandings) rather than research use as an outcome (simply focused on instrumentalist policy choices).

In sum, then, broader models of policy making open up more radical opportunities for research to have an influence, moving beyond expectations that it will simply support or refine current policy preoccupations to a hope that it will challenge those preoccupations or even stimulate paradigmatic shifts in thinking. In undertaking such a role it is to be expected that the sources and nature of evidence will be more inclusive and eclectic. This may pose problems for those who espouse a narrower, more restrictive definition of evidence as that based on rigorous – often academic – research. It will also pose significant new challenges as values, preferences, experience and tacit knowledge enter the dialogical mix, more often and more openly.

This view of a more dynamic network of actors engaged in processes of learning and reciprocal influence around evidence/research raises important questions about whether such networks are natural and emergent or whether they can be created, encouraged or stimulated by more deliberative action. Following from this, there are questions as to how such activities should be pursued and by whom: it is not at all clear what is the appropriate balance here between government activity and third-sector initiatives. Some of these issues we return to in Chapter Ten. In addition, any governmental or independent activity will inevitably be mediated by the wider national context. This will greatly influence the extent, activities and vibrancy of advocacy coalitions, and the opportunities for more inclusive and pluralistic engagement with research and other evidence. Thus, in the next (penultimate) section, we make some tentative observations about the national context within which policy activities and research advocacy take place that might have some influence on the role(s) that research may play in policy.

The national policy context

We have noted several times during the book that context is highly significant in understanding research use. This can be the rather specific context surrounding a particular policy area or specific piece of research, or it can be the more general cultural and institutional context of a country/region. In this section it is the latter national context that we are particularly interested in. As we noted in Chapter One, understanding national contextual arrangements – including cultural factors such as attitudes towards large-scale policy experimentation and constitutional issues such as unitary or federal government structures – is helpful as we seek to figure out research use/non-use. Sometimes these national characteristics are simply 'givens': factors affecting the potential for evidence use that need to be taken into account as strategies for promoting research uptake are developed, but largely not amenable to directed change. At other times these contextual factors could themselves be targets for change as part of strategies promoting increased research use. As elsewhere in this chapter, systematic study of these contextual factors and their influence on research use is largely absent. Published observations – scant as they are – are almost universally anecdotal. Our own contributions in this section should be assessed as similar and treated cautiously as a result.

Where to begin? Size, certainly, seems to matter. Nations differ greatly in size (geographically and by population) and more importantly, in terms of degree of economic development and the scale and scope of their governmental apparatus. All of these are likely to matter for research uptake. Of course, many large countries are federated, regionalised or otherwise segmented to ease the job of governance, and we shall comment on the influence of these arrangements shortly. Suffice to say, however, that smaller countries (that is, those with populations of, say, three to six million people) may have some advantages with regards to researchers' relative ease of access to ministers and civil servants, and the level of knowledge possible about what key people are working in various policy areas. This being the case, we might expect that interactions between these groups, and consequent increases in research/policy engagement, would be more possible in smaller countries than larger ones. However, smaller countries can also suffer from a lack of capacity in both research and policy terms, and may be less likely to be able to support the array of research production and research brokering activities that are possible in larger states. Finally, we have noted the potential importance of broader pluralistic research engagement – with active and vibrant policy networks – and it is unclear whether small country size may mean more focused advocacy or less effective and unsustainable coalitions due to a lack of capacity.

Thus, nation size may be important, but quite how will be difficult to discern as size and government configuration are inextricably bound up. Indeed, size may be a poor proxy for interconnectivity, with geography and/or extent of political integration perhaps having a greater influence. For example, densely populated countries such as Japan may find it easier to develop linkages than countries with sparse and far-flung populations such as Australia, although the degree of political integration and the availability of information and communications technologies are also likely to be important confounders to any such relationship.

National size and geography are givens, so perhaps of more interest is the influence of constitutional arrangements – or put more broadly, the overarching configurations of the machinery of government. We noted in Chapter Three that federal political structures tend to provide more distributed and interactive policy-making processes with greater opportunities for researchers to get engaged, and conversely that in centralised structures the civil service tends to have a stronger role. The issue is not just about the degree of federalism, but also about how policy is made within these political structures:

> In Europe, policy is overwhelmingly made by the civil service or by political parties (which tend to be hierarchical and centralised). In America independent policy entrepreneurs have lots of chances to influence it – partly because the civil service is weak and partly because the political process has lots of entry points, from the States to the Federal Government, from the White House to Congress. (*The Economist*, 2006b, p 64)

In making such comments, *The Economist* clearly sees advantages in the federal structure of the US when it comes to policy making and the potential influence of researchers and thinkers on that process. However, Wilensky (1997) argues conversely that the influence of social science in the (federal) US is in fact limited due to the nature of federal government, policy segmentation and the limited interaction of researchers with the executive arm of government. He claims that there is a tighter integration of knowledge and policy in such countries as Japan, Norway, Sweden, Austria, and to a lesser extent Belgium and the Netherlands:

> National differences in structures for bargaining shape the
> intellectual channels for influence.... If they were located
> in an interacting array of centralised labour federations,
> centralised employer federations, strong political parties, and
> at least moderately centralised governments with the
> capacity to implement policy, United States social scientists
> would have as much influence as their counterparts abroad.
> (Wilensky, 1997, p 1254)

From such paradoxical viewpoints we might draw the inference that
federal/central arrangements matter, but that they might play out
differentially – contingent on, for example, the policy issue in hand,
the interests of local knowledge agencies, or the shape of wider societal
values. The recent changes to governmental relations in the UK –
with significant devolution of social policy to its four constituent
countries – have offered fresh opportunities to explore such
contingencies in a changing set of national contexts. Nonetheless,
interesting as such work would be for the light that it could cast on
constitutional influences on research use, it is unlikely to offer radically
new avenues for change (it seems unlikely that fresh constitutional
arrangements will be driven by the desire to promote evidence use
alone).

Aside from the issue of constitutional arrangements, there is also the
much broader set of concerns about how services are organised and
delivered. National bureaucracies controlling public bodies charged
with service delivery may be more susceptible to evidence-influenced
change than, say, a diversity of providers embedded in market systems.
Oversight and scrutiny regimes, as we have seen, depending on their
terms of engagement, may also be influential parts of the national
infrastructure. Again, directing change at such arrangements as a means
of increasing research uptake, while not impossible, will not always be
realistic. Nonetheless, an understanding of such contextual influences
may at least keep expectations for research use within reasonable
bounds, and may help to shape more effective research use strategies.

Beyond service delivery arrangements, there is also the question of
the non-governmental institutions and networks that have grown up
within a country and that have an impact on the availability and use
of research. Given our earlier discussions of the potential for more
radical forms of research use being driven by active advocacy coalitions,
an examination of this 'knowledge-purveying infrastructure' may be
fruitful. Moreover, the nature, arrangement and opportunities for
interactions between governmental and non-governmental agencies

can rightly be seen as potential targets for change. For example, we have already noted the potential for think tanks and charities to act as intermediaries within the research use process, and the number and size of these varies enormously across countries.

The US, in particular, boasts a large number of lavishly funded think tanks (Rich, 2004). Their number has exploded in recent years, although Rich notes that there is an irony in that their influence seems to have eroded as their number has grown. He attributes this to the fact that they have changed from neutral, research-based organisations to ones that advocate particular ideologies. US think tanks have also become more aggressively self-promoting, and while this means that their research reaches policy makers and other stakeholders, recipients seem to be increasingly sceptical of it due to its ideological undertones (Rich, 2004). Their potential also seems to be impaired by another development – much of the work of the newer think tanks is directed at the final moments of policy making, when minds are largely made up.

By contrast, other countries such as the UK have far fewer think tanks and those that there are, are concentrated in London. In a way, for national policy making, London locations make sense, but such positioning is neglectful of distributed regional policy making and the potential for influence in such arenas. There are significant questions therefore about whether we have enough intermediary organisations of the right kind, and whether these are afforded the right opportunities for interaction. In the context of devolved government in Scotland, for example, it has been argued that there is a need to develop more of these intermediary bodies in order to improve research use and enhance policy debate and deliberation (SHEFC/US, 2005).

More generally, central and regional government may have an important role to play in nurturing the emergence of such intermediary organisations, providing them with access to policy teams, and setting ground rules for productive engagements. There is real scope here for the creation and reinvigoration of a variety of partnerships aimed at fostering a growth in research-informed dialogue. At the very least, there is untapped potential for a greater degree of interchange of personnel between different agencies: research outfits (university or otherwise), think tanks, charities, research brokering organisations and national/regional policy settings. From the analysis presented in this chapter, denser, well-functioning networks, consisting of experienced and knowledgeable participants with experience of each others' worlds, may help foster a more conducive national context for research use.

The alternative, as Wilensky commented, is a sidelining of research evidence:

> In the absence of effective coalitions of politicians, bureaucrats, and experts, and without a system for aggregating interests, achieving consensus, and integrating social and economic planning ... the voice of research, even scholarly analysis, is drowned out by noise. (Wilensky, 1997, p 1248) [We would note, however, that while we agree with Wilensky on the need for effective coalitions, we are less convinced about the likelihood – or even the necessity – of achieving consensus.]

Finally, in our consideration of national contexts, the role played by the national media may also be important, particularly the extent to which it takes on an investigative and/or adversarial role. In the UK, for example, the media play an important role not only in communicating government plans but also in questioning government and bringing it to account for the performance (or failure) of public services. While the degree of hostility towards government often seen in the UK print media may be unusually sharp and poses some distinctive challenges, it can certainly help to move concerns up the policy agenda. Moreover, many of the research advocacy agencies discussed earlier are adept at using the media to help shape the wider context, bring about new public consensus, or agitate for policy action. Indeed, the media are particularly important as a conduit for tactical and political uses of research, which, as we have suggested earlier, are not always to be deprecated.

Despite the potentially beneficial impacts of the media as a means of getting research heard, the approach is not without its problems. Research findings can be difficult to communicate in lay media, especially when methodological considerations have to be aired. There can be a tendency to either report findings completely uncritically or, worse, to hold challenging ideas up to ridicule. As the UK Commission on the Social Sciences reported in 2003: 'even in broadsheet newspapers, a kind of anti-intellectualism prevails ... [and they may] dislike findings that are critical of the socio-political *status quo*' (p 88). Perhaps as a result 'bad blood exists between many social scientists and journalists who, for better or worse, are gatekeepers to the passage of their work into the public domain' (p 91). Such a situation cannot be to the benefit of the sorts of pluralistic dialogue called for in the analysis of this chapter.

Concluding remarks

Overall in the UK, initiatives to improve research use in the policy process – particularly those instigated by government – have been focused on enhancing the supply of applied research, promoting the demand for such research by policy makers, and, sometimes, engendering the means of bringing these two together. Such initiatives are often underpinned by a linear, rational and instrumental model of the research use process, which views evidence from research as relatively straightforward facts to be weighed in the making of policy decisions. However, a focus on supply and demand issues fails fully to capture the complexity of the research/policy nexus, the political context or the contested nature of research evidence. As such, initiatives built around supply and demand tend to limit the influence of research to a consensus-based role; and they have often involved only small-scale and rather conservative changes to research and policy processes.

Alternative approaches to improving the use of research have by contrast begun to open up the policy process and establish different relationships between research and policy. The most radical of these have involved more grassroots activities by policy networks that operate beyond the executive arm of the government. They envisage a very different model of research use, which is dynamic and interactive, and that involves the interplay of values and interests that infuse both research and the policy process itself. As such they may challenge preconceptions of research findings as fixed and immutable, favouring instead the idea that the value of research is revealed through dialogue, contextualisation and assimilation with other forms of knowledge (such as experiential perceptions and tacit knowledge). Such interactive and pluralistic approaches bring values to the fore as central to the policy debates rather than sidelining them; they also emphasise the non-instrumentalist benefits of research engagement, such as open dialogue, conceptual reframing and 'enlightenment'. Thus, these approaches offer more diverse and more creative ways of thinking about embedding interactive research use in policy settings, ways that better reflect the complexity of the research–policy relationship. In doing so these more radical approaches unearth opportunities for more contentious and even paradigm-challenging roles for research in influencing policy.

These more radical approaches to evidence-influenced policy are not wholly new – but newer ways of understanding the evidence/policy nexus have rendered them more visible. Reactions to this range from attempts to stuff the genie back into the bottle (for example, by getting a firmer handle on more managed policy processes) to the development of more creative ways to capitalise on vibrant policy communities. While the former may be appropriate for certain areas of 'easy' policy making (for example, the approval and licensing of new health technologies), the latter has as yet largely untapped potential to stimulate radical and innovative approaches to the 'wicked' problems present in much of social policy. It will not, however, be an easy ride: these more open and interactive policy processes are time-consuming and often inconclusive. They require a loosening of central control that can be unsettling, may promote a widening of disagreement rather than convergence, and can lead to feelings of disillusionment or even burn-out among their participants. Establishing and sustaining vibrant policy communities will therefore be extremely challenging as well as contextually mediated. Our brief and tentative comments on national policy contexts go on to suggest some of the important mediating features of the local environment that may influence the ability to bring about these more radical approaches. They also point to some of the challenges and opportunities that lie ahead for those interested in promoting such approaches, a theme we return to in Chapter Ten.

Within all of the initiatives on increasing policy use of research, the same activities may be used in very different ways. For example, summaries of research may outline potential solutions to existing policy problems, or may detail new concepts and ideas that demand sustained debates and a fundamental shift in a prevalent policy paradigm. What is key, however, is the research use model that underpins how different activities are shaped and bundled together. This may mean that there are tensions and contradictions when different models of policy or research use are being served by a common set of activities. For example, under a 'supply-and-demand'-type framing, research synthesis may be seen as encouraging convergence of thinking on appropriate choices for action; under more pluralistic framings, the same synthesis may be seen as merely a springboard to a broader set of discussions that eventually undermine the very basis of the review. This means that an eclectic mix of strategies may not offer the best way forward as it is likely to contain significant tensions and incongruities. It is our hope therefore that greater understanding of the different models and mechanisms underpinning research use in policy will allow for greater discernment in how different research use strategies are mixed or emphasised, and, in less managed systems, will foster insights into the sources and nature of points of tension.

In our view, those initiatives that view research use as a complex, iterative and unpredictable process, which necessarily takes place within a political and politicised context, may be more promising because they reflect what we know about how research use most often happens on the ground (Chapter Four). Such initiatives are more likely to move research beyond a simplistic rational and consensus-based role in the policy process, and they are more likely to move thinking beyond a preoccupation with individual research users to a view that sees organisational contexts, processes and cultures as equally important. This is not to deny that promoting a rational ideal for the research–policy interface can be of some value, but to suggest that a better balance needs to be struck between these kinds of initiatives and those that allow a more open and interactive process for using research in policy.

NINE

How can we assess research use and wider research impact?

Throughout this book we have been concerned to document the complexities of research use, and the diversity of ways in which such use has been conceptualised. Building on these understandings we have then sought to explain how research use might be improved or enhanced in a wide variety of public service settings. This chapter takes these debates further by asking – given all the complexity, diversity and messiness of research use – how can both research use processes and the resultant impacts be assessed? As we shall see, work fully assessing research impacts, in particular work that takes account of the kinds of complexity and unexpectedness of research use highlighted in earlier chapters, has, to date, been somewhat underdeveloped. Thus, the material presented in this chapter is necessarily a little tentative. Rather than being able to explore and summarise a mature field of evaluative studies, we instead draw attention to the concerns and difficulties inherent in this kind of work, and provide a series of reflective questions to aid the design of future work. In doing so we draw heavily on the complex and nuanced understandings of research use laid out in previous chapters.

This chapter, then, addresses a central question first raised (and then swiftly put to one side!) in Chapter One: does research use make a difference? As anyone working in the field of research use knows, a central irony is the only limited extent to which evidence advocates can themselves draw on a robust evidence base to support their convictions that greater evidence use will ultimately be beneficial to public services. Our conclusions in this chapter are that we are unlikely any time soon to see such comprehensive evidence neatly linking research, research use, and research impacts, and that we should instead be more modest in our expectations about what we can attain through studies that look for these. A key theme of this chapter, then, is how we might integrate more sophisticated understandings of research use into better studies of research impact.

We begin by exploring in a little more detail the drivers from various quarters for the production of evidence on research impacts or, as it is sometimes called, research payback. We then consider the various ways the impact assessment task can be framed, and the methodological approaches that flow from these various framings. From here we move on to address some underpinning conceptual, methodological and practical issues, drawing heavily on the understandings elaborated in earlier chapters. We conclude by observing the need for a diversity of approaches to impact assessment, drawing attention to the potential for dysfunctional consequences arising from such activity, then setting out some broad recommendations for ways forward.

Why assess research impacts?

Researchers have always been concerned to influence other researchers with their findings, and it is a given of academic study that new research should build on existing bodies of knowledge. Thus, the influence and impact of research within *academic* communities are supported and encouraged in numerous ways, being woven into the fabric of academic practice. However, our focus here is on whether and how research findings are influential, get used, and have impacts, outside of the confines of academic life – what is sometimes termed their *non-academic* impacts – particularly those impacts in policy and practice arenas.

Since the mid 1990s there has been a growing interest in trying to understand these non-academic impacts – often with instrumental intentions of enabling better research management. There are many drivers of this, but two core concerns are political and practical. The political drivers highlight the need for research funding bodies, research advocates and other stakeholders to 'make the case' for direct spending on research as well as to justify the resources supporting research synthesis, translation, dissemination and other research promotion activities. As part of this justification, spending – and especially expenditure from the public purse – needs to be set in the context of the likely impacts and future societal benefits.

Related, but more practically, there are increasing demands for greater rigour in the prioritisation of research activity. This prioritisation covers not just the directions of research enquiry (aspects of the world under study), but also the balance between different modes of research funding (for example, the balance between projects, programmes, centres and various forms of research capacity building), and the organisation of the research efforts (for example, the strategies used to encourage user involvement and post-research uptake activity). It is in seeking evidence to underpin such choices that the spotlight has turned to assessing research use, and most especially, research impacts.

While we would agree that better information on the flows, uses and impacts of research may well feed into better exploitation of what social research has to offer, we should perhaps question whether all research activity should really be geared so strongly to use and impact. The complex and often unexpected routes by which research percolates through to public and professional discourse over longer time periods should caution us against too instrumentalist a view about what kind of research is 'worth' pursuing. Indeed, those involved in social research – producers, funders, brokers and (potential) users – are increasingly aware of the limitations of simple models (descriptive or prescriptive) connecting research, research use and research impact. Impact assessments need to take account of this broadening in thinking and should not be too narrowly cast.

There are some reasonable concerns about the narrowness of many existing assessments of social research. These have tended to focus on impacts within the academic community, such as peer review of work programmes, bibliometrics or citations. Even when assessments have gone outside of academic circles, they have often only looked for direct policy and practice applications of the research. Getting beyond this is difficult however: the diversity of social research, and the complexity of the means by which research may come into use, make understanding and assessing wider research impacts a challenging task. But these wider impacts do need to be drawn into any assessment of the worth of social research.

Added to this, different stakeholders (government, funding bodies, research assessment agencies, research provider organisations, user communities, and so on) may want information on impacts for different purposes – and it is a consideration of these purposes that should inform choices over what and how information on research impact is conceptualised, collected and presented.

The purpose and focus of assessing impact

Research impact assessments may be undertaken for many different reasons, singly or in combination. Typical goals in carrying out research impact assessments include:

- *Accountability* – providing an account of the activities and achievements of the unit being assessed (such as a funding agency, a research programme, or a research broker organisation).
- *Value for money* – demonstrating that the benefits arising from social research are commensurate with its cost.

- *Learning* – developing a better understanding of research use and research impact processes in order to enhance future impacts.
- *Auditing evidence-based policy and practice* – evaluating whether policy and practice in the UK (and elsewhere) are indeed using social research to support or challenge decision making and action.

Each of these is likely to entail different impact assessment strategies and therefore it is important to ensure clarity of purpose from the outset. It is also important to be clear about the most appropriate focal unit for impact assessment. At an organisational level, impact assessment could focus on the activities of a funding agency, a research production facility, a potential research user organisation and its staff, or even the entire research regime in a country. At the level of research itself, the assessment may consider the impact of individual projects, research syntheses or summaries, or whole programmes of work. Each of these would require different approaches.

In any assessment of research impact it is also important to take account of the different types of social research and the various roles that they play (see Chapters One and Two). This is not just a matter of making the familiar distinction between basic and applied research but also entails acknowledging that different forms of research lead to different types of knowledge. For example, knowing 'what works', knowing 'how things work', and knowing 'why things happen' are all likely to impact in different ways. Policy and practice communities are also interested in good description, analysis and critique as well as in evaluative research, and the impacts of these research activities too may need to be tracked. Good theory, particularly when it leads to new schema and novel testable hypotheses, can sometimes have significant impacts. Harder to trace are the impacts of research that challenges established ways of doing things or even undermines the very basis on which current decisions are being made. These contentious and paradigm-challenging roles for research (introduced in Chapter One) are likely to be resisted, discounted or marginalised in discussions of research use by research users, at least in the short to medium term, and hence their influence will be much more difficult to assess.

Assessment approaches may thus be needed that can capture the impact of each of these forms of research knowledge; that is, they should be designed not only with 'what works' research findings in mind, but also with a keen understanding of how the broadest array of research can be used more conceptually in processes of 'enlightenment' (Weiss, 1979). Of course, alongside this, any assessment of impact also needs to be based on realistic expectations about what research can and cannot do. As we discussed in Chapter One, research is only one form of knowledge, which often competes for attention with other forms of knowledge (both explicit and tacit).

In addition, it is not just the findings of social research that can have an impact but also the process by which that research is undertaken (Chapter Two). For example, an important impact of many projects that employ research assistants is the training of a new generation of researchers. Furthermore, projects that are undertaken in collaboration with specific policy or practice communities may result in improved understanding and more valuing of the research process among those communities (Huberman, 1990, 1993) or even lead to a rethinking of the outcomes sought from policy programmes (Patton, 1997, 1998). Thus, any comprehensive programme of impact assessment will also need to address such process impacts and not simply focus on outcomes.

Approaches to assessing impact

Following on from the different purposes and foci of assessments, there are several starting points from which an evaluation of research impacts can be approached (Figure 9.1). One obvious approach is to utilise forward-looking studies; that is, tracking from research, to research use and on to research impacts. Such studies would focus on how research outputs/findings (single studies, reviews or even whole programmes of work) make their way into user communities, and would assess the impacts that they have there, and how these ultimately play out in the design and outcomes of public services. Alternatively, we might take a backward-looking perspective; that is, working from actor behaviour to antecedent research. Here we are more concerned with research user communities themselves (for example, policy makers, service organisations or service provider practitioners), aiming to understand the extent and processes through which their decisions and actions are influenced by bodies of knowledge, including research. A third important perspective, given recent efforts to increase research uptake and use, may be a concern to assess the success or otherwise of a range of research enhancement initiatives. Examples here could include assessment of the effectiveness of specific interventions such as researcher outreach activity, or analysis of the impacts of research broker organisations. Such work would contribute to the evidence base outlined in Chapter Five. These different ways of framing the impact assessment task take very different perspectives and have at their heart different core questions of interest.

Figure 9.1: Starting points in assessing impacts

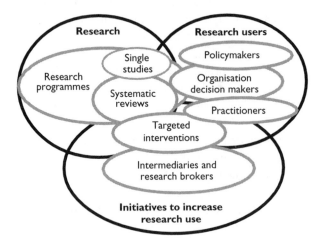

Each of the three approaches outlined poses distinct challenges. Tracking forwards from research to impacts raises important questions of what to look for, where to look, and over what timeframe. Tracking backwards from decisions or practice behaviours to identify research-based influences challenges us to disaggregate the impacts of multiple influences and multiple research strands. Finally, evaluations of research use enhancement activities will often struggle to identify causality and/or demonstrate the generalisability of any initiatives evaluated. Moreover, these three perspectives on impact assessment are somewhat interdependent: for example, the impacts of research projects or programmes cannot be understood separately from an understanding of the capacity of users to absorb and utilise findings; and any assessment of research use among user communities has to pay attention to the availability (or otherwise) of useable research findings. We could ask therefore: what are the relative advantages/disadvantages of tracking forwards from research to impacts, or backwards from change to antecedent research? And should we do either of these in the absence of initiatives to facilitate knowledge transfer and uptake? To help answer such questions, an elaboration of the challenges embedded in each of these three main approaches now follows.

Forward tracking from research to consequences

Traditionally, the success or otherwise of academic research has been judged in quite narrow ways, usually by an assessment of peer-reviewed published output. Extensions to this view have seen bibliometric analyses that have assessed not only the amount of published output, but also the quality of that output (for example, judged by peer esteem or by the impact factor of the outlets used), and the extent to which the output has influenced other academics in the same field (for example, by citation tracking). Such approaches have long been used to assess the 'productivity' of individual researchers, projects or programmes, or to map networks of relations between researchers (and between researchers and policy makers/practitioners) in similar or overlapping areas of study (Lindsey, 1989; Hicks, 1991).

More recently, attempts have been made to go beyond simply examining research outputs to describe and quantify the impacts of research, sometimes using models that call attention to 'return on investment' or 'research payback' (Buxton and Hanney, 1996; Hanney et al, 2002; Wooding et al, 2004). These approaches typically identify a number of categories where outputs/impacts might be expected from research, for example:

- knowledge production (for example, peer-reviewed papers, dissemination reports);
- research capacity building (for example, postgraduate training and career development);
- policy or product development (for example, input into official guidelines or protocols);
- sector benefits (for example, impacts on specific client groups); and
- wider societal benefits (for example, economic benefits from increased population health or productivity).

Assessments in each of these categories are derived from multiple data sources, including documentary evidence, routine data sets, bespoke surveys and interviews. The data gathered are sometimes then scored in each category, perhaps using Delphi-type methods (where panels of relevant experts share their assessments through repeated rounds of consultation). Such approaches to impact assessment can then provide a profile of scores across each category (sometimes referred to as measures of 'payback' [Buxton and Hanney, 1996; Wooding et al, 2004]); and these data can be used to compare profiles of impacts across projects, programmes or other 'units' of research activity.

While not in all cases going so far as to score impacts, a number of investigations and reports have taken similarly broad and inclusive approaches to assessing the benefits and impacts of research (see Box 9.1 for brief notes on a wide selection of these). For example, the study prepared for the Economic and Social Research Council (ESRC) (Molas-Gallart et al, 2000; see Box 9.1) developed two forward-tracking approaches to assessing impact. The first of these, termed 'networks and flows', mapped 'networks of researchers and relevant non-academic beneficiaries', before tracing the impacts of these interactions in many and diverse ways with an emphasis on qualitative description. Their second approach ('post-research tracing') examined the impact of a funded programme of research through the subsequent activities of funded researchers, including their employment outside academe, their consultancy/advisory roles, and the development of further research work. The contrast between this work and that, for example, of Wooding et al (2004), who developed specific scores of impact in five category areas when assessing the payback from charity-funded arthritis research (see Box 9.1), nicely illustrates the wide range of detailed study designs that can be accommodated within the forward-tracking approach. Thus, detailed study designs may emphasise the use of quantitative methods and relatively linear pathways between research products and research impacts, or may instead highlight non-linear interactive mechanisms of impact described through detailed qualitative study. Indeed, some studies incorporate multiple approaches, variants or hybrids, providing for a degree of triangulation, but these may also pose difficult challenges should the different approaches provide seemingly incongruous or even contradictory findings.

Box 9.1: Some examples of research impact assessment

'That full complement of riches': the contributions of the arts, humanities and social sciences to the nation's wealth

This is a first step towards identifying the broader contributions made by the arts, humanities and the social sciences, but one not fully focused on the research outputs or impacts in these areas. Five core areas are identified: cultural and intellectual enrichment; economic prosperity and wellbeing; major challenges facing the UK and the wider world; public policy and debate; and educational benefits. Although many examples of benefit are presented, these have largely been generated through wide consultation rather than by any formal methodology.

(The British Academy, 2004)

The returns from arthritis research

This evaluation attempts to improve understanding of how arthritis research funded by the Arthritis Research Campaign (a large charitable funder) is translated from 'bench to bedside'. It uses a payback model to identify and score research impacts in five categories, gathering data across 16 case studies, and using a modified Delphi process to create the category scores.

(Wooding et al, 2004)

The impact of academic research on industrial performance

An assessment of the contributions of academic research to the performance of five industry sectors: network systems and communications; medical devices and equipment; aerospace; transportation, distribution and logistics; and financial services. It concludes that research has made a substantial contribution to all five industries, including some significant impacts on performance. The data gathering used to come to these conclusions included: user-informed opinions; expert judgements; literature review; email surveys; workshop discussions; and panel deliberations.

(National Academy of Engineering, 2003)

The societal impact of applied health research: towards a quality assessment system

A methodology for the national evaluation of the societal impact of applied health research is presented based upon self-assessment by research institutes/groups and site visits. This is seen as something that complements the evaluation of the scientific quality of research outputs. Research teams are asked to self-assess based on (a) their mission with respect to societal impacts, and (b) their performance in relation to that mission. The report lists a number of relevant output categories, including: professional communication; guideline development; new programme/service development; and use of research output by targeted audiences.

(Council for Medical Sciences, The Netherlands, 2002)

The utilisation of health research in policy-making: concepts, examples and methods of assessment

An exploration of the nature of health policy making and the potential for cross-national studies of the utilisation of research in such policy making. Although previous work in this area is reviewed, and some potential approaches and possible tools are presented, no new empirical applications are developed.

(Hanney et al, 2002)

Assessing the outputs and outcomes of Alberta's Health Research Fund

A postal survey of active grant-holders identified a range of (self-reported) outputs (for example, presentations, publications and training) and outcomes (for example, influences on policy and practice, health system benefits and further knowledge discovery). These data were used to support and direct the activities of this major applied health research funder.

(Magnan et al, 2004)

Assessing research impact on non-academic audiences

An examination of social science impact on non-academic audiences that develops three pilot projects studying the impacts of two ESRC-funded projects. Three approaches are explored: a networks and flows model; a user-panel assessment; and tracing post-research activity (see main text). The report also develops and presents an impact assessment 'toolbox'.

(Molas-Gallart et al, 2000)

Understanding research use in user communities

Impact assessment work that begins with user communities usually takes a case-based approach but with a diversity of embedded methods (see Chapters Two and Three). Often these consist of simple surveys of policy makers (asking about their use of research), but more detailed and sophisticated studies are possible. For example, the ESRC study referred to above (Molas-Gallart et al, 2000) augmented its forward-tracking approaches with an additional study of 'user panels'. These panels consisted of individuals who might be expected to draw upon the results of research (Molas-Gallart et al, 2000), and to provide a longitudinal element these individuals were interviewed several times during the life of the project, as well as participating in a wrap-up workshop. Such an approach provided a means to trace not only the existing utilisation of the research outputs but also the forms of interaction between researcher and users. Such approaches provide a flexibility of investigation that can explore not just specific channels of communication (as would be done in forward-tracking methods) but can also identify unexpected channels, interactions and effects.

Hanney and colleagues (2002) developed similar ideas exploring research utilisation in health policy making. They suggested using documentary analysis, interviews (building on a stakeholder analysis) and questionnaires using scaling methods as a way of unpacking the role of research in influencing the development of health policy around specific policy themes. Their expectation was that this approach 'will produce its own narrative or story of what caused utilisation in the particular context' (Hanney et al, 2002, p vi), but they also highlight the need to 'structure all such studies around a conceptual framework' (Hanney et al, 2002, p v) (a point that we shall pick up on shortly; in this study Hanney and colleagues (2002) adopted a 'flows and interfaces' model). An example of such an application of this approach is that adopted by Jung (2005) in the criminal justice field. Here the use of research alongside other influences was examined in a case-based approach to see how it had shaped the policy response to a prominent newspaper campaign to change the law around sex offender community notification. (The *News of the World* newspaper ran a prolonged – but ultimately unsuccessful – campaign to get UK legislation equivalent to the US's 'Megan's Law', giving rights to community notification of sex offenders.)

Work with a stronger ethnographic flavour has also been used to explore the complexities of research application; for example, the work of Gabbay and colleagues among healthcare professionals that conceptualised these users as 'communities of practice' (Gabbay et al, 2003; and see Chapter Seven). The importance of this and other work by the same team (Gabbay and le May, 2004) lies in the way in which it draws attention to the unpredictable, non-linear and contingent nature of many research impact processes (discussed in detail in Chapters Three and Four). What is clear about such ethnographic approaches is that they are better able to produce rich descriptions of impact dynamics rather than any summative assessments.

Assessing initiatives aimed at increasing research impacts

A considerable research base has now been built up that examines the effectiveness of various strategies for increasing research impact (this was reviewed in Chapter Five). Such work may focus on increasing the uptake and use of specific research findings (for example, through guideline implementation), examine the role of knowledge brokers engaged in research translation activities, or even encompass the effects of agencies or intermediaries aimed at increasing research/practice connectivity. What links all these areas of study is their use of programme evaluation strategies: experimental and quasi-experimental, as well as action research and qualitative/ethnographic work. This aspect of impact assessment – assessing the effects of research use enhancement initiatives – of course merits detailed study in its own right. Yet while it is our hope that this book will contribute to the design of more effective research use enhancement initiatives, the subsequent evaluation of these is beyond the scope of this text (there is a wide general literature that explores programme impact assessment, and it is not our intention to duplicate this here; see, for example, Chen, 1990; Pawson and Tilley, 1997; Clarke, 1999; Davies et al, 2000b). Suffice to say that we note this perspective on research impact assessment partly for reasons of completeness but also to illustrate the need to ensure that consideration of impacts is not carried out in isolation from the wider context of these research uptake activities. That is, given what we know about the significant obstacles to research use, assessment of research impact in the absence of significant research use enhancement initiatives would need to be carefully justified.

While each of these three approaches to understanding research impact is distinctive, they do, however, share some common methodological challenges. Before identifying these, we recapitulate on some of the key conceptual issues covered in earlier chapters that should underpin thinking about research use and impact. In particular, we highlight the need for appropriately sophisticated models of the research use process (see Chapter Four).

The importance of conceptualising research use when exploring research impact

Many of the core conceptual issues surrounding research use (for example, what it means to use research, and how this use has been modelled) have already been introduced (Chapters Two to Four). They are revisited rather briefly here for their specific implications for the design of research impact assessment studies. Assessing wider research impact is about identifying the influences of research on policy, managerial and service delivery practices, or on political and public discourse. As we have seen, such impacts may be instrumental, influencing changes in policy, practices and behaviour, or conceptual, changing people's knowledge, understanding and attitudes towards social issues. There are various models that seek to capture both these different types of research impact and the various processes by which this impact occurs. These models are important because they shape, and provide a means of assessing the appropriateness of, different approaches to assessing research impact.

Simple staged models of research uptake

Some models focus on the micro-processes of research use (for more details see Chapter Four). This includes those that have described different stages of research communication and use, such as that developed by Knott and Wildavsky (1980), and elaborated by, among others, Landry et al (2001a, 2001b). This model characterises seven stages by which research can be seen to have increasing impact: transmission of research; cognition of findings; reference made to significant studies; efforts made to operationalise findings; adoption of findings into policy; influence seen on practice decisions; and impact on end-stage outcomes. While such staged models may be appealing in offering a straightforward framework for assessment, they can, however, tend to over-weight the instrumental uses of research at the expense of conceptual effects. They also have an implicit over-reliance on linear assumptions (for example, they tend to suggest that all stages will be traversed in sequence, that the stages are equally important and cumulative, and that similar efforts are required to move across stages).

Despite the popularity of staged models, as we have seen, the process by which research impacts occur is rarely as simple or as straightforward as these models imply (see Chapter Four). In order to capture this complexity and provide a framework for assessing impact, more sophisticated models of the research impact process may also be important. Different models are suited to different circumstances and it is unlikely that any single model will capture adequately the variety of different types of research, the different forms which impact can take, and the different reasons why we might be interested in these impacts.

Modelling more complex types of research use

Many empirical studies have shown that only rarely will research impacts be direct, instrumental and clearly identifiable, such as when research leads directly to specific policy choices, or when research is neatly captured and codified in tools and instruments such as guidelines, protocols or organisational processes (explored in Chapter Two). Instead, much important 'decision making' is diffuse, hard to identify and characterised by 'non-decisional processes' and the progressive establishment of new routines (Weiss, 1980, 1982). When this is the case, research provides 'a background of empirical generalisations and ideas that creep into policy deliberation' (Weiss, 1980, p 381). Research may also be absorbed and internalised into practitioners' tacit knowledge as it emulsifies with many other sources of knowledge (experience, anecdote, received wisdom, lay knowledge, and so on). In doing so, it may leave few telltale signs of its passage, role or impact. Thus, research can contribute not just to decisional choices, but also to the formation of values, to the creation of new understandings and possibilities, and to the quality of public and professional discourse and debate. Capturing these subtle and diverse impacts poses considerable conceptual, methodological and practical challenges.

In response to these challenges, some models have focused attention on the nature of researcher–research user interaction (Chapters Four and Five). Lavis et al (2003), for example, characterise three basic types of research–user interaction: *producer push, user pull,* and *exchange.* These are explained more fully in Chapter Four and exemplified in policy contexts in Chapter Eight, but in brief, the first of these emphasises the active role taken by researchers in communicating the messages from their research; the second highlights the need for potential research users to create an environment whereby research is actively valued, sought and used; and the third ('exchange') outlines models of interaction between researchers and users that emphasise joint actions in defining, creating, validating and using research. From this taxonomy, Lavis et al (2003) go on to identify where and how research impacts might be sought and measured in each case.

The three models outlined by Lavis et al (2003) map to, and are extended by, the typology developed first by Weiss (1979) for use in understanding the research/policy nexus, but used extensively by others (for example, Molas-Gallart et al, 2000; Hanney et al, 2002). Six models of research use are commonly identified (see Box 9.2), the first three of which largely duplicate those of Lavis et al (2003). These models encapsulate different types and processes of research use (elaborations on their implications can be found in Chapter Two) and each implies different ways of approaching the impact assessment task. In searching for research impacts (especially in policy arenas) such classifications can be helpful in structuring both data gathering and interpretation. However, some of the caveats about the relatively static nature of most of these typologies do need to be borne in mind – caveats that we will return to shortly.

Box 9.2: Typical policy models of research use

(1) *Classic, knowledge-driven model:* a linear view that research findings may be communicated to impel action.

(2) *Problem-solving, policy-driven model:* a second linear view that begins with the end users of research and the problems they face, before tracking back in search of useful findings.

(3) *Interactive model:* here the process is modelled as a set of non-linear, less predictable interactions between researchers and users, with research impact happening through complex social processes of 'sustained interactivity'.

(4) *Political model:* here research findings are seen as but more ammunition in adversarial systems of decision making.

(5) *Tactical model:* in this model, research becomes a resource to be drawn on whenever there is pressure for action on complex public issues, and may be used not just to bolster decision making but also to stall and deflect pressure for action.

(6) *Enlightenment model:* this model eschews the notion that research impacts are simple and instrumental in effect; instead, research is seen to impact through 'the gradual sedimentation of insight, theories, concepts and perspectives' (Hanney et al, 2002, p 12).

Modelling evidence use in practice settings

An additional useful way of thinking about research use, especially in practice settings, was proposed by Walter et al (2004b) (this was elaborated in some detail in Chapter Seven). This modelling of research use is not concerned with macro policy but instead focuses on the use of research in organisations charged with service delivery. Three broad models of how research is taken up and used in practice settings were proposed:

(1) The *research-based practitioner model:* this model highlights the role of skilled individual practitioners who are able to express their knowledge needs in terms of researchable questions, and then search for and appraise the research base to meet these needs.

(2) The *embedded research model:* in this model, research is distilled and codified before being incorporated into organisational processes, procedures, protocols and guidelines. In this view, the incorporation of research evidence is a policy and management

responsibility, together with the establishment and maintenance of suitable compliance regimes.

(3) The *organisational excellence model:* this understanding emphasises the importance of local strategies of continuous improvement that draw both on research and on local experimentation. What matters most here is reflexivity and research mindedness within organisations, together with a willingness to change.

The relevance of this typology is that it helpfully categorises research use environments and suggests the need for a customised approach to impact assessments contingent on the dominant modes of research uptake and use. For example, in environments characterised by research-based practitioners, impact assessments may focus on individual knowledge, skills and behaviour; in contrast, environments where the embedded research model operates require us to look for impacts in the organisational processes and routines. A further significance is that each model emphasises the unlikeliness of significant research impacts in practice settings unless substantial organisational initiatives are already in place to facilitate this. To our knowledge, these models have not yet been used explicitly in developing impact assessments, but the potential is clear.

Moving towards more interactive models

Prevalent in conceptualisations of research use is the idea that the research work has already been completed – and findings are available – before the processes of use are considered. However, increasingly, research impact is not seen as an end-stage activity to be achieved post-completion. Instead, researchers may seek to engage with those anticipated to be the main users of their research throughout the course of the research process. It is not uncommon therefore for researchers to target user-engagement activities around multiple stages, for example, developing the research questions, clarifying the research design, interpreting the research data and communicating the research implications. Process impacts may be particularly important in these earlier stages, with outcome impacts more to the fore latterly. Thus, impact assessments may need to be structured around capturing this potential diversity of activity/impact, with impacts being viewed more as ongoing processes and accumulations rather than one-off events (Huberman, 1994).

The metaphors of hierarchies and networks provide two rather different ways of viewing the connectivity between researchers and potential research users (see Chapter Eight), but increasingly networks are considered to reflect better the process by which interaction and use occur. However, there is a difference between defining networks as simply channels of dissemination and seeing them as complex social arenas within which knowledge is shared and developed (see Chapters Seven and Eight for discussions in the practice and policy contexts respectively). Understanding networks as complex social arenas for learning reflects current understandings about communities of practice, which emphasise the importance of situated knowledge (Chapter Six). In this view, knowledge is not seen as an object that can be disconnected from the community within which it develops; the emphasis instead is on situated processes of knowing that will usually involve multiple parties. Once we move towards models of knowledge co-production such as this, the idea of research impact cannot readily be captured by phrases such as knowledge transfer. At the very least we need to think in terms of knowledge exchange, knowledge mediation, knowledge interaction or knowledge integration. And when we make these shifts in thinking, it no longer makes sense to conceive of impacts as unidirectional – the impact of research on policy and practice – but instead reciprocal impacts need to be considered. Such a view also draws attention to research use as a process rather than an event, one with no clear beginning or obvious end.

Conceptual considerations such as those we have just outlined draw attention to the need to problematise simplistic conceptions of research use/impact, and highlight the importance of applying models of research use that can capture the diversity and subtlety of impacts that are of interest. Moreover, the appropriateness of any conceptualisation cannot readily be separated from the use/purpose of the research impact assessment. It is hoped that both these discussions and those earlier (in Chapters Two to Four in particular) will highlight this and allow the development of better conceived and more carefully targeted impact assessments.

Methodological considerations in research impact assessment

Whatever the overall approach to assessing research impact, and whatever the underlying conceptualisation or models of research use proposed, all studies face a broad range of practical questions during methodological development. Some of these are considered here.

Some general methodological concerns

Research impacts may be far removed temporally from the source research – so one important question is, *when* should impacts be assessed? What timeframes are most appropriate given the competing pressures of leaving it long enough so that impacts can reasonably occur, but not so long that the trail traversed by the research goes cold? Related to this is the issue of how wide to cast the net in looking for impacts, with a complicating factor being that potential research users are themselves not necessarily clearly defined or readily identifiable. As Shove and Rip (2000, p 175; emphasis added) comment: 'researchers and research funders have succumbed to the temptation of constructing and then believing in *users of their own making*'. Actual and potential users may not in fact map so readily to those identified beforehand by research teams, research funders or research impact assessors. This challenges those who would explore research impacts to think more creatively about how such user communities can be identified, a challenge equally for studies that trace forward from research to impacts as for those that begin with user communities.

Further methodological questions include: how can we balance qualitative descriptions with quantitative assessments, taking account of both subjective and objective judgements? How can (or indeed, should) impacts be scored or even valued within different categories? And how can we aggregate across different sorts of impact? There are few easy answers to these difficult questions and, in practice, all impact assessment studies are likely to involve a series of not wholly satisfactory compromises.

Methodological challenges in forward tracking

Impact assessments that take a forward-tracking or payback type of approach may labour under significant methodological challenges. First, the impacts from various projects, programmes, and so on may be diverse and idiosyncratic: there is no reason why such impacts should necessarily follow any ordered or recognisable distribution. Indeed, it may well be the case that some projects/programmes may have few or no apparent impacts while others, perhaps for serendipitous reasons, are seen to have large and unexpected influence. Given this, a case-sampling approach may provide an uneven or misleading picture, suggesting the need for full inclusion to capture the full range of impacts (with consequently serious resource implications). Second, forward-tracking models (and especially those that emphasise payback) can tend to highlight linearity and proportionality in moving from identification of research outputs to assessments of impacts. Such a view simplifies and under-specifies the complexity of the processes at work, and brings to the fore complex issues of attribution (was the research really the key driver?) and additionality (how does the contribution of the research compare to that of other drivers?). Finally, while case-based approaches may attempt more holistic assessment, forward-tracking approaches in general can often be comparatively neglectful of the context within which research is communicated and acted upon.

This context matters. Research uptake and subsequent impact are clearly not merely a function of the research findings themselves, but are likely to relate at least as strongly to the local environment within which those findings are delivered and considered. Impact assessments – however constructed – need, therefore, to take account of this. Core aspects of context that need to be considered include the concomitant activities that are in place to increase the degree of research receptivity, the extent of local 'absorptive capacity' for new information (Cohen and Levinthal, 1990) and an understanding of the unpredictable 'policy swirl' that sees issues surface/resurface as they compete for policy and/or organisational attention.

Methodological challenges when focusing on user communities

Research with a focus on user communities can be more subtle in the effects explored (non-linearity, complexities of use, and so on) and may be more able to take account of the contexts of that use. Nonetheless, studies on user communities can also suffer from a similar range of the methodological challenges we have just outlined (sampling, attribution, additionality, and so on). A major challenge is to disentangle the specific effects of research findings from the myriad other influences on decision makers. In particular, assessing impacts on major policy choices may be especially problematic as research that feeds into policy choices is often synthesised, integrated with other research/knowledge/expert opinion, pre-digested in various ways, and mediated through expert or political intermediaries (Jung, 2005). Further difficulties can include a lack of clarity over who indeed are the key decision makers for policy, the rapid turnover of staff in key policy roles and the shifting in and out of focus of what are seen as pressing contemporary issues (with consequent confusion as to where impact assessment should be directed).

Practical considerations can also have an important influence on methodological choices. Tracking impacts directly is likely to be costly and it may be possible and appropriate to develop proxy measures of research impact. Such proxy measures need to be defined in the context of specific project, programme or agency objectives. They rely on the specification of good logic models: that is, models that identify the main mechanisms and processes through which desired impacts are achieved. For example, in a knowledge linkage and exchange framing of research use, we might seek to track those activities which reflect this model of research use. Proxy measures might include assessments of, for example, research user involvement in research planning, or interactive research discussion sessions with users. The utility of the proxy measures will in part depend on the evidence base for such research use mechanisms within the logic model. The more robust that evidence base the greater the reliance that can be placed on assessing (actual or potential) impact by ensuring that a project, programme or agency is doing the right things to achieve that impact. Building credible linkages in this way is a significant methodological hurdle, but may make the impact assessment task more manageable.

Taken together, these conceptual and methodological considerations pose significant challenges to the design of robust and practical impact assessments. The next section draws on these and pulls together a set of reflective questions that attempt to capture the key considerations and trade-offs in impact assessment design.

Reflective questions to aid impact assessment design

A broad range of questions can help to frame the purpose and orientation of any impact assessment (Box 9.3). Crucially, such questions can help us to distinguish between assessments for learning and those intended to make judgements, and can help us set the balance between qualitative and quantitative enquiry. Other questions that address expectations about the nature of research impacts can force a degree of explicitness about our underlying assumptions on the nature of research use and the extent to which use can be expected in the absence of a supportive or facilitated environment.

Box 9.3: Important framing questions for impact assessment

- Who are the key stakeholders for research impact assessments, and why do they want information assessing specifically the *non-academic* impacts of research?

- Will any impact assessment be primarily for *learning* (hence examinations of process may need to be emphasised)? Or will the assessment be primarily to enable *judgements* to be made (hence examinations of output and outcomes will necessarily be privileged)?
- Will the dominant mode of assessment be *quantitative* or *qualitative* – and what are the implications of this? Is the balance here well matched to the purposes of the impact assessment?
- Are we interested primarily in *outputs* (what is produced by the research), impact *processes* (how research outputs are used), *impacts per se* (the initial consequences of research use in various decision arenas), or *outcomes* (the subsequent consequences of changes in decision arenas for clients or public)?
- For any programme of research work, what impacts are desired, expected, or reasonable? Should all research *have* identifiable impacts? What about the notion that individual studies should primarily feed into other academic work or into research synthesis?
- Should impacts be assessed in the absence of initiatives to increase research uptake, or only in tandem with significant facilitative efforts?
- What are the resource implications of carrying out impact assessments? How will we know what level of investment in impact assessment is worthwhile?

Some questions on the overall design of impact assessments are posed in Box 9.4. These address the focus of any impact assessment (that is, the research itself, user environments, or uptake initiatives), suitable timeframes, and the desirability (or otherwise) of attempting to quantify nebulous and elusive phenomena. Also posed are questions that highlight the problematic concerns of whether research should be valued for its *actual* or its *potential* impacts, as well as raising the extent to which impact assessments should address what might be termed dysfunctional impacts such as research *misuse* (although, as we noted in Chapter Two, it can be difficult to decide what types of research use are actually misuse).

Box 9.4: Overall design issues

- Where will the research impact assessment be directed? Will the focus be on research itself, user environments, or uptake initiatives?
- What are the relative advantages/disadvantages of tracking forwards from research to impacts, or backwards from change to antecedent research?

- When should impacts be assessed? What timeframes are most appropriate given the competing pressures of leaving it long enough so that impacts can reasonably occur, but not so long that the trail traversed by the research goes cold?
- How can we balance qualitative descriptions with quantitative measures of impact? How will subjective and objective assessments be used and reconciled?
- When does scoring the extent of impacts become a useful tool, and what are its potential dangers? And (how) can we aggregate across different sorts of impact?
- How can (or indeed, should) impacts be valued as part of an exploration of the cost/benefit ratios for research?
- Should we judge/value research on its *actual* impacts (which may, at the time of examination, be rather limited) or on its *potential* impacts (which may be much larger, but an assessment of which will require modelling based on some assumptions about research uptake and subsequent service change)?
- Should we also try to identify and examine unintended and/or dysfunctional impacts, such as the *misuse* of research (however defined)?

Finally, Box 9.5 elaborates a series of questions that draw on the more complex and nuanced conceptualisations of research use introduced in earlier chapters. Here the concern is to broaden thinking from an exploration of simple, linear, unidirectional impacts focused on individuals to a consideration of more complex processes of knowledge integration/co-production, in tandem with an alertness to organisational and/or collective effects.

Box 9.5: Questions arising from more complex ideas of research use

- What types of research use/impacts are of most interest (for example, instrumental or conceptual; immediate or longer term; consensus, contention or paradigm-challenging)? And what steps can be taken to guard against a bias towards privileging those impacts that are most instrumental, upfront and readily identifiable?
- Who are the actual and potential research users? Can we identify them all, even tracking through unexpected avenues of diffusion?
- Assessing impacts on policy choices may be especially problematic as research that feeds into policy choices is often synthesised, integrated

with other research/knowledge/expert opinion, and *digested*. How will this be addressed?

- In such complex circumstances, how can we disentangle the *specific impacts* of research, pay attention to *non-linearity* of effects, address issues of *attribution*, and identify the *additionality* of any research contribution?
- Can we identify research usage not just at the individual level, but also at the organisational and system level?
- How will we access the hidden or tacit use of research, especially as we think more in terms of the co-production of knowledge?
- How can we take into account the receptivity of context, not just in terms of the concomitant strategies used to increase uptake but also in terms of the political acceptability of findings or propitiousness of message/timing?
- In making judgements about impacts, how can we acknowledge the role played by serendipity and the opening up of windows of opportunity?

Taken together this wide range of questions could guide thinking in the development of new, more carefully targeted and more nuanced studies of research use and impact. It should also be clear that meeting such a wide-ranging array of challenging concerns will likely require not just ingenuity in the design of impact assessments but also a multiplicity of approaches.

Concluding remarks

To date, studies of research use and research impact have shed much interesting light on the former but have yet to make significant inroads into the latter. Indeed, the range and diversity of conceptual, methodological and practical problems discussed here suggest that comprehensive assessments of the wider impacts of research are likely to be difficult to achieve in any complete and robust manner. Much more achievable will be the attainment of greater insights into how any impacts are mediated and how they might be encouraged.

Whether such insights are obtained will depend in large part on the reach and sophistication of the models of research use that underpin future studies. We hope that the insights generated throughout this book will contribute to these more sophisticated and contingent approaches. Nonetheless, it should be clear that no single model or approach to assessing wider research impact is likely to suffice. Instead, the appropriateness of the impact assessment approach will be a function of many factors including, among other things, the purpose of the assessment, the nature of the research, the context of the setting and the types of impact of key interest. If the impact assessment uses a forward-tracking approach from research to use then one key concern will be the need for researchers and research assessors to agree beforehand the likely ways in which the funded research might make an impact, and for assessments to be planned in the light of that. Assessments will also need to take place, at the very least, in conducive contexts if the conclusions drawn from these are not to deliver overly pessimistic messages.

Throughout we have been keen to point to the establishment of a clear purpose before research impact assessments are carried out. This is important partly because of the complexity and diversity of research use but also because of the potential for the findings from impact assessments themselves to be used (as a type of research) in tactical and political ways. One danger here is that social research policy might find itself being shaped by findings from impact studies that are necessarily partial and possibly questionable in their robustness. It will be important therefore to figure out how we can draw reasonable research policy implications from impact assessments, whatever their flaws. There are also important questions over the resource implications of carrying out impact assessments, for example how will we know what level of investment in impact assessment is worth it?

We need to know, therefore, more about how the findings from impact studies are likely to be used by the various players in the research use arena. There is a risk that the development of various strategies of research impact assessment could generate some unintended and potentially dysfunctional consequences. For example, could the desire/need to demonstrate 'impact' influence funding bodies so that they alter their research priorities or even the nature of the research that they seek to fund? Will knowledge of the role of impact assessments by researchers influence the nature of the questions posed and methods applied, for example, to ensure production of readily absorbed 'policy messages' that challenge little but can readily be tracked through to impact? Such responses may be particularly likely when impact assessments are geared towards summative judgements on the importance or value of research. Researchers, in particular, are unlikely to be entirely passive in the face of additional scrutiny of their performance: they may well respond in sometimes unexpected and potentially opportunistic ways. For example, will savvy researchers begin to employ not just professional communicators but also media relations consultants as a means of ensuring some research impacts? And, if they did, would this necessarily be a bad thing? Of course, whether such responses are seen as enhancing or damaging to the research enterprise may depend on the perspective adopted vis-à-vis the tactical uses of research and the relative balance sought between instrumental and enlightenment uses, but certainly the range and scope of such responses should be investigated.

Despite all these potential difficulties it seems likely that assessing wider research impact will grow in importance (for the political and practical reasons previously elaborated). We should nonetheless be cautious in our expectations that impact assessment – even when done well – will always be a faithful guide. Most problematically, considerable research impact may not necessarily reflect longer-term 'worth' of the research in a societal sense. Two contrasting examples of research can serve to illustrate that immediate 'impact' and longer-term 'worth' should not be conflated: Andrew Wakefield's initial study suggesting a link between the measles-mumps-rubella (MMR) vaccine and Autism Spectrum Disorders (ASD) (Wakefield et al, 1998) undoubtedly had enormous impact; in contrast, Sir Douglas Black's careful examination of the nature and causes of health inequalities ('The Black Report') at first achieved almost no impact, knocking on a policy door firmly closed for well over a decade (Whitehead et al, 1992). Yet few would now disagree about the relative worth of these two studies as much later work has failed to support the Wakefield hypothesis (Demicheli et al, 2005) and The Black Report is now seen as seminal (Berridge and Blume, 2002). The problem at the heart of the worth–impact relationship is the contested nature of much of social research itself: impact might perhaps be thought to be worthwhile only if one is persuaded by the key messages that are having the impact, and such support can be – as we have argued throughout – political as well as methodological.

Research impact then is a somewhat elusive concept, difficult to operationalise, political in essence, and hard to assess in a robust and widely accepted manner. Such assessments that are achieved have the potential to contribute some insights into the role and value of research but are themselves likely to be contested and have the capacity to be misused. An overemphasis on demonstrable impacts may in turn lead to the neglect of the more elusive but nonetheless crucial role of research as value-shaper, problem reframer and moral critic. Our conclusions from this are that research impact assessment should be aimed more squarely at helping advance insights into research use processes and the improvement of these than at making summative assessments of worth. Thus, those arguing for a central role for research in policy and practice arenas may have to content themselves with theoretical and process-based arguments for the importance of research rather than being able to point towards any substantial bodies of work demonstrating incontrovertible beneficial impact. Within an instrumentalist framing of evidence-informed policy and practice such a situation is clearly highly unsatisfactory; within our own broader and more dialogical view of research influence this may be accepted as the best that can realistically be expected.

TEN

Drawing some conclusions on *Using evidence*

We began this book by highlighting that sometimes research has an impact and sometimes it does not. We made it clear that we were interested in understanding the processes of influence of research-based knowledge in policy and practice arenas, how such influence is mediated, blocked or amplified, and how the praxis of policy making and service delivery may change in the face of a deeper degree of research engagement. More than this, we pinned our colours to a positive agenda: a belief that by understanding research use processes we would be in a better position to encourage an increase in their scale, scope and effectiveness. Our clear expectation here is that such enhancements of research use (inclusively defined) will, for the most part, be to the betterment of democratic discourse, public policy making, service organisation and the quality of public services.

Of course, along the way we have noted the irony that any evidence that increases in research use have indeed made the world a better place is at best partial and contested, and some would say is largely absent. Moreover, we have been at pains throughout to acknowledge that radical criticism of the research use 'project' has been a constant feature of debates throughout. Indeed, some commentators (albeit largely from an academic base rather than from policy or practice settings, and often driven from narrow conceptualisations of what it means to 'use' evidence) would condemn the enterprise as being pernicious or, worse, outrageous and oppressive: for example, Holmes et al (2006, p 180) assert that 'the evidence-based movement in health sciences constitutes a good example of microfascism'.

Given the twin challenges of sustained theoretical critique and an absence of empirical evidence, we will begin drawing together the thesis of this book by remaking the case for a somewhat privileged role for research-based evidence in public policy and service delivery. In exploring how research might contribute, we will draw attention to the diversity of work that comes under the rubric 'social research' and we shall again make it clear that we are not concerned to defend hard-and-fast rules as to what actually counts as research, opting instead for an inclusive eclecticism. We also emphasise that 'use' takes many forms, with conceptual and 'enlightenment' uses being at least as important as instrumental applications. What follows from such inclusiveness is a belief that the lessons from this book – such as the reader may care to take – are likely to have applicability for the uptake and use of a wider variety of 'evidence' than that limited solely to the findings emerging from any narrow definition of academic research.

Having made the case for exploring research use as a potentially worthwhile endeavour, we then begin to summarise and integrate the arguments developed at the heart of the book. Examination of how research (and other evidence) actually gets used in policy and practice highlights the complex and contingent nature of research use. This begins to draw attention to the multichannelled, multifaceted, interactive, iterative and transformative nature of the process. It also heralds a shift away from understanding research use as primarily an individualised process to seeing it as something that is socially and organisationally situated. What follows in turn is that strategies to increase research use should be fully cogniscent of, and indeed designed to exploit, these enhanced understandings. Building on this, we would suggest that research use enhancement strategies that encourage a greater variety of voices in opportunities for dialogue have the potential to give research a substantial, sustained, and sometimes critical, role in debates about public services. We end the chapter by sketching out some potential future research directions, which, if pursued, may enable more informed elaboration of the agenda set out throughout the book.

Research does matter – but research, and its uses, are diverse

The absence of a strong and compelling evidence base documenting improvements in public services arising from increased research use should come as little surprise. The diversity and complexity of research use articulated throughout this book attest to the challenges of assessing research impact, and Chapter Nine explores in detail how these complexities militate against simple demonstrations of the 'worth' of research use outside of academic settings. Nonetheless, there is something in the character of (at least high-quality) research that, for many, makes research-based knowledge worthy of special attention. At the very least, the rhetoric and discourse around research and evidence that are now centre stage justify some attention to research as a specific type of knowledge.

As we laid out during Chapter One, our view of research covers 'any systematic process of critical investigation and evaluation, theory building, data collection, analysis and codification'. Thus, research differs from other ways of knowing by being more careful and deliberative in how observations and inferences are made, by acknowledging the need for a degree of robustness and replicability, and by opening itself up to peer scrutiny and appraisal. Whereas the extent and methods by which these are achieved may be open to question and critique, the mere fact that they are aspired to, debated and contested suggests that particular importance is indeed attached (by many) to knowledge of this type. It need hardly be said that, in our view, paying special attention to research-based knowledge does not necessarily mean disrespecting other ways of knowing. Indeed, it should be obvious from much of the book that we see important roles for diverse ways of knowing, with a major challenge for research use being how these various ways are brought together and, if not reconciled, then at least accommodated.

Paying specific attention to research may confer a number of potential benefits. Research can help to highlight the implications both of ways of thinking (for example, how client needs are conceptualised) and of decision choices (for example, the potential outcomes from alternative modes of service delivery). But our view of research goes much broader than the preoccupation with the 'what works?' type of instrumental knowledge central to the 'evidence-based everything' agenda. Careful research can, for example, surface and question assumptions, challenge tacit knowledge, and probe 'taken-for-granted' aspects of problem framing/problem solutions. For example, basic economic and sociological research can unpack the structures and operations of society in its broadest sense; more applied in-depth interview and ethnographic work can shed new light on the operation and dynamics of service contexts; and ethnomethodological approaches can provide significant insights into the day-to-day accomplishments of clients and service users.

Social research is also not just about empirical findings. Theorising, reconceptualising and inference drawing can all add insights, and can contribute to problematising of current ways of thinking, and gradual reframing over time. However, neither empirical nor theoretical research can be counted on to provide definitive answers (in the social world at least), and work can sometimes be frankly contradictory. Reflexive social science accommodates such contestation and contradiction by seeing all work as partial, contingent and provisional. While such indeterminacy is seen by some to undermine the evidence-based agenda, the more interactive and dialogical approaches suggested in this book can more readily accommodate these uncertainties.

Social research is also not just about codified knowledge of social artefacts. It can also help surface and articulate values and, over time, may begin to challenge and even to alter these. When such value-shifts can be seen among key players in the social policy landscape, more far-reaching change may be possible. Research acts as a stimulus to dialogue and reflection, and through such processes it can expand or reshape tacit as well as explicit knowledge.

We would argue therefore that research can enrich debates at every level, enhancing public discourse and giving shape to practice disputes. Its contribution can move beyond simply describing and analysing the social world to providing a counterpoint against which assumptions, beliefs and values can be tested. While noting that sometimes research can be used as a powerful driver for reshaped understandings and policy change, we would also contend that its contested nature will often mean that more questioning forms of engagement can be observed and should be encouraged. Thus, good research should be seen more as a stimulus to respectful dialogue and less often as a trump card to truncate any debate. Used in these more careful ways, then, we would suggest that research may also help to rebalance power between diverse stakeholders, perhaps giving (stronger) voice to otherwise marginalised views for example, through user-led research. This may be especially important in bringing to the fore user experience and challenging 'expert' perspectives on key social policy problems. Taken together – and a deconstruction of the role of research notwithstanding – these potential benefits seem to us powerful reasons to give a full consideration to more and better uses of research evidence in public service contexts.

Having made these comments in defence of special attention being paid to research, we now move to articulate and integrate the analysis presented through the book. Looking first at the complexities and contingencies of research use as it is seen to happen on the ground, we then build on this to explore the insights we have gained for more effective strategies for encouraging greater research use.

Research use is complex and contingent

In this section we integrate and reflect back on our discussions in Chapters One to Four in particular, and summarise what we know about how research is used in policy and practice settings.

Research use is a complex, multifaceted and dynamic social process

'Using research' – as Chapters Two and Three underline – is an intricate and multifaceted phenomenon. Much attention in the literature, and indeed in the policy and practice worlds themselves, has been focused on instrumental uses of research – where research evidence has a concrete and visible impact on the actions and choices of policy makers and practitioners. Yet research can be used in many diverse ways, which reach well beyond the direct use of findings in making decisions. In fact, if we expect research to come up with simple answers to policy and practice questions, we may both be hoping for too much – social research rarely provides such definitive evidence – and also falling short in our expectations of what social research can offer. We know that, on the ground, research is often used in more subtle, indirect and conceptual ways, to bring about changes in knowledge and understanding, or shifts in perceptions, attitudes and beliefs: altering the ways in which policy makers and practitioners think about what they do, how they do it, and why. Instead of simply giving answers to a problem, research – and particularly social research – can shed further light on the problem itself, and may even call into question what counts as a 'problem' in the first place. While sometimes difficult to pin down, such conceptual uses of research can in fact be very powerful. Although often hidden from view (even from those apparently 'using' research), such conceptual and 'enlightenment' influences can, over time, have a weighty impact, contributing to large-scale shifts in intellectual discourses, policy paradigms and social currents of thought.

Research, however, can be used in more strategic and tactical ways as well, and this is especially true within the highly politicised context of the policy arena. Research may be used to support a political stance or to undermine an opponent, to justify a decision that has already been taken, or to legitimate maintaining current policy and practice. Often – and particularly by researchers – such strategic uses of research are seen as *mis*use: an illegitimate deployment of findings in ways that the original researchers never intended and would not necessarily support. Yet research itself is always contested, and these strategic uses of research can play important roles in the political arena, supporting democratic debate and bringing the potential for more substantive impact from research where its advocates win through (Weiss, 1979). Attempts to define the misuse of research are thus far from straightforward, and will always encounter those questions of ethics, power and what constitutes 'legitimate' knowledge to which research use is intimately tied.

At the same time, while it is helpful – both descriptively and analytically – to distinguish the different forms research use can take, research use on the ground is a much more fluid and iterative process than these kinds of classification imply. Research use is best characterised as a continual and iterative flow among such 'types' of use. And this flow of research through the policy and practice communities will take place through many different channels and routes, more and less direct, and involving more and less translation/ transformation on the way. Interpersonal and social interactions are often key to the use of research, whether among policy and practice colleagues, or more directly with researchers themselves. This begins to suggest that research use means more than simple application, and may involve instead the complex social processing of research-based knowledge. Research use thus emerges as an elaborate and dynamic process, not a single event: it continually escapes neat definitions, easy categorisations and oversimplified descriptions.

Focusing on research use by individuals limits our understanding of the potential scope of this process

Chapters Two to Four also unearth a tendency in the literature to treat research use as primarily an individualised process. The dominant model of research use – for much conceptual work as well as for many empirical studies of the field – envisages individual policy makers and practitioners consciously seeking out and keeping up-to-date with research, and then applying the evidence they thereby glean in their day-to-day work. This means that we know much less about the potential for research to enter policy and practice at the organisational or system levels, in ways in which individuals may in fact be unaware. Much of what we do know about the use of research – how it takes place, and the barriers and enablers to this process – concerns individual-level processes alone. The potential roles that research may play at the organisational and system levels thus remain relatively unexplored, although the evidence we have suggests such uses of research may well be important. At the same time, the strength of interpersonal routes for using research suggests that research use may be a much more social and collective process than existing accounts often imply. Again, however, such collective uses of research have been relatively neglected in the literature, and knowledge of these processes remains thin. This imbalance in favour of individuals' research use encourages a skewed understanding of the use of research. We thus need to move beyond individualised framings of the research use process, and to capture what using research might mean within wider organisations and systems, and for groups and communities as well.

Research use is highly contingent and context-dependent

Our analyses in Chapters Two to Four have highlighted the multiple influences that will shape whether and how research gets used. Existing knowledge in the field suggests that key factors include the nature of the research itself, the characteristics of those actually using the research, and the ways these are both then linked together. Above all, however, it is the context for research use that emerges as core to understanding when research will be used, and in what ways. As Chapters Two and Three described, research use is a highly contingent process that shifts across settings and over time. Individuals engage with research in personal and idiosyncratic ways, ways that are shaped by the unique worldviews, knowledge and experience that they bring to the research use process. When we understand this and also attend to how using research interacts with local organisational priorities, cultures and systems of meaning, or with the highly politicised, dynamic and unpredictable policy arena, we can then begin to see how, as a process, research use is heavily contingent on the varied contexts in which it is played out.

The research use process is thus not wholly isolatable: the use of research is deeply interconnected with its environment and the often complex and capricious form that research use takes can only be fully understood through a contextual lens. Despite these contingencies, we have been able to draw out some insights (discussed shortly) that operate across diverse settings. That said, our knowledge of how and the extent to which research use is influenced by different contexts is partial and emergent: more in-depth studies of research use are needed to help us understand more completely how and why the use made of research may vary across different policy and practice settings.

Research is more likely to be adapted than simply adopted

As we have detailed, research use does not take place in a vacuum. It is always embedded in particular contexts, whose particular cultures, structures and politics will temper the ways in which research gets taken up by policy makers and practitioners. It is rare that research evidence can simply be adopted into such contexts: more often it needs to be adapted to fit local concerns and needs. Knowledge from research is itself the product of the context of its creation, and will acquire new meaning within the fresh contexts of its use. This suggests that frameworks advocating the faithful replication of research are unlikely to be helpful in all but fairly limited circumstances. Moreover, adhering strictly to research fidelity can stifle research-based innovation, as well as inhibiting a more wide-ranging view of the roles research can play in policy and practice settings. Advocating faithful adoption also tends to neglect or suppress the role of other forms of knowledge – local, situational, tacit – in the use of research.

To avoid this, effective research use is likely to involve the interaction of research-based evidence with these other types of knowledge. Research use involves people – individually and collectively – engaging with research, bringing their own and their organisation's beliefs, values, narratives, knowledge and experience with them. As such, policy makers and practitioners are not simply 'tabula rasa' to be inscribed with the latest findings from research, but will be active interpreters and participants in the process of research use. Our discussions in Chapters Two and Four suggest that research use may be best understood through constructionist accounts of learning, in which knowledge from research is seen to be filtered through and shaped by pre-existing understandings and experience, and then fused with other forms of knowledge that may be more local, tacit, anecdotal or experiential. Research is thus translated and transformed, not simply transferred, in the process of its use.

Interactive and social models of the research use process offer the most insight and understanding

Traditional research use models – described in Chapter Four – have tended to characterise the use of research as a rational, linear and instrumental process. Such models are grounded in positivist underpinnings, which depict research evidence as rather uncomplicated, providing more-or-less isolatable 'facts'. In addition, such models tend to view policy makers and practitioners as the passive 'targets' of research. Yet, as our discussion has highlighted, such models simply fail to fit the messy, contested and dynamic nature of research use on the ground. They represent an idealised version of the research use process, which, while potentially having value as a normative model, is less useful when it comes to understanding the complexity and contingency that characterises research use in everyday contexts.

Interpretive framings of research use seem to offer a better route to understanding the use of research. They envisage the potential for research to be used in much more iterative, interactive and social ways, and recognise that research will be interpreted and reconstructed – alongside other forms of knowledge – in the process of its use. Taken to their logical extreme, however, interpretive models suggest that all knowledge – including that from research – represents merely the social construction of a 'truth', and that no clear criteria exist against which to judge research's claims to offer useful knowledge for policy and practice. Such framings therefore run the risk of undermining the very project of research use that we seek to advance.

Instead, as we discuss in Chapter Four, it seems most productive to balance these two framings – positivist and interpretivist – in an interactive model of the research use process. This model suggests that it is the linkages between the research and the research user communities that hold the key to understanding whether and how research gets used. It conceives of research use as a dynamic, complex and mediated set of interactions between policy makers and practitioners, and researchers. Research use thus involves two-way rather than unilinear flows of knowledge, in which researchers and research users each bring their own experience, values and understanding to bear in interpreting research and its meaning for local contexts. Using research emerges as a social and collective, not merely individual, process, that takes place through intricate interactions, which in turn are open to more conceptual and symbolic, not just instrumental, uses of research.

Having examined the nature of research use, we now begin to explore the best ways forward in developing strategies to promote better use of research. In doing so, we emphasise the main conclusions to emerge from Chapters Five to Eight about these issues.

Insights for developing research use strategies

Interactive and social approaches seem to hold the most promise

Our conclusions from Chapters Two to Four – that interactive and social models of the research use process offer the most promising insight and understanding – hold firm when we come to examine what we know about enhancing the use of research. In Chapter Five we looked at the evidence about successful research use strategies, and concluded that those that draw on interactive mechanisms for enhancing the use of research – whether this involves formal partnership arrangements between policy makers, practitioners and researchers, or more simply just enhancing discussion and debate in research seminars and workshops to encourage greater two-way exchange – are most likely to be effective. Further, strategies acknowledging the typically social and collective nature of research use also seem more likely to lead to success. Such strategies might involve supporting social influence and social learning, for example by identifying local champions for research, or else be more facilitative, aiming to encourage the development of local organisational structures and cultures that support research and its use.

Our review in Chapter Six of other literatures that help shed light on the research use process – those on individual and organisational learning, knowledge management and the diffusion of innovations – bears out these findings. Such literatures re-emphasise the key roles played by collective learning and sense-making, and by organisational culture and action, in knowledge use. They reinforce our conclusions about the need to develop research use strategies that focus on mechanisms of interaction, social influence and local facilitation. Creating successful research use strategies may thus mean being clear about the often implicit mechanisms and theories underlying different approaches – in other words, how they aim to secure research use – in order to identify those that best fit our understanding of the use of research as an interactive and social process.

Research use strategies would benefit from taking a wider target than individual uses of research

Chapters Seven and Eight have demonstrated that much of the activity on the ground to promote research use – in both policy and practice – is implicitly underpinned by an individualised framing of the research use process. This dominant model, in which individual policy makers and practitioners are seen as the key drivers of research use in seeking out and applying evidence in their day-to-day work, encourages research use strategies that focus at the level of the individual. Under this framing, research use strategies include, for example, an emphasis on dissemination to key policy makers (with or without some degree of translation and interpretation), one-to-one contacts between researchers and research users, and the development of research appraisal skills among practitioners. Yet the literature reviewed in Chapter Six sheds light on the collective ways in which knowledge may be used, and the inherently social contexts in which knowledge sharing and application take place. This means more than simply being aware of the ways in which organisations shape and constrain individual uses of research: we need to recognise too that both research use and decision making may be collective and embedded, not merely individual processes.

Given that studies of research use strategies, and of barriers and enablers to using research, have often been framed by individualised understandings of what research use means, findings from these studies should be used with caution, as they may erroneously prompt us to develop primarily individualised approaches to the use of research. Instead, we need to think in new and very different ways about the kinds of research use strategies that look wider than individuals. Chapters Seven and Eight began to tease out what such strategies might entail. For example, groups and teams can be created that jointly engage with research, in ways that support more social forms of learning and the development of a 'research-minded' local culture. Learning across organisations can also be important, and networks might offer a way forward here. Further, relatively little attention has been paid to developing research use at the system level, for example by finding ways of incorporating research into strategies, procedures and practice tools, and into standards and scrutiny processes. As Chapter Seven describes, this approach may prove to be a more efficient and effective tactic, at least for certain forms of evidence and in certain public service settings, than encouraging individual practitioners to access research to solve problems that are, in any case, likely to be shared rather than unique. However, the evidence that we have about developing effective organisational- and system-level research use strategies, while emerging, is still fairly thin on the ground.

Enhanced research use strategies emerge when we focus beyond instrumental impacts from research

Existing research use strategies – as Chapters Seven and Eight detail – are most often geared towards achieving instrumental uses of research. They tend to assume that research is mostly of value when evidence provides some kind of direct input for policy or practice decisions. Yet as we have described, conceptual uses of research, which contribute to subtle but potentially weighty shifts in knowledge, understanding and discourse, can be hugely significant in policy and practice settings, not just as a means to more instrumental impact from research, but as an end in themselves. This is particularly true for social research, which is a key conduit not only for findings but also for new concepts, ideas and frameworks for understanding the social world. Research use strategies should not neglect this substantial potential role for research. As we saw in Chapters Five to Eight, interactive approaches seem a promising way of supporting more conceptual research use. They may also provide opportunities for 'process' uses of research to emerge – where the very act of conducting or considering research can lead to policy and practice changes, for example by enhancing communication among key stakeholders or by sharpening ideas about outcomes from public services and programmes. Much value lies in developing strategies that acknowledge, and can tap into, the potential for impacts to emerge from this close engagement between the process of research and its ultimate users.

Chapter Eight identified why it might be particularly important to move beyond instrumental research use strategies in the policy arena. Crucially, a focus on the instrumental use of research tends to relegate research to a consensus-based role in policy making – providing evidence on effective and efficient ways forward where policy goals have already been determined and, even if not agreed, are at least somewhat taken for granted. Yet a key role for social research lies in its capacity actively to challenge public policy – to question the appropriateness or value of particular ways forward, to change the way policy problems are framed, to act as a moral critic, even to pose alternative agendas and goals. Current strategies for increasing policy uses of research too often seem to narrow down the possible roles that can be envisioned for research in this arena, and thereby undercut the potential for social research to open up policy procedures and enrich policy debates. More tactical and strategic uses of research are often key here, where research is used to advocate particular courses of action; research use strategies may be needed that can legitimate and enable these political kinds of use. Such approaches are not without problems, of course, and in particular there is a risk that tactical and strategic uses will undermine the potential for more respectful forms of dialogue and debate. Above all, then, research use strategies need to open up rather than close down the potential for research to influence policy, in multiple ways and through multiple routes, and to engage multiple stakeholders within more deliberative processes.

Developing effective research use strategies means attending carefully to the contexts in which they are to be enacted

We know from our analyses in Chapters Two to Four that multiple influences on using research will be at play in any setting where we hope to support research use. In developing research use strategies we need to analyse and take account of any contextual and cultural mediating factors, including, but not limited to, the usual range of barriers and enablers (see Chapter Three).

Moreover, as Chapter Seven described, it is unlikely that any one approach – interaction, say, or social influence – will be effective alone. Different approaches will thus need to be combined, in nuanced ways that are sensitive to their local contexts for implementation. Our knowledge about how this might best be done remains somewhat limited, but, as we argued in Chapter Seven, such 'multifaceted' strategies need to be firmly rooted in a clear understanding or model of the research use process and how this might be enhanced within a particular context. Issues to be considered may include:

- the kinds of research use that are important (instrumental, conceptual);
- whether research replication or a degree of adaptation is sought;
- where the focus for research use should lie – at the individual, organisational and/or system level;
- whether a top-down or more decentralised approach is appropriate;
- the balance of interest between the dialogical and process benefits from research use as compared to the specific outcomes on decision making;
- the process of research use that is envisaged – more linear and rational, or more iterative, dynamic and interactive; and
- what constitutes 'evidence' for use.

As we have described, models that frame research use in rational, instrumental and linear ways have somewhat limited potential in supporting better use of research. But we have also seen – in Chapters Seven and Eight – that there are circumstances in which such framings may be appropriate and successful. This may be the case, for example, where research evidence is less contested, and where there are clear and agreed problems for which it might provide helpful answers. Similarly, while we would in general advocate for more interactive framings to support research use strategies, these are not a panacea. For example, it is likely to be difficult to 'scale up' interactive approaches to using research, and they also tend to bring heavy resource implications.

Taking a wider perspective, there are additional issues about creating balanced 'packages' of strategies within particular public service areas or across the policy arena. To what extent do different research use strategies – underpinned by different models and assumptions – fit comfortably together? Again, we have no definitive answers here, but there are likely to be tensions – as well as complementarities – between different approaches. For example, in practice settings, interactive strategies, which aim to adapt research to the contexts of its use, sit somewhat uncomfortably with more rational and replicative strategies demanding careful fidelity to the original research. Fundamentally different views of what constitutes evidence, how it might be used and the role and autonomy of practitioners within this process are at play here, which may not be neatly resolved. As we noted in Chapter Six, relevant literatures from elsewhere have similarly concluded that different models – for example codification and personalisation strategies for knowledge management – may not always readily be blended. A constructive approach is likely to involve careful analysis of the context for implementation, and some attempt to surface and manage the potential tensions that may arise where different approaches are combined. This will require clarity about the kinds of models that underpin the ways we seek to promote the use of research (some of these models are elaborated in Chapter Seven).

Some cognisance of the interplay of knowledge, politics and power in using research can help us to develop appropriate and successful research use strategies

The kinds of tensions outlined between different approaches to promoting the use of research underline those issues of politics and power at play in the process of using research, and hence in developing strategies to enhance research use. Research is contested knowledge, produced through structures that embed multiple relations of power. Further, any attempt to support research use necessarily contains innate assumptions about the kinds of evidence it is legitimate to use in developing public services and public policy, and in what ways that evidence can be deployed. It also points to the kinds of roles that different individuals and agencies might play in this process.

Critical and postmodern perspectives on research use – discussed in Chapters Four and Six – alert us to the interplay of the structures and relations of power entailed in the very act of using research, and remind us of the ways in which promoting the use of research is itself a political project. Such perspectives encourage us to surface these questions of power, influence and ideology in the use of research in any given context. Adopting this more critical lens is a significant agenda for future studies and understandings of the use of research. But it is important too for how we think about developing strategies to enhance research use. It encourages us to make transparent those interests that are being brought to the table in the process of using research. It also makes us question what we mean when we say we want to 'enhance the use of research'. Finally, it forces us to attend to those multiple, diverse other knowledges and views that can get excluded when we privilege evidence from research in thinking about and developing public services, and reminds us of the need for research use strategies that can listen to, rather than silence, these alternative voices. The use of specific deliberative processes (for example, those introduced in Chapter Eight) is just one way of addressing this, but other innovative approaches will need to be tried and evaluated.

In sum, then, it is clear from the preceding discussions that we now know much about research use processes and how these might be enhanced. From this knowledge there is much of practical value, with many implications for the various actors – individual and organisational – who are potential research users or who are engaged in encouraging research use. It is to these that we now turn.

Practical implications for increasing research use

It is not possible to draw out any straightforward or definitive set of practical prescriptions from the foregoing discussions. The implications to be drawn will inevitably vary contingent on a wide variety of factors, for example: the types of research of central interest; the relationships between this research and other forms of knowledge; the roles envisaged for the research; the contexts of use; the policy/service sector of prime interest; and the national and local arrangements for service delivery. For all this contingency, however, there *are* some fairly convincing generic messages about what might be done to increase research use, particularly in practice settings where the evidence base for action is often rather stronger and less contested than in policy settings.

In practice settings, taken together our review in Chapter Five, the literatures explored in Chapter Six, and the examination of practice models in Chapter Seven, begin to highlight some remarkably consistent themes that emerge from across different service sectors. One set of observations, summarised in Box 10.1, outlines a range of guiding principles, each of which contributes to the likelihood of evidence-based practice flourishing in local circumstances. These build on the emerging evidence about what sorts of mechanisms can best support increased research use in practice settings, which are summarised in Box 10.2. Of course, how these principles and mechanisms are operationalised in different service settings and contexts, and which of the guiding principles are given most weight and attention, will and should vary, in part due to the way that the task of increasing research use is framed. Chapter Seven outlined three relevant framings – the research-based practitioner model, the embedded research model, and the organisational excellence model – that can help sharpen our thinking as we seek to foster the flows and use of evidence in practice settings. Taken together, these principles, mechanisms and models offer some clear ways of thinking through research use enhancement. While none of this offers a simple blueprint or recipe for success, and all aspects require further development and evaluation, they do provide some grounds for optimism that practice can indeed be made more evidence aware in many different ways.

Box 10.1: Some guiding principles to support the use of research in practice

Research must be translated: To be used, research needs to be adapted for, or reconstructed within, local practice contexts. Simply providing the findings is not enough. Adaptation can take multiple forms, including tailoring research results to a target group, enabling debate about their implications, 'tinkering' with research in practice, or developing research-based programmes or tools.

Ownership is key: Ownership – of the research itself, of research-based programmes or tools, or of projects to implement research – is vital to uptake. Exceptions can, however, occur where implementation is received or perceived as a coercive process.

The need for enthusiasts: Individual enthusiasts or 'product champions' can help carry the process of getting research used. They are crucial to selling new ideas and practices. Personal contact is most effective here.

Conduct a contextual analysis: Successful initiatives are those that analyse the context for research implementation and target specific barriers to and enablers of change.

Ensure credibility: Research take-up and use is enhanced where there is credible evidence, endorsement from opinion leaders – both expert and peer – and a demonstrable high-level commitment to the process.

Provide leadership: Strong and visible leadership, at both management and project levels, can help provide motivation, authority and organisational integration.

Give adequate support: Ongoing support for those implementing change increases the chance of success. Financial, technical, organisational and emotional support are all important. Dedicated project coordinators have been core to the success of many initiatives.

Develop integration: To assist and sustain research use, activities need to be integrated within existing organisational systems and practices. All key stakeholders need to be involved. Alignment with local and national policy demands also supports research use.

Box 10.2: Some helpful mechanisms for increasing the use of research

- *Tailored dissemination* can promote the conceptual use of research and may support more direct use where it enables discussion of findings.
- *Interactive approaches*, such as partnerships that encourage greater communication and links between researchers and practitioners or policy makers, enable individuals to adapt and 'test out' findings from research within their local context in ways that support conceptual and sometimes instrumental use.
- *Social influence* strategies show promise, but most have yet to be shown to be widely effective in promoting increased use of research,
- *Facilitative approaches* that offer technical, financial, organisational and emotional support can aid the implementation of research-based protocols, tools and programmes.
- *Reminders and incentives* appear to be successful in encouraging research-based practice and promoting research use in some settings, but otherwise evidence about the effectiveness of reinforcement interventions is less clear.
- *Multifaceted interventions* may be effective, but more evidence is needed about what mechanisms work best in what contexts and about how different mechanisms interact.

Although derived largely from practice settings, many of the principles in Box 10.1 also seem to provide helpful guidance for action in policy contexts. This may be particularly so when, as we highlighted in Chapter Eight, much of the research use activity in policy contexts is aimed at addressing issues of research supply and, to some extent, research demand. However, one of the conclusions of our analysis was that there are limits to what can be expected from 'supply-and-demand'-type approaches to increasing the connection between research and policy. It is true that research supply can indeed be improved in many ways, especially by paying attention to the quality of research synthesis, its translation and communication. It also appears to be the case that amended policy processes have the potential to increase research demand and receptivity. Attention to both of these issues – as is ongoing in many areas – will likely reap some, although perhaps modest, beneficial impacts. However, it also seems necessary to be more attentive to the interplay between supply and demand. As already noted, interaction and intermediation seem to be the keys to getting a wider variety of research used in policy deliberations.

Interaction and intermediation – the drawing in of a multiplicity of voices and agencies into policy deliberations – offer many more opportunities for social research to become part of the policy discourse. The degree of contestation and debate that inevitably arises is likely to encourage more challenging roles for research: roles that go beyond simply supporting developments within current policy and service paradigms, to roles that question and challenge these paradigms. While clearly demanding in many ways, such open, pluralistic and interactive policy communities have exciting possibilities and democratising potential.

This vision for vibrant policy processes – involving active policy networks covering a wide variety of agencies and intermediaries – is most challenging for those who would like to see a centrally managed set of strategies for developing research-informed policy. It will involve a good deal of 'letting go' of policy debates and the evidence that shapes them. From the government side, there will need to be a willingness to get actively engaged with a wider range of actors – for all the difficulties, tensions and delays that might then ensue. Outside of government, there is already a growing awareness of what might be achieved through being policy-savvy, media-aware and advocacy-oriented. Some of these non-governmental agencies are already showing the way with creative mixed strategies involving vigorous attempts to shape the policy context, the creation of active alliances around key issues, and the development of demonstration projects that signal what can be done on the ground. There is much that governmental and non-governmental agencies can do, therefore, to help shape an environment where productive research-informed interactions are more likely than unproductive research-oblivious clashes.

Thus, there are a number of positive messages that we would draw about how research use might be better enabled. We could also go further to note that the knowledge that we have gleaned about research use may have wider applicability in helping us to understand the use of other forms of evidence. Because of this we will now begin to explore the implications of our analysis for a view of evidence that goes wider than simply research-based evidence; after this we will lay out some potential avenues for further study of research use and research use enhancement strategies.

Inclusive views of research – implications for wider evidence

The definition of research quoted earlier and elaborated on in Chapter One ('any systematic process of critical investigation...') could readily be interpreted as being inclusive of other forms of systematic enquiry beyond those that are carried out by recognised researchers in universities and other traditional research establishments. For example, systematic study by scrutiny agencies, analyses of routine service management data, stakeholder consultations through questionnaires or focus groups, might all be seen as so little different from formal research for any distinction to be rendered dubious. The conclusion we would draw from this is that there are few hard-and-fast distinctions between different categories of knowledge, that ambiguity and fluidity are the norm, and that knowledge labels (such as 'research' or 'evidence') are less technical descriptions than political value judgements. This is not to take away from the importance of traditional research as one very important form of knowledge worthy of particular attention, but it does draw attention to the need to examine the source, nature and use of *all* knowledge, research-based or otherwise.

With such an inclusive view of research/evidence, the issue then becomes more about what is the interpretation and meaning of the 'knowledge' in hand, and how persuasive is it to various stakeholders? Both of these (meaning and persuasiveness) are, of course, highly contextualised, and different stakeholders may come to rather different conclusions. Such an analysis also draws attention to issues of power and legitimacy (for example, who gets to decide what is persuasive and what is not?), as well as to the rhetorical and persuasive power of language (for example, when do observations become research? when does research get labelled as evidence?). While these challenges may become more acute as we broaden our categorisation of research, they are no different in kind to many of the concerns about the mutability of research that we have been at pains to draw attention to throughout the book. That is, sticking with a narrow and exclusive definition for research does not side-step the problems – they arise whenever different groups come together to discuss research in contexts other than that where the research work was completed; moreover, since no context is static, even these become different with the passage of time.

We would argue, then, that there are no clear lines of demarcation between research and other forms of systematically gathered information (matters of degree, yes, but not category shifts). Such a view, if taken to extremes, might be seen to undermine our advocation for a relatively privileged position for research; but operated modestly it does no more than recognise the contextual and contested nature of all knowledge, research included. This inclusivity of view about the nature of research/evidence opens up scope for broader lessons to be drawn from the messages contained in this book. It is our hope that readers will draw insights most particularly for research and research use, but will also use our analysis more widely for other sources of evidence and knowledge whose use they may be seeking to understand or promote.

Research use requires more study

While we now know much about research use, there is much yet still to uncover. Many of these knowledge gaps have been made explicit during discussions in earlier chapters, and Chapter Nine in particular highlighted the difficulties of developing comprehensive studies of research impact. Despite these difficulties, further research – if well cast in the light of the analysis so far – has the potential to augment our understanding about research use processes, as well to provide a richer, more nuanced evidence base on which to develop research use enhancement strategies. In our view, new research is probably best aimed at excavating insights for learning rather than comprehensive evaluations that seek to assess the full gamut of research use impacts on public policy/public services *per se*. This does not mean, however, that research use enhancement strategies cannot themselves be evaluated: on the contrary, such strategies can – and should – be researched both formatively and summatively as a means of contributing to the evidence base underpinning research use. More work in this area could, therefore, make a significant contribution both to showing how research use can indeed make a difference, and to showing how we can make a difference to research use.

Throughout this book we have stressed the importance of seeing research use as interactive and iterative, a collective and social process, and best understood through interpretive or social constructionist ways of seeing. It follows therefore that more research that takes on board these perspectives is likely to provide helpful new knowledge, adding to the accumulation of studies outlined in earlier chapters. Such approaches will, naturally and quite rightly, stress the importance of context as an important mediating factor, but context-dependent knowledge need not always mean atomised and incommensurate studies. Developments in research summary such as narrative synthesis, realist synthesis and meta-ethnography (Mays et al, 2005) have the potential not only to enhance the synthesis of research for policy and practice but also to help collate our knowledge about research use itself. As the field of 'research use studies' comes of age, we are already beginning to see such useful syntheses of previous work (Dopson and Fitzgerald, 2005).

Given the diversity of potential uses of research discussed so far, and the potential importance of process effects, it will be valuable for further study to examine these diverse aspects in more detail. In particular, we need more research on research use that moves away from a preoccupation with instrumental and consensus applications of evidence to examine the conceptual, enlightenment, challenging and even paradigm-shifting roles of research. Moreover, given the highly politicised environments within which research is used, more study of the strategic, political and tactical uses of research might help us to see how such use (often denigrated as misuse) can be an integral part of open and informed policy debates and decision making. In addition, research on research use has too often seemed to begin with the research part of the research/research user nexus; further study would do well to shift the emphasis from research to research users so that research use can be explored properly contextualised as one part of the many and varied influences on praxis.

In policy making, as the analysis of Chapter Eight showed, there is much more yet to uncover about how intermediaries and policy networks operate within more open and deliberative policy processes, how they use evidence (including research), how this might be encouraged, and what are the scale and scope for potential dysfunctions. Such work might consider, for example, what sorts of intermediaries or knowledge brokers might make a difference, how they might be encouraged to interact, the extent to which diverse voices are actually encouraged and heard in these environments, and the extent to which research findings do indeed begin to challenge embedded positions and vested interests. With all such work it will also be important to look widely for the subtle operations of power and the presence and effects of unintended consequences.

In practice settings, we set out in Chapter Seven some of the key models that might be used to describe activities aimed at increasing research uptake: the research-based practitioner model, the embedded research model and the organisational excellence model. Each of these deserves further study in its own right, perhaps drawing on the literatures outlined in Chapter Six, or moving more widely to embrace, for example, literatures on social marketing, communication processes or new conceptualisations of practice. Further study is also needed to see whether other models of evidence use are evident in different settings, the extent to which hybrids have or can be developed and, importantly, the implications and tensions arising from running various models in parallel.

But there is much of importance that lies between policy and practice settings that has been either ignored or lumped up or down into each of these categories. In particular, there is much debate and activity that takes place in service organisations that is not about the individual practitioner–client interaction but that cannot either be well described as 'policy'. Such organisational decision taking, and wider management activity, could (perhaps should) embrace evidence, but the means and processes by which it might do so have to date been little studied (Walshe and Rundall, 2001; Tranfield et al, 2003; Pfeffer and Sutton, 2006). Nonetheless, despite the relatively little activity so far, the role of evidence in this arena too is likely to be hotly contested (Learmonth and Harding, 2006). The relative absence of studies addressing evidence use at this meso organisational level, taken together with the importance of the collective nature of research use and its contextually situated nature, suggest that this is an important research gap in need of being filled.

A further significant area of neglect in understanding research use is the means by which greater and more effective use might be made of lay and/or service user perspectives. User-led research has been seen as one means of bringing user concerns to the fore but it remains in relative infancy. The research-based practitioner model introduced in Chapter Seven is also intended to have at its heart an integration of research evidence and client values/preferences, but the accomplishment of this integration is far from straightforward. In terms of shaping service delivery, it can sometimes seem that while the user's voice is being heard more in services (at least in the UK), such user input is often somewhat disconnected from debates about evidence. Indeed, when user perspectives and evidence do come into contact there can be a tendency to see these as incommensurate, with correspondingly little effort being made to advance towards shared perspectives. More open policy processes, and more responsive service delivery, cannot be achieved unless we can find ways of bringing together more effectively this plurality of voices, perspectives and knowledge. Research into knowledge intermingling and dialogical processes could have a significant role to play in bringing about more useful understanding of how disparate knowledge may be reconciled.

Finally, interest in research use processes is an international phenomenon. While much of this book has observed and commented from a UK perspective, we have at times taken the opportunity to draw more widely on an international literature. A more systematic drawing on this international literature might leverage additional insights, and we believe that there is much to gain from additional systematic study of international similarity and difference. Despite an ever-present warning on the particularity of context, such international study may enrich our local understandings and throw open the door to more creative strategies for encouraging research use.

Concluding remarks

From the evidence and arguments presented in this book, and through our wider experience, we would draw a number of conclusions. Good social research should matter, although what constitutes 'good' in research terms is diverse and eclectic – in its ontological and epistemological assumptions, its methods, theories and settings. Of course, assessments of research quality cannot readily be separated from the contexts of research use, and these contexts too are multifarious. The enormous growth of social research over recent decades, and the numerous potential openings for its use, are, therefore, both an opportunity and a challenge to those (like us) who seek greater connection between this knowledge resource and public services.

Studies of research use should look wider than instrumental impacts with identifiable policy/practice changes to embrace conceptual uses that challenge existing ways of thinking. Indeed, we believe that as much social good may come indirectly from the processes of research use (such as increased and more knowledgeable dialogue engaging a wider variety of voices) as may come more directly from identifiable changes in policy direction or practice shifts. Moreover, our view is that interactive, social and interpretive models of research use – models that acknowledge and engage with context, models that admit roles for other types of knowledge, and models that see research use as being more than just about individual behaviour – are more likely to help us when it comes to understanding how research actually gets used, and to assist us in intervening to get research used more.

There is now at least some credible evidence to underpin these conclusions: indeed, it has been a central mission of this book to collate and share that evidence. Nonetheless, we also recognise that there are many gaps and inadequacies in that evidence. It is therefore a secondary aim that the book should prompt further structured enquiry into addressing these evidential inadequacies.

In closing we would note that at several points in this book we have referred to the potential for social research to be part of 'respectful dialogue' between stakeholders in public services. While such use is not the only way in which research can have impact, we believe that, on the whole, constructive debate and dialogue drawing on research offers the best chance for a collective enhancement of knowledge and practice in public services. We hope that in teasing out the contingencies of research use and research enhancement strategies we will have contributed to further respectful dialogue in this field with similar effect.

References

Abbott, M., Walton, C. and Greenwood, C.R. (2002) 'Research to practice: phenomic awareness in kindergarten and first grade', *Teaching Exceptional Children*, vol 34, no 4, pp 20-7.

Addicott, R., McGivern, G. and Ferlie, E. (2006) 'Networks, organizational learning and knowledge management: NHS cancer networks', *Public Money & Management*, vol 26, no 2, pp 87-94.

Albaek, E. (1995) 'Between knowledge and power: utilization of social science in public policy making', *Policy Sciences*, vol 28, pp 79-100.

Anderson, M., Cosby, J., Swan, B., Moore, H. and Broekhoven, M. (1999) 'The use of research in local health service agencies', *Social Science and Medicine*, vol 49, pp 1007-19.

Antil, T., Desrochers, M., Joubert, P. and Bouchard, C. (2003) 'Implementation of an innovative grant programme to build partnerships between researchers, decision makers and practitioners: the experience of the Quebec Social Research Council', *Journal of Health Services Research and Policy*, vol 8, supp 2, pp 44-50.

Antman, E.M., Lau, J., Kupelnick, B., Mosteller, F. and Chalmers, T. C. (1992) 'A comparison of results of meta-analyses of randomized control trials and recommendations of clinical experts: treatments for myocardial infarction', *Journal of the American Medical Association*, vol 268, no 2, pp 240-8.

Argyris, C. and Schon, D.A. (1996) *Organizational learning II*, Reading, MA: Addison-Wesley.

Armfield, G., Armistead, C. and Kiely, J. (2002) *The COE learning network: Final Report*, Bournemouth: Centre for Organisational Effectiveness, Bournemouth University.

Armistead, C. and Meakins, M. (2002) 'A framework for practising knowledge management', *Long Range Planning*, vol 35, pp 49-71.

Audit Commission (1990) *A short cut to better services: Day surgery in England and Wales*, London: Audit Commission.

Auspos, P. and Kubisch, A. (2004) *Building knowledge about community change: Moving beyond evaluations*, New York: Aspen Institute Round Table on Community Change.

Ausubel, D.P., Novak, J.D. and Hanesian, H. (1986) *Educational psychology: A cognitive view* (2nd edition), New York: Werbel and Peck.

Baker, C.D. and Lorimer, A.R. (2000) 'Cardiology: the development of a managed clinical network', *British Medical Journal*, vol 321, pp 1152-3.

Balas, E.A., Austin, S.M., Mitchell, J.A., Ewigman, B.G., Bopp, K.D. and Brown, G.D. (1996a) 'The clinical value of computerized information services', *Archives of Family Medicine*, vol 5, pp 271-8.

Balas, E.A., Boren, S.A., Brown, G.D., Ewigman, B.G., Mitchell, J.A. and Perkoff, G.T. (1996b) 'Effect of physician profiling on utilization: meta-analysis of randomized clinical trials', *Journal of General Internal Medicine*, vol 11, no 10, pp 584-90.

Barab, S.A. and Duffy, T.M. (2000) 'From practice fields to communities of practice', in D.H. Jonassen and S.M. Land (eds) *Theoretical foundations of learning environments*, Mahwah, NJ: Lawrence Erlbaum Associates, pp 25-55.

Barker, K. (1994) 'Strengthening the impact of R&D evaluation on policy making: methodological and organisational considerations', *Science and Public Policy*, vol 21, no 6, pp 405-13.

Barratt, M. (2003) 'Organizational support for evidence-based practice within child and family social work: a collaborative study', *Child and Family Social Work*, vol 8, no 2, pp 143-50.

Bate, P. and Robert, G. (2002) 'Knowledge management and communities of practice in the private sector: lessons for modernizing the National Health Service in England', *Public Administration*, vol 80, no 4, pp 643-63.

Bell, S. (2004) 'Appropriate policy knowledge, and institutional and governance implications', *Australian Journal of Public Administration*, vol 63, no 1, pp 22-8.

Bemelmans-Videc, M.-L. (1989) 'Dutch experience in the utilization of evaluation research: the procedure of reconsideration', *Knowledge in Society*, vol 2, no 4, pp 31-48.

Bergmark, A. and Lundstrom, T. (2002) 'Education, practice and research: knowledge and attitudes to knowledge of Swedish social workers', *Social Work Education*, vol 21, no 3, pp 359-73.

Berman, P. and McLaughlin, M. (1978) *Federal program supporting educational change, volume 8: Implementing and sustaining innovations*, Santa Monica, CA: Rand Corporation.

Berman, P. and Pauley, E. (1975) *Federal programs supporting educational change, volume 2: Factors affecting change agent projects*, Santa Monica, CA: Rand Corporation.

Bero, L.A., Grilli, R., Grimshaw, J.M., Harvey, E., Oxman, A.D. and Thomson, M.A. (1998) 'Closing the gap between research and practice: an overview of systematic reviews of interventions to promote the implementation of research findings', *British Medical Journal*, vol 317, pp 465-8.

Berridge, V. and Blume, S. (eds) (2002) *Poor Health: Social Inequality before and after The Black Report*. London: Frank Cass Publishers.

Bessant, J., Kaplinsky, R. and Morris, M. (2003) 'Developing capability through learning networks', *International Journal of Technology Management and Sustainable Development*, vol 2, no 1, pp 19-38.

Bevan, G. and Hood, C. (2006) 'Have targets improved performance in the English NHS?', *British Medical Journal*, vol 332, pp 419-22.

Blackler, F., Crump, N. and McDonald, S. (1998) 'Knowledge, organizations and competition', in G. von Kogh, J. Roos and D. Kleine (eds) *Knowing in firms: Understanding, managing and measuring knowledge*, London: Sage Publications, pp 67-86.

Blunkett, D. (2000) 'Blunkett rejects anti-intellectualism and welcomes sound ideas', *DfEE News*, www.dfes.gov/uk/pns/DisplayPN.cgi?pn_id=2000_0043 accessed 20 December 2006.

Boaz, A. (2006) 'Systematic reviews as a source of evidence for policy: an in-depth exploration of a review of mentoring', PhD thesis, Queen Mary College, London.

Boaz, A., Ashby, D. and Young, K. (2002) *Systematic reviews: What have they got to offer evidence-based policy and practice*, Working Paper 2, London: ESRC UK Centre for Evidence-Based Policy and Practice (www.evidencenetwork.org).

Bogenschneider, K., Olson, J.R., Linney, K.D. and Mills, J. (2000) 'Connecting research and policymaking: implications for theory and practice from the Family Impact Seminars', *Family Relations*, vol 49, no 3, pp 327-39.

Bolam, R. (1994) 'The impact of research on policy and practice in continuing professional development', *British Journal of In-Service Education*, vol 20, no 1, pp 35-46.

Booth, S.H., Booth, A. and Falzon, L.J. (2003) 'The need for information and research skills training to support evidence-based social care: a literature review and survey', *Learning in Health and Social Care*, vol 2, no 4, pp 191-201.

Bradley, P., Nordheim, L., De La Harpe, D., Innvaer, S. and Thompson, C. (2005) 'A systematic review of qualitative literature on educational interventions for evidence-based practice', *Learning in Health and Social Care*, vol 4, no 2, pp 89-109.

Brechin, A. and Siddell, M. (2000) 'Ways of knowing', in R. Gomm and C. Davies (eds) *Using evidence in health care*, Buckingham: Open University Press, pp 3-25.

Bridgman, P. and Davis, G. (2003) 'What use is a policy cycle? Plenty, if the aim is clear', *Australian Journal of Public Administration*, vol 62, no 3, pp 98-102.

Brown, G. (1995) 'What is involved in learning?', in C. Desforges (ed) *An introduction to teaching: Psychological perspectives*, Oxford: Blackwell, pp 11-33.

Brumner, J. (1990) *Acts of meaning*, Cambridge, MA: Harvard University Press.

Bukowitz, W.R. and Williams, R.L. (1999) *The knowledge management fieldbook*, Harlow: Financial Times Prentice Hall.

Bullock, H., Mountford, J. and Stanley, R. (2001) *Better policy making*, London: Cabinet Office, Centre for Management and Policy Studies.

Bullock, K., Erol, R. and Tilley, N. (2006) *Problem-oriented policing and partnerships: Implementing an evidence-based approach to crime reduction*, Cullompton: Willan.

Bullock, R., Gooch, D., Little, M. and Mount, K. (1998) *Research in practice: Experiments in development and information design*, Dartington Social Research Series, Aldershot: Ashgate Publishing Ltd.

Bulmer, M. (1986) 'The policy process and the place in it of social research', in M. Bulmer (ed) *Social science and social policy*, London: Allen & Unwin, pp 3-30.

Buntinx, F., Winkens, R., Grol, R. and Knottnerus, J.A. (1993) 'Influencing diagnostic and preventive performance in ambulatory care by feedback and reminders: a review', *Family Practice*, vol 10, pp 219-28.

Buxton, M. and Hanney, S. (1996) 'How can payback from health research be assessed?', *Journal of Health Services Research & Policy*, vol 1, pp 35-43.

Buysse, V., Sparkman, K.L. and Wesley, P.W. (2003) 'Communities of practice: connecting what we know with what we do', *Exceptional Children*, vol 69, no 3, pp 263-77.

Cabinet Office (1999) *Professional policy making for the twenty first century*, London: Cabinet Office, Strategic Policy Making Team.

Cabinet Office (2000) *Adding it up: Improving analysis and modelling in central government*, London: Cabinet Office, Performance and Innovation Unit.

Cabinet Office (2003a) *The Magenta book: Guidance notes for policy evaluation and analysis*, London: Cabinet Office, Government Chief Social Researcher's Office.

Cabinet Office (2003b) *Trying it out: The role of 'pilots' in policy making: Report of the review of government pilots*, London: Cabinet Office, Government Chief Social Researcher's Office.

Campbell, D. (1969) 'Reforms as experiments', *American Psychologist*, vol 24, pp 409-29.

Caplan, N. (1979) 'The two-communities theory and knowledge utilization', *American Behavioral Scientist*, vol 22, no 3, pp 459-70.

CfPS (Centre for Public Scrutiny) (2005) *The Scrutiny Map: Charting the range and reach of scrutiny bodies across the public sector*, London: CfPS.

CfPS (Centre for Public Scrutiny) (2006) *CfPS Annual Conference*, London, 28 June (www.cfps.org.uk/events/indexphp - accessed 20 December 2006).

Chalmers, I. (2005) 'If evidence-informed policy works in practice, does it matter if it doesn't work in theory?', *Evidence & Policy*, vol 1, no 2, pp 227-42.

Chassin, M. R. (2006) 'Does paying for performance improve the quality of health care?' *Medical Care Research and Review*, vol 63 no 1, pp 122S-25S.

Chen, H.-T. (1990) *Theory-driven evaluations*, London: Sage Publications.

CHSRF (Canadian Health Services Research Foundation) (2000) *Health services research and evidence-based decision making*, Ottawa: CHSRF.

CHSRF (2006) *Weighing up the evidence, making evidence informed guidance accurate, achievable, and acceptable: A summary of the workshop held on September 29 2005*, Ottawa: CHSRF.

Clarence, E. (2002) 'Technocracy reinvented: the new evidence-based policy movement', *Public Policy and Administration*, vol 17, no 3, pp 1-11.

Clark, G. and Kelly, L. (2005) *New directions for knowledge transfer and knowledge brokerage in Scotland*, Edinburgh: Scottish Executive, Office of the Chief Researcher.

Clarke, A. (1999) *Evaluation research: An introduction to principles, methods and practice*, London: Sage Publications.

Cleaver, H., Wattam, C. and Cawson, P. (1998) *Children living at home: The initial children protection enquiry; Ten pitfalls and how to avoid them; What research tells us / Assessing risk in child protection*, London: NSPCC.

Cohen, M., March, J. and Olsen, J. (1972) 'A garbage can model of organizational choice', *Administrative Science Quarterly*, vol 17, pp 1-25.

Cohen, W. and Levinthal, D. (1990) 'Absorptive capacity: a new perspective on learning and innovation', *Administrative Science Quarterly*, vol 35, no 1, pp 128-52.

Colebatch, H. K. (2005) 'Policy analysis, policy practice and political science', *Australian Journal of Public Administration*, vol 64, no 3, pp 14-23.

Commission on Social Sciences (2003) *Great Expectations: The social sciences in Great Britain*, London: Academy of Learned Societies for the Social Sciences (www.the-academy.org.uk).

Conrad, D.A. and Christianson, J.B. (2004) 'Penetrating the "black box": financial incentives for enhancing the quality of physician services', *Medical Care Research & Review* vol 61, no 3, pp 37S-68S.

Coopey, J. (1995) 'The learning organisation: power, politics and ideology', *Management Learning*, vol 26, pp 193-214.

Coopey, J. and Burgoyne, J. (2000) 'Politics and organisational learning', *Journal of Management Studies*, vol 37, no 6, pp 869-86.

Coote, A., Allen, J. and Woodhead, D. (2004) *Finding out what works: Building knowledge about complex, community-based initiatives*, London: King's Fund.

Cordingley, P. and Bell, M. (undated) *School-Based Research Consortia Initiative: An overview report* (unpublished).

Cordingley, P., Baumfield, V., Butterworth, M., McNamara, O. and Elkins, T. (2002) 'Lessons from the School-Based Research Consortia', Paper presented at the British Educational Research Association Annual Conference, University of Exeter, 12-14 September.

Council for Medical Sciences, The Netherlands (2002) *The societal impact of applied health research: Towards a quality assessment system*, Amsterdam: Council for Medical Sciences.

Court, J. and Young, J. (2003) *Bridging research and policy: Insights from 50 case studies*, London: Overseas Development Institute (ODI).

Court, J., Hovland, I. and Young, J. (2005) *Bridging research and policy in development: evidence and the change process*, Rugby: ITDG Publishing

Cousins, J.B. and Leithwood, K.A. (1986) 'Current empirical research on evaluation utilization', *Review of Educational Research*, vol 56, no 3, pp 331-64.

Cousins, J.B. and Leithwood, K.A. (1993) 'Enhancing knowledge utilization as a strategy for school improvement', *Knowledge: Creation, Diffusion, Utilization*, vol 14, no 3, pp 305-33.

Cousins, J.B. and Simon, M. (1996) 'The nature and impact of policy-induced partnerships between research and practice communities', *Educational Evaluation and Policy Analysis*, vol 18, no 3, pp 199-218.

Crane, J. (ed) (1998) *Social programs that work*, New York: Russell Sage Foundation.

Crewe, E. and Young, J. (2002) *Bridging research and policy: Context, evidence and links*, London: Overseas Development Institute (ODI).

CRG (2001) *Evaluating the Connexions Card Demonstration and Pathfinder Projects*, Department for Education and Skills Research Report 318, London: DfES.

Crow, I., France, A., Hacking, S. and Hart, M. (2004) *Does Communities that Care work? An evaluation of a community-based risk prevention programme in three neighbourhoods*, York: Joseph Rowntree Foundation.

Culyer, A. and Lomas, J. (2006) 'Deliberative processes and evidence-informed decision making in health care: do they work and how might we know?', *Evidence & Policy*, vol 2, no 3, pp 357-71.

Cumbers, B.J. and Donald, A. (1998) 'Using biomedical databases in everyday clinical practice: the Front-Line Evidence-Based Medicine project in North Thames', *Health Libraries Review*, vol 15, no 4, pp 255-65.

Currie, G. (ed) (2006) 'Managing knowledge across organisational and professional boundaries within public services', *Public Money and Management*, vol 26, no 2, pp 83-130.

Dahler-Larsen, P. (2000) 'Surviving the routinization of evaluation: the administrative use of evaluations in Danish municipalities', *Administration and Society*, vol 32, no 1, pp 70-92.

Daley, B.J. (2001) 'Learning and professional practice: a study of four professions', *Adult Education Quarterly*, vol 52, no 1, pp 39-54.

Davenport, E. (2001) 'Knowledge management issues for online organisations: "communities of practice" as an exploratory framework', *Journal of Documentation*, vol 57, no 1, pp 61-75.

Davenport, T.H. and Glaser, J. (2002) 'Just-in-time delivery comes to knowledge management', *Harvard Business Review*, vol 80, no 7, pp 107-111.

Davey Smith, G., Ebrahim, S. and Frankel, S. (2001) 'How policy informs the evidence', *British Medical Journal*, vol 322, pp 184-5.

Davies, H.T.O. and Harrison, S. (2003) 'Trends in doctor–manager relationships', *British Medical Journal*, vol 326, pp 646-9.

Davies, H.T.O. and Nutley, S.M. (1999) 'The rise and rise of evidence in health care', *Public Money and Management*, vol 19, no 1, pp 9-16.

Davies, H.T.O. and Nutley, S.M. (2000) 'Developing learning organisations in the new NHS', *British Medical Journal*, vol 320, pp 998-1001.

Davies, H.T.O., Nutley, S.M. and Smith, P.C. (1999) 'What works? The role of evidence in public sector policy and practice' *Public Money and Management*, vol 19, no 1, pp 3-5.

Davies, H.T.O., Nutley, S.M. and Smith, P.C. (eds) (2000a) *What works? Evidence-based policy and practice in public services*, Bristol: The Policy Press.

Davies, H.T.O., Nutley, S.M. and Tilley, N. (2000b) 'Debates on the role of experimentation', in H.T.O. Davies, S.M. Nutley and P. Smith (eds) *Evidence-based policy and practice in public services*, Bristol: The Policy Press, pp 251-75.

Davies, H. T. O., Nutley, S. M. and Walter, I. (2005) 'Approaches to assessing the non-academic impact of social science research', Report of the ESRC symposium on assessing the non-academic impact of research, 12-13 May, Research Unit for Research Utilisation, University of St Andrews (www.ruru.ac.uk/publications.html).

Davies, P. (1999) 'What is evidence-based education?', *British Journal of Educational Studies*, vol 47, pp 108-21.

Davies, P. (2004) 'Is evidence-based government possible? Jerry Lee Lecture 2004', Paper presented at the 4th Annual Campbell Collaboration Colloquium, Washington, DC, 19 February.

Davis, D. (1998) 'Does CME work? An analysis of the effect of educational activities on physician performance or health care outcomes', *International Journal of Psychiatry in Medicine*, vol 28, no 1, pp 21-39.

Davis, D., O'Brien, M.A.T., Freemantle, N., Wolf, F.M., Mazmanian, P. and Taylor-Vaisey, A. (1999) 'Impact of formal continuing medical education: do conferences, workshops, rounds, and other traditional continuing education activities change physician behavior or health care outcomes?', *Journal of the American Medical Association*, vol 282, no 9, pp 687-874.

Davis, D.A. and Taylor-Vaisey, A. (1997) 'Translating guidelines into practice: a systematic review of theoretic concepts, practical experience and research evidence in the adoption of clinical practice guidelines', *Journal of the Canadian Medical Association*, vol 157, no 4, pp 408-16.

Dawson, S., Sutherland, K., Dopson, S., Miller, R. and Law, S. (1998) *The relationship between R&D and clinical practice in primary and secondary care: Cases of adult asthma and glue ear in children: Final Report*, Cambridge and Oxford: Judge Institute of Management Studies, University of Cambridge and Saïd Business School, University of Oxford.

De Corte, E. (2000) 'High-powered learning communities: a European perspective', Paper presented at the First Conference of the Economic and Social Research Council's Research Programme on Teaching and Learning, Leicester, 9-10 November.

Demicheli, V., Jefferson, T., Rivetti, A. and Price, D. (2005) 'Vaccines for measles, mumps and rubella in children', *Cochrane Database of Systematic Reviews 2005*, issue 4, art. no.: CD004407. DOI: 10.1002/14651858.CD004407.pub2.

Denis, J.-L. and Lomas, J. (2003) 'Convergent evolution: the academic and policy roots of collaborative research', *Journal of Health Services Research and Policy*, vol 8, supp 2, pp 1-5.

Denton, C., Vaughn, S. and Fletcher, J. M. (2003) 'Bringing research-based practice in reading intervention to scale', *Learning Disabilities Research & Practice*, vol 18, no 3, pp 201-11.

Department of Health (1995) *Child Protection: messages from the research*, London: HMSO.

Desforges, C. (2000) 'Putting educational research to use through knowledge transformation', Keynote lecture to the Further Education Research Network Conference, Coventry: Learning and Skills Development Agency, December.

Dickey, L.L., Gemson, D.H. and Carney, P. (1999) 'Office system interventions supporting primary care-based health behavior change counseling', *American Journal of Preventive Medicine*, vol 17, no 4, pp 299-308.

DiMaggio, P. and Powell, W. (1983) 'The iron cage revisited: institutional isomorphism and collective rationality in organisation fields', *American Sociological Review*, vol 48, pp 147-60.

Dodgson, M. (1993) 'Organisational learning: a review of some literatures', *Organization Studies*, vol 14, pp 375-94.

Donald, A. (1998) *The Front-Line Evidence-Based Medicine Project*, London: NHS Executive North Thames Regional Office (Research and Development).

Dopson, S. (2006) 'Debate: Why does knowledge stick? What we can learn from the case of evidence-based health care', *Public Money & Management*, vol 26, no 2, pp 85-6.

Dopson, S. and Fitzgerald, L. (eds) (2005) *Knowledge to action: Evidence-based healthcare in context*, Oxford: Oxford University Press.

Dopson, S., Locock, L., Chambers, D. and Gabbay, J. (2001) 'Implementation of evidence-based medicine: evaluation of the Promoting Action on Clinical Effectiveness programme', *Journal of Health Services Research and Policy*, vol 6, no 1, pp 23-31.

Dopson, S., Locock, L., Gabbay, J., Ferlie, E. and Fitzgerald, L. (2005) 'Evidence-based health care and the implementation gap' in S. Dopson and L. Fitzgerald (eds) *Knowledge to action: evidence-based health care in context*, Oxford: Oxford University Press, pp 28-47.

Downe, J. and Martin, S. (2005) 'Inspecting the inspectors: an empirical analysis of the external inspection of local government services', Paper presented at the International Research Symposium on Public Management, Milan, April.

Dror, Y. (1983) *Public policymaking reexamined*, New Brunswick, Canada: Transaction Books.

Drummond, M. and Weatherly, H. (2000) 'Implementing the findings of health technology assessments: if the CAT got out of the bag, can the TAIL wag the dog?', *International Journal of Technology Assessment in Health Care*, vol 16, no 1, pp 1-12.

Duke, K. (2001) 'Evidence-based policy making? The interplay between research and the development of prison drugs policy', *Criminal Justice*, vol 1, no 3, pp 277-300.

Duncan, S. (2005) 'Towards evidence-inspired policy making', *Social Sciences*, News from the ESRC September 2005, issue 61, pp 10-11.

Eagar, K., Cromwell, D., Owen, A., Senior, K., Gordon, R. and Green, J. (2003) 'Health services research and development in practice: an Australian experience', *Journal of Health Services Research and Policy*, vol 8, supp 2, pp 7-13.

Effective Health Care Bulletin (1994) 'Implementing clinical guidelines: can guidelines be used to improve clinical practice?', *Effective Health Care Bulletin*, vol 1, no 8, pp 1-12.

Effective Health Care Bulletin (1999) 'Getting evidence into practice', *Effective Health Care Bulletin*, vol 5, no 1, pp 1-16.

Eisenstadt, M. (2000) 'Sure Start: research into practice; practice into research', *Public Money & Management*, vol 20, no 4, pp 6-8.

Ekblom, P. (2002) 'From the source to the mainstream is uphill: the challenge of transferring knowledge of crime prevention through replication, innovation and anticipation', in N. Tilley (ed) *Analysis for crime prevention*, Crime Prevention Studies, Volume 13, Monsey, NY: Criminal Justice Press, pp 131-203.

Estabrooks, C.A., Floyd, J.A., Scott-Findlay, S., O'Leary, K.A. and Gushta, M. (2003) 'Individual determinants of research utilization: a systematic review', *Journal of Advanced Nursing*, vol 43, no 5, pp 506-20.

Everton, T., Galton, M. and Pell, T. (2000) 'Teachers' perspectives on educational research: knowledge and context', *Journal of Education for Teaching*, vol 26, no 2, pp 167-82.

Fairhurst, K. and Huby, G. (1998) 'From trial data to practical knowledge: qualitative study of how general practitioners have accessed and used evidence about statin drugs in their management of hypercholesterolaemia', *British Medical Journal*, vol 317, pp 1130-4.

Fear, W. and Roberts, A. (2004) *The state of policy in Wales: A critical review*, Cardiff: Wales Funders Forum.

Feldman, P.H., Nadash, P. and Gursen, M. (2001) 'Improving communication between researchers and policy makers in long-term care: or, researchers are from Mars; policy makers are from Venus', *The Gerontologist*, vol 41, no 3, pp 312-21.

Fennessy, G. (2001) 'Knowledge management in evidence-based healthcare: issues raised when specialist information services search for the evidence', *Health Informatics Journal*, vol 7, no 1, pp 4-7.

Ferlie, E. (2005) 'Conclusion: from evidence to actionable knowledge?', in S. Dopson and L. Fitzgerald (eds) *Knowledge to action? Evidence-based health care in context*, Oxford: Oxford University Press, pp 182-97.

Ferlie, E. and Addicott, R. (2004) *The introduction, impact and performance of cancer networks: A process evaluation*, London: Centre for Public Services Organizations, Royal Holloway.

Finch, J. (1986) *Research and policy: The use of qualitative methods in social and educational research*, London: Farmer Press.

Fisher, T. (1997) 'Learning about child protection', *Social Work Education*, vol 16, no 2, pp 92-112.

Foucault, M. (1977) *Discipline and punish*, Harmondsworth: Penguin.

Freemantle, N., Harvey, E.L., Wolf, F.M., Grimshaw, J.M., Grilli, R. and Bero, L. A. (2002) 'Printed educational materials: effects on professional practice and health care outcomes', *The Cochrane Library*, no 2, Oxford: Update Software.

Fulop, N., Protopsaltis, G., King, A., Allen, P., Hutchings, A. and Normand, C. (2005) 'Changing organisations: a study of the context and processes of mergers of health care providers in England', *Social Science & Medicine*, vol 60, pp 119-30.

Fulop, N., Protopsaltis, G., Hutchings, A., King, A., Allen, P., Normand, C. and Walters, R. (2002) 'Process and impact of mergers of NHS trusts: multicentre case study and management cost analysis', *British Medical Journal*, vol 325, p 246.

Funk, S.G., Tornquist, E.M. and Champagne, M.T. (1995) 'Barriers and facilitators of research utilization: an integrative review', *Nursing Clinics of North America*, vol 30, no 3, pp 395-407.

Furniss, J. and Nutley, S.M. (2000) 'Implementing What Works with Offenders – The Effective Practice Initiative', *Public Money & Management*, vol 20, no 4, pp 23-8.

Gabbay, J. and le May, A. (2004) 'Evidence based guidelines or collectively constructed "mindlines"? Ethnographic study of knowledge management in primary care', *British Medical Journal*, vol 329, p 1013.

Gabbay, J., le May, A., Jefferson, H., Webb, D., Lovelock, R., Powell, J. and Lathlean, J. (2003) 'A case study of knowledge management in multi-agency consumer-informed "communities of practice": implications for evidence-based policy development in health and social services', *Health: An Interdisciplinary Journal for the Social Study of Health, Illness and Medicine*, vol 7, no 3, pp 283-310.

General Teaching Council for England (2004) *The impact of collaborative Continuing Professional Development (CPD) on classroom teaching and learning*, London: General Teaching Council for England.

General Teaching Council for England (2005) *Continuing Professional Development*, London: General Teaching Council for England.

Gibson, B. (2003) 'Beyond "two communities"', in V. Lin and B. Gibson (eds) *Evidence-based health policy: Problems and possibilities*, Melbourne: Oxford University Press, pp 18-32.

Giddens, A. (1987) *Social theory and modern sociology*, Cambridge: Polity Press.

Gill, P.S., Makela, M., Vermeulen, K.M., Freemantle, N., Ryan, G., Bond, C., Thorsen, T. and Haaijer-Ruskamp, F.M. (1999) 'Changing doctor prescribing behaviour', *Pharmacy World and Science*, vol 21, no 4, pp 158-67.

Gira, E., Kessler, M.L. and Poertner, J. (2004) 'Influencing social workers to use research evidence in practice: lessons from medicine and allied health professions', *Research on Social Work Practice*, vol 14, no 2, pp 68-79.

Glasziou, P. and Haynes, B. (2005) 'The paths from research to improve health outcomes', *ACP Journal Club*, vol 142, no 2, pp A8-A10.

Goering, P., Butterill, D., Jacobson, N. and Sturtevant, D. (2003) 'Linkage and exchange at the organizational level: a model of collaboration between research and policy', *Journal of Health Services Research and Policy*, vol 8, supp 2, pp 14-19.

Goh, S.C. (1998) 'Toward a learning organisation: the strategic building blocks', *Advanced Management Journal*, vol 63, no 2, pp 15-22.

Goldblatt, P. and Lewis, C. (1998) *Reducing offending: An assessment of research evidence on ways of dealing with offending behaviour*, Home Office Research Study 187, London: Home Office.

Golden-Biddle, K., Reay, T., Petz, S., Witt, C., Casebeer, A., Pablo, A. and Hinings, B. (2003) 'Toward a communicative perspective of collaborating in research: the case of the researcher–decision maker partnership', *Journal of Health Services Research and Policy*, vol 8, supp 2, pp 20-5.

Gomm, R. (2000) 'Would it work here?', in R. Gomm and C. Davies (eds) *Using evidence in health and social care*, Buckingham: Open University Press, pp 171-89.

Gomm, R. and Davies, C. (eds) (2000) *Using evidence in health and social care*, Buckingham: Open University Press.

Gorman, D. (2005) 'Complexity, evaluation and evidence-based practice in the 21st century', *The Evaluator*, Winter, pp 12-14.

Government Social Research (2002) *Annual report 2001-2*, London: Government Social Research Heads of Profession Group.

Granados, A., Jonsson, E., Banta, D.H., Bero, L.A., Bonair, A., Cochet, C., Freemantle, N., Grilli, R., Grimshaw, J., Harvey, E., Levi, R., Marshall, D., Oxman, A., Pasart, L., Raisanen, V., Rius, E. and Espinas, J. A. (1997) 'EUR-ASSESS project group subgroup report on dissemination and impact', *International Journal of Technology Assessment in Health Care*, vol 13, no 2, pp 220-86.

Green, L.W. and Kreuter, M.W. (1992) 'CDC's Planned Approach to Community Health as an application of PRECEDE and an inspiration for PROCEED', *Journal of Health Education*, vol 23, no 3, pp 140-7.

Greenberg, D., Linksz, D. and Mandell, M. (2003) *Social experimentation and public policymaking*, Washington, DC: The Urban Institute Press.

Greenberg, D.H. and Mandell, M.M. (1991) 'Research utilization in policymaking: a tale of two series (of social experiments)', *Journal of Policy Analysis and Management*, vol 10, no 4, pp 633-56.

Greenhalgh, T., Robert, G., Bate, P., Kyriakidou, O., Macfarlane, F. and Peacock, R. (2004) *How to spread good ideas: A systematic review of the literature on diffusion, dissemination and sustainability of innovations in health service delivery and organisation*, London: National Co-ordinating Centre for NHS Service Delivery and Organisation R & D (NCCSDO).

Greenwood, C.R., Tapia, Y., Abbott, M. and Walton, C. (2003) 'A building-based case study of evidence-based literacy practices: implementation, reading behavior, and growth in reading fluency, K-4', *Journal of Special Education*, vol 37, no 2, pp 95-110.

Grilli, R. and Lomas, J. (1994) 'Evaluating the message: the relationship between compliance rate and the subject of a practice guideline', *Medical Care*, vol 32, no 3, pp 202-13.

Grilli, R., Ramsay, C. and Minozzi, S. (2002) 'Mass media interventions: effects on health services utilisation', *The Cochrane Library*, no 2, Oxford: Update Software.

Grimshaw, J.M., Eccles, M.P., Walker, A.E. and Thomas, R.E. (2002) 'Changing physicians' behavior: what works and thoughts on getting more things to work', *Journal of Continuing Education in the Health Professions*, vol 22, no 4, pp 237-43.

Grimshaw, J.M., Shirran, L., Thomas, R.E., Mowatt, G., Fraser, C., Bero, L.A., Grilli, R., Harvey, E., Oxman, A. and O'Brien, M.A. (2001) 'Changing provider behavior: an overview of systematic reviews of interventions', *Medical Care*, vol 39, no 8, pp II-2-II-45.

Grimshaw, J.M., Thomas, R.E., MacLennan, G., Fraser, C., Ramsay, C.R., Vale, L., Whitty, P., Eccles, M.P., Matowe, L., Shirran, L., Wensing, M., Dijkstra, R. and Donaldson, C. (2004) 'Effectiveness and efficiency of guideline dissemination and implementation strategies', *Health Technology Assessment*, vol 8, no 6, pp 1-351.

Grol, R. and Grimshaw, J.M. (1999) 'Evidence-based implementation of evidence-based medicine', *Journal on Quality Improvement*, vol 25, no 10, pp 503-13.

Gross, P.A. and Pujat, D. (2001) 'Implementing practice guidelines for appropriate antimicrobial usage', *Medical Care*, vol 39, no 8, pp II-55-II-69.

Haas, P.M. (1992) 'Introduction: epistemic communities and international policy coordination', *International Organization*, vol 46, no 1, pp 1-35.

Hagell, A. and Spencer, L. (2004) 'An evaluation of an innovative method for keeping social care staff up to date with the latest research findings', *Child and Family Social Work*, vol 9, pp 187-96.

Halladay, M. and Bero, L. (2000) 'Implementing evidence-based practice in health care', *Public Money & Management*, vol 20, no 4, pp 43-51.

Hammersley, M. (2001) 'Some questions about evidence-based practice in education', Paper presented at the Annual Conference of the British Educational Research Association, University of Leeds, 13-15 September, available at www.leeds.ac.uk/educol/documents/00001819.htm

Hannan, A., Enright, H. and Ballard, P. (1998) 'Using research: the results of a pilot study comparing teachers, general practitioners and surgeons', *EDUCATION-LINE*, available at www.leeds.ac.uk/educol/documents/000000851.htm, accessed August 2004.

Hanney, S.R., Gonzalez-Block, M.A., Buxton, M.J. and Kogan, M. (2002) *The utilisation of health research in policy-making: Concepts, examples and methods of assessment. A report to the World Health Organization, Health Economics Research Group*, Uxbridge: Brunel University.

Hansen, M.T., Nohria, N. and Tierney, T. (1999) 'What's your strategy for managing knowledge?', *Harvard Business Review*, March–April, pp 106–16.

Hargreaves, D.H. (1997) 'In defence of research for evidence-based teaching: a rejoinder to Martyn Hammersley', *British Educational Research Journal*, vol 23, no 4, pp 405–19.

Hargreaves, D.H. (1998) *Creative professionalism: The role of teachers in the knowledge society*, London: Demos.

Harry, R., Hegarty, P., Lisles, C., Thurston, R. and Vanstone, M. (1997–98) 'Research into practice does go: integrating research within programme development', *Groupwork*, vol 10, no 2, pp 107–25.

Hartley, J. and Benington, J. (2006) 'Copy and paste, or graft and transplant? Knowledge sharing through inter-organizational networks', *Public Money & Management*, vol 26, no 2, pp 101–8.

Hartley, J., Radnor, Z., Rashman, L. and Morrell, K. (2005) 'Rich aunts and poor cousins: a comparison of service improvement through audit and inspection and through sharing good practice', Paper presented at the International Research Symposium on Public Management, Milan, April.

Harvey, J., Oliver, M. and Smith, J. (2002) 'Towards effective practitioner evaluation: an exploration of issues relating to skills, motivation and evidence', *Educational Technology & Society*, vol 5, no 3, pp 3–10.

Hatton, N. and Smith, D. (1995) 'Reflection in teacher education: towards definition and implementation', *Teaching and Teacher Education*, vol 11, no 1, pp 33–49.

Hayes, S. (1981) 'Single case experimental design and empirical clinical practice', *Journal of Consulting and Clinical Psychology*, vol 49, pp 193–211.

Heclo, H. (1978) 'Issue networks and the executive establishment', in A. King (ed) *The new American political system*, Washington, DC: American Enterprise Institute for Public Policy Research, pp 87–124.

Hedberg, B. (1981) 'How organizations learn and unlearn', in P. Nystrom and W. Starbuck (eds) *Handbook of organizational design vol 1*, Oxford: Oxford University Press, pp 3–27.

Heisig, P. and Vorbeck, J. (2001) 'Benchmarking survey results', in K. Mertins, P. Heisig and J. Vorbeck (eds) *Knowledge management: Best practices in Europe*, Berlin: Springer, pp 97–126.

Hemsley-Brown, J. and Sharp, C. (2003) 'The use of research to improve professional practice: a systematic review of the literature', *Oxford Review of Education*, vol 29, no 4, pp 449–70.

Hicks, D. (1991) 'A cautionary tale of co-citation analysis', *Research Evaluation*, vol 1, pp 31-6.

Hildebrand, C. (1999) 'Making knowledge management pay off', *CIO Enterprise Magazine*, 15 February.

Hillage, J., Pearson, R., Anderson, A. and Tamkin, P. (1998) *Excellence in research on schools*, London: The Institute for Employment Studies/ Department for Education and Employment.

Hodson, R. (2003) *Leading the drive for evidence based practice in services for children and families*, Totnes: Research in Practice.

Hollin, C.R. (1995) 'The meaning and implications of "programme integrity"', in J. McGuire (ed) *What works: Reducing reoffending – guidelines from research and practice*, Chichester: John Wiley & Sons Ltd, pp 195-208.

Holmes, D., Murray, S.J., Perron, A. and Rail, G. (2006) 'Deconstructing the evidence-based discourse in health sciences: truth, power and fascism', *International Journal of Evidence Based Healthcare*, vol 4, pp 180-6.

Home Office (1999) *Reducing crime and tackling its causes: A briefing note on the crime reduction programme*, London: Home Office.

Homel, P., Nutley, S.M, Webb, B. and Tilley, N. (2004) *Investing to deliver: Reviewing the implementation of the UK Crime Reduction Programme*, Home Office Research Study 281, London: Home Office.

Hope, T. (2004) 'Pretend it works: evidence and governance in the evaluation of the reducing burglary initiative', *Criminal Justice*, vol 4, no 3, pp 287-308.

Howard, C. (2003) 'The policy cycle: a model of post-Machiavellian policy making?', *Australian Journal of Public Administration*, vol 64, no 3, pp 3-13.

Huberman, M. (1987) 'Steps towards an integrated model of research utilization', *Knowledge: Creation, Diffusion, Utilization*, vol 8, no 4, pp 586-611.

Huberman, M. (1990) 'Linkage between researchers and practitioners: a qualitative study', *American Educational Research Journal*, vol 27, no 2, pp 363-91.

Huberman, M. (1993) 'Linking the practitioner and researcher communities for school improvement', *School Effectiveness and School Improvement*, vol 4, no 1, pp 1-16.

Huberman, M. (1994) 'Research utilization: the state of the art', *Knowledge and Policy: The International Journal of Knowledge Transfer and Utilization*, vol 7, no 4, pp 13-33.

Hughes, M., McNeish, D., Newman, T., Roberts, H. and Sachdev, D. (2000) *What works? Making connections: linking research and practice*, Ilford, Essex: Barnardo's (Research and Development Team).

Hulscher, M.E.J.L., Wensing, M., van der Weijden, T. and Grol, R. (2002) *Interventions to implement prevention in primary care, The Cochrane Library*, no 2, Oxford: Update Software.

Hunt, D.L., Haynes, R.B., Hanna, S.E. and Smith, K. (1998) 'Effects of computer-based clinical decision support systems on physician performance and patient outcomes: a systematic review', *Journal of the American Medical Association*, vol 280, no 15, pp 1339-46.

Hutchinson, J. R. (1995) 'A multimethod analysis of knowledge use in social policy', *Science Communication*, vol 17, no 1, pp 90-106.

Innvaer, S., Vist, G., Trommald, M. and Oxman, A.D. (2002) 'Health policy-makers' perceptions of their use of evidence: a systematic review', *Journal of Health Services Research and Policy*, vol 17, no 4, pp 239-244.

Jackson, P. (1971) 'The way teachers think', in G. Lesser (ed) *Psychology and educational practice*, Chicago, IL: Scott Foresman, pp 10-34.

Janowitz, M. (1972) *Sociological models and social policy*, Morristown, NJ: General Learning Systems.

Jaworski, B. (2000) 'Collaborating with mathematics tutors to explore undergraduate teaching', Paper presented at the Economic and Social Research Council Teaching and Learning Research Programme Conference, Leicester, November.

Jenkins-Smith, H.C. and Sabatier, P.A. (1994) 'Evaluating the Advocacy Coalition Framework', *Journal of Public Policy*, vol 14, no 2, pp 175-203.

Jenkins-Smith, H.C., St Clair, G.K. and Woods, B. (1991) 'Explaining change in policy subsystems: analysis of coalition stability and defection over time', *American Journal of Political Science*, vol 35, no 4, pp 851-80.

John-Steiner, V. and Souberman, E. (1978) 'Afterword', in M. Cole, V. John-Steiner, S. Scribner and E. Souberman (eds) *Mind in society: The development of higher psychological processes*, Cambridge, MA: Harvard University Press, pp 121-34.

Johnston, M.E., Langton, K.B., Haynes, R.B. and Mathieu, A. (1994) 'Effects of computer-based clinical decision support systems on clinician performance and patient outcome', *Annals of Internal Medicine*, vol 120, no 2, pp 135-42.

JRF (Joseph Rowntree Foundation) *Findings* (2000) *Linking research and practice*, September, York: Joseph Rowntree Foundation (www.jrf.org.uk).

Jung, T. (2005) 'Networks, evidence and lesson-drawing in the public policy process: the case of Sarah Payne and the British debate about sex offender community notification', PhD thesis, University of St Andrews.

Kelly, J. (2003) 'The Audit Commission: guiding, steering and regulating local government', *Public Administration*, vol 81, no 3, pp 456-76.

Kingdon, J.W. (1984) *Agendas, alternatives and public policies*, Boston, MA: Little, Brown.

Kitson, A., Harvey, G. and McCormack, B. (1998) 'Enabling the implementation of evidence based practice: a conceptual framework', *Quality in Health Care*, vol 7, pp 149-58.

Kitson, A., Ahmed, L.B., Harvey, G., Seers, K. and Thompson, D.R. (1996) 'From research to practice: one organizational model for promoting research-based practice', *Journal of Advanced Nursing*, vol 23, pp 430-40.

Klein, S.S. and Gwaltney, M.K. (1991) 'Charting the education dissemination system', *Knowledge: Creation, Diffusion, Utilization*, vol 12, no 3, pp 241-65.

Kluge, J., Stein, W. and Licht, J. (2001) *Knowledge unplugged*, Basingstoke: Palgrave.

Knott, J. and Wildavsky, A. (1980) 'If dissemination is the solution, what is the problem?', *Knowledge: Creation, Diffusion, Utilization*, vol 1, no 4, pp 537-78.

Knowles, M., Holton III, E. and Swanson, R. (2005) *The adult learner* (6th edition), London: Elsevier Butterworth Heinnemann.

Landry, R., Amara, N. and Lamari, M. (2001a) 'Utilization of social science research knowledge in Canada', *Research Policy*, vol 30, no 2, pp 333-49.

Landry, R., Amara, N. and Lamari, M. (2001b) 'Climbing the ladder of research utilization', *Science Communication*, vol 22, no 4, pp 396-422.

Lavis, J., Ross, S., McLeod, C. and Gildiner, A. (2003) 'Measuring the impact of health research', *Journal of Health Services Research and Policy*, vol 8, no 3, pp 165-70.

Lavis, J.N., Davies, H.T.O., Gruen, R.L., Walshe, K. and Farquhar, C.M. (2006) 'Working within and beyond the Cochrane Collaboration to make systematic reviews more useful to healthcare managers and policy makers', *Healthcare Policy*, vol 1, no 2, pp 21-33.

Lavis, J., Davies, H.T.O., Oxman, A., Denis, J.-L., Golden-Biddle, K. and Ferlie, E. (2005) 'Towards systematic reviews that inform health care management and policy-making', *Journal of Health Services Research and Policy*, vol 10, no 1, pp S1: 35-48.

Law, M. (2000) 'Strategies for implementing evidence-based practice in early intervention', *Infants and Young Children*, vol 1, no 2, pp 32-40.

Laycock, G. and Farrell, G. (2003) 'Repeat victimization: lessons for implementing problem-oriented policing', *Crime Prevention Studies*, vol 15, pp 213-37.

Learmonth, M. and Harding, N. (2006) 'Evidence-based management: the very idea', *Public Administration*, vol 84, no 2, pp 245-66.

Leicester, G. (1999) 'The seven enemies of evidence-based policy', *Public Money & Management*, vol 19, no 19, pp 5-7.

Levitt, R. (2003) *GM crops and foods: Evidence, policy and practice in the UK: A case study*, Working Paper 20, London: ESRC UK Centre for Evidence Based Policy and Practice, Queen Mary, University of London (www.evidencenetwork.org, accessed August 2004).

Lia-Hoagberg, B., Schaffer, M. and Strohschein, S. (1999) 'Public health nursing practice guidelines: an evaluation of dissemination and use', *Public Health Nursing*, vol 16, no 6, pp 397-404.

Liddle, H.A., Rowe, C.L., Quille, T.J., Dakof, G.A., Mills, D.S., Sakran, E. and Biaggi, H. (2002) 'Transporting a research-based adolescent drug treatment into practice', *Journal of Substance Abuse Treatment*, vol 22, no 4, pp 231-43.

Liebowitz, J. (2000) *Building organizational intelligence: A knowledge management primer*, London: CRC Press.

Light, S.C. and Newman, T.K. (1992) 'Awareness and use of social science research among executive and administrative staff members of state correctional agencies', *Justice Quarterly*, vol 9, no 2, pp 299-324.

Lindblom, C.E. (1968) *The policy-making process*, Englewood Cliffs, NJ: Prentice Hall.

Lindsey, D. (1989) 'Using citation counts as a measure of quality in science: measuring what's measurable instead of what's valid', *Scientometrics*, vol 15, pp 189-203.

Little, M.E. and Houston, D. (2003) 'Research into practice through professional development', *Remedial and Special Education*, vol 24, no 2, pp 75-87.

Little, S. and Ray, T. (eds) (2005) *Managing knowledge*, London: Sage Publications.

Locock, L., Dopson, S., Chambers, D. and Gabbay, J. (2001) 'Understanding the role of opinion leaders in improving clinical effectiveness', *Social Science and Medicine*, vol 53, pp 745-57.

Lomas, J. (1991) 'Words without action? The production, dissemination, and impact of consensus recommendations', *Annual Review of Public Health*, vol 12, pp 41-65.

Lomas, J. (1997) *Improving research dissemination and uptake in the health sector: Beyond the sound of one hand clapping*, Policy Commentary C97-1, Hamilton, Ontario: McMaster University, Centre for Health Economics and Policy Analysis.

Lomas, J. (2000) 'Using "linkage and exchange" to move research into policy at a Canadian foundation', *Health Affairs*, vol 19, no 3, pp 236-40.

Lomas, J., Fulop, N., Gagnon, D. and Allen, P. (2003) 'On being a good listener: setting priorities for applied health services research', *Milbank Quarterly*, vol 81, no 3, pp 363-88.

Louis, K.S. (1998) 'Reconnecting knowledge utilization and school improvement: two steps forward, one step back', in A. Hargreaves, A. Lieberman, M. Fullan and D. Hopkins (eds) *International handbook of educational change: Part two*, Dordrecht: Kluwer Academic Publishers, pp 1074-95.

Lovell, R. and Kalinich, D. (1992) 'The unimportance of in-house research in a professional criminal justice organization', *Criminal Justice Review*, vol 17, no 1, pp 77-93.

McAdam, R. and Reid, R. (2001) 'SME and large organisation perceptions of knowledge management: management comparisons and contrasts', *Journal of Knowledge Management*, vol 5, no 3, pp 231-41.

Macdonald, G. (2000) 'Social care: rhetoric and reality', in H.T.O. Davies, S.M. Nutley and P.C. Smith (eds) *What works? Evidence-based policy and practice in public services*, Bristol: The Policy Press, pp 117-40.

McGuinness, C. (2000) 'ACTS (Activating Children's Thinking Skills): a methodology for enhancing thinking skills across the curriculum (with a focus on knowledge transformation)', Paper presented at the First Conference of the Economic and Social Research Council's Research Programme on Teaching and Learning, Leicester, 9-10 November.

McKenna, H., Ashton, S. and Keeney, S. (2004) 'Barriers to evidence based practice in primary care: a review of the literature', *International Journal of Nursing Studies*, vol 41, no 4, pp 369-78.

McKinlay, A. (2005) 'Knowledge management', in S. Ackroyd, R. Batt, P. Thompson and P. Tolbert (eds) *The Oxford handbook of work and organization*, Oxford: Oxford University Press, pp 242-62.

Magnan, J., L'Heureux, L., Taylor, M. and Thornley, R. (2004), 'Assessing the outputs and outcomes of Alberta's Health Research Fund', Poster presented at the *First annual conference of the Canadian Association for Health Services and Policy Research*, Montreal, QC, Canada (May 2004).

Maguire, M. (2004) 'The Crime Reduction Programme in England and Wales', *Criminal Justice*, vol 4, no 3, pp 213-37.

Mannion, R., Davies, H.T.O. and Marshal, M.N. (2005) 'Impact of "star" performance ratings on English NHS Trusts', *Journal of Health Services Research and Policy*, vol 10, no 1, pp 18-24.

March, J. and Olsen, J. (1976) *Ambiguity and choice in organisations*, Englewood Cliffs, NJ: Prentice Hall.

Marston, G. and Watts, R. (2003) 'Tampering with the evidence: a critical appraisal of evidence-based policy making', *The Drawing Board: An Australian Review of Public Affairs*, vol 3, no 3, pp 143-63.

Marteau, T.M., Sowden, A.J. and Armstrong, D. (2002) 'Implementing research findings into practice: beyond the information deficit model', in A. Haines and A. Donald (eds) *Getting research findings into practice*, London: BMJ Books, pp 68-76.

Martin, S. (2002) 'Modernisation of UK local government: markets, managers, monitors and mixed fortunes', *Public Management Review*, vol 4, no 3, pp 291-307.

Mays, N., Pope, C. and Popay, J. (2005) 'Systematically reviewing qualitative and quantitative evidence to inform management and policy-making in the health field', *Journal of Health Services Research and Policy*, vol 10, supp 1, pp 6-20.

Megginson, D. and Pedlar, M. (1992) *Self-development: A facilitator's guide*, Maidenhead: McGraw-Hill.

Mihalic, S., Fagan, A., Irwin, K., Ballard, D. and Elliott, D., (2004a) *Blueprints for violence prevention*, Boulder, CO: Centre for the Study and Prevention of Violence, University of Colorado/Office of Juvenile Justice and Delinquency Prevention, US Department of Justice, available at www.ojjdp.ncjrs.org/publications/PubAbstract.asp?pubi=11721, accessed August 2004.

Mihalic, S., Irwin, K., Fagan, A., Ballard, D. and Elliott, D. (2004b) *Successful program implementation: Lessons from Blueprints*, Washington, DC: US Department of Justice, Office of Juvenile Justice and Delinquency Prevention, available at www.ojjdp.ncjrs.org/publications/PubAbstract.asp?pubi=11719, accessed August 2004.

Miles, A., Grey, J., Polychronis, A. and Melchiorri, C. (2002) 'Critical advances in the evaluation and development of clinical care', *Journal of Evaluation in Clinical Practice*, vol 8, no 2, pp 87-102.

Miles, A., Grey, J., Polychronis, A., Price, N. and Melchiorri, C. (2003) 'Current thinking in the evidence-based health care debate', *Journal of Evaluation in Clinical Practice*, vol 9, no 2, pp 95-109.

Milewa, T. and Barry, C. (2005) 'Health policy and the politics of evidence', *Social Policy and Administration*, vol 39, no 5, pp 498-512.

Mintzberg, H., Ahlstrand, B. and Lampel, J. (1998) *The strategy safari*, New York: Free Press.

Molas-Gallart, J., Tang, P. and Morrow, S. (2000) 'Assessing the non-academic impact of grant-funded socio-economic research: results from a pilot study', *Research Evaluation*, vol 9, no 3, pp 171-82.

Moulding, N.T., Silagy, C.A. and Weller, D.P. (1999) 'A framework for effective management of change in clinical practice: dissemination and implementation of clinical practice guidelines', *Quality in Health Care*, vol 8, no 3, pp 177-83.

Mukherjee, S., Beresford, B. and Sloper, P. (1999) *Unlocking key working: An analysis and evaluation of key worker services for families with disabled children*, Bristol/York: The Policy Press/Joseph Rowntree Foundation.

Mulgan, G. (2003) 'Government, knowledge and the business of policy making', *Canberra Bulletin of Public Administration*, vol 108, pp 1-5.

Mulhall, A. and le May, A. (1999) *Nursing research: Dissemination and implementation*, Edinburgh: Churchill Livingstone.

Musson, G. (undated) *Qualitative evaluation of the facts Aspirin Programme*, Sheffield: *facts*/Centre for Innovation in Primary Care, www.innovate.org.uk/library/aspquarep/GillsQualRep.html (accessed 16 July 2002).

NAO (National Audit Office) (2004) *Connexions Service: Advice and guidance for all young people*, London: The Stationery Office.

National Academy of Engineering (2003) *The impact of academic research on industrial performance*, Washington, DC, United States: National Academies Press, http://books/nap.edu/catalog/10805.html?onpi_newsdoc10092003.

NCDDR (National Centre for the Dissemination of Disability Research) (1996) *A review of the literature on dissemination and knowledge utilization*, Austin, TX: NCDDR.

NCSL (National College of School Leadership) (2005a) *International perspectives on networked learning: Key messages emerging from Phase 1 of the external evaluation of the NCSL Networked Learning Communities*, Nottingham: NCSL.

NCSL (2005b) *Evaluating the NCSL Networked Learning Communities Programme: Summary of the overall approaches to the evaluation*, Nottingham: NCSL.

Neilson, S. (2001) *IDRC supported research and its influence on public policy: Knowledge utilization and public policy processes: A literature review*, Ottawa: International Development Research Centre.

NESS (National Evaluation of Sure Start) (2005) *Early impacts of Sure Start local programmes on children and families*, Sure Start Report 13, London: HMSO.

Newell, S., Edelman, L. and Bresnean, M. (2001) 'The inevitability of reinvention in project-based learning', Paper presented at the 17th EGOS Conference 'The Odyssey of Organising', Lyon, 5-7 July.

Nicholas, E. (2003) 'An outcomes focus in carer assessment and review: value and challenge', *British Journal of Social Work*, vol 33, no 1, pp 31-47.

Nonaka, I. and Takeuchi, H. (1995) *A knowledge-creating company: How Japanese companies create the dynamics of innovation*, Oxford: Oxford University Press.

Norman, L. (2004) *Research-policy interaction: A study of a series of DfES convened seminars*, NERF Working Paper 8.1, London: National Education Research Forum (NERF; www.nerf-uk.org, accessed January 2006).

Novak, J.D. (1998) *Learning, creating, and using knowledge: Concept maps™ as facilitative tools for schools and corporations*, Mahwah, NJ: Lawrence Erlbaum Associates.

Nutley, S.M. and Davies, H.T.O. (1999) 'The fall and rise of evidence in criminal justice', *Public Money and Management*, vol 19, no 1, pp 47-54.

Nutley, S.M. and Davies, H.T.O. (2000) 'Making a reality of evidence-based practice: some lessons from the diffusion of innovations', *Public Money and Management*, vol 20, no 4, pp 35-43.

Nutley, S.M. and Davies, H.T.O. (2001) 'Developing organizational learning in the NHS', *Medical Education*, vol 35, pp 35-42.

Nutley, S.M. and Homel, P. (2006) 'Delivering evidence-based policy and practice: lessons from the implementation of the Crime Reduction Programme', *Evidence & Policy*, vol 2, no 1, pp 5-26.

Nutley, S.M. and Webb, J. (2000) 'Evidence and the policy process', in H.T.O. Davies, S.M. Nutley and P.C. Smith (eds) *What works? Evidence-based policy and practice in public services*, Bristol: The Policy Press, pp 13-42.

Nutley, S.M., Bland, N. and Walter, I. C. (2002) 'The institutional arrangements for connecting evidence and policy: the case of drug misuse', *Public Policy and Administration*, vol 17, no 3, pp 76-94.

Nutley, S.M., Percy-Smith, J. and Solesbury, W. (2003a), *Models of research impact: a cross-sector review of literature and practice*, London: Learning and Skills Research Centre.

Nutley, S.M., Walter, I. C. and Davies, H.T.O. (2003b) 'From knowing to doing: a framework for understanding the evidence-into-practice agenda', *Evaluation*, vol 9, no 2, pp 125-48.

O'Brien, T.M.A., Oxman, A., Davis, D., Haynes, B.R., Freemantle, N. and Harvey, E.L. (2002a) 'Educational outreach visits: effects on professional practice and health care outcomes', *The Cochrane Library*, no 2, Oxford: Update Software.

O'Brien, T.M.A., Oxman, A., Davis, D., Haynes, B.R., Freemantle, N. and Harvey, E.L. (2002b) 'Audit and feedback versus alternative strategies: effects on professional practice and health care outcomes', *The Cochrane Library*, no 2, Oxford: Update Software.

O'Brien, T.M.A., Oxman, A., Davis, D., Haynes, B.R., Freemantle, N. and Harvey, E.L. (2002c) 'Audit and feedback: effects on professional practice and health care outcomes', *The Cochrane Library*, no 2, Oxford: Update Software.

Oh, C. (1996) *Linking social science information to policy-making*, Greenwich, CT: JAI Press Inc.

Oh, C. (1997) 'Explaining the impact of policy information on policy-making', *Knowledge and Policy*, vol 10, no 3, pp 25-55.

O'Neill, H.M., Pouder, R.W. and Buchholtz, A.K. (1998) 'Patterns in the diffusion of strategies across organisations: insights from the innovation diffusion literature', *Academy of Management Review*, vol 23, pp 98-114.

Øvretveit, J. (2002) 'How to run an effective improvement collaborative', *International Journal of Health Care Quality Assurance*, vol 15, pp 33-44.

Oxman, A.D., Thomson, M.A., Davis, D.A. and Haynes, B.R. (1995) 'No magic bullets: a systematic review of 102 trials of interventions to improve professional practice', *Journal of the Canadian Medical Association*, vol 153, no 10, pp 1423-31.

Palmer, C. and Fenner, J. (1999) *Getting the message across: Review of research and theory about disseminating information within the NHS*, London: Royal College of Psychiatrists.

Parker, G. (1990) 'Informal care, social research and social policy: real influence or wishful thinking?', *Social Policy Research Unit Working Paper* CP 750 11/90, York: University of York.

Parsons, W. (1995) *Public policy*, Cheltenham: Edward Elgar.

Parsons, W. (2002) 'From muddling through to muddling up: evidence-based policy making and the modernisation of British government', *Public Policy and Administration*, vol 17, no 3, pp 43-60.

Parsons, W. (2004) 'Not just steering but weaving: relevant knowledge and the craft of building policy capacity and coherence', *Australian Journal of Public Administration*, vol 63, no 1, pp 43-57.

Patton, M.Q. (1997) *Utilization-focused evaluation*, Thousand Oaks, CA: Sage Publications.

Patton, M.Q. (1998) 'Discovering process use', *Evaluation*, vol 4, no 2, pp 225-33.

Pawson, R. (2002) 'Evidence-based policy: the promise of realist synthesis', *Evaluation*, vol 8, no 3, pp 340-58.

Pawson, R. and Tilley, N. (1997) *Realistic evaluation*, London: Sage Publications.

Pawson, R., Greenhalgh, T., Harvey, G. and Walshe, K. (2005) 'Realist review: a new method of systematic review designed for complex policy interventions', *Journal of Health Services Research and Policy*, vol 10, supp 1, pp 21-34.

Pawson, R., Boaz, A., Grayson, L., Long, A. and Barnes, C. (2003) *Types and quality of knowledge in social care*, Bristol/London: The Policy Press/Social Care Institute for Excellence.

Pedlar, M. and Aspinwall, K. (1998) *A concise guide to the learning organisation*, London: Lemos & Crane.

Pedlar, M.J., Burgoyne, J.G. and Boydell, T.H. (1997) *The learning company: A strategy for sustainable development*, Maidenhead: McGraw-Hill.

Percy-Smith, J., Speller, V. and Nutley, S.M. (2006) *Evidence-informed policy and practice: A review of approaches used in health improvement in Scotland*, Edinburgh: NHS Health Scotland.

Percy-Smith, J., Burden, T., Darlow, A., Dowson, L., Hawtin, M. and Ladi, S. (2002) *Promoting change through research: The impact of research in local government*, York: Joseph Rowntree Foundation.

Petersen, L.A., Woodard, L.D., Urech, T., Daw, C. and Sookanan, S. (2006). 'Does Pay-for-Performance Improve the Quality of Health Care?', *Annals of Internal Medicine*, vol 145, no 4, pp 265-72.

Pfeffer, J. and Sutton, R. I. (2000) *The knowing-doing gap: How smart companies turn knowledge into action*, Boston, MA: Harvard Business School Press.

Pfeffer, J. and Sutton, R. I. (2006) *Hard facts, dangerous half-truths and total nonsense: Profiting from evidence-based management*, Boston, MA: Harvard Business School Press.

Philip, K.L., Backett-Milburn, K., Cunningham-Burley, S. and Davis, J. B. (2003) 'Practising what we preach? A practical approach to bringing research, policy and practice together in relation to children and health inequalities', *Health Education Research*, vol 18, no 5, pp 568-79.

Phillips Report (2000) *The BSE Inquiry Report*, www.bseinquiry.gov.uk/index.htm (accessed 20 December 2006)

Polanyi, M. (1967) *The tacit dimension*, New York: Doubleday.

Price, L., Ravenscroft, J. and Nutley, S. (2006) 'Fostering voices and fostering messages: an evaluation of new strategies to promote research utilisation', *Adoption and Fostering*, vol 30, no 1, pp 6-17.

Prime Minister's Strategy Unit (2006) *The UK government's approach to public service reform: A discussion paper*, London: Cabinet Office.

Quinn, M. (2002) 'Evidence-based or people-based policy making? A view from Wales', *Public Policy and Administration*, vol 17, no 3, pp 29-42.

Qureshi, H. and Nicholas, E. (2001) 'A new conception of social care outcomes and its practical use in assessment with older people', *Research Policy and Planning*, vol 19, no 2, pp 11-26.

Ramey, C., Campbell, F., Burchinal, M., Skinner, M., Gardner, D. and Ramey, F. (2000) 'Persistent effects of early childhood education on high risk children and their mothers', *Applied Developmental Science*, vol 4, no 1, pp 2-14.

Reber, A.S. (1993) *Implicit learning and tacit knowledge: An essay on the cognitive unconscious*, New York: Oxford University Press.

Reid, F. (2003) *Evidence-based policy: Where is the evidence for it?*, Bristol: School for Policy Studies, University of Bristol (www.bristol.ac.uk/sps, accessed January 2005).

Rein, L. (1976) *Social science and public policy*, Harmondsworth: Penguin Education.

Rich, A. (2004) *Think tanks, public policy and the politics of expertise*, Cambridge, MA: Cambridge University Press.

Rickinson, M. (2005) *Practitioners' use of research*, NERF Working Paper 7.5, London: National Education Research Forum (NERF; www.nerf-uk.org, accessed January 2005).

Robinson, G. (2001) 'Power, knowledge and "what works" in probation', *The Howard Journal*, vol 40, no 3, pp 235-54.

Rodger, J. and Cowen, G. (2005) *National evaluation of the Connexions Card: Final Report*, York: York Consulting Ltd.

Rogers, E.M. (1995) *Diffusion of innovations*, New York: Free Press.

Rogers, E.M. (2003) *Diffusion of innovations* (5th edition), New York: Free Press.

Ross, S., Lavis, J., Rodriguez, C., Woodside, J. and Denis, J.-L. (2003) 'Partnership experiences: involving decision makers in the research process', *Journal of Health Services Research and Policy*, vol 8, supp 2, pp 26-34.

Rushmer, R.K. and Davies, H.T.O. (2004) 'Unlearning in health care', *Quality and Safety in Health Care*, vol 13, supp II, pp 10-15.

Sabatier, P. (1998) 'The advocacy coalition framework: revisions and relevance for Europe', *Journal of European Public Policy*, vol 5, no 1, pp 98-130.

Sabatier, P. and Jenkins-Smith, H.C. (1993) *Policy change and learning: An advocacy coalitions approach*, Boulder, CO: Westview Press.

Sabatier, P. and Pelkey, N. (1987) 'Incorporating multiple actors and guidance instruments into models of regulatory policymaking: an advocacy coalition framework', *Administration and Society*, vol 19, no 2, pp 236-63.

Sackett, D.L., Rosenberg, W.M.C., Gray, J.A.M., Haynes, R.B. and Richardson, W.S. (1996) 'Evidence based medicine: what it is and what it isn't', *British Medical Journal*, vol 312, no 7023, pp 71-2.

Sanderson, I. (2002) 'Evaluation, policy learning and evidence-based policy making', *Public Administration*, vol 80, no 1, pp 1-22.

Sanderson, I. (2006) 'Complexity, "practical rationality" and evidence-based policy making' *Policy and Politics*, vol 34, no 1, pp 115-32

Scarborough, H., Swan, J. and Preston, J. (1999) *Knowledge management: A literature review*, London: Institute of Personnel and Development.

Schein, E. (1996) 'Organisational learning as cognitive re-definition: corrective persuasion revisited', available at www.sol-ne.org/res/wp/index.html, last accessed 9 October 2006.

Schon, D.A. (1967) *Technology and change: The new Heraclitus*, New York: Delacorte Press.

Schon, D.A. (1971) *Beyond the stable state*, London: Norton & Company.

Schweinhart, L. and Weikart, D. (1993) *A summary of significant benefits: The high/scope Perry pre-school study through age 27*, London: Hodder Stoughton.

Scottish Executive (2003) *The Lifelong Learning Strategy for Scotland*, Edinburgh: Scottish Executive (www.scotland.gov.uk/publications/2003/02/16308/17776 – accessed 20 December 2006).

Selby Smith, C. and Selby Smith, J. (2002) 'Reflections on the impact of research on policy development: a case study of user choice', *Australian and New Zealand Journal of Vocational Education Research*, vol 10, no 1, pp 69-93.

Seligman, M., Steen, T., Park, N. and Peterson, C. (2005) 'Positive psychology progress: empirical validation of interventions', *American Psychologist*, vol 60, no 5, pp 410-21.

Senge, P.M. (1990) *The fifth discipline: The art and practice of the learning organization*, New York: Doubleday Currency.

SEU (Social Exclusion Unit) (1998) *Bringing Britain together: A national strategy for neighbourhood renewal*, Cm 4045, London: SEU.

SEU (Social Exclusion Unit) (2001) *A new commitment to neighbourhood renewal: national strategy action plan*, London: Cabinet Office

SEU and CMPS (Social Exclusion Unit and Centre for Management and Policy Studies) (2002) *The Social Exclusion Unit's policy action team approach to policy development: The views of participants*, London: SEU.

Shanley, C., Lodge, M. and Mattick, R.P. (1996) 'Dissemination of research findings to alcohol and other drug practitioners', *Drug and Alcohol Review*, vol 15, no 1, pp 89-94.

Shannon, S.I. and Norman, G.R. (1995) 'A critical appraisal of critical appraisal skills teaching interventions', in A. Rothman (ed) *The 6th Ottawa conference on medical education*, Toronto: University of Toronto.

SHEFC/US (Scottish Higher Education Funding Council/ Universities Scotland) (2005) *Knowledge transfer from Scotland's higher education institutions: Progress and prospects. Report of the joint SHEFC/ Universities Scotland task force on knowledge transfer*, Edinburgh: Scottish Funding Council (RKTC/05/08/Annex 1).

Sheldon, B. (1998) 'Evidence-based social services', *Research, Policy and Planning*, vol 16, no 2, pp 16-18.

Sheldon, B. and Chilvers, R. (2000) *Evidence-based social care: A study of prospects and problems*, Lyme Regis, UK: Russell House.

Sheldon, B. and Chilvers, R. (2002) 'An empirical study of the obstacles to evidence-based practice', *Social Work and Social Sciences Review*, vol 10, no 1, pp 6-26.

Sheldon, T. (2005) 'Making evidence synthesis more useful for management and policy-making', *Journal of Health Services Research and Policy*, vol 10, supp 1, pp 1-5.

Shove, E. and Rip, A. (2000) 'Users and unicorns: a discussion of mythical beasts in interactive science', *Science and Public Policy*, vol 27, pp 175-82.

Shulha, L.M. and Cousins, J.B. (1997) 'Evaluation use: theory, research and practice since 1986', *Evaluation Practice*, vol 18, no 3, pp 195-208.

Simon, H.A. (1957) *Models of man*, New York: John Wiley and Sons.

Simons, H., Kushner, S., Jones, K. and James, D. (2003) 'From evidence-based practice to practice-based evidence: the idea of situated generalisation', *Research Papers in Education*, vol 18, no 4, pp 347-64.

Sinclair, R. and Jacobs, C. (1994) *Research in personal social services: The experiences of three local authorities*, London: National Children's Bureau.

Sloper, P., Mukherjee, S., Beresford, B., Lightfoot, J. and Norris, P. (1999) *Real change not rhetoric: Putting research into practice in multi-agency services*, Bristol/York: The Policy Press/Joseph Rowntree Foundation.

Smith, P. (1995) 'On the unintended consequences of publishing performance data in the public sector', *International Journal of Public Administration*, vol 18, pp 277-310.

Smith, W.R. (2000) 'Evidence for the effectiveness of techniques to change physician behavior', *Chest*, vol 118, no 2, pp 8-17.

Sobell, L. (1996) 'Bridging the gap between scientists and practitioners: the challenge before us', *Behaviour Therapy*, vol 27, no 3, pp 297-320.

Spencer, L., Ritchie, J., Lewis, J. and Dillon, L. (2003) *Quality in qualitative evaluation: A framework for assessing research evidence*, London: Cabinet Office.

SPICE (Scottish Parliament Information Centre) (1999) *Approaches to tackling poverty and social exclusion*, Research note RN42, Edinburgh: SPICE.

Spittlehouse, C., Acton, M. and Enock, K. (2000) 'Introducing critical appraisal skills training in UK social services: another link between health and social care?', *Journal of Interprofessional Care*, vol 14, no 4, pp 397-404.

Sprague, J., Walker, H., Golly, A., White, K., Myers, D.R. and Shannon, T. (2001) 'Translating research into effective practice: the effects of a universal staff and student intervention on indicators of discipline and school safety', *Education and Treatment of Children*, vol 24, no 4, pp 495-511.

Stein, D. (1998) *Situated learning in adult education*, Syracuse, NY: Eric Clearinghouse on Information Resources (ERIC Digest Reproduction Service No. ED 418 250).

Steuer, M. (2003) *The scientific study of society*, London: Kluwer Academic Publishers.

Stocking, B. (1985) *Initiative and inertia: Case studies in the NHS*, London: Nuffield Provincial Hospitals Trust.

Stoker, G. (1999) *Notes on keynote address*, ARCISS conference, London, 27 January (www.arciss.ac.uk/pages/publications.html – accessed 20 December 2006).

Stone, D. (2001) *Bridging research and policy*, Warwick: Warwick University.

Stroot, S., Keil, V., Stedman, P., Lohr, L., Faust, R., Schincariol-Randall, L., Sullivan, A., Czerniak, G., Kuchcinski, J., Orel, N. and Richter, M. (1998) *Peer assistance and review guidebook*, Columbus, OH: Ohio Department of Education.

Sunesson, S. and Nilsson, K. (1988) 'Explaining research utilization: beyond "functions"', *Knowledge: Creation, Diffusion, Utilization*, vol 10, no 2, pp 145-55.

Swan, J. and Scarborough, H. (2001) 'Knowledge management: concepts and controversies', *Journal of Management Studies*, vol 38, no 7, pp 913-21.

Tang, P. and Sinclair, T. (2001) 'Exploitation practice in social science research', *Science and Public Policy*, vol 28, no 2, pp 131-7.

The British Academy (2004) *'That full complement of riches': The contributions of the arts, humanities and social sciences to the nation's wealth*, London: The British Academy.

The Economist (2005) 'Child care a faltering start', 10 December, pp 34-5.

The Economist (2006a) 'Teaching reading: fast, first – effective', 25 March, pp 36 and 41.

The Economist (2006b) 'Lexington/the battle of ideas', 25 March, p 64.

Thomas, L., McColl, E., Cullum, N., Rousseau, N. and Soutter, J. (1999) 'Clinical guidelines in nursing, midwifery and the therapies: a systematic review', *Journal of Advanced Nursing*, vol 30, no 1, pp 40-50.

Thomas, L., Cullum, N., McColl, E., Rousseau, N., Soutter, J. and Steen, N. (2002) 'Guidelines in professions allied to medicine', *The Cochrane Library*, no 2, Oxford: Update Software.

Thomas, L., McColl, E., Cullum, N., Rousseau, N., Soutter, J. and Steen, N. (1998) 'Effect of clinical guidelines in nursing, midwifery, and the therapies: a systematic review of evaluations', *Quality in Health Care*, vol 7, pp 183-91.

Tilley, N. (1993) *After Kirkholt: Theory, method and results of replication evaluations*, London: Home Office Police Department, Police Research Group.

Tilley, N. (2004) 'Applying theory driven evaluation to the British Crime Reduction Programme: the theories of the programme and its evaluation', *Criminal Justice*, vol 4, no 3, pp 255-76.

Toynbee, P. (2005) 'We must hold our nerve and support deprived children', *The Guardian*, 13 September.

Tozer, C. and Ray, S. (1999) '20 questions: the research needs of children and family social workers', *Research, Policy and Planning*, vol 17, no 1, pp 7-15.

Tranfield, D.R., Denyer, D. and Smart, P. (2003) 'Towards a methodology for developing evidence-informed management knowledge by means of systematic review', *British Journal of Management*, vol 14, pp 207-22.

Trinder, L. and Reynolds, S. (2000) *Evidence-based practice: A critical appraisal*, Oxford: Blackwell Science.

Tsoukas, H. (2005) 'Do we really understand tacit knowledge?', in S. Little and T. Ray (eds) *Managing knowledge*, London: Sage Publications, pp 107-26.

Tsoukas, H. and Vladimirou, E. (2001) 'What is organization knowledge?', *Journal of Management Studies*, vol 38, no 7, pp 973-93.

Tyden, T. (1993) *Knowledge interplay: User oriented research dissemination through synthesis pedagogics*, Uppsala Studies in Education 50, Uppsala: Uppsala University.

Tyden, T. (1994) 'Trained research consumers – a key to better knowledge utilization?', Paper presented to the conference 'When Science Becomes Culture', Montreal, 10-13 April.

Tyden, T. (1996) 'The contribution of longitudinal studies for understanding science communication and research utilization', *Science Communication*, vol 18, no 1, pp 29-48.

Upshur, R.E. (2002) 'If not evidence, then what? Or does medicine really need a base?', *Journal of Evaluation in Clinical Practice*, vol 8, no 2, pp 113-20.

Van de Ven, A.H., Polley, D.E., Garud, R. and Venkataraman, S. (1999) *The innovation journey*, Oxford: Oxford University Press.

Vaughn, S. and Coleman, M. (2004) 'The role of mentoring in promoting use of research-based practices in reading', *Remedial and Special Education*, vol 25, no 1, pp 25-38.

Wakefield, J. and Kirk, S. (1996) 'Unscientific thinking about scientific practice: evaluating the scientist practitioner model', *Social Work Research*, vol 20, no 2, pp 83-95.

Wakefield, A., Murch, S., Anthony, A., Linnell, J., Casson, D., Malik, M., Berelowitz, M., Dhillon, A., Thomson, M., Harvey, P., Valentine, A., Davies, S. and Walker-Smith, J. (1998) 'Ileal-lymphoid-nodular hyperplasia, non-specific colitis, and pervasive developmental disorder in children', *The Lancet*, vol 351, no 9103, pp 637-41.

Walshe, K. and Rundall, T.G. (2001) 'Evidence-based management: from theory to practice in health care', *The Milbank Quarterly*, vol 79, no 3, pp 429-57.

Walker, D. (2000) 'You find the evidence, we'll pick the policy', *The Guardian*, 15 February.

Walter, I., Nutley, S.M. and Davies, H.T.O. (2003a) *Research impact: A cross-sector review*, St Andrews: Research Unit for Research Utilisation, University of St Andrews, available at www.ruru.ac.uk/publications.html, accessed January 2006.

Walter, I.C., Nutley, S.M. and Davies, H.T.O. (2003b) *Developing a taxonomy of interventions used to increase the impact of research*, Discussion Paper 3, St Andrews: Research Unit for Research Utilisation, University of St Andrews, available at www.ruru.ac.uk/home.html, accessed January 2006.

Walter, I., Davies, H.T.O. and Nutley, S.M. (2003c) 'Increasing research impact through partnerships: evidence from outside healthcare', *Journal of Health Services Research and Policy* vol 8, no 2, pp 58-61.

Walter, I.C., Nutley, S.M. and Davies, H.T.O. (2004a) *Assessing research impact. Report of RURU seminar 3, 15-16 January 2004*, St Andrews: Research Unit for Research Utilisation, University of St Andrews, available at www.ruru.ac.uk/publications.html, accessed January 2006.

Walter, I., Nutley, S., Percy-Smith, J., McNeish, D. and Frost, S. (2004b) *Improving the use of research in social care. Knowledge Review* 7, Bristol/London: The Policy Press/Social Care Institute for Excellence.

Walter, I., Nutley, S.M. and Davies, H.T.O. (2005), 'What works to promote evidence-based practice? A cross-sector review' *Evidence & Policy*, vol 1, no 3, pp 335-64.

Ward, H. (1995) *Looking after children: Research into practice*, London: HMSO.

Ward, L. (2005) 'Doubts over value of £3 billion Sure Start', *The Guardian*, 13 September.

Waterman, H., Tillen, D., Dickson, R. and de Konig, K. (2001) 'Action research: a systematic review and guidance for assessment', *Health Technology Assessment*, vol 5, no 23 (www.hta.nhsweb.nhs.uk).

Watkins, J.M. (1994) 'A postmodern critical theory of research use', *Knowledge and Policy*, vol 7, no 4, pp 55-77.

Webb, S.A. (2001) 'Some considerations on the validity of evidence-based practice in social work', *British Journal of Social Work*, vol 31, pp 57-79.

Webber, D.J. (1986) 'Explaining policymakers' use of policy information', *Knowledge: Creation, Diffusion, Utilization*, vol 7, no 3, pp 249-90.

Webber, D.J. (1991) 'The distribution and use of policy knowledge in the policy process', *Knowledge and Policy: The International Journal of Knowledge Transfer and Utilization*, vol 4, no 4, pp 6-35.

Weiss, C.H. (1979) 'The many meanings of research utilization', *Public Administration Review*, vol 39, no 5, pp 426-31.

Weiss, C.H. (1980) 'Knowledge creep and decision accretion', *Knowledge: Creation, Diffusion, Utilization*, vol 1, no 3, pp 381-404.

Weiss, C.H. (1982) 'Policy research in the context of diffuse decision making', *Journal of Higher Education*, vol 53, no 6, pp 619-39.

Weiss, C.H. (1987) 'The circuitry of enlightenment: diffusion of social science research to policy makers', *Knowledge: Creation, Diffusion, Utilization*, vol 8, no 2, pp 274-81.

Weiss, C.H. (1995) 'The haphazard connection: social science and public policy', *International Journal of Educational Research*, vol 23, no 2, pp 137-50.

Weiss, C.H. (1998) 'Have we learned anything new about the use of evaluation?', *American Journal of Evaluation*, vol 19, no 1, pp 21-33.

Weiss, C.H. (1999) 'The interface between evaluation and public policy', *Evaluation*, vol 5, no 4, pp 468-86.

Weiss, C.H., Murphy-Graham, E. and Birkeland, S. (2005) 'An alternative route to policy influence: how evaluations affect DARE', *The American Journal of Evaluation*, vol 26, no 1, pp 12-13.

Wenger, E. (1998) *Communities of practice: Learning, meaning and identity*, Cambridge, MA: Cambridge University Press.

Wenger, E., McDermott, R. and Snyder, W. (2002) *Cultivating communities of practice*, Boston, MA: Harvard Business School Press.

Westphal, J. D., Gulati, R. and Shortell, S. M. (1997) 'Customization or conformity? An institutional and network perspective on the content and consequences of TQM adoption', *Administrative Science Quarterly*, vol 42, pp 366-94.

Weyts, A., Morpeth, L. and Bullock, R. (2000) 'Department of Health research overviews – past, present and future: an evaluation of the dissemination of the Blue Book, *Child protection: messages from research*', *Child and Family Social Work*, vol 5, no 3, pp 215-23.

Whitehead, M., Townsend, P. and Davidson, N. (eds) (1992) *Inequalities in Health: The Black Report and the Health Divide*, London: Penguin.

Whiteman, D. (1985) 'Reaffirming the importance of strategic use: a two-dimensional perspective on policy analysis in Congress', *Knowledge*, vol 6, pp 203-24.

Wikeley, F. (1998) 'Dissemination of research as a tool for school improvement?', *School Leadership and Management*, vol 18, no 1, pp 59-73.

Wilensky, H. (1997) 'Social science and the public agenda: reflections on relation of knowledge to policy in the United States and abroad', *Journal of Health Politics, Policy and Law*, vol 22, no 5, pp 1241-65.

Williams, D., McConnell, M. and Wilson, K. (1997) *Is there any knowledge out there? The impact of research information on practitioners*, Boston Spa: British Library Research and Innovation Centre.

Williams, M. (2005) 'The evaluation of Sure Start', *The Evaluator*, Winter, pp 10-12.

Willinsky, J. (2003) 'Policymakers' online use of academic research', *Education Policy and Analysis Archives*, vol 11, no 2, pp 1-17, available at http://epaa.asu.edu/epaa/v11n2/, accessed January 2005.

Wilson, R., Hemsley-Brown, J., Easton, C. and Sharp, C. (2003) *Using research for school improvement: The LEA's role*, Local Government Association Research Report 42, Slough, Berkshire: National Foundation for Educational Research (NFER).

Wingens, M. (1990) 'Toward a general utilization theory: a systems theory reformulation of the two communities metaphor', *Knowledge: Creation, Diffusion, Utilization*, vol 12, no 1, pp 27-42.

Wolfe, R.A. (1994) 'Organisational innovation: review, critique and suggested research directions', *Journal of Management Studies*, vol 31, no 3, pp 405-31.

Wood, E. (2003) 'The power of pupil perspectives in evidence-based practice: the case of gender and underachievement', *Research Papers in Education*, vol 18, no 4, pp 365-83.

Wood, M., Ferlie, E. and Fitzgerald, L. (1998) 'Achieving clinical behaviour change: a case of becoming indeterminate', *Social Science and Medicine*, vol 47, no 11, pp 1729-38.

Wooding, S., Hanney, S., Buxton, M. and Grant, J. (2004) *The returns from arthritis research. Volume 1: Approach, analysis and recommendations*, Arthritis Research Campaign, RAND Europe (www.rand.org/pubs/monographs/MG251/ - accessed 20 December 2006).

Woolgar, S. (2000) 'Social basis of interactive social science', *Science and Public Policy*, vol 27, no 3, pp 165-73.

Wye, L. and McClenahan, J. (2000) *Getting better with evidence: Experiences of putting evidence into practice*, London: King's Fund, available at www.kingsfund.org.uk, accessed July 2004.

Yano, E.M., Fink, A., Hirsch, S.H., Robbins, A.S. and Rubenstein, L.V. (1995) 'Helping practices reach primary care goals: lessons from the literature', *Archives of Internal Medicine*, vol 155, no 11, pp 1146-56.

Young, K., Ashby, D., Boaz, A. and Grayson, L. (2002) 'Social science and the evidence-based policy movement', *Social Policy and Society*, vol 1, no 3, pp 215-24.

Zeuli, J.S. (1994) 'How do teachers understand research when they read it?', *Teaching and Teacher Education*, vol 10, no 1, pp 39-55.

———

Index

Page references for notes are followed by n